BRUCE MANSFIELD is Emeritus Professor and Deputy Vice-Chancellor (Academic) of Macquarie University, Australia.

This book is the story of the decline, fall, and recovery of a reputation. As it traces the history of opinion about Erasmus and his work from his death to the Enlightenment, it shows how his changing reputation reflected shifts in the intellectual climate over succeeding generations and contributes to a new understanding of Erasmus himself by examining long-established stereotyped judgments about him.

Around 1550 there were those among both Catholics and Protestants who wrote sympathetically about Erasmus. As the religious division deepened, each side rejected him as a temporizer, and by the end of the century his reputation was submerged.

Different forms of the Protestant Reformation each tended to fashion its own version of Erasmus. The Arminians were the first to revive his reputation in the seventeenth century, for they saw their controversy with orthodox Calvinists as a continuation of his fight with the monks and scholastic theologians. Similarly, the Jansenists and irenicists in the Gallican church of the late seventeenth and early eighteenth century identified their struggles against a prevailing orthodoxy with his. German pietists went further and, like some earlier religious radicals, identified him as one of the few who were God's instruments for the reformation of the church.

With the beginnings of the Enlightenment and the emergence of a religion of reason or of sentiment, Erasmus again became a figure of the cultural majority, presented, in the biographies of Samuel Knight and John Jortin in England and Jean Lévesque de Burigny in France, as a model of enlightened religion.

Bruce Mansfield's study of two centuries of opinion is an accomplished piece of intellectual history and an invaluable contribution to Erasmus scholarship; another volume is planned that will continue the theme.

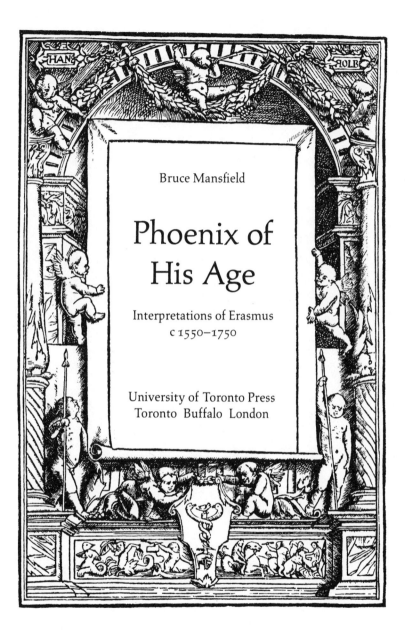

Bruce Mansfield

Phoenix of His Age

Interpretations of Erasmus
c 1550–1750

University of Toronto Press
Toronto Buffalo London

© University of Toronto Press 1979
Toronto Buffalo London
Printed in Canada

Library of Congress Cataloging in Publication Data

Mansfield, Bruce E
Phoenix of his age.

(Erasmus studies ; 4)
Bibliography: p.
Includes index.
1. Erasmus, Desiderius, d. 1536 –
Criticism and interpretation – History.
I. Title. II. Series.
PZ8518.M355   199'.492 [B]   79-14960
ISBN 0-8020-5457-9

The decorated border on the cover and title page
is from Erasmus *Epistola ad Dorpium*
(Basel: Froben 1516)
and is by Hans Holbein the Younger.

TO JOAN
for 1974

Contents

✣

Illustrations

❧

Preface

This work was begun with the modest aim of providing students of Erasmus with a ready reference to the history of his reputation across the generations. Its form was to be a collection of readings from writers about Erasmus with editorial introduction and commentary. But the historian's itch for analysis, for setting his matter in temporal context and continuous prose prompted a change to the present form, an attempt to locate Erasmus' reputation in the changing controversies of two centuries, but naturally without departing from the primary aim. A sequel is intended to carry the account to the present day.

A quarter of a century ago Andreas Flitner published his admirable *Erasmus im Urteil seiner Nachwelt: Das literarische Erasmusbild von Beatus Rhenanus bis zu Jean Le Clerc.* It might be asked whether the work – done once with judgment and sophistication – needs to be done again. Those twenty-five years have produced a library of works on Erasmus himself, notably in the quincentenary exercises which, given the uncertainties about his date of birth, could with a good conscience be spread over five years.[1] Any development in Erasmus scholarship, any deepening in our understanding of the man and his environment, alters our line of vision on the tradition about him; an accumulation makes a full review worthwhile. Similarly, there have been changes since 1952 in the interpretation of some of those who wrote about

1 There are references to various of the quincentenary works through the text. For bibliographies of recent work on Erasmus, see eg, Jean-Claude Margolin *Douze Années de bibliographie érasmienne (1950–61)* and the 'Bibliographia erasmiana' in *Scrinium Erasmianum* II 621–78. A culmination was the appearance of the first volumes of the *Opera omnia* (North-Holland Publishing Company, Amsterdam) and the *Collected Works of Erasmus* (University of Toronto Press).

Erasmus. While no more is known (or probably can be known) about the obscure encyclopedists, local historians, or theological writers who for one reason or another included him in their works from generation to generation, major figures are constantly reappraised, and the meaning of their retrospective encounters with Erasmus changes correspondingly.

The history of successive generations' understanding of an historical figure – the fate of a name and a reputation – has become an established form of historical writing.[2] It has its own dangers and difficulties. One must, above all, avoid the mechanical effect of stringing interpretations together one after the other. Not only does this make for a wooden kind of writing; it also evades the peculiar challenge of this form of intellectual history. For the subject remains an actor in the drama. Different generations interpret him according to their needs. But he goes on exercising an influence, and what they discover may be a fresh and neglected side of a many-sided nature. Erasmus remains a subject of continuing concern, someone to be reckoned with in the great debates of European history.

That is why this study presents him as a controversial figure, asking how he was handled by the warring parties of early modern Europe. From this approach may come a liveliness and sense of continuity in the narrative. It may also promote a gross simplification – the categories may be too ready and too glib. In the following chapters writers may be grouped as 'Catholics,' 'Protestants,' 'Arminians,' and so on; that is not to suggest a closer identity among them than their real opinions and associations justify; it is primarily to identify areas of controversy.

Each writer about Erasmus stands in two necessary relationships – one to previous writers about Erasmus, the other to his own intellectual, cultural, and social environment. There are correspondingly two demands on the observer: to analyse and explain the work of these

2 Pieter Geyl's *Napoleon: For and Against* was a model, and Wallace K. Ferguson's enduring *The Renaissance in Historical Thought: Five Centuries of Interpretation* the most influential work on a theme in early modern history. With the so-called Luther renaissance came various studies of how Luther has been seen in the German intellectual tradition: E.W. Zeeden's *Martin Luther und die Reformation im Urteil des deutschen Luthertums* on the period up to Lessing; Heinrich Bornkamm's *Luther im Spiegel der deutschen Geistesgeschichte*, which operated over a wider front, on the nineteenth and twentieth centuries. There has been special interest in the Catholic writers on the Reformers. See, eg, A. Herte *Das katholische Lutherbild im Bann der Lutherkommentare des Cochläus*; R. Stauffer *Luther vu par les catholiques*; F. Büsser *Das katholische Zwinglibild: Von der Reformation bis zur Gegenwart*.

writers in historical context; to contribute by a kind of historical
introspection to the understanding of Erasmus himself. Does understanding deepen from generation to generation? Or do stereotypes
establish themselves early and then hold sway over those that follow?
How powerful are the cross-currents set up by the religious or political
tumults of the age? How pervasive in this kind of literature is the
changing mental or emotional climate?

To answer one kind of question is essentially a scholarly task – the
commentator is tracing dependences and establishing affiliations,
testing for staleness or freshness, assessing clumsiness or finesse in the
handling of materials. The other kind of question calls for a host of
little histories and biographies. Each writer belonged to his own world;
his interpretation of Erasmus and his whole social and cultural world
must be related. That belief impels this enquiry. Some are major
figures – Beza, Grotius, Bayle, Bossuet, Gottfried Arnold – and the
task is to set their interpretations of Erasmus against current understandings of their thought and significance. Of others – minor and
obscure figures – one can but speculate and make a sketch.

This is a history of the interpretations of Erasmus, not a history of
his influence or of Erasmianism. Our subject is those who wrote about
Erasmus and deliberately addressed themselves to what the twentieth
century would call the problem of Erasmus. For our purposes Erasmus
must be mentioned by name; memorialists and biographers deserve a
place, naturally, but also those encountering him in controversy,
challenging him or associating themselves with him.[3] In its limited
way this may serve the larger and grander theme which would, of
course, also require an appreciation of the unacknowledged borrow-
ings, influences, and associations. Great essays have been attempted on
that larger theme, and some will be mentioned in what follows.
Synthesis will call for many more and will then depend on talents well
beyond those of the author of these pages.

I have said elsewhere: 'There is a history of writing about [Erasmus]
which is a history of important strains in the making of modern
civilization.'[4] Ultimately, the only justification for a study like this is
that it should show the great changes of early modern history – from

3 In any case, one cannot pretend to completeness but can hope only for a
reasonably representative coverage of the different areas of controversy.
The basis of any bibliography must be part 3 of F. Vander Haeghen
Bibliotheca Erasmiana. Editions of Erasmus' works have by and large not
been drawn into my analysis, though occasionally a preface or commentary
has seemed of such importance as to require inclusion in this kind of study.
4 'Erasmus of Rotterdam: Evangelical' 1

Reformation to Enlightenment – refracted in the interpretation of one influential but enigmatic human being. There are, of course, dangers of circularity: the Enlightenment may be expected to produce an Enlightenment Erasmus. I hope to have done better justice to the element of the unpredictable and the unforeseen in this story of the generations in encounter with Erasmus. Let me repeat: above all, I hope to have given the study life and actuality by showing how Erasmus was drawn into the encounters of the generations and the parties and the traditions with one another.

Acknowledgments

The idea of this book emerged in correspondence with Dr R. Schoeffel of University of Toronto Press and Professor J.K. McConica, Pontifical Institute of Mediaeval Studies. I wish to thank them for constant encouragement and for precious time spent on reading fragments of the work presented untimely for appraisal and criticism. The late Professor Beatrice Corrigan welcomed with characteristic generosity an unknown antipodean visitor to Toronto in 1974.

Many friends and colleagues have in their turn encouraged the work. May I without attempting a list of names express my gratitude? To one association I must, however, pay tribute. Since we first met at Yale University in 1965, Professor Roland Bainton has shown for my work that lively interest he brings to all scholarly efforts in Reformation history and Erasmian studies. I thank Professor Hugh Trevor-Roper, Dr Dominic Baker-Smith, and Dr Margaret Mann Phillips for a hospitable welcome and particular suggestions. Naturally, responsibility for the fate of such suggestions is mine.

Macquarie University has supported the undertaking with research grants, especially for books and microfilm and with a grant of study leave in 1974. I thank the officers of the Macquarie University Library for their patience with apparently bizarre requests for inter-library loans.

Library collections used were those of the J.P. Robarts Research Library, the Centre for Reformation and Renaissance Research (where Professor Harry Secor was a welcoming director), the Knox College and Emmanuel College Libraries of the University of Toronto, Yale University Library, the Newberry Library, the British Library, the Warburg Institute, the University of London Library, the Bodleian Library, Christ Church Library (to whose beautiful precincts I was

introduced by my friend Professor John McManners), the Gemeentebibliotheek, Rotterdam, and the Fisher Library of the University of
Sydney. Many acts of assistance in these places deserve more than
conventional expressions of appreciation. A note elsewhere marks the
ready response of the Bibliothèque de l'Arsenal in Paris to a query
about an important manuscript which was made available on
microfilm.

The book has been published with the help of grants from the
Canadian Federation for the Humanities, using funds provided by the
Social Sciences and Humanities Research Council of Canada, and from
the Publications Fund of the University of Toronto Press.

Mrs Jean Scott, Mrs Betty Williams, and Mrs Maureen Tyler have
typed the manuscript in its various parts and stages with much care and
– one might say – fortitude.

My son Nicholas helped to assemble the bibliography. I would also
like to thank Margaret Parker for her meticulous preparation of the
manuscript and Joyce Acheson for assistance with the index and proofs.

The work is dedicated with affection to my wife.

Abbreviations

꽃

Allen	P.S. and H.M. Allen *Opus epistolarum Des. Erasmi Roterodami* 12 vols, Oxford 1906–58
ADB	*Allgemeine deutsche Biographie* 56 vols, 1875–1912
ARG	*Archiv für Reformationsgeschichte*
BHR	*Bibliothèque d'humanisme et renaissance*
Biographie nationale	*Biographie nationale de Belgique* 27 vols, 1866–
Cath Enc	*The Catholic Encyclopedia* 12 vols, New York 1907–12
CWE	*The Collected Works of Erasmus* Toronto 1974–
DBF	Dictionnaire de biographie française 1933–
DNB	*Dictionary of National Biography* 21 vols, 1921–2
DTC	*Dictionnaire de théologie catholique* 15 vols, 1903–50
Gedenkschrift	*Gedenkschrift zum 400. Todestage des Erasmus von Rotterdam* Basel 1936
Hoefer	*Nouvelle Biographie générale depuis les temps les plus reculés jusqu'à nos jours* ed J.C.F. Hoefer, 46 vols, 1853–66
HR	*Humanisme et Renaissance*
LB	Erasmus. *Opera omnia,* ed J. Le Clerc, 10 vols, Leiden 1703ff
Michaud	*Biographie universelle (Michaud) ancienne et moderne* founded by J.F. Michaud and L.G. Michaud, new ed, 45 vols, 1842–65
NDB	*Neue deutsche Biographie* 1953–
New Cath Enc	*New Catholic Encyclopedia,* 15 vols, New York 1967
NNBW	*Nieuw Nederlandsch Biografisch Woordenboek* 10 vols, 1911–37

RE 3	*Realencyklopädie für protestantische Theologie und Kirche* 3rd ed, 21 vols (and Register) 1898–1909
RGG	*Die Religion in Geschichte und Gegenwart* 3rd ed, 6 vols (and Register), 1957–65
Scrinium Erasmianum	J. Coppens (ed) *Scrinium Erasmianum, Mélanges historiques publiés sous le patronage de l'Université de Louvain à l'occasion du cinquième centenaire de la naissance d'Erasme* 2 vols, Leiden 1969

PART ONE

IN THE CONFESSIONAL AGE

ONE

Introduction to Part One

ﷺ

ERASMUS LIVED AN EMBATTLED LIFE. Born illegitimate, he had to find his own footing in a world where family connection counted above everything else. Wishing to live free in a corporate society, where belonging was valued more than independence of mind, he must allay suspicion, attract patrons, and conjure friends – in short create an accepted status for himself. A monk of convenience, living outside his monastery, he must discover a personal vocation; not surprisingly there were years of uncertainty as he was pulled in different directions, as the intellectual influences of his youth and early manhood played over his essentially receptive and eclectic mind: traditional piety, *devotio moderna*, Italian humanism, the Fathers. The compass set steady only when he was already in full manhood. As publicist for a renewal and vast reconstruction of Christian society, he was bound to arouse enmities, to irritate vested interests, to provoke the defenders of entrenched positions and the apologists for established ways. An easy fluency and an at times astonishing candour or negligence of expression could stir up controversy, and the sensitive, suspicious, defensive strains in his personality helped keep that controversy alive.

There were warm friendships and spontaneous, unstinted admiration. One thinks of Erasmus' triumphant journey along the Rhine in 1514 and the greetings of his Strasbourg friends.[1] On another journey he met a customs officer, Christopher Eschenfelder, who leapt for joy when he discovered whom he had for a guest, shouting his happiness and calling his children, his wife, and all his friends.[2] That association

1 See Roland H. Bainton *Erasmus of Christendom* 159.
2 Erasmus to Beatus Rhenanus, Louvain, [c 15 October] 1518, Allen Ep 867, III 395

endured. Years later Eschenfelder was said to have kissed with the deepest emotion Erasmus' handwriting on a letter.[3] In 1518 Eobanus Hesse paid a visit of homage to Erasmus at Louvain, bearing letters and presents from the humanist circle at Erfurt.[4] Long separations and differences of inner direction or outward experience could not destroy his intimacy with his English friends, Colet, Fisher, and More.

Enmity was no less active and persistent than friendship. Noël Beda and the Sorbonne pursued him with stubborn rancour as the fount of heresies and author of all the church's troubles. His old age was beset with accusation and reproach, much of it strident, some of it grotesque. Luther called him an 'epicurean,' a 'wormy nut,' a 'stratagem of Satan,' 'without God.'[5] Julius Caesar Scaliger portrayed him as a drunkard, a restless parasite, an enemy to Jesus Christ, and a stirrer of tempests and threw his illegitimate birth in his teeth.[6]

This study of interpretations of Erasmus from the decade or so after his death to the middle years of the eighteenth century cannot leave unmentioned the extravagances of a Luther or a Scaliger. The judgments of the one naturally had unrivalled authority in German Protestantism; the influence of the other may be traced among Catholic controversialists, in the 'Mediterranean' reception of Erasmus, and in the reverberations of the Ciceronian affair. In a sense, the interpretation of Erasmus in the mid- and late sixteenth century was but a continuation of the controversies of his lifetime.

On the other hand, changes in the historical situation – the lightening or darkening of the historical landscape – were also registered in the interpretations of Erasmus. Fifteen fifty was no longer 1536, and 1563 or 1572 or 1610 all represented distinctive vantage-points. When the sources in use were limited and rhetoric generally carried the day over sober criticism, judgments received from authoritative figures of the past were bound to be for ever reiterated. Beating against them, however, and modifying them constantly were the flow of events and, above all, the changing fortunes in the confessional struggles. The primary interest of this study is in Erasmus' reputation as a barometer of the changing atmosphere.

3 Konrad Nyder to Erasmus, 20 December 1534, Allen Ep 2984, XI 57
4 Allen IV 405
5 *Luther's Works* (American edition) LIV *Table Talk* 19, 50, 73, 312
6 *J. Caes. Scaligeri pro M. Tullio Cicerone* ... 9–10, 27, 54. Scaliger to Le Ferron, 31 January 1535, in *Jul. Caes. Scaligeri epistolae aliquot* ... Ep 15, 45–6. Cf Vernon Hall Jr *Life of Julius Caesar Scaliger (1484–1558)* 100–3, 113.

The situation when he died was threatening but not hopeless. The reunion of Christians – the hope of his last years – was still on the agenda of church and state. Iconoclasm, riot, persecution fell short of civil war. The church remained unreformed, but there were evidences of good will and of serious intention. Might reform come without fixing the divisions and alienating half of christendom? It was not to be. Erasmus saw men returning from the evangelical preaching in Basel not milder but more morose and sour in spirit: 'I have never entered your churches, but now and then I have seen the hearers of your sermons come out like men possessed, with anger and rage painted on their faces ... They come out like warriors, animated by the oration of the general to some mighty attack ... Are not riots common among this evangelical people? Do they not for small causes take themselves to force?'[7] He may or may not have been fair to those he saw, but this account was prophetic of the growing bitterness and the deepening savagery which the religious conflict was to bring to Europe. Of these things Erasmus' own reputation was to be a victim. Interpretation of Erasmus in the first two generations was the barometer of a deteriorating atmosphere.

7 *Epistola contra quosdam, qui se falso jactant evangelicos* (1529) (LB X (col) 1578–9) Eng tr in Preserved Smith *Erasmus: A Study of His Life, Ideals and Place in History* 391–2

TWO

Catholicism:
Friends and Enemies

❧

IN THE LAST MONTHS OF HIS LIFE Erasmus was caught in indecision about moving or settling. In May 1535 he had come back to Protestant Basel, which he had left for religion's sake six years before. He had true friends there, and the whole temper and atmosphere of the city-state was congenial to him. Yet there were times when he longed to be in Catholic territory and even under the Habsburg shadow. Throughout his life he had been the enemy of a prevailing clericalism and dynasticism and at the end he did not deny those struggles. Nevertheless in his last fatal weakness expressions of a deep and abiding loyalty were forced from him: 'If only Brabant were closer!'[1] If he wanted the complete renewal of the spirit that informed them, he yet belonged to the old church and the old Europe. A study of the fate of Erasmus' reputation rightly begins with the generation of Catholics who considered themselves his heirs.

The first 'interpretations' of Erasmus after his death were the elegies and epitaphs of his friends and admirers. Their picture of Erasmus belonged to the war propaganda of humanism against its enemies: Erasmus turned back barbarism, purified literature, instructed youth in better ways, brought the sacred books again to light. But beneath the humanist periods with their echoing of literary and academic feuds there was genuine grief for the loss of a friend and master. Doctrinally and ideologically these pieces represented a kind of Catholicism which in the brutal confrontations of the later sixteenth century was to be trampled down, a more open and moderating, less defensive and

---

1   To Conradus Goclenius, 28 June 1536, Allen Ep 3130, XI 337. Cf C. Reedijk
     'Das Lebenende des Erasmus.'

militant Catholicism than triumphed finally at the Council of Trent and in the new religious orders. More particularly they represented the different circles or settings where Erasmus' memory was cherished: among the reforming bishops, in the Habsburg entourage, especially among the court humanists of the east European lands of the dynasty, where Christendom was face to face with catastrophe, and of the Netherlands, and among the literate and learned of the German cities.

When within a month of Erasmus' death, Fridericus Nausea (1480–1552) wrote his *Monodia* on that event, he spoke of a grief which distracted and incapacitated him.[2] From boyhood he had loved Erasmus as a teacher and a guide of incomparable virtues and divine gifts.[3] When still a young man, though after completing legal and theological studies in Italy, Nausea reissued some of Erasmus' educational works (1522–4).[4] The two men met in Basel in 1525 when Nausea was accompanying Cardinal Campegio on his mission to Germany over the Luther affair.[5] Their relationship endured – close but sometimes clouded, as was unavoidable for the friends of the aging and testy Erasmus. It was the relationship of master and disciple; the master did not forebear a 'trenchant criticism' of the disciple's literary work, his lack of discrimination, his too easy succumbing to the 'itch of writing.'[6] In his own career Nausea represented a moderate Catholicism. He sustained a many-sided homiletic activity as cathedral preacher at Mainz but he also stood out against the Reformers. Later Erasmus recognized him as a spokesman for his ideas at the court of Vienna.[7] He was to become bishop of Vienna in 1541 and fight in the Council of Trent for King Ferdinand's moderating proposals of clerical marriage and communion in both kinds. An irenic strain ran through his endeavours.

The *Monodia* circles around two themes: Erasmus' qualities and his place in the life of his time, in intellectual history, and, one may say, in salvation history.

The first theme needs little development. Erasmus is presented as the pattern of the Christian humanist. His fertility of mind and

2 Dedication to King Ferdinand, 18 August 1536, Allen Ep 3139, XI 350
3 *Friderici Nauseae ... Monodia* LB I 8* 3ᵛ
4 On Nausea, Allen VI 78–9; ADB 23: 321–5; RGG 4, cols 1384–5; J. Metzner *Friedrich Nausea aus Waischenfeld, Bischof von Wien*
5 *Monodia* 8* 4ʳ
6 Erasmus to Nausea, 8 March 1526, Allen Ep 1673, VI 278
7 Erasmus to Johann Koler, 19 February 1534, Allen Ep 2906, X 357: 'Is de offensis Romanis mea Concordia pertulit in aulam Ferdinandi ... '

rhetorical power put him ahead of any rival. He wrote so well in every branch of philosophy that he outshone the specialists in each and made their works appear insipid by contrast with his; he wrote more than others could read and filled a whole library while others were putting together mere parts. His intellectual fertility did not weaken with age – he carried on the study of letters as vigorously at seventy as he had done in his youth. To eloquence Erasmus added the higher qualities of innocence of life and a more than human wisdom. His religion was as free from superstition as his life from the vices which disfigured the lives even of the philosophers. There was in him a concord of virtues so that 'his gaiety never in any way detracted from his seriousness nor his simplicity from his gravity nor his humanity from his dignity.'[8]

The second theme, interwoven with the first through the whole piece, requires a more complex development. Erasmus' immediate setting must be determined, and his links with antiquity and posterity established, even beyond the assertion that in his virtues examples abounded 'which posterity will wish to follow and antiquity, if the nature of things allowed, would like to have claimed for itself.'[9]

First, the question, much beloved by the humanists, of Erasmus' *patria*: was he French or German? It is no surprise that Nausea, born Friedrich Grau of Waischenfeld near Bamberg, should associate him with Germany, of the European lands 'omnium longe nobilissimam.'[1] But his true *patria* was Holland, whose inhabitants were celebrated – here Nausea follows Erasmus' own words on the adage 'Auris Batava' – not only in war but for simplicity and sincerity in manners, for humanity, for learned piety and pious erudition, for freedom from treachery and deceit. Erasmus was a model of these characteristics of his people: prudent, simple and sincere, trusting, generous – even to the unworthy.[2]

Nausea touches lightly on the strictly biographical problems. Erasmus' illegitimacy, which Scaliger denounced with savage rancour and which later biographers were to handle with differing degrees of incredulity, embarrassment, and candour, was covered by a veil of words: only the worthiest of parents could have produced such a son; the fruit proves the quality of the tree; in any case, true nobility stems not from his parents but from the man himself ...[3] The circumstances

8 *Monodia* 9* 1[r]
9 Ibid 8* 4[r]
1 Ibid
2 Ibid 8* 4[v]
3 Ibid

of Erasmus' death in a Protestant city were also to embarrass Catholic apologists; Nausea again relied on a rhetorical solution: could a death, whatever the manner or place or time, be bad when so holy a life had gone before?[4]

Secondly, Nausea refers to Erasmus' place in the intellectual battles of his age. For those wanting to know and understand divine things his writings were a boundless store from which to draw counsel and advice and a defence against the heretics. He had enemies, but only among those whose god was their belly, the ignorant among the monks and theologians, falsely accusing him of heresy. Blame from them was true praise.[5]

Socrates and the Athenians, Erasmus and Christians: Nausea made the comparison, the first of many historical analogies to play through the Erasmus literature. Ingratitude towards Erasmus would be more reprehensible than the ingratitude of the Athenian towards Socrates – that corresponded with the scale of the two achievements. Socrates taught profane knowledge to the youth of one city; Erasmus taught the sacred and evangelical disciplines to men and women of all ages through the whole world – his voice, like that of any apostle, was heard to the farthest ends of the earth. Who of recent times more happily than Erasmus brought gospel truth forth from darkness? Who more wisely than Erasmus discovered the pearl of great price lying hidden in a field? 'To whom do we owe it that in our age the ploughman at his plough thinks on some part of the Gospel? Is it not to Erasmus? And that the weaver accompanies his labours at the loom with something from the Gospel? Is it not to Erasmus?'[6] As Philip of Macedon rejoiced that his son was born in the time of Aristotle, as Christ bade the disciples rejoice because they saw in Him a sight denied to the great kings and prophets who had gone before, so contemporary Christians should thank God to have lived in the time of Erasmus. Through his work they see and hear Christ as the disciples did, since, in the sacred writings which he made available, Christ lives and breathes more efficaciously than when He moved among men, if only they have eyes

4 Ibid 9* 1ᵛ
5 Some of the expressions were Erasmus' own. In a letter of 10 June 1527 he advised Nausea to look to Christ alone and attribute victory only to Him. It would mean nothing to have Luther put down, 'si victoriam intercipiant Pharisaici quidam, qui gulae ventrique suo serviunt, non Jesu Christo' (Allen Ep 1834, VII 81).
6 *Monodia* 9* 2ʳ. One is reminded of the famous passage from the *Paraclesis* about the vernacular scriptures.

to see and ears to hear.[7] So Erasmus takes his place in sacred history. The recollection of his great virtues shining like stars will inspire others to virtue and light the way to Christ. He belonged to the company of saints. 'Sanctus,' said Nausea to King Ferdinand, 'enim erat Erasmus.'[8]

The tones of Nausea's portrait of Erasmus were bright though the background was sombre: schism in Germany, intransigence in the citadels of the old faith, catastrophe in eastern Europe. This brightness expressed the still undimmed hopes of the moderating party. Both the sombre experience of Nausea and his hopes were shared by the great Hungarian humanist Nicolaus Olahus (1493–1568), whose elegy on the master's death may be taken as a representative utterance of the circles in which he moved – the humanists about the Hungarian court, the makers of religious policy in the Habsburg government, the Erasmians of the Netherlands.

Olahus, it has been said, belonged to a second generation of Hungarian humanists who not only were taken with Erasmus' critical and satirical works but penetrated more deeply into his thought.[9] Born in Transylvania (he might be called the 'first humanist of Romanian origin'),[1] he entered the Hungarian court in his youth. Ecclesiastical preferment came easily to the young man. In the fateful year 1526 he became secretary to the young king Louis II; within months the king was dead, the nobility decimated, the survival of the kingdom itself left uncertain by the great Turkish victory at Mohacs. Olahus remained in the service of the widow, the Habsburg princess Mary. In 1531, when Mary became regent in the Netherlands for her brother, Charles V, Olahus came to Brussels, helping to make the conjuncture between Hungarian and Netherlandish humanism, between the Habsburg administration and the reforming party in the church. With Mary at the Diet of Augsburg in 1530 he had delivered two discourses in line with Erasmus' views, insisting on the dangers of religious division in Europe before the growing power of the Turk.[2] Correspondence between Olahus and Erasmus began at that time; it was from Olahus that the letters were to come persuading Erasmus to return to the Netherlands and trying to set at rest his anxieties about his health, his incapacity for

7   Ibid
8   Dedication 350
9   Tibor Kardos 'L'esprit d'Erasme en Hongrie' 205
1   Constantia Crisan 'Erasme en Roumanie' 182
2   Imre Trencsényi-Waldapfel 'L'humanisme belge et l'humanisme hongrois liés par l'esprit d'Erasme' 219

life at court, the animosity of the monks.[3] The exchanges were lively, the friendship warm.

When the news of Erasmus' death arrived in Brussels elegiac verses were quickly fashioned in the humanist circle. Olahus, burdened by affairs, was reluctantly persuaded to take part by Frans von Cranevelt, humanist and jurist, member of the Grand Council of Malines; in a few days he 'poured out rather than wrote' his poem.[4]

The traveller standing before Erasmus' grave is told of Erasmus' life and virtue.[5] He gave evidence of genius as a boy; his youth was dedicated to intense study, not least of the scriptures; old age did not take away his powers but made him in everything more fruitful. He outstripped other men in virtue as the sun surpasses the stars. Of this his writings bore witness – they showed the way to the summits of virtue and to the kingdom of heaven. A brittle rhetoric, perhaps. Yet what follows makes the real bearing clear: Mary wanted Erasmus to return to Brabant to pursue there sacred learning. Erasmus was the leader of those who sought renewal through learning: that is the point of substance beneath Olahus' lines. The conceit in a second, briefer epitaph says much the same: Erasmus longs to be present at the reforming council; God, however, calls him to join the heavenly host, saying that the council has his writings to approve; He wishes Erasmus to live with Him.[6] Olahus here represents the program of the moderate, reforming party for the coming council. In the responsible and difficult years of his return to Hungary after 1542 he was not altogether to abandon that program.[7]

Even more than in the entourage of the great dynasty for whose imperialism he could feel little sympathy, Erasmus was regretted in

3　Eg, Olahus to Erasmus, 26 July 1532, Allen Ep 2693, x 69–72
4　Ladislaus Juhász 'De carminibus Nicolai Olahi in mortem Erasmi scriptis' 317
5　'Elegia ad sepulchrum Erasmi Roterodami' in ibid 317–19. Also in LB I 9*2ᵛ–3ʳ. First published in D. Erasmi Roterodami epitaphia per clarissimos aliquot viros conscripta (Louvain 1537).
6　Juhász 'Carminibus' 319–20:
　　　Jussu pontificis Pauli cum doctus Erasmus
　　　　Concilio patrum gestit adesse sacro,
　　　Tunc Deus omnipotens superas transvexit ad auras,
　　　　Coetibus ut divum redderet aethereis.
　　　Concilio patrum poterunt tua scripta probari,
　　　　Vivere te mecum malo, ait ipse Deus.
7　Bishop of Zagreb 1543, of Eger 1548; primate and archbishop of Esztergom 1553 (Allen vIII 468)

many of the more humble courts of the German Empire; even more than in the marches of eastern Europe one finds his traces in the borderlands of the Rhine valley, where he so often travelled in his lifetime. In the Duchy of Cleves on the Lower Rhine there had long been a reforming tradition in the sober and sincere spirit of the 'devotio moderna.' Erasmus himself gave advice on church regulations in the duchy in 1532–3. Those regulations – in their gradualism and modera- tion, their biblicism and irenicism, their call for preaching and teaching and for the recovery of the values of the primitive church – took on an 'Erasmian colouring.'[8] Cleves, in the face of many difficulties and uncertainties, stood for the moderating Catholicism whose under- standing of Erasmus has taken first place in our discussion.

A funeral oration of 1536 by Guilielmus Insulanus (Wilhelm von Grevenbroich, d 1556) consciously associated Erasmus with this at- mosphere at the Cleves court.[9] Dedicated to the prince William, who in 1539 was to succeed his father, John, in the hazardous pursuit of the middle way[1] and who valued Erasmus' memory, it regretted the loss to the Christian commonwealth on the eve of a general council which was to moderate its conflicts and right its wrongs.[2] The biographical treat- ment is sketchy but sufficient to establish the tone. Erasmus was born at Rotterdam of humble but honest parents; at a time when good letters were beginning to raise their head in Germany he was educated at Deventer by the learned and pious Alexander Hegius. From the seed there cultivated, a great harvest was later to arise; he entered and then left the monastery – this was no desertion but an honest self- awareness, for he saw that he was destined for other and better things.[3] A free man, Erasmus pursued the study of wisdom in many lands. He enjoyed the friendship of the learned and the great; his name began to

8 John Patrick Dolan *The Influence of Erasmus, Witzel and Cassander in the Church Ordinances and Reform Proposals of the United Duchies of Cleve during the Middle Decades of the Sixteenth Century* 9–23; Jean-Claude Margolin 'La politique culturelle de Guillaume, duc de Cleves'
9 *Oratio funebris in obitum Desiderii Erasmi Roterodami* ...
1 It is disputed how far William swung towards Protestantism. Dolan argues that Cleves held to a reformist Catholicism but that William personally trod an unsure path (*Influence* 25). Margolin has a more positive appreciation ('Politique culturelle').
2 In 1533 Insulanus wrote a piece proposing Cologne as the seat of the Council (ADB IX 648–9). Bonifacius Amerbach was another who wished that Erasmus could be present at the Council (to Johann Paumgartner, 1 February 1537 (preface to *Catalogi duo*), Allen Ep. 3141, XI 351–6).
3 'Oratio funebris' 1850B–1851A

shine so that when, for example, he visited Italy, he was already famous and sought after. From a mastery of classical learning (revealed in his *Adagia*) he turned to sacred letters, working at Basel with Froben, the printer. Here in a holy work he transcended himself and all his other achievements.[4]

One may find a certain humanistic blandness in this oration. It is wordy and badly proportioned. The space given to a defence of Erasmus against a charge of cupidity seems ludicrously excessive – the part of a philosopher, it is solemnly said, is the sober use of wealth, not its complete abrogation.[5] Much is made of the envy from which Erasmus suffered, and again he is defended from his enemies on both sides of the religious division, but the defence lacks bite. Ecumenical mildness or lack of passion? To Erasmus himself is attributed an unusual modesty and patience and constancy of spirit. He referred all to Christ alone. How then could he dread the ill will of those who misunderstood his spirit and intention?[6] The tone is too didactic, even a little sentimental, but there is a true perception as well: the mind of Erasmus had roots in the teaching of the pious and learned Hegius. Above all, Insulanus sees clearly Erasmus' place in the history of Christian thought; he belonged with those who, without putting orthodoxy into question, wanted to free theology from too mechanical a method and too sterile a spirit. He regretted that theology had been reduced 'ad summulas ac indices'; he wished that the time and energy given to disputations which made men more learned rather than better, and perhaps not even more learned, were spent on reading the Old and New Testaments and the best and oldest commentators on scripture. His enemies accused him of pride for condemning the more recent theologians and of an intellectual restlessness which led to sedition – he was said to have offered ammunition to Luther. On the other side, Luther's associates accused him of frivolousness for not joining them. Erasmus was caught at a crossroads. Yet he was determined to show his colours clearly on the matters in dispute. He was not hypocritical and opportunist but open and candid.[7]

It is a sober and defensible judgment, and Insulanus showed himself in contact with an accurate tradition and perhaps with the Erasmus circle itself when he came at the end to write about Erasmus' last days

4 Ibid 1851C–1852F
5 Ibid 1856D–1857E
6 Ibid 1854E
7 Ibid 1855C–F

and death. Erasmus was patient, calling with constancy of mind on the mercy of God. He was said to have passed away crying, 'Miserere mei, Deus.'[8] Such an ending was true to the Erasmus of Insulanus' depiction – the moderate, devout Catholic Christian who set a pattern for the reforming and irenic endeavours in the Duchy of Cleves.

A Cleves tradition about Erasmus persisted. Konrad Heresbach (1496–1576) belonged to the humanist confraternity in the 1520s. Friendship with Erasmus himself led him in turn to an association with Froben, to the chair of Greek at Freiburg, and to the service of the Cleves court, first as tutor to the prince William. By 1535 he was privy councillor; already he had helped fashion the church regulations of the duchy. To religious questions he brought the mediating party's spirit of reconciliation – no break with the old church but also no persecution and no stifling of reform. He condemned equally those princes who forced changes on the church in order to establish their own tyranny or enhance their wealth and those who stubbornly defended church abuses for fear of losing lucrative dignities or appointments for their children or friends. All that is Erasmian enough, and so is a sense of the public weal, expressed in efforts for school and law reform in the 1550s and even for the improvement of agriculture – Heresbach wrote the first full account of agricultural conditions in the German region.[9]

In his own setting Heresbach also contributed to the 'mirror of princes' literature. His treatise *On the Education and Upbringing of the Children of Princes, destined for rule, and on the administration of the Christian commonwealth* gave him an opportunity later in life to proclaim his esteem for Erasmus. Why should he take up a subject so well and so fully treated by others and not least by Erasmus in his *Institutio principis christiani?* 'I must indeed confess that that man, whose name should be introduced only in honour and who deserves the best of all the learned, wrote purely and fully on many matters of the greatest usefulness and importance for our religion and age ...'[1] Heresbach himself makes use of his advice and commends it to all princes and teachers of princes. But since Erasmus wrote circumstances have changed; there are storms and agitations, and Christendom faces its greatest crisis in eight hundred years. Princes must be forearmed for facing new and terrifying conditions. If Erasmus were writing now, he

---

8 Ibid 1858c
9 NDB VIII 606–7; ADB XII 103–5; *Erasme: Declamatio de pueris statim ac liberaliter instituendis* 29–40
1 *De educandis erudiendisque principum liberis ...* A4ᵛ

Beatus Rhenanus
An early engraved portrait by an unknown artist
Bibliothèque Municipale de Sélestat

would be attuning his advice to these dangerous times.[2] Here is the moderate Catholic faith in the continuing value of Erasmus' counsel as the crisis deepened in the sixteenth century. Heresbach was but adding what Erasmus himself could no longer add. Also, there was a wisdom which Erasmus could not know which comes only from the experience of ruling; Heresbach could not forgo the 'practical' statesman's little sniff of superiority over the scholar's remoteness from affairs.[3]

To go from the princely courts to the cities of Alsace and the Upper Rhine is to move into the Erasmian heartland.[4] Erasmus was a city man; a certain bourgeois feeling runs through his appeals for peace and moderation in government. He lived longest in two German-speaking cities of the Upper Rhine, Basel and Freiburg. Beatus Rhenanus (Beat Bild from Rheinau, 1485–1547), one of the most attractive personalities in the Upper Rhine circle of humanists, was bound to Erasmus not only by a self-effacing friendship but also by a common experience of life in the cities of the region.[5] They were associated for five years in the Froben press in Basel. Beatus Rhenanus had already done editorial work for Estienne in Paris and Schürer in Strasbourg; he belonged to the world of the scholarly printers who offered a kind of alternative university to the lay, bourgeois society of the time. Between him and Erasmus there grew up a comradeship of work on this intellectual frontier. In 1526 Rhenanus returned to Sélestat, where he had gone to school, to continue his philological and historical labours, but their relationship was unbroken. It is not surprising that the one little masterpiece in the first generation of writing about Erasmus should come from the pen of Rhenanus and out of the Upper Rhine humanist circle; it was commissioned as preface to the Froben edition of the *Opera omnia* (Basel 1538–40).

The opening theme of Rhenanus is Erasmus' fame; Rotterdam, where he was born, and Deventer, where he went to school, may justly boast of their association with his fame.[6] His reputation was estab-

---

2 Dangerous not least for Cleves. Duke William's attempt to strengthen Cleves politically and territorially and to extend its influence as a pioneer of moderate church reform in the Lower Rhine was severely checked by a war with Emperor Charles v over Guelders, 1543 (Dolan *Influence* 27; H. Holborn *A History of Modern Germany: The Reformation* 222–3; K. Brandi *Emperor Charles v* 501–3).
3 *De educandis* 5ʳ
4 Cf G. Ritter *Erasmus und der deutsche Humanistenkreis am Oberrhein*.
5 NDB I 682–3; Allen II 60
6 Text in Allen I 56–71. I use the English translation by John C. Olin *Desiderius Erasmus: Christian Humanism and the Reformation, Selected*

lished early: a teacher, delighted with his progress, prophesied that he would reach the very summit of learning.[7] This theme, plainly stated at the beginning, runs through the whole work. Nowhere, however, is it separated from another and more robust theme – Erasmus' vocation in scholarship and its social and cultural significance. All the military exploits of the Batavi did not bring as much glory to Holland as this one scholar. If soldiers who defend their country are honoured, how much more justly is he 'who of his own accord consumed, not any brief time, but his whole life in the service of letters, employing his talents to the public advantage, unmindful of his own enjoyment?' As a young man he, with his friend Willem Hermans, devoted his time to study while their fellows were feasting or fooling or sleeping. So throughout his life 'he preferred the public usefulness of his studies to all honors and to the crass pleasures of this life.'[8]

In Paris (in the 1490s) he surpassed all others in reputation for learning and faithful teaching. That reputation went before him to England and later to Italy; he took into Italy the erudition which others were accustomed to bring away.[9] Reputation, however, counted less than vocation: Rhenanus himself strikes the balance. For Erasmus, writer and editor, what mattered was not the applause but the joy in the work itself. ' "Here I am on my own field of action," he said. And so he was.'[1]

From his own knowledge and from talk within the Erasmus circle, Rhenanus put into the biographical record items that were to be the essential staple of biographies of Erasmus until the eighteenth century: the evil guardian who placed him in a monastery, his studies there with Willem Hermans, his new life with Henry of Bergen, bishop of Cambrai, his becoming a Scotist under the bishop's patronage at the University of Paris, his friendships in England and in Italy at Bologna, Venice, Padua, and Rome. Some unhappy episodes became favourites among the early biographers: how he nearly came to grief at Dover

---

Writings 31–54. Cross-reference may be made to an earlier sketch in Rhenanus' dedication of Erasmus' edition of Origen to Hermann von Wied, the reforming archbishop of Cologne, 15 August 1536 (Allen I 52–6).

7 Olin *Desiderius Erasmus* 32. This was Jan Synthen, one of the Brothers of the Common Life. Melanchthon (see next chapter) associated the episode with Rodolphus Agricola, the pioneer German humanist, but Allen considers Rhenanus the better authority (I 57, n25).

8 Olin *Desiderius Erasmus* 32–3, 46

9 Ibid 34, 36, 39

1 Ibid 43; ' "Hic sum" inquit "in meo campo." Et sic erat' (Allen I 64).

when his fortune was confiscated by customs and at Bologna when his dress was confused with that of the plague doctors.[2] To Rhenanus' famous description of his physical appearance all later pen portraits were indebted: 'He had a fair complexion, light blond hair in his youth, bluish gray eyes, a pleasant expression ...'[3] But about his parentage there was silence, except for an oblique reference to the papal dispensation affecting his illegitimacy.[4] The works were not presented systematically: 'His books are extant, nor is it necessary to recount them by name.'[5]

What savour does Rhenanus leave of Erasmus' personality? He speaks of his charm, candour, and amiability and makes much of his generosity.[6] He distinguishes this portrait from the mere conventional image of the good man by touching also on his more angular qualities, his sense of personal freedom and his writer's courage: he was prepared to make severe judgments, 'clear proof of the most resolute and discerning character.'[7] His death was truly pious. In a brief forerunner to the life composed much closer to the event Rhenanus had written with great feeling on this contentious point. Amid acute sufferings Erasmus, with a scholar's heroism, 'never ceased to write.' At the end he gave clear proof of Christian patience and bore witness that all his hope was in Christ.[8]

The associations and allegiances of Erasmus as Rhenanus describes them will be the best clue to the tendency of this work and to its historical context. Clearly the esteem felt for Erasmus in Rome counts a good deal with Rhenanus. Nor is it surprising in a work dedicated to Charles v to find much made of his Burgundian and Habsburg connections. Who honoured and esteemed the emperor more? But Rhenanus

2 Olin *Desiderius Erasmus* 33–7
3 Ibid 52
4 Ibid 37
5 Ibid 50. It seems less remarkable now than it did to Alfred Hartmann in 1936 that Rhenanus did not highlight the *Moriae encomium* and the *Colloquia*, the two writings of Erasmus 'die allein die Jahrhunderte überdauern sollten' ('Beatus Rhenanus: Leben und Werke des Erasmus' 11). Rhenanus mentions the *Adagia* a number of times and the work on the New Testament and the Fathers.
6 Olin *Desiderius Erasmus* 34, 53
7 Ibid 45, 50
8 The preface to Hermann von Wied, Allen I 53. Rhenanus, with the advice of Bonifacius Amerbach, established the authoritative tradition about the circumstances of Erasmus' death. (Insulanus, as we have seen, was already acquainted with it.) Cf Reedijk 'Das Lebenende.'

goes too far. An un-Erasmian imperialism is one note that does not ring true: 'Indeed Erasmus has always sought ... to give honor to the most noble House of Austria, cradle of so many Caesars, whose empire is scarcely limited by the Julian and Rhaetian Alps and by the northern ocean.'[9] Nevertheless no claim is made to an exclusive allegiance. The honour paid to Erasmus by the emperor's enemies – Henry VIII, Clement VII, Francis I – is given its due.

The cities too are mentioned – Erasmus had from them the honours paid to magnates and ambassadors.[1] In fact, nowhere better than in Rhenanus' picture of Erasmus revising proofs 'amid the din of the presses' in Froben's press at Basel does one sense the actualities of Erasmus' life. Here he is at work among his bourgeois friends.[2] It is revealing of the work's orientation that Rhenanus, writing to Charles V, praised the moderation of the Basel Reformation; in his earlier sketch he had pointed to the signs of mutual attachment between the man and the city: the sense of public loss at his death, the presence of all the light and learning of Basel at his funeral, the thoughtful and generous provisions of his will for the city's young and needy.[3]

Rhenanus places Erasmus' work within the classic humanist understanding of the Renaissance. 'In Germany and France letters lay cold and lifeless ... And behold, immediately when the *Adagiorum chiliades* and the *De copia verborum et rerum* were published, the knowledge of languages began to come forth, like the sun breaking through the clouds.'[4] His aims were not at all precious or merely literary. The fruits of scholarship were to be made accessible to all. And at the end of his whole effort was the reform of theology and the church. Here Erasmus again stands forth as the spokesman of moderate, reforming Catholicism; Rhenanus' 'Life' is in fact the best account of that way of seeing him. Erasmus saw the danger of speaking too freely (in retrospect he regretted some of his own expressions) but he said what was necessary: recognizing 'that ecclesiastical discipline had declined far from the purity of the Gospels, that the Christian people were weighed down with many practices, and that the consciences of men were ensnared by various tricks,' he attacked the arrogance,

9 Olin *Desiderius Erasmus* 44. On the national enthusiasm of the Upper Rhine humanists, of which Rhenanus' historical work was a superior expression, see Ritter *Erasmus* 22.
1 Olin *Desiderius Erasmus* 45
2 Ibid 42
3 Ibid 51; Allen I 54
4 Olin *Desiderius Erasmus* 46

greed, and superstition responsible.[5] Rhenanus shared this understanding of the needs of the church, which had points of contact also with the state of mind of Charles v himself around 1540, that time in the German empire when attempts at religious reunion came closest to success.[6]

The *Commentaria ... de actis et scriptis Martini Lutheri* of Johannes Cochlaeus (Mainz 1549) belongs to a different time; one is tempted to say that it breathes a different spirit. Germany had had its first taste of religious war; the emperor had made the first (as it proved, futile) attempt to impose a solution on the parties. Cochlaeus (c 1479–1552) had come out from the beginning against Luther; he was a vigorous polemicist, one of the stalwarts of the 'pre-Tridentine controversial theology' which struggled in vain against the seemingly irresistible flood-tide of Lutheran propaganda.[7] Yet even then simple categories will not do. One is not dealing with mutually exclusive schools or firm Catholic 'parties,' the moderates and the intransigents. Cochlaeus was not an intransigent or a backwoodsman. He was an educational reformer, a humanist, and a comrade of Nausea.[8] They shared the friendship of Erasmus. We have not yet crossed the watershed beyond which Erasmian humanism and the reform movements of the early sixteenth century are seen only through a cloud of suspicion and Erasmus is condemned equally with Luther as an enemy of the faith.[9]

In the *Commentaria* Erasmus' judgments on Luther are treated as authoritative, a stick for beating the heresiarch. Erasmus is described as a 'man of the highest learning, eloquence and authority in Germany.' He shook the faith of many in Luther's teachings, which until then had seemed evangelical, with his diatribe on free will.[1] For a long time Luther did not deign a reply, since Erasmus had written in Latin and not for the unlettered multitude whom Luther favoured. He was stirred to reply at last by the translation of Erasmus' work into German. Characteristically he showered Erasmus with calumnies but mixed them with blandishments, either to gratify his moderate associates or cunningly to weaken Erasmus' reputation with the or-

5 Ibid 48–9
6 W. Teichmann 'Die kirchliche Haltung des Beatus Rhenanus: Eine kirchengeschichtliche Studie'; H. Jedin *History of the Council of Trent* I
7 Jedin *History* I 393–6
8 Allen VII 145
9 That judgment had, of course, been anticipated by Aleander, with whom Cochlaeus was associated at Worms in 1521.
1 *Commentaria Joannis Cochlaei ...* 140

thodox.[2] Luther's judgments on Erasmus were pure expediency: as long as he hoped to win him to his side, Erasmus was a great theologian; now he was more ignorant than the scholastics.[3] Erasmus made a worthy reply, especially in the second part of his *Hyperaspistes*; Luther's arguments were here so vigorously and so plainly refuted that neither he nor his henchmen thereafter dared a reply. Erasmus saw from Luther's violent language and the depraved manners of the so-called evangelicals the spirit that inhabited them.[4]

So Erasmus is subdued to a purely polemical purpose. Cochlaeus may quote his moving reply to Luther's charge that he wished to restore paganism,[5] but Erasmus does not here speak for his own values and purposes. One senses that the age of fragmentation, of partial and partisan judgments, where writings are raked over for telling phrases for or against, has already come.[6]

One may use the word *fragmentary* of the famous collection of *Elogia* of illustrious men by Paolo Giovio (1483–1552). This kind of work reduced complex lives to little sketches, to quick touches of the brush, to suggestive or ironic remarks. Giovio, whose formal career lay elsewhere, in medicine and the church (after 1528 he was bishop of Nocera in the Kingdom of Naples, although he continued to live in northern Italy), had from his youth the *idée fixe* of collecting, in copy or in the original, the portraits of those great in thought or action.[7] The gallery he gathered in his villa at Como was in a long classical and Renaissance tradition, the cult of fame. Giovio published his sketchy *Elogia* of those represented in the gallery but never realized his ambition of engraving and reproducing the portraits themselves. That was to be done twenty years after his death by another Italian, the printer Perna, who came as a refugee to Basel and its more open intellectual atmosphere.[8] He had woodcuts made of a selection of the most important portraits – not without some serious distortions – and published them with the texts in two beautiful in-folios in 1575–7. This work,

2 Ibid 142
3 Ibid 157
4 Ibid 158–61
5 Ibid 268
6 For the polemical-historical importance of the *Commentaria*, see Adolf Herte *Das katholische Lutherbild im Bann der Lutherkommentare des Cochläus*.
7 Eugène Müntz 'Le Musée de portraits de Paul Jove: Contributions pour servir à l'iconographie du moyen âge et de la Renaissance'; Michaud xvi 511–15
8 Werner Kaegi 'Machiavelli in Basel,' especially 130–9

which made the reputation of Giovio's collection, was an outcome of the Italian intellectual dispersion of the sixteenth century and a late fruit of Renaissance aspirations. Oddly Erasmus was among those denied a portrait in the Basel edition.[9] It could be that his portrait was well enough known in the north, but the lack somehow symbolizes the shadowy understanding of the northern humanist and reformer in this late Italian Renaissance work. In Catholic historical writing about Erasmus here is a much cooler performance than the tributes from within his own circle which have occupied us so far.

Giovio suggests a certain lightness of temperament in Erasmus. A religious resolve in adolescence led him into joining the monks as though he despised human ambitions. 'Soon after, however, weary of a rash vow which had condemned him to untimely servitude, he leaped over the enclosure of his sacred order and took to wandering through all the academies of Europe freely cultivating his mind.'[1] He was driven by a great ambition, seeking the heights of glory through a command of literature and learning achieved by immense reading and an uncommon memory. With these few strokes Giovio put into the literature Erasmus, the rootless individualist. To this Erasmus the *Moriae encomium* first brought renown, scattering as it did his stinging Lucianic shafts. Certainly the work deserved its reputation – the wit sprinkled through it was a delight – still it did not become a priest to seem so to play with holy things. Always there is the same judgment: the younger Erasmus was not to be taken seriously as a Catholic thinker. Then – again in a few words – Giovio set another pattern for the biography of Erasmus. There was a turning-point after the *Moria* : Erasmus took up sacred letters and by the exertions of a very vigorous mind produced more translations and editions than anyone else. This was some appreciation of Erasmus' solid achievement.

A new current now set in across these cool Catholic judgments; Giovio renewed the Ciceronian quarrel. Erasmus would have won a higher reputation if he had imitated seriously the creators of the Latin tongue rather than giving free rein to his eager, precipitate mind. He sought fame by novelty of expression and showed in the *Ciceronianus* an unmistakable spleen. There follows a rather demeaning metaphor; Erasmus was like an ever-pregnant girl: 'He was so fertile by nature that his womb was always full; delighted by the manifold and hurried offspring of a luxuriant mind, he was forever giving birth to something

9 Müntz 'Le Musée' 272
1 *Elogia doctorum virorum* ... 208

new for the printers, who were like earnest midwives.'[2] Here is a certain Italian contempt for the precipitate publication of a northern Johnny-come-lately. The factual insecurity of Giovio's little biographical sketch is revealed by its one ostensible hard fact (apart from Erasmus' birth 'ex insula Batavorum'): he died in Swiss Fribourg or, as some say, in Basel. The last touch seems on the face of it absurdly inconsequential: Erasmus died in the year Charles v carried his war against the king of France into Provence. Is this an intended irony? Hardly. Perhaps the uncertainty about the place of death and the final obeisance to the emperor are meant to obscure Erasmus' association with the great Protestant city where he spent his last days.

In their different ways Cochlaeus and Giovio were to be quarries for writers later in the sixteenth century and beyond. Across Europe in the 1550s and 1560s apologists seeking to hold the line for the old church and prepare its counter-attack were still, like Cochlaeus, using Erasmus as evidence against the innovators. In Poland especially that way of seeing Erasmus persisted.[3] Erasmus' Catholic reputation remained resilient there; the chapter of Cracow in its instructions for the synod of 1551, which – inspired by Stanislaus Hosius and Martin Kromer – took the first steps towards Catholic reform, recommended the Enchiridion and the De modo orandi Deum for the edification of the Polish clergy.[4] Hosius, an old Erasmian, was one of the architects of the Counter-Reformation in Poland, a many-sided reformer and defender of the church, not the least of whose services to the Catholic cause was to bring the Jesuits to Poland in 1564.[5] Among his prolific writings was a broadside against the Protestant Reformers quite in the spirit of Cochlaeus.[6] Luther, moved by cupidity and led by the devil, first disturbed the long established peace of the church, in Poland as elsewhere. The sowing of dissension was always a sign of the devil's work. Erasmus' criticism of the temper of the new evangelicals was used in passing.[7]

Controversialists in the West made use of Hosius and through him of Cochlaeus. The Netherlander Lindanus (Van der Lindt 1525–88)

2 Ibid 209
3 Maria Cytowska 'Erasme en Pologne avant l'époque du Concile de Trente' 14–15
4 C. Backvis 'La Fortune d'Erasme en Pologne' 195
5 The Cambridge History of Poland 399–408
6 De origine haeresium nostri temporis. Satirical and critical writing against Luther had begun early in Poland (Cambridge History 398).
7 De origine haeresium 40

was an inquisitor of the faith under Philip II; he was intended by the king for one of the new bishoprics created by the reorganization of the church in 1562 but was prevented from taking it up by the onset of the troubles. He has been described as 'one of the first historians of the Protestant "variations," ' a far precursor of Bossuet.[8] His Luther portrait owed most to Cochlaeus; like him Lindanus called on the testimony of Erasmus. Thus Erasmus saw in Luther a man furious, driven, frantic with hatred.[9] In fact, Lindanus goes far beyond the evidence of Luther's temperament left by contemporaries like Erasmus (also, of course, this is a very imperfect rendering of Erasmus' many-sided judgment on Luther's personality). He enters into a nightmare world of demonology: Luther was in league with the devil. Erasmus is a valuable witness because of what he says about the public conse-quences of the Reformation: 'At his first taste of Luther's writings Erasmus rightly foresaw that the affair would issue in sedition.'[1]

A third controversialist, Gabriel Prateolus or Du Préau (1511–88), found Lindanus' and Hosius' polemic of use in another critical situa-tion, the France of the first decade of religious war.[2] He intended to show that the ancient heresies and those of his own age were identical.[3] As might be expected of a trained humanist treating the heresies of the early church, he tried there to work from good sources, but for contemporary history he simply pillaged Lindanus and Hosius without apparently realizing that behind them both stood Cochlaeus.[4] He used Erasmus as they had done: as Hosius saw, Erasmus blamed the new gospel for opening the door to evils of every kind; as Lindanus saw, Luther in Erasmus' view was impelled by an insane and diabolical spirit and with his fellows created a world of 'templa sine aris, forum sine justitia.'[5]

These books all belong to a time of degeneration into religious war. From one side they may be seen as giving vent to the wretched, intemperate, uncritical polemics characteristic of such times; in another way they express the heroic effort of the old church to regather

---

8 DTC IX 1 cols 772–6 at col 774; cf *Biographie nationale* XI cols 212–16.
9 *Dubitantius de vera certaque per Christi Jesu Evangelium ... 66*. Based on Erasmus *Purgatio adversus epistolam non sobriam Martini Lutheri* 1534, LB X 1537–58, eg, at 1547E–8A.
1 *Dubitantius* 272
2 *De vitis, sectis, et dogmatibus omnium haereticorum ...*
3 DTC XII 2 cols 2786–8
4 Herte *Das katholische Lutherbild* I 50–2
5 Prateolus *De vitis* 160, 162, 272

its forces and stem the rout of the first generation or so after 1520. That effort was dragging in its train historical distortions of various kinds. In these works, however, the moderates like Erasmus were not yet lumped in with the heretics; they remained independent Catholic witnesses to the errors of the false 'evangelicals.' Cochlaeus' way of seeing Erasmus could thus hold up into the 1560s. It could not, however, endure much longer. At the Council of Trent and with the emergence of the new religious orders an ever more exclusive spirit was being imposed on the past. Lindanus and Prateolus argued that the worst of ancient heresies – Arianism, Pelagianism – revived under the shadow of Protestantism: commentators on Erasmus in the next generation were to make him equally responsible with the Protestant Reformers for these poisonous regrowths, in that way renewing the polemic of his orthodox enemies during his lifetime and wiping out the generation of favourable judgments from Nausea to Hosius and beyond.

The effect of the Council of Trent could only be to undermine the moderate Catholic judgment of Erasmus. Certainly in the first sessions Erasmus had distinguished partisans; the Christian humanist method of scriptural study could be recommended to the clergy and Erasmus' *Enchiridion* included among works available for their formation. But at the same time his errors – on original sin and baptism – were listed for condemnation.[6] In the discussion of the sacrament of marriage during the Bologna interlude of the council Erasmus' views were identified with those of the Reformers, and his expressions favouring marriage over virginity were explicitly condemned.[7] As division deepened through the 1550s and into the last period of the council's life (1562–3), Erasmus was left for Catholics more and more on the far side of the gulf. The history of the Index makes the point. The Index of Paul IV (1559) placed Erasmus in the first class of heretics whose whole output was condemned, the unusual elaboration being given 'with all his commentaries, annotations, *scholia*, dialogues, letters, opinions, translations, books and writings, even if these include nothing against or about religion.'[8] If this frantic judgment was an aberration, the

6 Jedin *History* II: 99–100, 153, 371. Cf A. Michel *Histoire des Conciles* x, part 1: 33, 173; Arthur Allgeier 'Erasmus und Kardinal Ximenes in den Vorhandlungen des Konzils von Trient' 193–205.
7 H. Jedin *Geschichte des Konzils von Trient* 3: 143, 152
8 F.H. Reusch, *Der Index der verbotenen Bücher: Ein Beitrag zur Kirchen- und Literaturgeschichte* 347

revised Index of Pius IV (the 'Council Index,' 1564) still revealed a profound suspicion of him. In the council commission it was argued that all restriction should be removed from his writings in recognition of his services to the church and to Christian scholarship, but the majority considered it a favour that he was kept in memory by the expurgation of some of his works and the suppression of others. The *Moria*, the *Colloquia*, the work on Christian marriage, the *Lingua*, and an Italian translation of the paraphrase on St Matthew were forbidden absolutely, the other religious writings until they were expurgated by the faculties of Paris or Louvain.[9] Erasmus was more and more isolated. Ranke's hard words about the 'moderate Catholicism' of the noble Contarini could seem apt for Erasmus, his admirers, and the whole Erasmian tradition in the 1560s: 'Having failed in securing its benevolent and world-embracing designs, it now became a question whether it would even maintain its own existence.'[1]

The new mood was indicated by the widely read history from which, says Herte, two generations of Catholic readers drew their knowledge of the Reformation, Laurentius Surius' continuation into the sixteenth century of the chronicle of Joannes Nauclerus.[2] While a student at Frankfurt-am-Oder in the uncertain years before 1540 Surius (Lorenz Sauer 1522–78) had been attracted to Protestantism, but the influence of Canisius won him back to a firm faith; in 1540 he entered the Carthusian order, and in 1543 he was ordained priest.[3] His major literary service to Catholic renewal was his histories of the saints, which anticipated the work of the Bollandists. The *Commentarius* was an answer to the first generation of Protestant historiography, especially to Johannes Sleidan. Surius studied, says a pious biographer, to expose the divergencies, absurdities, falsities, and lies of the heretical historians.[4] He saw his own work as a counter-offensive. It is not insignificant that his book was dedicated to Albert, duke of Bavaria, at a time when the foundations of the most effective of Counter-Reformation régimes were being laid in that land. Religious admonitions and devotional reflections added to its attractiveness for Catholic readers, but its essence was a denunciation of the lack of integrity and

9 Ibid. On the above there is a good, fuller discussion in A. Flitner *Erasmus im Urteil seiner Nachwelt* 33–46.
1 *History of the Popes* 128
2 *Commentarius brevis rerum in orbe gestarum* ... Cf Herte *Das katholische Lutherbild* I 17–18.
3 RGG VI col 529; DTC XIV 2 cols 2842–9; ADB XXXVII 166
4 'Vita' (by George Garnefelt) in *Vitae sanctorum*

of the fierce dissensions and altercations among Luther and his follow-ers.[5] The theme of 'Protestant variations' had a long history before Bossuet mixed with it his genius in the later seventeenth century. For his Luther portrait Surius was slavishly dependent on Cochlaeus[6] but in his treatment of Erasmus he moves far from him. Erasmus is still used as a witness against the enemies of the church, but he is no longer seen as essentially Catholic. From Cochlaeus to Surius we have crossed a watershed.

The Protestant historians were embarrassed by Erasmus' appear-ance as a witness against them. Sleidan, for example, played down his work of 1529 against the false evangelicals.[7] Sleidan felt himself pinched, Surius says, by Erasmus' authority, then so great among so many. Erasmus had indeed said nothing more truly than that among the innovators none was made better but all were made worse. Yet Erasmus incautiously encouraged the heretics. The Zwinglians wrongly claimed him for themselves, but his writings gave them grounds. He wrote against them but not with the warmth that the case required.[8] He must share responsibility for exciting the tumults in religion. Despite the late admission that he would have written and acted differently if he had foreseen how the age would turn out, he seems to have made few corrections, for example in his pernicious *Colloquia*. Why should he teach susceptible youth to condemn or call in doubt the constitutions and ceremonies of the church? There was much imprudence and much seditious opinion. He hatefully be-laboured the monks and theologians and frightened young people away from the monastic life, to which Surius fervently affirms his loyalty. Erasmus, laying aside his monastic dress, chose to live in the world, not without causing scandal to many (shades perhaps of Giovio); Surius prefers with the Fathers to flee its dangers.[9] In sum, Erasmus relied too much on his own judgment; he ought not to be trusted too lightly. 'Would that he had never touched theological subjects or that he had treated them more devoutly or more modestly,' Surius says in a refrain of the Counter-Reformation literature on Erasmus.[1] (Inconsistently perhaps, Surius adds that he should have written more energetically

5 'Epistola dedicatoria' in *Commentarius* a4^v–5^r
6 Herte *Das katholische Lutherbild* 22
7 *Commentarius* 234–5. Cf introduction, above. On Sleidan's handling of Erasmus, see below, 82–6.
8 *Commentarius* 199
9 Ibid 371–3
1 Ibid 374

against Luther.) There is another hallmark of the Counter-Reformation literature: Surius attempts to drive a wedge between Erasmus and Thomas More. The denial of the comradeship-in-arms of the two Christian humanists became a necessity of the interpretation of Erasmus that was emerging.[2]

The watershed of the 1550s can also be charted in the Spanish and English Catholic literature. There is a stark contrast between the works of two Spanish Franciscans, one, Alfonso de Castro, publishing in the 1530s, the other, Antonius Ruvio, in the 1560s. Their interpretations of Erasmus belong to different worlds; it is a measure of the change in his standing and of a profound change in Spain itself. An understanding of the deep penetration of Erasmus' thought into the Spain of Charles v has been a precious possession of scholarship on Erasmus since the appearance of Marcel Bataillon's magisterial study *Erasme et l'Espagne* in 1937. Equally important for the history of Erasmus' reputation is the closing-off of Spain to such influences in the next generation; in the redoubt of the Counter-Reformation, the defensive, militant Spain of Philip II, fine distinctions could not be made between heretics, and tentative and inclusive minds stood condemned.[3]

Alfonso de Castro (1495–1558) was a luminary of his order, a teacher at the University of Salamanca, confessor of the Spanish kings and preacher at their court, theologian of the Council of Trent.[4] His book *Adversus omnes haereses libri xiiii* (Paris 1534) was an armoury for Catholic controversialists and for the Council of Trent itself. That in such a book Erasmus should be handled in a warm and friendly way indicates the ground won by his influence in those years.[5] Castro challenges Erasmus on a sensitive issue – the vernacular bible, which for him was the fount of heresies.[6] Yet he in no way diminishes Erasmus' claim to be Catholic and devout: 'a most learned man, deserving well of good literature and in my judgment truly pious.'[7]

---

2 Ibid. On the More literature, see below.
3 Cf 'The battle between Erasmians and anti-Erasmians may thus have been in some respects a conflict between opposing ideas about the future course to be taken by Spain ... It was, indeed, intensively fought from the 1520s to the 1560s, and it ended in victory for the traditionalists: by the end of the 1560s the "open" Spain of the Renaissance had been transformed into the partially "closed" Spain of the Counter-Reformation' (J.H. Elliott, *Imperial Spain 1469–1716* 208).
4 DTC II 2 cols 1835–6; *Cath Enc* III 415; Jedin *History* passim
5 Marcel Bataillon *Erasme et l'Espagne* 543–4
6 For Castro's role at Trent on this issue, see Jedin *History* II 71, 83.
7 Castro *Adversus* 28E

Castro bears witness to his piety precisely because there are some who dare to deny it; he wants it to be clear that his differences with Erasmus are like those between any two good Catholics and are not a questioning of his faith and piety. Erasmus should have recognized the evil consequences of the vernacular bible. 'I think,' Castro concludes, 'that he would have taken it in good part that I have disagreed with him on this matter, for he himself says more than once that anyone is free to differ from the opinion of another man, even from that of a saint, so long as he does it with respect and by reasoned argument.'[8] Similarly, Castro disagrees with Erasmus' reading of one of the Trinitarian texts, but not to accuse him of Arianism. The debate arises not because Erasmus belongs to the Arian party but because he reads a text badly – that is not suprising, for Homer sometimes nods.[9] For later commentators such readings were enough to damn Erasmus.

Later versions of his work registered a growing restraint on Castro's own judgment. In the Cologne edition of 1539 the more explicit expressions in favour of Erasmus' piety and orthodoxy were omitted, though Castro still refused to taint him with Arianism. However, the work defended Erasmus in a curiously backhanded way. It printed as an appendix the determination of the Paris faculty against Erasmus but introduced this with the ironic note:

> You see, reader, that Erasmus, whom certain enemies place among the heretics, is free of the charge of heresy in the opinion not only of this author but of many other good and learned men, inasmuch as he frequently submits his errors to the judgment of the church. Devout and astute people may find things in his books to carp at, and we often face the objection that he treats serious and sacred subjects more childishly or frivolously than is decent, not to say (as they do) that he misrepresents them. They assert that many things in his books should therefore be abbreviated, some should be changed and others utterly condemned and blotted out. I on the other hand think it sufficient to add at the end of this book the judgment of the University of Paris, with an indication of what in his works is to be read with caution.[1]

8 Ibid 29B
9 Ibid 92DE
1 Bataillon raises the possibility that the addition is the work of other hands, of Cologne Erasmians responsible for re-issuing the work (*Erasme et L'Espagne* 544).

This version also includes without introduction or commentary a letter of Erasmus in favour of monasticism – a tacit association of the humanist with orthodoxy.[2] A further hardening may be traced in the edition of 1543 (Paris), but even here the spirit is not especially hostile. The essential change lies across the great divide of the 1550s.

How well Ruvio's work epitomizes this change is indicated by the censor's introduction: 'Such is Spain's integrity, such her zeal for the faith that she not only watches to drive the church's enemies away but strives with all her strength to root out anything that may do it harm.'[3] This is a siege mentality. In these days, it is said, heresies come not singly or in succession, as in the past, but all swarming together. To the ills of so mad an age no mild unguent can bring relief, but only fire and sword. Erasmus and Ruvio are given fit parts for such a drama, the one an image of the hidden enemy sowing poison secretly and therefore worse than an open foe showing the bold front of heresy, the other from the ranks of the religious ever on guard in the time of danger, exposing the serpent, penetrating the whited sepulchre: 'Slaying the beast he comes safely from the labyrinth.'[4]

Ruvio's own dedication was to Philip II. There is the same picture of Erasmus, the secret enemy; as the polyp resembles the colour of its rock to deceive the fisherman, he took on a Catholic colour to avoid condemnation.[5] The vision is apocalyptic: the dragon of the apocalypse – with Luther and Erasmus as its tail – is devouring the children of faith as they are born. By teaching not contempt for but love of the world's vanities they are responsible for the overthrow of all order. Total subversion follows. For a time Ruvio feared even for the Spanish kingdoms themselves, but under the king's protection they have been kept safe. Philip is indeed the new Constantine, 'the sole defence of the Catholic religion.'[6] The dedication finishes with a paean of praise to the ecclesiastical, civil, and military leaders of Spain, a perfect expression of Spain militant, mortal enemy of Turk and heretic.

The prologue to the reader includes a fragment of Ruvio's autobiography.[7] When a boy, he says, he often heard Erasmus' books praised for their good Latinity; on the other hand, he heard but did not

2 Cf Allen VII 198.
3 *Assertionum catholicarum adversus Erasmi Roterodami* ... 'Censura Fratris Joannis de la Vega' 3[r]
4 Ibid 3[v]
5 Ibid 6[r]
6 Ibid 8[v]
7 In this part of the text, there is no pagination.

at first understand the saying that Erasmus laid the egg that Luther hatched; preserved from heresy by God's grace, he came, while still a youth, to see in Erasmus the teachings the inquisitors condemned in Luther. While in his student days many were being carried away by Erasmus, he determined to drag into the daylight the Erasmian pestilence which was secretly turning sure teachings into doubt and controversy. He was encouraged by the censures of the Sorbonne, by the exposure of Erasmus' errors at a conference of theologians at Valladolid in 1527 (where admittedly some favoured him, but these have since come to a bad end!) and by the Index of Paul IV.[8] What is the justification of his book when there have been so many catalogues of heresies, including those of Castro, Ruvio's teacher and father? Erasmus' opponents, Beda, Carpi, and the others, had the wolf by the ears but could not finish it off – its ears were too short and its teeth too sharp. But now that Erasmus' errors are apparent to the whole Christian world, Ruvio will overthrow them utterly.

The book's method is to state the erroneous assertions culled from works like the *Colloquia* and the annotations on the New Testament and, without elaborating them in the text, to lay out the judgments of the Fathers and Councils. They do not seem to come in any particular order (the first errors mentioned concern the immortality of the soul, purgatory, indulgences, the angels, and abstinence from meats),[9] and the balance also seems strange: the great issues like the Trinity and justification are passed over quickly. There is nevertheless no hesitation in attributing Arianism to Erasmus: like the hyena described by Pliny he disinterred and sucked the bones of that dead heresy and renewed its life.[1] The book is evidence for the recovery of scholasticism and of the ecclesiastical hierarchy in the Counter-Reformation. At one point Ruvio says that Erasmus was deceived by his ignorance of scholastic theology.[2] Passing expressions are treated as theological propositions, weighed, and found wanting. It is indicative that one of the longest sections condemns Erasmus' association of the saying of the office and the canonical hours with Judaism.[3] Through all runs the crude but simple historical argument: Erasmus drew his heresies from the same sources as Luther and was his fellow-traveller, indeed his fellow-worker. In the great restoration of faith and church under

8   On the Valladolid conference, see Bataillon *Erasme et l'Espagne* ch 5.
9   Respectively at 1, 30[r], 34[r], 40[v], 41[v]
1   151[r]
2   71[r]. Book 8 attacks Erasmus for his criticisms of scholastic theology.
3   120[r]–149[r]

Spanish leadership both must be crushed. From Castro to Ruvio the judgment hardens, reflecting the changes in Spain from the middle years of Charles v to the early embattled years of Philip II.

In the sixteenth-century books on Sir Thomas More we find a similar deterioration; that is an expression of the stiffening Catholic recusant resistance to the Protestant settlement in England. The friendship between More and Erasmus became an embarrassment to those wishing to mark sharply the battle-lines between faith and heresy, the church and its enemies, as indeed it has been down to our own time for all Catholic writers wishing to ascribe to Erasmus a culpable liberalism.[4]

Nicholas Harpsfield (1519–75), the first biographer of More, escaped the embitterment of a later recusant generation, despite a long imprisonment under Elizabeth.[5] His work was written in the 1550s after he had returned from exile at Louvain in the time of Edward VI and while, as archdeacon of Canterbury and a close associate of Reginald Pole's, he was serving the Marian restoration. Its purpose was devotional – to present More as a Catholic lay martyr who lived a life unmarked by breaks or contradictions, all of a piece.[6]

Erasmus appears first as one of the More circle, in effect a member of the family; he corresponded with More's children and praised their learning and virtue. To More's daughter, Margaret, whom he called 'the flowre of all the learned matrones in Inglande,' he dedicated a commentary on Prudentius.[7] The friendship of Erasmus and More is recognized; so strong was More's regard for his friend that, at Erasmus' urging, he suppressed his book against the French humanist Brixius (Germain de Brie), though More had the better of the argu-

4 On the background in the recusant literature, see James K. McConica *English Humanists and Reformation Politics under Henry VIII and Edward VI* appendix 2, 285–94. The sharp article by Marie Delcourt, 'Recherches sur Thomas More: La tradition continentale et la tradition anglaise,' is very stimulating, though some of its judgments have been shown to be exaggerated. See also J.K. Sowards 'Thomas More and the Friendship of Erasmus, 1499–1517: A Study in Northern Humanism' appendix A 247–54.
5 *The life and death of Sir Thomas Moore, knight, sometymes Lord High Chancellor of Englande, written in the tyme of Queene Marie* introduction by R.W. Chambers, cxciii. The contemporary work by More's son-in-law, William Roper, *The Lyfe of Sir Thomas Moore, knighte,* is not a biography but rather personal notes for Harpsfield's use. It does not deal with the Erasmus friendship.
6 Chambers intro to Harpsfield *Sir Thomas Moore* xlvii, xlix
7 Harpsfield *Sir Thomas Moore* 78, 80

ment between them.[8] More spoke of his entire love for Erasmus who, for his part, 'of all men in the world [most] delighted in the companye of Sir Thomas More, whose helpe and frendshipp he muche used when he had any affaires with king Henrye the eight.'[9] Nothing, however, is said of their common battles for humanism and church reform.

Across the warm picture there falls like a chill shadow a story which, embellished or subtly transformed, was to reappear in the Catholic literature on Erasmus. More, Harpsfield says, was a fair controversialist; he was willing to recognize and correct his mistakes:

The like he counsailed his learned frendes, especially Erasmus, to doo, and to retracte many thinges that he had written, whose counsaile (wherein he had a notable president so to doo in the woorthy doctour St Augustine) if Erasmus had folowed, I trowe his bookes would be better lyked of our posteritie, which perchaunce shal be faine either utterly to abolishe some of his woorkes, or at least to redresse and reforme them.[1]

This passage calls for a number of comments. First, it arises from a remark about More's controversial manner: what is said of Erasmus must relate to his theological writings, but it is given no dogmatic substance and there is no explicit suggestion of heresy. Later writers were to become explicit, notably Thomas Stapleton, whose version of the story was to be most influential. Secondly, in Harpsfield's account the passage can be seen as something of an interloper; later in his work Harpsfield resumes his customary tone: Erasmus is that 'great excellent Clerke, of fine and excellent wittes a meete and convenient Judge,' here used as witness to More's great talents.[2] Yet, thirdly, the passage must have registered the discussions of the 1550s which were to issue in the placing of Erasmus on the Index. Harpsfield's expressions in fact correspond to the eventual fate of Erasmus' works on the Index: some were completely suppressed and others were expurgated. Surius had the story and drew the conclusion: the present judgment of the church on Erasmus' writings fulfils the prophecy which he attributed to More himself.[3]

8 Ibid 101–2
9 Ibid 136
1 Ibid 109
2 Ibid 208
3 Surius *Commentaria* 374. Surius had the story 'ex quodam docto et gravi viro.' It derived presumably from the recusant exiles. Harpsfield's account, of course, remained unpublished until this century. On the foundation of the story, see the discussion of Stapleton below.

Harpsfield referred to Erasmus in another work likewise published long after his death, his *Historia anglicana ecclesiastica*. The reference comes in a chapter on William Warham, archbishop of Canterbury, 1503–32. Warham, Harpsfield says, was a generous patron of studies who had a particular regard for Erasmus, conferring upon him a living in his own diocese which Erasmus refused from an awareness of his inability fruitfully to fulfil the pastoral office in the unfamiliar tongue.[4] That is the extent of the published version, which appears, in comparison with the manuscript, to be severely truncated. The original goes on to elaborate the archbishop's high opinion of Erasmus: his rare gifts, his great eloquence and learning would benefit the universal church and would (to use Warham's own words) bring it lustre like a star. England, too, for which Erasmus showed a preference, abandoning his prospects in other countries to live there, would gain much from his presence. There follows a listing of Erasmus' English friends and patrons (of whom Warham was the chief), and the long account finishes with pleasantries passed in correspondence with Warham about Erasmus' suffering from the stone.[5] Acton thought the abbreviation of this passage an act of censorship by Harpsfield's seventeenth-century editor which might be taken to illustrate the argument of this chapter, namely, that in the history of the Counter-Reformation between 1550 and 1600 Erasmus' reputation as Catholic writer and scholar plummeted.[6] One need not go so far in interpreting the deletions of 1622; the substance after all remained in the published version – Warham's warm friendship for Erasmus – and much of the excised material could be counted irrelevant in a *Historia anglicana ecclesiastica*, the check-list of Erasmus' friends, for example, and jokes about the stone. Nevertheless the main point stands unaffected; Harpsfield wrote still in living connection with the More circle and shared its appreciation of Erasmus.[7] The retraction passage in the More biography may come like a sudden wind heralding a change of season, but it is still no more than a forewarning. By the time Thomas Stapleton (1535–98) wrote about More the season was far advanced.

4 *Historia* 632. Cf Allen I 501.
5 British Library, Arundel MS 73, 96ᵛ–97ᵛ
6 In the *Academy* ix (1876) 609–10, quoted in Chambers intro to Harpsfield *Sir Thomas Moore* cxciii–iv
7 'The distinctive feature in Harpsfield's character is his admiration for Erasmus. He remained true to the memory of the great Iconoclast, and continued to defend his reputation long after his influence had become extinct in the Church, when his writings were proscribed, and the last of his friends had passed away' (ibid).

The deleted passage from Harpsfield
Historia anglicana ecclesiastica (Arundel MS 73, 96ᵛ)
Courtesy of the British Library Board

Stapleton's work, better founded than Harpsfield's, more scholarly and more sophisticated, was published in the year of the Armada; it breathes a more polemical spirit, it belongs to the great 'cold war' between the schismatic England of Elizabeth and Counter-Reformation Spain.[8] Stapleton himself belonged to the later recusant generation, an émigré who studied at Louvain and Paris and taught at Douai; pre-eminent in learning among his contemporaries, he was in 1590 appointed by Philip II (of whom he described himself as 'a true and trusty servant') to the chair of Holy Scripture at Louvain.[9] He was moved to write first by his devotion to the glory of God and his love for the Catholic church, then by pity for his country. He drew on written sources like Erasmus' correspondence (the Basel edition, 1540) and on oral tradition among the exiles.[1]

Stapleton recognized the friendship between More and Erasmus, but it was not a comradeship of equals, morally speaking: on More's side there was graciousness and a making of allowances, on Erasmus' side a kind of spiritual dependence. 'More's friendship for Erasmus honoured Erasmus more than it benefited More. But as that Protestant heresy increased, for which Erasmus had so widely sown the accursed seed, More's love towards him decreased and grew cool.'[2] The bond was good letters; this was a literary friendship. Certainly Erasmus' labours for literature were very meritorious; yet More loved him 'more than he deserved.'[3] The personal power was More's. When Maarten Dorp condemned Greek studies, More persuaded him to change his mind, 'a thing which Erasmus, who employed against the same Dorpius the weapon of sarcasm rather than solid reason, was never able to do.'[4]

The retraction passage in Stapleton is a development from Harpsfield's. Towards the end of his life More realized that many things in Erasmus' writings needed to be corrected and in a letter earnestly admonished him to follow Augustine's example and issue a book of

8   *Tres Thomae* ... Eng tr by P.E. Hallett *The Life and Illustrious Martyrdom of Sir Thomas More*
9   DNB XVIII 988–91; Marvin R. O'Connell *Thomas Stapleton and the Counter Reformation*
1   Hallett *Sir Thomas More* xiii, xvi
2   Ibid 39. 'Fuit tamen amicitia Mori cum Erasmo ipsi Erasmo magis hon-orifica quam Moro utilis. Sed & crescente hac haeresi, cuius ova tam multa & mala Erasmus posuit, decrevit ac refrixit Mori erga Erasmum amor' (*Tres Thomae* 54).
3   Hallett 51; *Tres Thomae* 67
4   Hallett 54; *Tres Thomae* 71

THOMÆ
STAPLETONI
ANGLI, SACRAE
THEOLOGIÆ DOCTÒRIS,
ET PROFESSORIS REGII.
DVACI PRIMO·DEINDE LOVANII
Opera quæ extant omnia,

NONNVLLA AVCTIVS ET EMENDATIVS,
quædam iam anteà Anglicè scripta, nunc primùm studio & diligentia
Doctorum virorum Anglorum Latinè reddita.

IN QVATVOR TOMOS DISTRIBVTA QVORVM

Elenchum Pagina decima-nona indicabit.

TOMVS PRIMVS.

LVTETIÆ PARISIORVM.
M· D C X X
CVM PRIVILEGIO CHRISTIANISSIMI REGIS.

Thomas Stapleton
Portrait on the title page of his *Opera quae extant omnia*
By permission of the Board of Directors
Union Theological Seminary, New York City

'Retractions.' John Fisher, bishop of Rochester, did the same. 'But Erasmus, who was as unlike St Augustine in humility as he was in doctrine, refused and destroyed More's letter so that it should not be included in his collected correspondence.'[5] New touches here are More's deliberate judgment against Erasmus' doctrine (the setting of More's own modesty in literary controversy has been removed) and the harsh contrast with Augustine. The detail of the letter's destruction left an impression unflattering to Erasmus. It also rendered the foundations of the whole story insecure, as they have remained.[6] The story must have rested on received tradition among the exiles. Stapleton's account of Erasmus came out of the world of the English mission, the resistance to the Elizabethan settlement, and the Counter-Reformation challenge to Elizabeth's throne. May one read here too a contemptuous dismissal of the Erasmian strain in the Anglican tradition?[7]

The later life of More by his great-grandson, Cresacre (1572–1649), adds little.[8] Dedicated by another hand to the Queen of Charles I, it expresses a sense of the Catholic minority's alienation after nearly one hundred years: More is seen as 'raysed by God to be one of the first famous warriours in this our long persecution.'[9] It is, on the other hand, disfigured by a certain triviality of mind; Cresacre offers his

5 Hallett 40; *Tres Thomae* 54
6 It is impossible to confirm the story. It is hardly consistent with More's last letters to Erasmus in 1532 (Allen Epp 2659, 2831, X 31–4, 258–61), where he identifies himself with Erasmus against his critics. Cf McConica *English Humanists* 287–9, Delcourt 'Recherches' 29–32. The strongest argument in its favour is that it must have come ultimately from John Harris, More's secretary (Harpsfield *Sir Thomas Moore* 339–40, Chambers' note; McConica 291). A confusion with a letter of Cuthbert Tunstall, 24 October 1529 (Allen Ep 2226, VIII 290–2), urging Erasmus to overcome his Catholic critics by holding to the orthodox faith and submitting his writings to the judgment of the church as the Fathers had done has been suggested (E.E. Reynolds *Thomas More and Erasmus* 221).
7 Cf Craig R. Thompson 'Erasmus and Tudor England,' especially 57–60.
8 Written about 1630, published in Louvain or Paris in 1631, and attributed to Cresacre's brother, Thomas, until the edition of Rev Joseph Hunter in 1828 (DNB XIII 895–6). Michael A. Anderegg, in a full and more sympathetic account of Cresacre's work than is customary, puts the dates for composition and publication somewhat earlier and suggests Douai as the place for the latter ('The Tradition of Early More Biography'). The edition used is *The Life of Sir Thomas More, Kt. Lord High Chancellour of England under K. Henry the Eighth, and His Majesty's Embassadour to the Courts of France and Germany* London 1726.
9 *Sir Thomas More* xxx

entering into part of More's inheritance as evidence of a 'particular furtherance and blessing' by More's prayers in heaven – this in the same breath as a homily on the perils of living in the world![1] Cresacre rightly makes no pretence of rivalling Stapleton in skill or, one might add, in depth. He takes the retraction story from his more talented predecessor. To earlier accounts he adds only an extended observation on the apocryphal story of the first incognito encounter between More and Erasmus when More is said to have cried: 'Aut tu es Erasmus, aut diabolus.'[2] Cresacre More takes literally this reference to the devil and, in a confusion of metaphors and a remarkable inversion of the famous remark about the egg of heresy and its hatching says:

> Because at that time he was strangely disguised, and had sought to defende impious propositions; for although he was a singular Humanist, and one that could utter his minde in a most eloquent phrase, yet had he alwaies a delight to scoffe at religious matters, and find fault with all sorts of Clergie men. He took a felicitie to sett out sundrie Commentaries upon the Fathers workes, censuring them at his pleasure, for which cause he is tearmed *Errans-mus*; because he wandreth here and there in other mens harvests; yea in his writings he is sayd to have hatched manie of those egges of heresie, which the apostata Fryer *Luther* had before layde; not that he is to be accounted an heretike, for he would never be obstinate in anie of his opinions, yet would he irreligiously glaunce at all antiquitie and finde manie faultes with the present state of the Church.[3]

Here are strong traces of the polemic against Erasmus in the Jesuit literature of the late sixteenth century. To the analysis of this we will shortly come.

Among the English Catholic exiles the sympathetic judgments of Erasmus possible in the first decades after his death had thus been modified or undermined by the end of the century. This was the common pattern in Catholic Europe. Yet in the Catholic Netherlands, in that part of the Netherlands saved for Catholicism as the desperate struggle between the Spanish king and his rebellious subjects dragged on into its second generation, the two views of Erasmus – those we

1 Ibid xxvii–xxviii. Delcourt describes his as 'un esprit fort médiocre' ('Recherches' 33).
2 Cf Sowards 'Thomas More' 89.
3 *Sir Thomas More* 83

have called respectively the 'moderate Catholic' and the 'Counter-Reformation' views – remained in some kind of balance.

In his lifetime Erasmus had had friends and enemies, critics and supporters at Louvain, at once a citadel of the traditional learning and, through the Trilingual College in whose institution Erasmus himself had had a large hand, a training-ground for the new.[4] So it continued. In the 1550s, as the gulf between the confessions widened, a fresh review of his theological errors was undertaken in Louvain. An erudite Dominican, John Henten (1500–66), followed Erasmus through his *Opera omnia* volume by volume and page by page and, at the invitation of the faculty of theology, composed in 1552 a list which distinguished erroneous and scandalous opinions and more manifest heresy. One entry indicates the received view of Erasmus among the theologians of Louvain: 'Erroneous teaching of Erasmus included under no particular heading and his inordinate recommendation of himself.'[5] The themes of the diffuseness and equivocation of Erasmus' thought and of his falling into error through too great confidence in his own judgment were to be commonplaces of the Jesuit polemic against him. A complementary listing attached to one manuscript of Henten's work was by Tilman Clercx (Clerici), president of the College of the Pope at Louvain between 1527 and 1550 and a friend of Loyola and Canisius.[6] Another pointer to the theological outlook at Louvain in these years may be found in the commentary by the distinguished chancellor of the university, Ruard Tappaert, *Explicationis articulorum* ... [7] Here Erasmus is placed firmly among the erring. He is especially taken to task for remarks on marriage and celibacy: what he said about sexuality in the *Encomium matrimonii* was naturalist and Pelagian; the ideas on divorce he advanced as probable were taken for certain by Luther and other heretics; his arguing in the *Colloquia* against the admission of young people to monasteries without their parents' consent showed a poor appreciation of the evangelical counsels and the religious life.[8]

There were contrary voices. The Council of Brabant, invited by

4 See, eg, M.A. Nauwelarts 'Erasme à Louvain: Ephémérides d'un séjour de 1517 à 1521.'
5 R. Crahay 'Les censeurs louvanistes d'Erasme' 233–5
6 Ibid. 240–8. Henten's work was meant to guide the Council of Trent in a condemnation of Erasmus' errors. In fact, it provided the groundwork for the treatment of him in the Antwerp *Index expurgatorius* (1571), which subjected his works to expurgation but also within limits left them available (ibid passim).
7 On Tappaert, see *Biographie nationale* XXIV cols 555–77.
8 *Explicationis* 42, 329, 349, 354–6

Philip II to comment on a catalogue of prohibited books proposed by the University of Louvain, opposed the inclusion of Erasmus' book of 1533 on mending the peace of the church. It held, like Charles V and his advisers, that Erasmus had either cleared himself from all censure or made up for any failing by his great services to the church. The Protestant Reformers had never accepted him as one of theirs, popes had approved several of his writings, and he had always made clear his submission to the church's teaching. The Fathers, too, fell into errors, but that did not make them heretics. The book concerned, the *De sarcienda ecclesiae concordia*, remained in the catalogue, but this was not really a defeat for the moderate party. The latter – led, it would seem, by the king's formidable adviser, Granvelle – had resisted pressure from the Rome of Paul IV to follow its lead by condemning everything Erasmus had written.[9]

A satirical dialogue aimed at Ruard Tappaert himself was located more problematically in a no-man's land between Catholic reform and the advancing Reformation in the Netherlands.[1] In its criticism of the Roman hierarchy it represented a certain royalist and national sentiment; it also sympathized with the first Protestant martyrs in the Netherlands. Tappaert, seen contesting with St Peter for his admission to heaven, is caricatured as an enemy of scripture and of good learning and as a busy inquisitor; Erasmus by contrast had taught men to turn to the scriptures – for that the Inquisition condemned him as the worst of heretics.[2] These touches reveal an awareness of Erasmus' deteriorating position among the orthodox; they also show him favourably handled by a Reformation still in touch with Christian humanism and its reformist aspirations.

The attitudes of writers in the next generation were darkened by the troubles themselves. Cornelius Loos (Latin Callidius, 1546–95) was stimulated to write against the innovators and conciliators by earlier Catholic Netherlandish polemicists like Tappaert and Lindanus but he had also been chased from Gouda, his birthplace, and wrote in the bitterest years of the struggle.[3] His work on Erasmus appears in a

9 For the above, see Ernest Gossart 'Un livre d'Erasme réprouvé par l'Université de Louvain,' especially 436–9.
1 Verus Gratianus (pseud) *Clariss. theologi D. Ruardi Tappaert Enchusani* ... The author was probably Henry Geldorp, who after a humanist training had gone over to the Reformation and left Brabant for Germany (1557).
2 Ibid 590, 602–4, 612. See the introduction, 567–76, and Gossart 'Un livre d'Erasme' 440–5.
3 On Loos, see DTC IX 1 cols 930–3; ADB XIX 168–9.

biographical collection of no particular merit on the lives of Catholic German and Netherlandish writers.[4] It is a strange mixture. The foundation is the piece by Giovio, but this is rather inconsistently elaborated from the More literature and the developing Jesuit polemic against Erasmus. After repeating most of Giovio with some minor additions on Erasmus' early and monastic years, Loos makes a remark that is to become part of the stock-in-trade of Catholic writers for the next century: would that Erasmus, in line with his great natural gifts, had remained within the limits of literary endeavour. Then he would have won for himself everlasting fame. This hardly seems consistent with the condescending Ciceronianism of Giovio recapitulated in the preceding passage. Indeed, Loos goes on: 'For in carefully cultivating and adorning humane letters he either surpassed the first authors and tenderers of the Latin tongue or at least showed himself their equal.'[5] His failure was in the moral or religious sphere. Precocious minds with a fortunate disposition are inclined to pride. There is extant, says Loos, repeating Surius, a letter of Thomas More's exhorting Erasmus to retract and correct his writings in the manner of St Augustine and adding that otherwise they would be rejected by the church. In a mocking reply Erasmus refused to heed this advice, which was by no means vain: today the church's judgment is apparent in the Index of the Council of Trent.[6] To this mixture Loos adds at the end some touches of local knowledge – he was, after all, from Gouda, where Erasmus himself grew up. He corrected Giovio's ignorance – Holland is not an island – and referred to the Spanish soldiery's destruction of a stone statue of Erasmus in the market-place of Rotterdam in 1572.[7] Above all, he brought again to light Erasmus' illegitimacy: if the tradition of the old folk in the locality is to be accepted, his father was a Gouda priest who hid the pregnancy of his servant and had her give birth in the neighbouring city (of Rotterdam).

Loos' portrait of Erasmus is not particularly flattering. Yet to his own story there was a not irrelevant sequel: towards contemporary belief in sorcery and witchcraft he showed 'a critical sense unusual for his time.'[8] At Trier in 1592 he was forced to recant his teachings against witch-trials and magic; later he was imprisoned at Brussels for the

4 *Illustrium Germaniae scriptorum catalogus.* The work has no regular
   pagination: Erasmus is to be found at D5[4–8] to E[1–2].
5 Ibid D5[6]
6 Ibid [7]
7 Cf N. Van der Blom 'The Erasmus Statues in Rotterdam.'
8 DTC IX 1 col 932

same views. Was there here in this mind fashioned by the Counter-Reformation and embittered by the struggle against Calvinism and the rebellion in the Netherlands a persistence of Erasmus' own distrust of superstition and the irrational?

The printers of Antwerp and Louvain produced for the readers of the southern Netherlands a variety of biographical dictionaries, national encyclopedias, and general works of reference in the early decades of the seventeenth century, a sign perhaps of the definition of a new political and cultural identity after the division of the Netherlands. Erasmus had his place in most of them. The *Opus chronographicum orbis universi* of Petrus Opmeer (1526–95), written in the north in the 1570s but published posthumously in the south at Antwerp in 1611, was a history of the world from creation to 1569. Its account of Erasmus was the best informed of its period. Opmeer was plainly in touch with the Erasmus tradition: he had been educated by Alaard of Amsterdam, the editor of the first great northern humanist, Rodolphus Agricola, and by Nicolaas Kan, who had been *famulus* and valued collaborator of Erasmus himself between 1524 and 1530.[9] The circumstances of Opmeer's family were such that he could devote his life to study; the range of his studies was astonishingly wide – the classics (like Erasmus himself he learned Greek as an adult), medicine, and jurisprudence. With the inrush of Calvinism he turned to theology, in particular to the Fathers, to prepare himself for the defence of the old religion. He worked to confirm the citizens of Amsterdam and later of Delft in the old faith. But he was not at all a bigot: 'cum Catholicis syncere, cum hereticis caute agebat ... ' said an early biographer.[1]

Opmeer's treatment of Erasmus' biography is unusually exact and based among other things on a sharp sense of locality. One notices the many precise references to places in the Netherlands. Erasmus' father was a priest at Gouda (Opmeer knows of his older brother, Pieter); the boy was first among the learned young men produced by Hegius' school at Deventer; in the monastery at Stein with his (named) companions he first showed the quality of his erudition; called into the service of the bishop Henry of Bergen for his lively mind and learning, he wrote his *Antibarbari* in the castle at Halsteren.[2] Opmeer has criticisms of Erasmus that are severe enough. He had a Lucianic

9 On Cannius, see Franz Bierlaire *La familia d'Erasme: Contribution à l'histoire de l'humanisme* 72–6.
1 Valerius Andreas in preface to *Opus chronographicum*. Cf NNBW v cols 404–5.
2 *Opus chronographicum* 426, 436, 438

temper, he was a carper;[3] he spared neither his hosts nor (with particular unfairness) his own brother.[4] The wit of the *Moriae Encomium* was very amusing but not too decent in a theologian. Criticisms of it in fact turned him to sacred studies. His work in that new sphere and his relation to the Reformation are judged moderately and sympathetically. To those who called on him to take up the Gospel, he replied, 'Each seems to make his own gospel.' He showed decisively his disapproval of the Reformation proceedings at Basel. At the time of his death in that city he was *en route* to Belgium at the summons of the ruling house.[5] This way of putting it was characteristic of the moderate Catholic and south Netherlandish view.

The treatment of Erasmus in Aubertus Miraeus' *Elogia illustrium Belgii scriptorum* is more in the Counter-Reformation spirit.[6] Miraeus himself (Aubert le Mire, 1573–1640) belonged to the Counter-Reformation Netherlands of the Habsburg archdukes Isabella and Albert.[7] His family was deeply attached to the old religion and to the government of Philip II; his father, a cloth merchant, was a magistrate at Brussels after the Duke of Parma's reconquest in 1585. Miraeus studied at Douai and Louvain. He was admitted to the Antwerp chapter in 1601 and exercised a real influence in the diocese as personal secretary to his uncle, John, who had been named bishop of Antwerp by the archdukes. In 1615 he became chaplain to the court at Brussels, in 1624 dean of Antwerp. Encouraged by his friend, Justus Lipsius, he had thrown himself into historical researches, but always in the service of the faith and the dynasty. He wrote to defend the papal authority, to vindicate monasticism, and 'to exalt the political ideas which then prevailed in Belgium.'[8] He wrote in Latin for members of the clergy and the bureaucracy, for the official class of the Habsburg Netherlands.

The biography of Erasmus in the *Elogia* is characteristic of Miraeus' researches – right enough as far as it goes, but sketchy and showing

3 'Carpendi alios morbo tum (quod dolendum) laborabat D. *Erasmus* etiam vehementer ... ' (ibid 454).
4 His references to Erasmus' brother demonstrate Opmeer's care in research. See Flitner *Erasmus* 66 on his use of otherwise unknown or neglected sources.
5 *Opus chronographicum* 454, 457, 463, 476
6 Full title, *Elogia illustrium Belgii scriptorum, qui vel ecclesiam Dei propugnarunt, vel disciplinas illustrarunt, centuria, decadibus distincta,* Antwerp, 1602.
7 *Biographie nationale* XIII cols 882–95, for what follows. Cf Cathleen Flanagan 'Aubertus Miraeus, An Early Belgian Librarian.'
8 *Biographie nationale* XIII col 885

Aubertus Miraeus
Portrait by Erasmus Quellin, 1642
prepared for Balthasar II Moretus, a descendant of
Christopher Plantin, the famous printer of Antwerp
Plantin-Moretus Museum, Antwerp

signs of haste. Miraeus presents Erasmus as a pioneer in the restoration of good letters, Greek as well as Latin. He renews Giovio's picture of the wandering celebrity. Above all, he repeats the paradox of Loos and of Scaliger long before: Erasmus' reputation would have been higher had he not aimed so high ('major & apud posteros futurus, si minor esse voluisset'); if he had stuck to the literary studies which were natural to him, he could have rivalled the Latin authors.[9] But he had theological ambitions; relying on his own cleverness, he took too much on himself and presumptuously acted the critic of the scriptures and the Fathers. Would that he had shown more modesty and like Augustine written a retraction ... ![1] Here once again is the influence of the More tradition, but above all of the Jesuit polemic against Erasmus as theologian. In one version, Miraeus' sketch ends with a long quotation from Canisius.[2]

Miraeus is critical but not especially hostile or bitter. That is the outlook of the southern Netherlands. It is maintained by two other writers of compilations; the first, Valerius Andreas (Valère André, 1588–1655), in student days a friend of Miraeus, was professor of Hebrew at the Trilingual College (1611) and later (1628) professor of Roman law and historian of the Belgian provinces and of the University of Louvain; the second, Franciscus Sweertius (Sweerts, 1567–1629), followed his father in business but, well trained in the humanities, gave all his leisure to literature. Brought up a zealous Catholic, Sweertius yet kept a connection with the Protestant scholars of the northern Netherlands. His *Athenae Belgicae* (Antwerp 1628) was built on Andreas' *Bibliotheca Belgica* (Louvain 1623) – this led in fact to charges of plagiarism – but the works were, it is claimed, planned independently.[3] In factual matters, they represent a decline from Opmeer. Erasmus' *Compendium vitae*, with its more romantic version of his parents' relationship, had meantime been published (Leiden 1607), and the suggestion that Erasmus' father was a priest is indignantly repudiated.[4] The judgments of Andreas and Sweertius are if anything milder than those of Miraeus and in a quite different spirit from the harsh rejection now standard elsewhere in Catholic Europe. Erasmus is certainly not seen as an enemy of religion. He was a great man, the

9 *Elogia* 147
1 Ibid 148
2 In Miraeus' *Bibliotheca ecclesiastica sive de scriptoribus ecclesiasticis ...* 139–40
3 *Biographie nationale* I cols 281–90, XXIV cols 362–9
4 *Bibliotheca Belgica* 229

light of the Netherlands, a miracle of nature, the phoenix of his age: reviving letters owed both life and spirit to him.[5] He spoke too freely on theological subjects; no Catholic writer could now avoid that judgment, to which the Jesuit writers were, as we shall see, giving a magisterial expression, but there was a Netherlandish mitigation. The wish here is not that he had refrained altogether from theological writing but rather that he had taken more care over it.[6] Beyond the recent polemic, which they could not, of course, ignore, these Belgian writers linked up with the first generation of Erasmus' admirers, with Insulanus and Beatus Rhenanus, to whom in fact they referred.

Through the sixteenth century in Catholic Europe, a hardening of attitude towards Erasmus, seen more and more as a corrosive influence, weakening structures and easing the way for the assault of the heretics – that is the theme of this chapter. Such a hardening may be seen among those on whom the church especially relied for its defence, renewal, and restoration, the Society of Jesus. A famous passage has been held to define a sharp contradiction between Erasmus and the Jesuits from the beginning: Ignatius Loyola is said in his student days to have read Erasmus' *Enchiridion* and 'observed that the reading of that book chilled the spirit of God in him and gradually extinguished the ardour of devotion.'[7] But the passage comes from the *Life* by Pedro Ribadeneira written in the late 1560s and already affected by the changed atmosphere of the previous two decades. There are grounds for believing that Ignatius was not especially hostile to Erasmus, who early had an accepted if not an honoured place in the reading of the Society, though before his death in 1556 he showed signs of disquiet, 'reflective of a general attitude toward Erasmus that began to harden in these years and of a climate of opinion that was superorthodox, suspicious, and unbending.'[8]

One still finds sobriety of language and a certain balance of judgment (though with an unmistakable tilt) in a work of 1577 by Peter Canisius, the pioneer of Catholic restoration in Germany. This was his

5 *Athenae Belgicae* 206
6 *Bibliotheca Belgica* 230–1; *Athenae Belgicae* 207–8
7 *Vita Ignatii Loiolae* in *Fontes narrativi de S. Ignatio de Loyola* IV (Rome 1965) 172–5, quoted by John C. Olin 'Erasmus and St Ignatius Loyola' 116. I follow Olin in this paragraph.
8 Ibid 121. Of Ribadeneira's work Olin says: 'I must confess that I see it as embodying an attitude toward Erasmus and a handling of the delicate problem of Ignatius and Erasmus more in keeping with the anti-Erasmian spirit of the Counter Reformation, that is of the time in which it was written, than with the actual facts of the case' (ibid).

book on the Virgin Mary,[9] of whose vastness (and of the strains its composition imposed on its author) a contemporary (his half-brother, Theodoric) said: 'We and all who know his studies consider it almost a miracle that he has not been overwhelmed and killed some time ago by the immensity of his labours ... '[1] The effort was part of a response to the great propagandist Protestant history, the Magdeburg *Centuries*, and a measure of the importance Canisius gave to the Marian doctrine in the Counter-Reformation struggle in Germany.

How does Erasmus stand to the Marian devotion?[2] Canisius' answer strikes a balance, but not a perfect balance, as I have said – the tilt is unfavourable. This is consistent with Canisius' whole judgment of Erasmus: he was justly celebrated in studies with a happy genius, many-sided learning, and rare eloquence – he stimulated good studies and freed them from barbarism; yet, in matters of faith and theology, he did much harm – he used and taught others to use an inordinate freedom in judging the writings of the Fathers, the constitutions of the church, the opinions of the theologians, indeed in disturbing and overthrowing them. He prepared the way for Luther; the difference between them was that, while Luther was the turbulent leader of a sect, Erasmus advanced his opinions and errors with caution and moderation.[3] He wrote about what deserved condemnation and correction in the church but (wittingly or unwittingly) too much in the spirit of the jester.[4] In his writings on Mary, too, there is much to condemn and somewhat to praise.

Much to condemn: Erasmus called devotion to Mary superstition, injurious to the Son, as if those paying this devotion put more trust in Mary than in Christ Himself. Prayers to Mary (like those of the pilgrims satirized in the colloquy 'A Pilgrimage for Religion's Sake' or those of the sailors satirized in 'The Shipwreck')[5] 'were not unknown to the Fathers and have been offered for many centuries in the universal church. Thus they may be appropriately interpreted, as the learned have often shown, and can be kept in use without any dishonour to Christ ... ' Is there anyone so foolish or ignorant of true piety as to pray to Mary in the belief that the Mother is superior to the Son?[6] Because some have fallen into such clownish errors, ought Erasmus to bring

9 *De Maria virgine incomparabili ...*
1 Quoted in James Brodrick sj *Saint Peter Canisius* 743
2 Erasmus is discussed at book 5, ch 10, 600–4.
3 Ibid 600
4 Ibid 601
5 *The Colloquies of Erasmus* 138–46, 285–312
6 *De Maria virgine* 601

into contempt genuine devotion paid to Mary? In his Marian doctrine there is a characteristic uncertainty and ambiguity; the more he tried to explain himself, the less credible and the more a follower of the Pyrrhonian or sceptical theology he seemed.[7]

Somewhat to praise: there are places where Erasmus spoke far more reverently of the Marian cult and himself furthered the cult (the *Virginis matris apud Lauretum cultae liturgia.*)[8] In this matter he was more on the side of the Catholics than of their opponents – the Protestants cannot fairly claim him. His damaging expressions may even be forgiven because he later regretted them vehemently; he did not anticipate the time that was to come, predicting an age of spiritual freedom whereas those who emerged under the cloak of evangelical freedom gave way to the licence of the flesh. He himself was left giving satisfaction to neither party, a sign of God's marvellous judgment on one who wished to accommodate both.[9]

In another work, the preface to his edition of Jerome's letters, Canisius gave its classic expression to the view, which we have already encountered in Miraeus and others, that Erasmus should have stuck to his literary last. Would that he had not defiled his own edition of St Jerome with theological comments, 'administering the poison instead of the antidote and, so to speak, selling coals for gold.'[1] He should have left sacred studies alone entirely or at least shown a less supercilious spirit in judging the works of the Fathers. 'When he began to play the theologian, he took on something beyond his powers and trusted too much in his own judgment; he was more attentive to words than to realities and often proved himself unnecessarily severe and hypercritical.'[2] He was merciless towards others but too lenient towards himself. Consequently his authority was shaken more by the man himself than by his opponents; he carries no more weight with the pious than many impious do. Yet there are still Erasmians to be found ('ô mores, ô tempora'), taught by Folly and corrupted by vicious Colloquies, thinking themselves learned when they undermine 'human constitutions' (as they are pleased to call the monastic orders), tickle the ears of the multitude with disparagement of the religious and, like their

7 Ibid 602
8 (Basel 1523) LB V 1327
9 *De Maria virgine* 604
1 *D. Hieronymi Stridoniensis epistolae selectae* ... a vii[r]. The expression is 'carbones (ut aiunt) pro auro vendidisset.'
2 Ibid a vii[v]: 'Nam revera postquam Erasmus Theologum agere coepit, abusus ille ingenio, nimium sibi tribuit ac sumpsit: tum verborum quam rerum studiosior, severum se praebuit saepe Aristarchum, ubi nihil erat necesse.'

Lucian, impurely, not to say impiously, scoff at sacred things. Through them he remains a disturber of the church.[3]

That is the language of the Counter-Reformation in battle for German minds. Despite its comparative restraint and moderation, Canisius' handling of Erasmus belongs to an age when the uncertain, the mediating, or the detached have already gone to the wall. To move on to another great Jesuit missioner, Antonio Possevino (1533/4–1611), is to enter a new stage of the Catholic rejection of Erasmus. The tone deteriorates, and there is a frankly abusive, even scatological strain: throwing off all authority, of the Fathers, of the church, of sacred theology, Erasmus implanted his 'filthy feet' on the sacred books; he wrote in bitter jest or madness; his dregs were licked by many, drained by Luther ... More important, one moves into a new historical setting, eastern Europe, where the ecclesiastical foundations seemed more shifting and insecure and the future of the Catholic faith more open and problematical than in Germany itself.

From his entry to the Society of Jesus in 1559 Possevino was on mission in places where the church was threatened.[4] In the 1570s and 1580s he was preoccupied with a kind of northern and eastern mission – incognito to Sweden to restore King John III Vasa to the Catholic faith (1577, 1579), to Moscow to mediate in the wars between Poland and Muscovy and to seek a union of the Russian and Catholic churches (1581–2), in the steps of Hosius to Poland, where he founded colleges to further Catholic restoration (1582–5), and to Transylvania where he met the Reformation in its theologically most radical form, antitrinitarianism.[5] He first wrote his judgment on Erasmus after he had confronted the antitrinitarians of eastern Europe, *Judicium de confessione (ut vocant) Augustana ... De Des. Erasmo ad quem novi Ariani provocant* (Posnan 1586). Back in Padua in the later 1580s he drew on his studies and experiences in composing works for the upbuilding of the church or the discomfiting of its enemies. One volley was aimed at an unlikely group, the Huguenots La Noue and Du Plessis Mornay, the *politique* Bodin – and Machiavelli; the judgment on Erasmus was repeated here for good measure.[6] His larger works, *Bibliotheca selecta* and *Apparatus sacer*, were comprehensive surveys of theological,

3 Ibid a viii[r]. Cf Brodrick *Peter Canisius* 458.
4 DTC XII 2 cols 2647–57
5 See Oskar Garstein *Rome and the Counter-Reformation in Scandinavia* passim. Possevino's larger plans were mostly unsuccessful. On antitrinitarianism in Poland and Transylvania, see, eg, G.H. Williams *The Radical Reformation*.
6 *Judicium, de Nuae ... scriptis ...*

biblical, and other studies, among the most considerable things of their kind so far seen.[7] The piece on Erasmus recurs in both. From the literary Possevino passed once more to the active prosecution of the church's interests when he went to France in the critical time of Henry IV's conversion. Ludwig Pastor's solemn periods are just: 'In addition to his vast learning, Possevino was a man of big ideas, unwearied application, great missionary zeal, dexterity and versatility, and besides all this was firm in his principles and indefatigable in carrying out his plans and projects.'[8]

In all Possevino's writing there are echoes of the battle in eastern Europe. Printed with the work against La Noue and the others was a treatise addressed to Stephen Batory, the dynamic king of Poland, Catholic but tolerant, on the expediency of holding, under the aegis of the secular authority and for the sake of civil peace, colloquies about religion with the heretics. Possevino's answer was unequivocal – all should be settled by the Catholic Church, to which Christ had committed the authority.[9] More indicative was the prominence given to the Trinitarian question. 'First,' Possevino begins the version of the Erasmus piece in Bibliotheca selecta, 'I will say who Erasmus was, then why he fell into various errors and, finally, why he is justly condemned. For this will perhaps be useful to open the eyes of the new Arians who appeal to him ... '[1] In Apparatus sacer he is more explicit; his purpose is to expose the many-headed error sprung from Erasmus' life and writings: 'For some years ago I tried to do this very thing when, with other learned men, I strove to eradicate from Poland, Hungary, and especially Transylvania (where I then was) opinions spawning Arianism and other enormities which the heretics were imbibing from his writings.'[2] Writers from Beatus Rhenanus on have praised Erasmus to the skies; thus in Catholic lands they have insinuated his name and willy-nilly opened the door to heresy.

The judgment of Erasmus that follows is summary, though much is owed to earlier controversialists. From Loos comes the story of Eras-

7   *Bibliotheca selecta qua agitur de ratione studiorum in historia ... ; Apparatus sacer ad scriptores Veteris & Novi Testamenti ...* Sommervogel called the latter 'le catalogue le plus considérable des écrivains ecclésiastiques anciens et modernes qu'on eût encore vu ... ' (quoted in DTC XII 2 col 2656).
8   *History of the Popes from the Close of the Middle Ages* XX 424–5
9   *Judicium, de Nuae ... scriptis* 319–36; cf *Cambridge History* 386.
1   *Bibliotheca selecta* 91
2   *Apparatus sacer* I: 419

mus' bastardy; from Giovio the picture of a renegade monk wandering the academies of Europe, lusting for human glory, giving free rein to his genius, and heaping up errors as rapidly as he published books so that, in Scaliger's words (now repeated as we know by many others), he would have been greater if he had been content to be less. In his restless pride, supported by no legitimate authority and certainly not by solid theology, he opened wide the window for the new Arians, as the Transylvanian ministers themselves recognize.[3] He sowed the seed of doubt in many minds, especially over the divinity of Christ. These dregs, licked by many, Luther drained ... In particular, he prepared the ground for Protestant questionings of the Trinity. Through him Satan undermined faith in the Apostles' Creed. In editing the Fathers, once he had gone beyond the purely literary or linguistic, he showed not only the fallibility but also the malignancy of his judgment.[4] Saying sometimes 'yea,' sometimes 'nay', he mixed heaven and hell. He never made his promised recantation and died leaving a name behind him, certainly, but one full of offence.

In Possevino's 'Erasmus' the Counter-Reformation is in full cry. Always the lines are drawn between sound theology, resting on texts which at one and the same time support the authority of the church and have their own authenticity guaranteed by the church, and the presumption of half-Catholics, half-heretics like Erasmus.[5]

From the time of Possevino, Erasmus the Arian joined other Erasmuses (the scoffer, the progenitor of Luther) in the heretics' gallery. The great Jesuit controversialist Robert Bellarmine gave its classic formulation to this charge. Bellarmine was indeed the very image of a perfect controversialist, in the calmness of his deportment, in the lucidity of his expression, in the directness of his blows. His principal work, which includes his comments on Erasmus, was a version of

---

3 See below, 108–10.
4 *Apparatus sacer* 420. In particular, he cast doubt on the authenticity of writings attributed to Augustine in defence of the monastic life.
5 The English Jesuit Robert Persons, while aiming at a distinctively English target, John Foxe the martyrologist, who included Erasmus in his own canon (see below, 111–14), essentially recapitulated Canisius and Possevino, including more than one reference to Erasmus' responsibility for 'all the pestilent sect of new Arians in our days.' See the full discussion in Thompson 'Erasmus and Tudor England' 62–4. The references are to the unfinished and unpublished *Certamen ecclesiae anglicanae* (quoted in Joseph Simons *Robert Persons, S.J., Certamen ecclesiae anglicanae: A study of an Unpublished Manuscript* Assen 1965) and the *Third Part of a Treatise of Three Conversions of England* 1604.

lectures delivered from his chair of controversy at the Roman College between 1576 and 1588, his *Disputationes de controversiis christianae fidei adversus huius temporis haereticos*.[6]

Everywhere, Bellarmine says, the Protestants attack the anti-trinitarians, but their own prophets, Erasmus and Luther, were unsound on this question.[7] With justice the Transylvanian ministers called Erasmus the precursor of *their* prophet, Servetus. His saying, in *scholia* to Jerome's letters, that the Arians were not so much heretics as schismatics, almost equal in number to the Catholics and their superior in learning and eloquence, earns this ironic address: 'Lo, the distinguished protector of the Arians who vindicates them from heresy and makes them more learned than the Catholics. What else remains but to call the Arians Catholics and the Catholics heretics?'[8] Erasmus had doubted the conventional reading of texts traditionally considered Trinitarian (Romans 9:5, Philippians 2:6) and indeed considered some of them unnecessary for the defence of the orthodox doctrine.[9] So, says Bellarmine, he does all he can to disarm the Catholics and wrest their weapons from their hands.[1]

Around Bellarmine's work, like a castle on the open plain, the enemy controversialists gathered.[2] Erasmus does not figure prominently in the Calvinist attacks on Bellarmine. He is quoted against the Catholics but in this literature seems alienated from both parties.

6 I use the later edition *Disputationum ... de controversiis christianae fidei ...* (Ingolstadt 1601). On Bellarmine, see, eg, E.A. Ryan *The Historical Scholarship of Saint Bellarmine*, who *inter alia* emphasizes the effect on Bellarmine of the controversial atmosphere of Louvain, where he spent the years 1569–76, first as a remarkably effective preacher, then as a teacher of theology at the Jesuit College. The chair of controversy at the Roman College was especially created for him in 1576. He was later rector of that college (1592) and archbishop of Capua (1602–5). Ranke called Bellarmine the greatest controversialist of the Roman Church. DTC II 1 cols 560–99.

7 *Disputationum* I 267–8. This discussion is in a preface to the 'Secunda controversia generalis. De Christo capite totius ecclesiae.'

8 Ibid 268

9 On Erasmus' handling of the texts concerning the deity of Christ, see J.B. Payne, *Erasmus: His Theology of the Sacraments* 56–9.

1 One example: the orthodox Fathers interpreted Philippians2:9 ('Non rapinam arbitratus est esse se aequalem Deo') thus – to claim equality with God could not be robbery, since Christ was by nature God. But Erasmus took the Arian reading: 'Non usurpavit sibi cum Deo aequalitatem.' So Bellarmine: 'I ask you, Erasmus, had you been paid a fee by the Arians, could you have put their case more assiduously?' (*Disputationum* 268–9).

2 Titles listed in Carlos Sommervogel sj *Bibliothèque de la Compagnie de Jésus* I cols 1165–80

William Whitaker (1548–95), master of St John's College, Cambridge, and regius professor of divinity, champion of the teaching of the Church of England 'interpreted in its most Calvinistic sense,' dedicated his *Disputation on Holy Scripture* against Bellarmine to William Cecil in the year of the Armada; it was aimed at dissipating 'the pestilential vapours' called up by the Jesuits to obscure 'the clear and cheerful lustre' of the Gospel.[3] Whitaker criticized Erasmus on one biblical question (inerrancy) but used him on another (the apocrypha). He was not really papist: of the various Catholic authors who admit the existence of apocrypha, 'the church of Rome acknowledges them all as her sons and disciples; except perhaps Erasmus, whom she hath expelled, as he deserves, from her family ...'[4] Franciscus Junius (François du Jon, 1545–1602), a Huguenot refugee who served William of Orange and taught at both Heidelberg and Leiden, challenged Bellarmine's association of Erasmus with the Protestants.[5] Erasmus, he says, does not belong to us. He held off out of judgment or cowardice or prudence or a dislike of partisanship. Yet in the index to Junius' *Animadversiones* Erasmus is included with Protestant writers among the 'theologi neoterici,' not among 'scholastici & pontificii scriptores'! For these controversialists of the harsh 1590s, Erasmus was not securely located anywhere; broken from one allegiance, he had not taken on another. He was left – in a time when lines were drawn hard – isolated, wandering.

On the other side, there was the same judgment. Thus in Germany, Jacob Gretser, SJ: 'He seems not to deserve a home among Catholics. The sectarians take him reluctantly into their camp. In his lifetime he wished to be neutral, so now he occupies a place apart, on neither side.'[6] Gretser (1562–1624) defended Bellarmine vigorously and marshalled an army of controversial works against the Protestants in the bitter, tragic years leading to the Thirty Years War. A historian of Bohemia speaks of the vigour of the extremes around the turn of the century and 'the failure of the centre.'[7] The reputation of Erasmus went down finally in that failure. Gretser was student and teacher

---

3 *A Disputation on Holy Scripture against the Papists, especially Bellarmine and Stapleton* 3. On Whitaker, see DNB XXI 21–3.
4 *Disputation* 37, 49, 66
5 *Animadversiones ad controversiam secundam christianae fidei* ... at cols 545–6. On Junius, see NNBW IX cols 481–3.
6 *Controversiarum Roberti Bellarmini ... defensio* col 938
7 R.J.W. Evans *Rudolf II and His World: A Study in Intellectual History 1576–1612* 115

(professor of scholastic theology, 1592) at the University of Ingolstadt, citadel of the Counter-Reformation in South Germany.[8] Early he had turned from the humanities to the certitudes of scholasticism. He did not stand apart from the fierce public struggles. He took a leading role in the Colloquy of Regensburg in 1601, whose failure signalled the coming catastrophe in Germany. He was adviser to Ferdinand II, the architect of the last attempt to carry the Counter-Reformation through politically in the Empire. His formidable reputation as a controversialist rested on his erudition and indefatigable activity but also on his grounding on the scholastic certitudes. Inevitably he condemned one who reserved his judgment on many of the theological issues: Erasmus was 'fickle and unsteady and changed with the wind.'[9]

In the first volume of his defence of Bellarmine against Whitaker, Junius, and their like, Gretser includes an attack on Erasmus' version of the New Testament. His bold corrections of the Vulgate were aimed at making his version more marketable among those who preferred novelty to antiquity.[1] The approval of Pope Leo X cannot be quoted in Erasmus' favour; the pope approved Erasmus' labours, not his errors, nor indeed his presumptuous handling of the Vulgate. In any case, it was not then clear how dangerous Erasmus was; he was a wolf in sheep's clothing, and many at Rome were deceived.[2] He did not so much interpret as corrupt the New Testament.[3] His editorial work on the Fathers is written off sarcastically. The Protestant writers who relied on it were cutting the critical knots with a blunt sword. Erasmus used it in fact as a vehicle for his doctrinal errors, for example, his Pelagianism ('Erasmo, Pelagii amico, & non occulto patrono'). In the second volume Gretser takes up again the Trinitarian question, attacking Erasmus' statement in the preface to his edition of Hilary (to this Bellarmine, too, had objected): the Fathers did not dare call the Holy Spirit God. For all the smokescreen of words he put up, Erasmus could not hide his blasphemy.[4]

Gretser's controversial manner was lively, but savage and sarcastic, a true child of its time. That of the last of the Jesuit writers to be considered here was more rhetorical, less scholastic, ultimately less

---

8 DTC VI 2 cols 1866–71
9 *Defensio* I col 374
1 Ibid col 725
2 Ibid col 558
3 Ibid col 963: ' ... multis locis novum testamentum non vertit, sed pervertit.'
4 *Defensio* II cols 21–5. The preface, addressed to John Carondelet, is at Allen V 172–92 (see page 182).

serious, as befits an essentially literary polemic. François Garasse (1585–1631) was a successful preacher in the France of Louis XIII, that is, to a generation more affected than any of its predecessors in France by the deeper strains in the Catholic Reformation. His eloquence, however, had a rough edge – in the written as well as the spoken form. An unsympathetic nineteenth-century biographer described his most celebrated work as amusing, alive with burlesque energy but without method, filled 'with bad proofs, with inexact facts and inconclusive citations.'[5] *La Doctrine curieuse des beaux esprits de ce temps, ou pretendus tels* was aimed at *politique* and 'libertine' writers, at the sceptical spirit which the last terrible years of the French wars of religion had engendered in some observers.[6] On its title-page was an engraving of the decapitated Holofernes bleeding copiously and Judith delivering up his head with remarkable *savoir faire* and a motto from Judith 13: 'Confirma me Domine Deus in hac hora.' Garasse needed little encouragement in his assault on the wickedness and stupidity of the sect of 'atheists' as he called them.[7] Erasmus appears in a book devoted to the libertine maxims that belief is free and should not be forced, that the articles of faith should be reduced to a minimum. His particular folly was, with Zwingli, to teach that the good pagans would be saved. So paradise is filled with 'plus grandes ordures,' with Hercules, Socrates, Theseus, infamous in their lives, atheist in their beliefs, immoral in their writings.[8] None can be saved except by faith in Jesus Christ, explicit or implicit (as with the patriarchs); whether an implicit faith might be efficacious for the pagan philosophers we do not know. Certainly, we must reject the libertine teaching that those who believe in one God and live a good life even among the pagans are as assured of salvation as those who punctually and expressly practise their faith in Paris or in Rome. Erasmus, with his heaven filled pell-mell with the good and the bad, is like the agnostic emperor 'who kept in his cabinet the images of Jesus Christ on one side and Venus on the

5   Hoefer XVIII cols 426–9; cf René Pintard *Le libertinage érudit dans la première moitié du XVIIᵉ siècle* I 32, 394.
6   The subtitle reads: 'Contenant plusieurs maximes pernicieuses à l'Estat, à la Religion, & aux bonnes Mœurs.'
7   On this usage, see L. Febvre *Le Problème de l'incroyance au XVIᵉ siècle: La religion de Rabelais* 149. Cf Joseph Lecler 'Un adversaire des libertins au début du XVIIᵉ siècle: Le P. François Garasse (1585–1631),' especially 558; P.O. Kristeller 'Le mythe de l'athéisme de la Renaissance et la tradition française de la libre pensée' 343.
8   *La Doctrine curieuse* 250–1

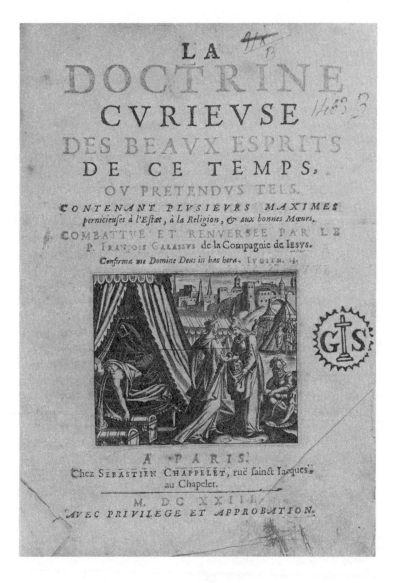

LA
DOCTRINE
CVRIEVSE
DES BEAVX ESPRITS
DE CE TEMPS,
OV PRETENDVS TELS.
CONTENANT PLVSIEVRS MAXIMES
pernicieuses à l'Estat, à la Religion, & aux bonnes Mœurs.
COMBATTVE ET RENVERSEE PAR LE
P. FRANÇOIS GARASSVS de la Compagnie de IESVS.
Confirma me Domine Deus in hac hora. IVDITH. 13.

A PARIS,
Chez SEBASTIEN CHAPPELET, ruë sainct Iacques,
au Chapelet.
M. DC XXIII.
AVEC PRIVILEGE ET APPROBATION.

Title page of François Garasse
La Doctrine curieuse des beaux esprits de ce temps, ou pretendus tels
depicting Judith as a symbol of the faith in mortal combat with its enemies
Reproduced by permission of the
Thomas Fisher Rare Book Library, University of Toronto

other, of David and Priapus, of Abraham and Flora.'[9] The libertines have so expansive a heaven in order to find a way in for themselves.[1]

France had known conflicts more tragic than the extravagant polemics and rhetorical feudings of a Garasse. The scars of two generations of civil war mark the historiography of the century's end. Florimond de Raemond (c 1540–1602) had lived through the religious wars (he became councillor of the *Parlement* of Bordeaux in the year of St Bartholomew) and as judge and writer had fought his own fight against the Huguenots; his reconversion after a time of attraction to Calvinism had made his Catholic zeal all the warmer.[2] His work *L'Histoire de la naissance, progrez et decadence de l'heresie de ce siècle*, written at the end of the religious wars and edited and published by his son François, drew on Catholic historians and polemicists of the sixteenth century, Cochlaeus, Surius, Hosius, and Prateolus, but added rich, dark, apocalyptic colours of its own.[3] These times were a wretched age of iron ('ce miserable siècle de fer'), a true night of the world.[4] History was a battle of cosmic forces. His own work was a combat for the church against 'roaring lions, ravening wolves, monstrous dragons, mordant vipers.' In François' dedication to Pope Paul v, we see the same evidences of the spirit of religious war: heresy was 'a fury come out from hell … a monster with a hundred heads …' The heretics have declared war openly against God, altars have been destroyed, priests martyred, states overthrown. Europe has become 'a circus, a battlefield of gladiators and fencers to the death.'[5]

The depiction of Erasmus also is touched by dark colours, without being especially hostile to the man himself. The German Reformation began with quarrels of monks, filled with envy, hate, and pride, over indulgences, quarrels characteristic of the church of the time, with pride and dissoluteness rife among the orders and gross ignorance among the people. Some participants came to regret stirring up these

9 Ibid 265–6
1 Ibid 267. On the salvation of the good pagans, see Hans Baron 'Erasmus-Probleme im Spiegel des Colloquium "Inquisitio de Fide." ' Garasse makes one other reference to Erasmus, in a section on the authority of scripture. From criticism of the scholastics he hastened into an impious handling of scripture, indeed into an abyss of impiety and buffoonery (647).
2 Michaud xxxv 74–5
3 Herte *Das katholische Lutherbild* I 165–9
4 1623 Rouen edition 3–4
5 Ibid aii^v–aiii

troubles, like Erasmus, who in his youth produced polemical works against the monks but later said that, had he foreseen the madness of Luther, he would have avoided fathering such children. He became the great enemy of the Lutheran sect, though the Lutherans sought in his writings expressions which would attach him to their cause. A sound reading of Erasmus in fact imprints piety and the fear of God in men's hearts.[6]

The Reformation for Raemond was a catastrophe, but also unwittingly a purification, a providential torrent. Luther's heresy should have been snuffed out by force; however, 'Heaven had decided otherwise and our sins deserved the worst and cried out for vengeance. If the true causes are hidden from us, we should not consider them other than just, since they come from the just prime mover, whose works are always justice ...'[7]

What role did Erasmus play in this great shaking?[8] In describing its ambiguity, Raemond draws on most of the Catholic literature of the century. At the beginning of the Reformation some battled on among the ruins and saved a part of the Christian people. Should Erasmus, that great man of letters, be placed among this number? He was wavering and doubtful in some things. Though avowedly an enemy of Luther and all sectarians, the antitrinitarians have claimed him as the precursor of their prophet, Servetus.[9] He began as the satirist of the clergy and up to 1529 seemed to favour Luther's revolt. But he never separated himself from the unity of the church and in the end showed that he had written, not against the dignity of the offices, but against the failings of the men. He was carried away by scholarly conceit ('la presomption de son sçavoir'). He would have been a greater man (as Scaliger said) ... ! In his last years, however, by his writings and example he turned many from following the heretics. He was prevented by death from publishing his book of retractions, 'often' requested by Thomas More![1] At times he seemed to wound the honour of the Virgin Mary but he also made vows and composed a liturgy in her honour.[2]

6 Ibid 46–7, 50
7 Ibid 59
8 The fullest treatment of Erasmus is at book 5, ch 1, entitled 'Quels furent ceux qui firent teste au commencement à l'Heresie?'
9 Ibid 516. Cf Bellarmine. Elsewhere Raemond says that Erasmus approaches the errors of the antitrinitarians in only one place, the Hilary preface (230).
1 Ibid 517
2 Ibid 518. Cf Canisius (above).

This picture of Erasmus – somewhat apart from the struggle but never finally going over to the other side – is confirmed by a strange apocryphal story. In 1534 Martin Bucer introduced Calvin to Erasmus: '... fearful of what he saw in this man's spirit, [Erasmus] said to Bucer, pointing out Calvin, "I see a great pestilence arise in the church against the church."'[3]

Raemond had lived through a holocaust. He saw the Reformation under Providence as the work of passionate, wilful, misguided spirits. It shook the foundations of civilization. Erasmus was not one of those perverse spirits. He recognized the appalling consequences of what they were about. Yet he did stand somewhat apart; he did not fully come up to the measure of the events through which he lived. The great providential torrents of the sixteenth century left moderate and uncertain spirits on the strand. These were understandable judgments from one who had known a lifetime of religious war.

The civil wars had prompted different reflections in others. In many there remained a powerful nostalgia for the broken unity of Christendom, but in the desperate 1580s and 1590s some were ready to accept a lesser solution, the salvaging of national unity by the civil power even at the expense of religious uniformity. These *politiques* might look back to Erasmus, not as the herald of their solution, which he could not be, but as one who foresaw the terrible outcome of unchecked religious passion and party spirit.[4]

That he was remembered is indicated by references in the *Mémoires-Journaux* of Pierre de l'Estoile. On Saturday 4 August 1607 l'Estoile bought for five *sols* a copperplate portrait of Erasmus and recalled that Claude d'Espence, a spokesman of moderate Catholicism and seeker after reconciliation in the first years of the religious wars, had called him 'the fifth doctor of the church.'[5] In October of the same year a friend lent him Erasmus' *Epistola ad fratres Inferioris Germaniae* (Paris 1545):[6] he read it many times over the following year and a half. All who loved the unity and concord of the church would, he said, share its opinions. Yet it made clear that Erasmus was neither Lutheran nor Huguenot.[7] In his own youth l'Estoile had been ad-

---

3   Ibid 890. Raemond recognizes the model character of this story: a similar story was told of Berengarius and Fulbert, bishop of Chartres.
4   On the different solutions to the problems of religious conflict, see, eg, Joseph Lecler *Histoire de la tolérance au siècle de la Réforme* II 428–38.
5   *Mémoires-Journaux* VIII 328. On Claude d'Espence (1511–71), see DBF XII cols 1503–4; DTC V 1 cols 603–5.
6   Cf LB X 1589–1632.
7   *Mémoires-Journaux* VIII 352, IX 250

monished by his father, who belonged to one of the parliamentary families, to remain in the Catholic church but not subject to its abuses or superstitions. 'This last wish of his father,' it has been said, 'remained graven on his soul and became the rule of his whole life.'[8] He hated the extremists of the Catholic League in Paris in 1588–9 and was suspect in their eyes. He rallied to Henry IV, but not openly enough to avoid for a time the suspicion of both sides.[9] He was moderate, royalist, irenic. A relation, Felix Vialar, published in 1609 a book called *Le Chemin à l'athéisme, fraié par les hérétiques de ce siècle*. Its intemperate zeal and grotesque injuries would, l'Estoile considered, serve to make the division between Christians perpetual and irremediable rather than bring about reunion and the reformation of the church desired by all men of good will. 'In this he does not imitate that great man Erasmus, whose authority he nevertheless uses against the errors and vices of the Protestants.'[1]

In 1610–11 l'Estoile was much afflicted by illness and close to death. He vowed henceforth to make the Bible his principal reading. On 2 March 1611 he finished a complete reading begun on 1 January; he had read with more fervour and attention than ever before and had found true Erasmus' saying: there is little profit in a perfunctory reading of the gospels (as Erasmus himself had discovered), but he who gives to them a careful and constant study feels a strength found in no other books.[2] Here in the depths of the confessional age, after two generations of religious war, is a pocket of Erasmian piety; against the stream, a cautious Parisian *politique* holds to the moderate Catholic interpretation of Erasmus of sixty years before.

The great jurist and servant of Henry III and Henry IV, enemy also of the Catholic League, Jacques-Auguste de Thou (1553–1617), identified himself with Erasmus in a similar way. In the famous preface to his *Histoire universelle*, begun amid the clash of arms, he expressed a *politique* disillusion with the policy of maintaining religious unity by force.[3] Persecution in France and the Netherlands over forty years had

8 'Notice sur Pierre de l'Estoile' ibid XII iv–v
9 Ibid viii–x
1 Ibid x 46–7
2 Ibid XI 85. Cf 'Notice ... ' xvi.
3 *Histoire universelle* I xli–vi. For the complicated history of the French translations of de Thou's History, see Henry Harrisse *Le Président de Thou et ses descendants, leur célèbre bibliothèque, leurs armoires et les traductions françaises de J.A. Thuani Historiarum sui temporis*; Samuel C. Kinser 'The Historiography of Jacques-Auguste de Thou' ch 2. In a visit to Basel in 1579 de Thou saw in the home of Basilius Amerbach various objects

placed both the state and religion in peril; it would be better to follow the path of prudence – Protestantism diminished in times of peace, expanded in times of war.[4] There are Erasmian echoes in this preface: in peace men may choose the best in religion – 'I mean,' says de Thou, 'what most conforms to antiquity.'[5] The preface finishes with an ardent prayer for the pacification of the kingdom through the royal house and for an end to schism and novelties in religion – a mingling of the two strains, the Erasmian and the *politique*.

De Thou knew that his intention to deal impartially with the Protestants, 'to publish nothing false and to say the truth boldly,' would be ill received by more zealous Catholics. A poem, 'A la posterité,' in his *Mémoires*, ostensibly written by a friend, was a kind of *apologia*. De Thou speaks:

> Virtue I honour wherever I find it
> Without favour of rank or country or party.[6]

He has esteemed all who love peace. His criticism of unworthy popes and his praise of worthy Protestants lessen neither this attachment to the ancient and unchanging faith nor his hatred of schism.[7] Thus the poet comes to Erasmus. De Thou could not bring himself to tarnish the memory of this great man's rare talents. If he was sometimes in error, he should be excused – he was human and could be deceived. What if one searched the lives and hearts of his enemies with the rigour they use towards him? What would one not find – real crimes, errors, frightful maxims? Young – for every age has its failings – he gave too free rein to his biting pen. Let us think rather of his Christian and Catholic death and judge his soul and his opinions by his last letters.[8]

This poem reflects the state of mind on the Catholic side by the early seventeenth century: Erasmus can be defended only by avowing his faults and declaring his enemies worse. Yet in the final reference to his Catholic and Christian death there is a link back to the Erasmus portraits of Insulanus and Nausea.

In a letter of 1615 to his younger friend, Hugo Grotius, de Thou

once belonging to Erasmus (Peter G. Bietenholz *Basle and France in the Sixteenth Century: The Basle Humanists and Printers in their Contacts with Francophone Culture* 211, 215).

4 *Histoire universelle* I xlviii
5 Ibid liii. Cf Kinser 'Historiography' 228–32.
6 *Mémoires de la vie de Jacques-Auguste de Thou, Conseiller d'Etat, et Président à Mortier au Parlement de Paris* 211
7 Ibid 212–15
8 Ibid 217

expressed his own feelings more directly.[9] The origins of the schism of the sixteenth century lay in blindness on the one side and extremism on the other. The theological controversies in which Grotius was then engaged in Holland revealed the danger of endless division.[1] It was dangerous to break away from the original unity. Now on both sides reunion was sought in vain. Irenicists like 'your Erasmus' and 'our d'Espence' had done all that they could by word and writing to bring peace to the church, but in face of the hatred of both parties they had had amid sighs to give up. One can only turn to God and put one's trust in Him. There could be no more fitting conclusion to the story of deepening distrust and division unfolded in the present chapter than this sombre letter, full of a deeply felt resignation.

9 De Thou to Grotius, 29 July 1615, *Briefwisseling van Hugo Grotius* I 402–3
1 See below, 140–3.

THREE

Protestantism:
Erasmus and the Patterns
of Reformation

THE STORY OF ERASMUS' REPUTATION among Catholics in the sixteenth century has a simple shape; it is a story of decline and fall. The bitter controversy which attended the last twenty years of his life was momentarily stilled at his death. His friends and followers took the word first – in the Basel circle, in the Habsburg entourage, among the controversialists fighting a desperate rearguard against the Protestants in the years before the Council of Trent, among the mediators and irenicists hoping against hope to divert the gathering storm. It could not last. By 1560 the mood had changed decisively, the last Erasmian generation had passed away, and the smell of battle was in the air. The Catholic Reformation required an intense concentration of moral energies, a new discipline – not only for the living but also, so to speak, for the dead. Those like Erasmus, who, without denying ultimately their loyalty to the church, had yet rejected the very notion of religious militancy, were doomed. The new mood was reflected in the essayists, historians, controversialists. He who before 1550 had been a witness against the heretics now shared the dock and scaffold with them. One can trace the change in a body of literature like the biographical tradition about Sir Thomas More. Above all, the front-line troops of Counter-Reformation, the Society of Jesus, treated Erasmus as the ally of the enemies they fought on different battlefields – the Anglicans, the Huguenots, the Lutherans, the Socinians. Only a few isolated pockets of the older interpretation survived, in the Southern Netherlands, among the *politiques*, but here too concessions had to be made to the now prevailing interpretation or, as in de Thou's sad letter to Grotius, one finds an almost wistful regret for possibilities lost beyond recall.

The shape of any treatment of Protestant interpretations of Erasmus in the sixteenth century cannot be so simple; there were different

The philosophers grubbing in the sand
From an edition of the *Cymbalum mundi*
by Prosper Marchand, Amsterdam 1732
Princeton University Library

'patterns of Reformation.' The model of waves rolling out from a single centre like Luther's Saxony will not suffice. One cannot ignore, for example, the broad, ill-defined movement known as *évangelisme*, although some of its adherents remained formally Catholic and the doctrine of others may seem impenetrable. Erasmus' personal experience of the Reformation was in its distinctive Basel form. Each of the Swiss and German cities had its own Reformation history, and at least Strasbourg and St Gallen offered something substantial to the story of Erasmus interpretation. The new orthodoxies, Lutheranism in the Empire and Calvinism in Western Europe, had to settle with Erasmus in the second half of the sixteenth century; religious radicalism in its various forms had been coming to terms with him from the beginning and had finally to place him in its precarious succession of witnesses. A picture of Erasmus was necessary, too, for the propagandists of England's unique religious settlement. In this chapter we will fit the reputation of Erasmus into these different patterns of Reformation.

Let us begin with *évangelisme*, a name for widely dispersed impulses towards spiritual renewal and church reform, with no precise limits or exclusive ecclesiastical orientation, especially as they appear in France and Italy in the 1520s and 1530s.[1] Here is a dialogue of 1537 illustrating one such impulse. An enigmatic god, Mercury, has broken the philosopher's stone, distributed the pieces in the sand of the arena where the philosophers are disputing, and promised them knowledge and power from the fragments. The philosophers are grubbing in the sand like little children. None has found a thing, but all claim great heaps making much more than the original stone: 'One boasts that he has more than his fellow who replies that his is not the true stone.' Two who come on disputing are Rhetulus and Cubercus. The latter says that Rhetulus should allow others their pieces of stone: Mercury who gave the stone did not wish them to shower abuse on one another but rather to love one another as brothers. But Rhetulus brusquely replies: 'The rest of you have found only sand.' A third character, Drarig, appears and the dialogue proceeds:

> DRARIG You lie. Here is a piece belonging to the true philosopher's stone and better than yours.
> RHETULUS Aren't you ashamed to produce that as philosopher's

1 For a recent discussion, see D. Fenlon *Heresy and Obedience in Tridentine Italy: Cardinal Pole and the Counter Reformation* 13–16, 18–21, and the references there indicated.

stone? Can't you see that it is only sand? Fie, fie, take it away.
DRARIG Why have you made me drop it? It will be lost. Were I a
man of war or carried a sword, I could die of rage if I did not kill
you on the spot. How will I ever find it now? I have taken so much
trouble looking for it and now this wretch has made me lose it!
RHETULUS You have lost nothing of importance. Don't trouble
yourself.
DRARIG Nothing of importance! I would not have exchanged it
for any treasure in this world. What madness could be driving
you! Oh, envious traitor! Couldn't you have wronged me somehow without making me lose in a moment the efforts of thirty
years? I will be revenged, no matter how long it takes.[2]

Rhetulus and Cubercus had long been recognized as anagrams for
Luther and Bucer, and the characterizations have some telling features.
In the middle of the eighteenth century Drarig was identified with
Erasmus through his family name of Girard.[3] Knowing that, let us now
interpret the above encounter. Luther with characteristic brutality has
upset the 'philosophy' which is the vehicle of Erasmus' vanity. The
latter's response is petulant and vindictive, despite his claim to be a
man of peace. In short, this dialogue represents a rejection of both the
Erasmian reform and the Protestant Reformation.

It belongs to a set of dialogues first printed in Paris in 1537 without
the author's name and called *Cymbalum mundi*. In character they are
partly satirical, partly spiritual, and, however difficult intepretation
may be, the tone is unmistakable – a scepticism about all the loudly
proclaimed solutions to the problems of the age, a dark, pessimistic
vision of the world as a scene of confusion and agitation. The author
was Bonaventure des Périers, whose life began in obscurity (1510–15)
and ended in suicide (1544), a good humanist who entered the
evangelical circle around the king's sister, Marguerite of Navarre, and
was perhaps protected by her when Francis I ordered an investigation of
the book and the pursuit of its printer.[4]

The book required interpretation. Generally it was seen as a work of
unbelief – contemporaries would have said, of impiety. In the most
extended modern version of this interpretation (Lucien Febvre's) Des
Périers owed his doubt and irreverence to a reading of Origen's *Contra*

2 Bonaventure des Périers *Cymbalum mundi* 16
3 By J.-B. Michault (ibid 46)
4 Lucien Febvre 'Une histoire obscure: La publication du "Cymbalum
   mundi" '

Celsum – Celsus, Origen's Epicurean opponent, won a belated victory from the pages intended to refute him.[5] But such an interpretation – against the grain of Febvre's other writing on sixteenth-century religious history – requires a 'stupefying precocity' in Des Périers. It will not do. The clue to an understanding of the *Cymbalum mundi* rests rather in his association with Marguerite and the evangelicals.[6]

For us the problem is: how can a humanist and biblical scholar of the 1530s be so scornful of Erasmus? The answer to that question helps capture the mood of the evangelical circle after 1536. There has been a movement from the humanist and Protestant cult of the word to a cult of silence, from the 'évangelisme prédicant' of Erasmus to an 'évangelisme taciturne.'[7] Words provoke quarrels and brawls, tempt to presumption and self-assertion. Truth on the contrary resides with reticence and renunciation and tranquillity of spirit.

Another work, published in Erasmus' life-time and of whose existence he was aware, had expressed a similar outlook, Etienne Dolet's *Dialogus, de imitatione Ciceroniana, adversus Desiderium Erasmum Roterodamum, pro Christophoro Longolio*, a severe attack on Erasmus from the Ciceronian quarter.[8] Dolet, perhaps a little older than Des Périers, belonged to a generation which had escaped Erasmus' spell.[9] In the Ciceronian controversy itself, in the debate about style, literary and human, Dolet's *Dialogus* opposes to the common-sense solutions of Erasmus the pure flame of his own fanaticism, an absolute commitment to an ideal of perfection.[1] More fundamental and more interesting to us (though also analogous in the religious sphere to his Ciceronianism in the literary) is Dolet's attack on Erasmus' *philosophia Christi*, which he sees not as clarifying but as obscuring the

---

5 Lucien Febvre 'Origène et Des Périers ou l'enigme du *Cymbalum mundi*'
6 V.-L. Saulnier 'Le sens du "Cymbalum mundi"'
7 Ibid 162–3. The title is indicative if it indeed derives from St Paul's 'tinkling cymbal' (cf Peter H. Nurse in Des Périers *Cymbalum mundi* xxxii). For an interpretation of the work as more comic and less didactic, see now Ian R. Morrison 'The *Cymbalum Mundi* Revisited.' The satire on the philosophers with their bombast and pathetic trust in their own words and opinions is, however, unaffected.
8 Lyon 1535. Most of the *Dialogus* reappeared in sections of Dolet's *Commentariorum linguae Latinae, tomus primus* (Lyon 1536), though the latter may in fact have been prepared first. See the editor's introduction to the most recent edition of the *Dialogus, L'Erasmianus sive Ciceronianus d'Etienne Dolet (1535)* 42, 65. Cf Allen Ep 3005, XI 108–9.
9 *L'Erasmianus* 22
1 Ibid 57

gospel, as a muddying of the waters, a dangerous confusion of the sacred and the profane.

It is, says his spokesman in the dialogue, blindness to believe that divine causes can be advanced by human efforts. So he baits Erasmus. Unless Erasmus and other babbling theologians come its its aid the divine Word lacks efficacy! Erasmus' loquaciousness fills up what is lacking in the Holy Spirit![2] True reverence is not advanced or protected but rather dissipated or undermined by talk. The claims of the Reformers to remove superstition and restore religion are full of arrogance.[3] Erasmus pounds away at us with words but achieves nothing. The itch to interpret the scriptures produces no fruit but only excites endless brawling. Even the admitted abuses in the church do not justify the restless agitations of an Erasmus or a Luther.[4]

The association of Erasmus and Luther gives a clue to the character of these writings; they represent a quietist reformation, while the two men – in their different ways – are seen as brawlers for religion's sake. In this pattern of reform Erasmus is condemned for what his friends most praised, his services to biblical scholarship and Christian renewal through an easy command of words.[5]

Another setting for an interpretation of Erasmus was the small city in eastern Switzerland, St Gallen, whose history consisted of a balancing of relationships – with the great abbey in its midst, with the German Empire, with its partners near and far in the linen trade, with neighbouring states, especially Zürich. From his youth Joachim von Watt (Vadianus, 1484–1551) reflected on these relationships; his roots were deep in the soil of St Gallen.[6] After a successful academic career at Vienna and a saturation in humanist learning, he returned as town physician to St Gallen (1518). He was soon to become town councillor and in 1525 burgomaster. He presided over the coming of the Reformation to St Gallen; deeply influenced by Erasmus, he saw no need to make a choice between Erasmus and Luther. He observed at first hand the crisis years between 1529, when the ancient abbey was forcibly

2 Facsimile of 1535 edition, in ibid 35 (the facsimile carries the original pagination distinct from that of Telle's introduction).
3 Ibid 36
4 Ibid 38–9
5 Cf Telle's introduction, ibid 48–9; Nurse in Des Périers Cymbalum mundi xi; Saulnier 'Le sens' 162–3.
6 For a brief introduction, see Gordon Rupp Patterns of Reformation 357–78. The essential work is Werner Näf Vadian und seine Stadt St Gallen.

secularized, and 1531, when a small St Gallen contingent shared the Protestant defeat at Kappel. His historical work, which includes a striking reference to Erasmus, began seriously in these years – it came out of his concern for the city and was accompanied by a sense of the complexity of its historical experience.[7]

First between 1525 and 1533 Vadianus wrote a chronicle of the abbots of St Gallen from the high Middle Ages (1199) to his own childhood (1491). In time this was to be enriched by the study of the records of the secularized abbey. In the late 1530s he resumed the work, stimulated again to take up his German historical writing – after immersion in practical activities and humanist and theological works – by an association with Johannes Stümpf's chronicle of the Swiss Confederacy, to which he was to contribute the section on the abbots. He was determined at the one end to go back to the beginnings of monasticism in St Gallen and at the other to come through to the crisis of 1530. The whole work goes well beyond local history, relating the town and the abbey to the history of Western Christendom and the German Empire. In addition, two intentionally broader and more discursive studies preceded the revised chronicle, one on the character of monasticism and the other a general account of the history of cloisters and foundations.[8]

Erasmus appears in two connections in Vadianus' writings; he is given a place first in the history of monasticism and secondly in the coming of the Reformation. Monasticism, according to Vadianus, began as a withdrawal in the time of persecutions; at their end it continued by free choice and in the belief that it was well pleasing to God.[9] One subsequent kind of monastic life – without binding rules, adopted not for selfish or self-indulgent reasons but for the study of the Bible, each suiting the demands to his needs and measuring all by the teaching of scripture – is honoured among Christians. Among monks of this kind were Jerome and Simplicianus, who was the teacher of Augustine. To them may 'in our own time' be added 'der teur und hochgelert man Erasmus von Rotterdam.'[1]

7 *Chronik der Aebte des Klosters St Gallen* in Joachim von Watt *Deutsche Historische Schriften* 2 vols
8 For the above, Näf *Vadian* II 377–421; Ernst Götzinger, Introduction, *Chronik* I. Stümpf included in his chronicle most of the works Vadianus made available to him, but in an altered or abbreviated form; this was their only printing at the time. Götzinger did not print them in the true order because he himself established that order only in the course of the editorial work (Näf II 383, 401).
9 'Von dem Mönchsstand ... ' in *Chronik* I 3–4
1 Ibid 6

Erasmus did not live as a hermit but among pious and learned folk in the towns, unmarried and without public office, leading an upright, Christian, unspotted life. From his youth in various lands he strove to acquire good letters and to master the languages necessary for the understanding of scripture. So he prepared himself for the work which various patrons, especially the nobles and bishops of England, were to support. Then he came into Germany, of which he was a native, settled in Basel, and brought to light the fruits of his labours. 'In furthering the true Christian life and our holy faith through the correction and explanation of the biblical texts and the teachings of the Fathers he did greater service and reverence than any Latin writer for a thousand years.'[2] Often pope and emperor wished to promote him to bishop or cardinal, but he did not seek the burden of such honours as they exist in the present time; but to the end of his life he gave himself freely and unstintingly to studies – for God's honour and the betterment of the church. He did more for the churches by his labours than any bishop, abbot, or monk. By his will he provided for the support of poor, deserving scholars that they might come to a good understanding and, according to their gifts, serve the Christian community.[3]

In this brief portrait Erasmus appears as the representative of true monasticism, with its double commitment to piety and learning. Another kind of monasticism had been dominant in the last centuries. With the mendicant orders came the doctrine of merits and rewards, and studies and schools, once the best fruits of monasticism, declined. Vadianus, however prudently, accepts the view, common among the Reformers of all persuasions, that the church had passed through stages of decline, that Christian history was the history of the fall of the church.[4] The nadir came – in a conjuncture of general history and the history of St Gallen – with Abbot Ulrich VIII Rösch (1463–91), rich, political, dominating, a symbol of the corruptions of the modern church enmeshed in worldly affairs.[5]

Here is the background to Vadianus' Reformation and to Erasmus' place in the succession of Reformers. Christendom was in darkness after the burning of Hus at the Council of Constance; the truth was

2 Ibid 7
3 Ibid
4 Näf *Vadian* II 390–1, 417
5 Abbot Ulrich's period occupies one-third of the original text of the chronicle (the so-called 'Grosse Chronik'). It retained its importance in the revised version (the 'Kleine Chronik'). Götzinger, Introduction, *Chronik* I xxi; Näf *Vadian* II 412–15.

suppressed, until God made the power of His Word appear again through three men – Erasmus of Rotterdam, Martin Luther in Saxony, and Ulrich Zwingli in the Swiss Confederacy – and the monkish deceptions collapsed.[6] Even before Luther began to write against indulgences in 1518 'der teur und gelerte man Erasmus von Rotterdam' had begun at Basel to put in print the books of St Jerome and other ancient and saintly interpreters of holy scripture.[7] He had criticized the false notions sown by the papacy, for example, the idea of the crusade, saying that Christ's church cannot be maintained or extended by war.[8] As a Reformer, Erasmus was, for the humanist and bourgeois Vadianus, the great castigator of the impure in life and studies. He represented the hope of a great purification of the church through rectitude and learning. But in the gathering confessional controversy Vadianus gave him another significance – he captured him for the Protestant side.

We have described the cities of the Upper Rhine as the Erasmian heartland and found in Beatus Rhenanus the best representative of their humanist circles.[9] In this section we come to the 'Protestant' phase in the history of that urban, bourgeois, reformist culture. Beyond the great divide of the Basel iconoclasm and the bringing in of the new religious order (1528–9), the pattern of that culture persists, and the distinctive Reformation of the Rhine city takes on an Erasmian colouring, as Erasmus' own last dispositions towards it make clear.[1]

The links between Heinrich Pantaleon (1522–95) and the Basel culture and Reformation are obvious. He was born in the city, the son of a tailor who had migrated there twenty years before and had supported the reforming party in the 1520s.[2] In his adolescence he was drawn away from Basel by the splendours of a wider social world, especially in the German Empire, but in 1543 he returned. Marriage in 1545 associated him with the leading families of the city; in 1548 he was appointed to the chair of rhetoric at the university. In the conflicts of 1549–50 between the clergy and the city government over the form of the civic oath, he sided with the civil power. These controversies put

6 *Chronik* I 469 (from the 'Grosse Chronik')
7 Ibid II 399 (from the 'Kleine Chronik')
8 Ibid I 226
9 See above, 17.
1 C. Reedijk 'Das Lebenende des Erasmus' 51–4
2 For what follows, see Hans Buscher *Heinrich Pantaleon und sein Helden-buch* 1–43.

View of Basel
Drawing by Conrad Morand, 1513
Historisches Museum, Basel

an end to his theological studies and plans for a clerical career. He turned instead to medicine and joined the medical faculty in the late 1550s. He had a particular devotion to the university library, which supported his literary work. Through both work and career ran the influence of Erasmus; as a boy he had been present at the obsequies of the great man and saw himself always as Erasmus' disciple, 'the representative of that particular humanist and ecclesiastical standpoint which seemed possible only in Basel, where refugees and religious fugitives of every kind came together from all sides and where the memory of Erasmus lived on.'[3]

The book which made Pantaleon famous, his collection of German heroes, combined that irenic tradition with other ideas which Erasmus would have considered alien to it, an intense German patriotism and Habsburg imperialism.[4] Pantaleon was the heir of the patriotic humanists of the early years of the Reformation and in Basel itself a spokesman for those – a diminishing group – who wished to bind the city to the German Empire. Not by chance was he called to be poet laureate by Emperor Maximilian II (1564–76). His irenicism and impartiality among the religious parties (which stopped short of Calvinism, a sign of a certain coolness between Basel and Geneva, about which more may be said later) not only expressed the ethos of Basel, a haven for refugees, but also corresponded to the emperor's plans for a religious accommodation in the German Empire through a national council.[5] The epistle dedicating to Maximilian II the third part of the work, embracing the heroes of the present age, expresses admirably its spirit. Previous parts had presented the German heroes before 1500; the author could not forbear carrying his collection forward into a time – a true golden age – when Germany 'greatly surpassed all other nations in piety, in strength, in courage and in knowledge of arts and languages.'[6] In religion he would fulfil the function of the good historian, not swayed by emotion but giving each, of either side, his due.[7] In Pantaleon's biographies the idealization characteristic of medieval hagiography persists, now partly secularized and in the service of a policy of national reconciliation.[8]

For his Erasmus portrait Pantaleon could turn to eyewitness ac-

3 Ibid 31
4 *Prosopographiae heroum atque illustrium virorum totius Germaniae ...*
5 Buscher *Heinrich Pantaleon* 46–8, 225–6, 229
6 *Prosopographiae* part 3, a3^r
7 Ibid a4^r
8 Buscher *Heinrich Pantaleon* 132

counts of contemporaries; he was a friend of Johannes Ulricus Zasius, the son of Udalrichus Zasius, the eminent jurist and Erasmus' friend in his Freiburg days.[9] Nevertheless there is a close literary dependence on Beatus Rhenanus. The work is very much in the spirit of Rhenanus, follows by and large the pattern of his 'Life,' and appropriates many of its more striking formulations. Thus Pantaleon begins, like Rhenanus, with the early appearance of Erasmus' great qualities of mind: he was devoted to studies from his childhood and at Deventer he shone out beyond all his fellows, Synthen forecasting his future fame.[1] Both writers go on to his burgeoning reputation in all the civilized centres of the West: despite the death of his parents and the betrayal of his guardian, he persisted in his studies with his friend Willem Hermans, attracted the attention of the bishop of Cambrai by the eminence and agreeableness of his mind, studied in Paris, and became known, eventually by visiting their country, to the most distinguished scholars of England. Similarly, in Rhenanus' words: 'He took into Italy the reputation and erudition which others were accustomed to bring away.'[2] In Rome the highest positions opened before him, but he turned away.[3] Anecdotes which Rhenanus helped write into the Erasmus record are repeated by Pantaleon – the change of dress at Bologna, for example.[4] His physical and moral dispositions are recalled in Rhenanus' terms: a delicate constitution easily disturbed by change, fair complexion, thin voice, grave manner ... ;[5] he 'could have lived in splendour at the court of any king he chose, he could have spent his days in ease and pleasures but he preferred the public utility of his studies to all honours and the crass pleasures of this life.'[6]

There are three main themes in Pantaleon's work on Erasmus. First, Erasmus is presented as the teacher of the whole Christian world. He wrote books of every kind, accommodating himself to the least as to the greatest. Through him letters not only revived in France and Germany, where great barbarism had reigned before, but flourished more

9 Ibid 220
1 *Prosopographiae* part 3, 46
2 Ibid: 'Unde dignitatem & eruditionem in Italiam importavit, quam caeteri inde reportare consuevêre.' Cf Olin *Desiderius Erasmus* 36.
3 *Prosopographiae* part 3, 47
4 Ibid 46
5 Ibid 49. Cf Olin *Desiderius Erasmus* 52–3.
6 *Prosopographiae* part 3, 48: 'Potuisset ergo Erasmus apud quosvis reges in splendore vivere, potuisset in ocio, in voluptatibus versari, sed praetulit communem studiorum utilitatem universis honoribus, & huius vitae crassis delitiis.' Cf Olin 46.

in Italy itself, so that he could be considered the very founder of literature. Who in a thousand years wrote more on letters both sacred and profane? Whose books were more widely dispersed and more eagerly read? Like the sun rising in mist, the knowledge of languages began to emerge with the appearance of his *Adagia* and *De copia*. He was honoured not only by princes and bishops but also by the cities of Germany; he was favoured by the learned of all nations.[7] Thus his significance was recognized in his own lifetime. This image of Erasmus, the teacher of the nations, was essentially Rhenanus'; the very words were often also his.

Secondly, there is a strain of German patriotism, and this, too, has a counterpart in Rhenanus, as we have seen. Pantaleon begins by calling Erasmus 'Germaniae phoenix';[8] he finishes with an 'Epicedion' written in his youth on 'Erasmo de patria mea, adeoque tota Germania bene merito.' To Erasmus, says the latter in one passage, the Romans and mendacious Greece give way, to Erasmus who has the favour of Teutonic muses.[9]

Thirdly, Pantaleon claims Erasmus for Basel, projects a Basel atmosphere, identifies a Basel way. Rhenanus had not overlooked the attachment between Erasmus and the city, but here at last a change in tone or emphasis can be discerned. In Pantaleon's portrait of Erasmus the Basel Reformation has a centrality it could never have had for Rhenanus. Between the contending theologians he sought a middle way, reform and purification without seditions and tumults – but that was Basel's preferred way, too. He urged moderation on both parties. 'But when he saw at Basel, by the prudence of the magistrates, everything carried through calmly and the study of literature come again to life ... he returned to the city.'[1] To Rhenanus Erasmus was coming to Basel on the way to Brabant, the Burgundian Habsburg homeland; to Pantaleon he was returning to his true spiritual home.

To sum up: between these two understandings of Erasmus there was a close sympathy and much common ground. To recognize this is to be aware of the risks in organizing authors, as I have done in these chapters, into a 'Catholic' series and a 'Protestant' series. Yet, there is apparent also a difference in emphasis fairly represented by phrases like 'moderate Catholic' (Beatus Rhenanus) and 'Basel Reformation' (Heinrich Pantaleon).

7 *Prosopographiae* part 3, 47–8
8 Ibid 46
9 Ibid 50
1 Ibid 49

Erasmus' relation to the Swiss Reformation appears in a more ambiguous light in a work much more curious than Vadian's or Pantaleon's. This is the *Pasquillus ecstaticus* of Celio Secundo Curione (1503–69). It belongs to a particular stage in the pilgrimage of its author. The essential outlines of that pilgrimage were: humanistic and juristic studies in various centres in north Italy, an interest in Protestant books and a sharing in the personal, spiritual aspirations characteristic of the Italian Reformers, flight in face of imprisonment and prosecution, four years teaching at Lausanne (1542–6), where Curione was most directly under the influence of the Zürich Reformation of Zwingli and Bullinger, and finally after 1546 settlement in Basel – as ever drawing the refugee – where he taught in the university, joined humanist circles, pursued scholarly work, and almost certainly indulged freer, more radical religious musings.[2]

The *Pasquillus ecstaticus* arose from Curione's Lausanne years, a time when he was most committed to the cause of the Reformation and most constrained by an orthodoxy.[3] It is to be seen, therefore, as an anti-papal, generally Protestant work.[4]

In a preface attributed to the printer but probably by Curione himself, *Pasquillus ecstaticus* is described as one of those books which touch on serious matters lightly ('iocando').[5] In another place Curione is frank: the dialogue is concerned with 'corrupto religionis statu.'[6] His concern is to distinguish true and false sainthood. Pasquillus ironically recounts to Marforius, hitherto a simple, unquestioning Catholic believer, ecstatic experiences which revealed to him two heavens:

2 C. Schmidt 'Celio Secundo Curioni'; RE3 IV 353–7; D. Cantimori *Italienische Haeretiker der Spätrenaissance*; M. Kutter *Celio Secundo Curione: Sein Leben und sein Werk (1503–1569)*

3 Kutter *Celio Secundo Curione* 90–2. In 1546 Curione wrote a work, *Pro vera & antiqua ecclesiae Christi autoritate*, which was a defence of the Zürich, Bullinger position against other Protestant positions. Here Curione appears as the defender of the Swiss Reformation. There is a marked difference from the more individual religiosity of his earlier work, *Araneus* (1540). Kutter 111, 117.

4 The name is connected with the antique torso to which in the Rome of Leo X lampoons, epigrams, and satirical writings were attached. Curione put together a number of pasquinades brought from Italy or gathered (by others) in Germany in his *Pasquillorum tomi duo* (Basel 1544). It included the very first form of *Pasquillus ecstaticus*, which was mostly his own but perhaps carried traces of interlocutors. Ibid 98–103.

5 *Pasquillus ecstaticus non ille prior, sed totus plane alter, auctus & expolitus* ... A2^v

6 Ibid A5^v

Christ's, where all is equality and a place is prepared for all believers, and the pope's, ruled by a rigid hierarchy.

He visits first the pope's heaven and, turned back at massive gates to which the false Donation of Constantine is affixed, enters by mines and tunnels dug by Luther and Zwingli.[7] A council is in progress, its business the restoration of Germany to the Roman obedience by entreaty, by bribes, by force of arms. There are grounds for hope since (a Zwinglian touch!) the German Reformers – Luther, Melanchthon, and Bucer – retain much of popery, though in the end hopes of betrayal will be belied.[8] From this council go out angels of war, dissension, and death.[9]

Then Pasquillus passes to Christ's heaven, and on that journey encounters Erasmus in the sphere of Mercury.

PASQUILLUS Many shades were there tossed about in various ways. Among them I saw one hanging on a rope between two poles. On his head he had two stag's horns, and from his feet hung a sack. His body was turning in ceaseless motion, for between his horns hung a sail like those we see on ships. As a favouring wind filled the sail he was carried in a circle as though he seemed to wish to beat heaven with his feet; but, the wind dropping for a little while, he was brought back to his feet by the weight of the sack. Thus he was driven up and down, to and fro.
MARFORIUS Could you recognize the man?
PASQUILLUS I could not; but my accompanying angel told me that it was Desiderius Erasmus of Rotterdam ... [1]

How is this restless agitation to be explained? Here the different versions of Curione's work leave a real ambiguity. In the first separate edition (Basel? 1544?, soon reprinted at Geneva in 1544),[2] Marforius and Pasquillus regret the fate of the learned and witty Erasmus, and the latter goes on: 'He had many enemies on both sides ... However, among those who pursued him with hatred he felt none more hostile to him than the monks,' as the circulation of a nasty epitaph concocted by some monk indicates.[3] Such is the outcome for those who want to have

7 Ibid 30–3
8 Ibid 154–6
9 Ibid 165–6
1 Ibid 170–1
2 The Geneva text has been used above.
3 'Hic jacet Erasmus, qui quondam pravus erat mus,
   Rodere qui solitus, roditur à vermibus' (ibid 171).

one foot on earth and one in heaven. Well might it be remembered by any tempted by fear or avarice or ambition to conceal or deny the truth. This Erasmus portrait is being used to persuade his fellows in Italy to follow Curione's path of exile rather than to dissimulate or swing indecisively between the two sides.[4] It represents a Reformation rejection of Erasmus, but not, however, without explaining or excusing; if Erasmus was inclined to be unstable, he was also tossed about by the hatred of both sides.

By contrast, the version in *Pasquillorum tomi duo* on which an Italian and an English translation were based offers a notably blacker picture.[5] The passage on the enmity of the two sides and the monkish epitaph are not included, and an unflattering exegesis is. In particular, the sack is now said to be full of coins. In the words of the Tudor translation: 'The harts hornes signifie his fearefulnesse, and the Pursse his covetousnesse, which two things were so muche in him, that the one whyle the one, an other whyle the other, made him bowe, now this way, now that waye, so that it coulde not be discerned whether he drewe neerest to Gods heaven, or to the Popes heaven, & therefore is he placed in the middes between them both.'[6] If Erasmus' qualities are mentioned in passing, he is now explicitly charged with avarice, and no mitigation is allowed from the ill will of others.

One may have to admit that it is impossible to identify Curione's personal judgment with either version, but one is tempted to think that he brought the harsher version from the circle of Italian Reformers who were growing cooler towards Erasmus as they were forced into exile and sharper opposition to the old church, and that he fashioned the milder in a Swiss (Reformed) atmosphere, always more sympathetic to Erasmus. What one may clearly say is this: these two texts represent a milder and a more severe Protestant criticism of Erasmus in the mid-1540s. But in neither may be found the warmth – to be felt in Pantaleon's words – flowing from the intimacy between Erasmus and Basel.

St Gallen, Basel ... Strasbourg. Strasbourg has a distinctive place in the history of the German Reformation; it had, 'even in the Middle Ages, a reputation for religious vitality, variety, and toleration, a trait which

4 Ibid 172
5 *Pasquino in estasi nuovo ... Pasquine in a Traunce ...* The English is based on the Italian translation.
6 75^r

persisted into the Era of Reformation.'[7] Distinctiveness meant independence but also a peculiar vulnerability, which was to be expected
anyway from the city's geographical and political position. It would be
bound to seek wider associations for support and survival in the crisis
years of the Reformation.[8]

Erasmus himself had a changing relationship with Strasbourg: the
warm expressions of 1514 ('monarchy without tyranny, aristocracy
without factions, democracy without uproar, wealth without extravagance, happiness without impudence')[9] gave way to the irritations of
1530 as the Reformation established itself there and the Reformers at
one and the same time called on his name and diverged from his
teaching. The city of classical balance and moderation had become 'a
nest of hungry tricksters.'[1] Yet beyond his death the Strasbourg
Reformers remained true to his moderate and ecumenical ideal.[2]

Johannes Sleidan (1505–56) would take his place in this story as the
first historian of the German Reformation.[3] But Strasbourg and its
preoccupations are the setting for his work and his understanding
of Erasmus.[4] Sleidan had approached the Reformation through humanism – among the Reformers he was drawn especially to Melanchthon.[5] In 1533 he was in Paris studying with Johann Sturm
(1507–89), a young Rhineland humanist already attracted to the Reformation.[6] Sturm introduced Sleidan to a distinctive political and
cultural milieu. Sturm's patrons were Jean and Guillaume Du Bellay,
who in French politics stood for a close association between France and
the German Protestant states.[7] Strasbourg, a Rhine bridgehead and
culturally a crossroads, was an important element in that policy. By
1538 Sturm was established in Strasbourg, and Sleidan was acting on
Du Bellay's behalf as go-between with the city and other German

7 G.H. Williams *The Radical Reformation* 242
8 See, eg, M.U. Chrisman *Strasbourg and the Reform: A Study in the
   Process of Change* 202.
9 Erasmus to Wimpfeling, 21 September 1514, Allen Ep 305, II 19
1 Erasmus to Bucer, 2 March 1532, Allen Ep 2615, IX 454
2 For Erasmus' relations with Strasbourg, see *Erasme, l'Alsace et son temps*.
3 *Joan. Sleidani de statu religionis et reipublicae, Carolo Quinto Caesare,
   commentarii*
4 See especially W. Friedensburg *Johannes Sleidanus: Der Geschichtsschreiber und die Schicksalmächte der Reformationszeit*.
5 Ibid 9–10
6 On Sturm, P. Mesnard 'The Pedagogy of Johann Sturm (1507–1589) and
   its Evangelical Inspiration'
7 Friedensburg *Johannes Sleidanus* 17–18

Protestant states.[8] In the end, when the Du Bellay influence at the French court had waned, Sleidan himself settled in Strasbourg. Indeed, the great project of his life, the history of the German Reformation – he had already undertaken historical work indicative of his current French associations, for example, editions of Froissart and Commynes – was in its beginnings a Strasbourg project: the chief minister of the city, Martin Bucer, and its political leader, Jakob Sturm, both encouraged it.[9]

This work was, however, to be more – the official history of the Reformation sponsored by the Lutheran League of Schmalkalden.[1] Sleidan wrote it over years of crisis for German Protestantism and for Strasbourg itself: he began in the lowering days when Charles v was preparing to restore unity to the Empire by destroying the Schmalkaldic League (1547); he finished as the Lutheran Estates, back from the brink, were forcing compromise on the emperor's representatives: the *Commentaries* were published as the Diet to settle Germany's affairs was actually meeting at Augsburg (1555).[2]

This is the history of a religious movement but in its connection with national politics: Luther is a centre of interest, naturally, but the depiction of the great Habsburg emperor is not unsympathetic. The tone is urbane rather than bitter, which accords well with the Strasbourg tradition and Sleidan's own Christian humanist piety.[3]

Sleidan uses Erasmus in three ways: as a witness to Luther's force and integrity and to the ill will of his enemies, as a sober observer of German affairs, and, of course, as a foil to the Reformers. The last use also is without bitterness, and Sleidan's summing-up of Erasmus is favourable. Letters of 1519–20 from Erasmus to Frederick, elector of Saxony, to Albert, archbishop of Mainz, to Cardinal Campegio, to Luther himself – written at a critical moment in Luther's career (and therefore coming at a high-point in Sleidan's first book) – bear Erasmus' witness to Luther. Luther's books, Erasmus wrote to Frederick, are welcomed by good and learned men; no one criticizes his life, which bears no trace of avarice or ambition. The theologians of Louvain assail him on all occasions as a heretic and Antichrist. When Luther but

8   Ibid 21–3
9   Ibid 37–8
1   Ibid 38–9
2   Ibid 43, 47
3   Sleidan's sources included the Strasbourg archives, the first volumes of the Wittenberg edition of Luther's Latin works (1545–57), and observations of contemporaries (ibid 49–53).

proposes debate and submits his judgment to others, they cry heresy and create a disturbance unworthy of Christians and theologians. Of course (he wrote to Mainz and Campegio), the sophists cannot tolerate the study of languages and eloquence or any purer teaching. He warmly commended a letter of Luther's demonstrating sharpness of mind and breathing a Christian spirit. He added only that more would be gained by politeness and moderation than by impetuousness.[4]

Erasmus' sober judgment of German affairs is illustrated by a letter to Campegio written during the great confrontation at Augsburg in 1530. The emperor, he said, is not in complete control of the situation in Germany; the war drags on in France and Italy, and the Turkish danger is ever present. Certainly the Protestants and those who favour them deserve condemnation, but primary now must be, not the suppression of heresy, but the safety of the commonwealth. It would be prudent to concede to the Lutherans the toleration granted the Bohemians: 'Though a grave step, it would be a lesser evil than war.'[5] Sympathy for the emperor in his difficulties, suspicion towards Rome, hatred of war and discord, prudent faith in toleration – these elements in the Erasmian outlook are those Sleidan chooses to emphasize.

In Sleidan's handling of the free-will controversy and of Erasmus' criticisms of the Reformers, Erasmus is treated as a foil, but never as an enemy. In recording the revival of the free-will controversy in 1534 Sleidan allows most of the running to Luther with his wilder charges: Erasmus brings the Christian faith into doubt, scorn, or despite; he imposes himself by his eloquence but sports equivocally with theological subjects when he should speak openly. Sleidan himself makes no comment here; he does not approve or disapprove but is content to report: 'To Luther's writing Erasmus replied, and sharply enough, for he feared above everything else that his writings would lose esteem and authority.'[6] Similarly, there is a report without elaboration of Erasmus' controversy with the Rhineland theologians in his book against the false evangelicals (which was in effect an attack on the whole Protestant movement): Erasmus knew no one who had not been made worse by the new gospel. 'To Erasmus' writing the theologians of

---

4 *Commentarii* 1555 ed, 17^{r-v}; 1785–6 ed, I 84–5. The letters to Frederick and Luther are to be found at Allen III 527, 605. The former was available to Sleidan in vol I of the Wittenberg edition. He could use various collections of Erasmus' letters.

5 1555 ed, 105^{v}, 106^{r}; 1785–6 ed, I 415–16; text of letter at Allen IX 13

6 1555 ed, 133^{r}; 1785–6 ed, I 508

Strasbourg replied since he dealt mostly with them and with their fellows at Basel but especially with Bucer.'[7]

The summing-up: in his chronicle for the year 1536 Sleidan mentions Erasmus' death at Basel (he is explicit about the return from Freiburg). 'How great a man he was and how eloquent and how much literary studies owe to him his monuments testify.'[8] But there are sequels, references to the plan of Paul III to raise Erasmus to the cardinalate and, above all, to the criticism of Erasmus' *Colloquia* in the *Consilium ... de emenda ecclesia* of a famous reforming commission in Rome (1537). And so Sleidan:

> Among the many writings with which Erasmus wonderfully advanced the study of literature, a collection of dialogues, composed for young people and later often enriched, was read most eagerly. A man of outstanding genius and supreme eloquence, he played there with various subjects drawn from the observation of nature and the life of men and with marvellous skill and elegant turns of speech, he taught the precepts of manners and of piety and, as occasion offered, pointed up long established errors and vices. Hence this complaint against him.[9]

Sleidan, the official historian of the Lutheran League, is not trapped in a Lutheran animosity towards Erasmus.[1] For all the contretemps between Strasbourg and Erasmus in his last bitter years, the relationship remained, if not quite with the Basel cordiality. In Sleidan's few short passages on Erasmus, that relationship persists.

Sleidan spoke for Strasbourg. But he also wrote the first official Protestant history of the great crisis in the German Empire. Naturally it drew the attention of later historians down to Ranke. It also attracted immediate controversy; there were attacks, not least on his use of Erasmus. Thus Surius' *Commentarius* accuses him of a prudent selectivity in his handling of Erasmus' book against the false evangelicals. The historian, who is profuse enough when retailing Protestant

7 1555 ed, 97^v–98^r; 1785–6 ed, I 382–3
8 1555 ed, 162^v; 1785–6 ed, II 48
9 1555 ed, 183^v–184^r; 1785–6 ed, II 118. The reference to the cardinalate is at, respectively, 180^r and II 103–4. The criticism of the *Colloquia* in the text of the *Consilium* is in B.J. Kidd *Documents Illustrative of the Continental Reformation* 315.
1 Paul Kalkoff 'Die Anfangsperiode der Reformation in Sleidans Kommentarien' 319–20 seems to overstate Sleidan's dependence on the Wittenberg view.

calumnies against the Roman Church, can spare this book scarcely three words, for he feels the pressure of Erasmus' authority. Thus, says Surius, the Protestants underestimate the witness of Erasmus against them.[2] In the time of Sleidan and Surius it still mattered where the weight of his authority was placed.

Likewise one of the great Catholic controversialists of the third quarter of the century – a contemporary of Surius, Hosius, and Lindanus – attacked Sleidan for misuse of evidence from Erasmus. Johannes Nas (1534–90) had been attracted by the Lutheran preachers in travels about the Franconian cities as a journeyman tailor, but a reading of the *Imitation of Christ* had restored him to the Catholic faith. He became a Franciscan, studying first in the cloister at Munich and later, after ordination (1557), with the Jesuits at Ingolstadt. There and throughout south Germany he won a great reputation as a popular preacher, giving his Protestant rivals no quarter and moving the people profoundly.[3] Written polemics followed. His *Centuriae* (Ingolstadt 1565–70) were replies in kind to the gross effusions of the Lutheran controversialists. Nas did not fall behind his opponents in bitterness. The Protestants, he said, know only how to lie and scorn and swear; if he uses gross language, it is because he is replying to them.[4]

More sober apologists like Sliedan were caught up in this controversial storm. This lying historian, says Nas, claimed that the renowned scholar Erasmus of Rotterdam praised Luther and held his teaching to be most sure.[5] The falseness of this claim is not difficult to demonstrate. Erasmus' view of the Protestants grew worse all the time, and in the end he rejected them utterly. He was himself Catholic; in his last book, *Ecclesiastes*, he submitted himself to the church, which has not damned his works but rather sought their correction. (He would, like Augustine, have willingly prepared a book of retractions).[6] His controversies against Luther show that he did not honour him; on the contrary, he thought him diabolical. In Luther and his followers was to be found no reliable teaching but only endless change and division. Luther offered nothing but gross abuse and ancient heresy.[7]

2 Surius *Commentarius* 234–5. Cf above, 27–9.
3 A. Herte *Das katholische Lutherbild* I 52–9; Johann B. Schöpf *Johannes Nasus, Franziskaner und Weihbischof von Brixen (1534–90)*
4 Schöpf *Johannes Nasus* 20–5. Nas drew on Surius, Prateolus, and Cochlaeus. Herte says that in his handling of Luther he even exaggerated Cochlaeus (*Das katholische Lutherbild* 59).
5 In letters to Frederick of Saxony (*Secunda Centuria* (1570) 185^r)
6 Ibid 185^v
7 Ibid 186. The debt to Hosius, Lindanus, and Surius is apparent.

At the end of this chapter, a broadside against Sleidan, Nas returns to Erasmus. He did not praise Luther. He did not die a Lutheran; he was Catholic more surely at the end than earlier.[8] Here is an attempt to refute the Protestant claim to him, to deny the sympathy suggested by Pantaleon and Sleidan between him and the great Reformation cities like Strasbourg and Basel. Still in the 1550s and 1560s (though it was the eleventh hour) Erasmus seemed a valuable possession over whom the controversialists thought it worthwhile to struggle.

How Erasmus was to be valued had been disputed in the Lutheran camp from the beginning. His relationship with Luther is one of the more familiar parts of Erasmus' biography – an early apparent comradeship-in-arms followed by misgivings and misunderstandings, confusion brought on by the intrigues and polemics of third parties, then serious theological debate, all ending in open enmity and controversy with high denunciation on one side and wounded feelings on the other. But even under Luther's shadow there were those who kept their connection with Erasmus and valued his friendship. Luther's associates, members of his household or entourage, represented rival views to the second generation of Luther's followers.

In what has been seen as the last work to emerge from Luther's personal circle and the first major biography of Luther,[9] the sermons of Johannes Mathesius (1504–65), pastor of Joachimsthal, Erasmus is judged for his part in Luther's story and from Luther sources. Mathesius, a Saxon by birth, entered Luther's circle and lived in his house in 1540 when he returned to studies at Wittenberg as a mature man – he had been there already in 1529–30 after earlier studies at Ingolstadt (1523–4) and meantime he had taught in the Latin school at Joachimsthal, a mining boom town in northern Bohemia (1532–40). Later he was to occupy a long pastorate there and become (it has been said) the most important Lutheran preacher of the century after Luther himself.[1] His personal experiences fed directly into the biographical

8 Ibid 187^r. Other references to Erasmus in Nas' *Centuriae* include his well-known critique of the effect of their 'gospel' on the lives and countenances of the Protestants – the tree is known by its fruit (*Sexta centuria* (1569) 127) – and the charge that his *Moriae encomium* prepared the way for Luther's evil-speaking while he himself (though in this respect 'Luthers erster Herolt und einfurirer') prudently withdrew (*Quinta centuria* (1570) 194). Here the new mood is already apparent.

9 E.W. Zeeden *Martin Luther und die Reformation im Urteil des deutschen Luthertums* I 35

1 H. Volz *Die Lutherpredigten des Johannes Mathesius: Kritische Untersuchungen zur Geschichtsschreibung im Zeitalter der Reformation* 1–7

sermons since Mathesius himself was one of the recorders of Luther's table-talk.[2] Otherwise – for these sermons prepared at the end of his life – he drew on the Wittenberg editions of Luther's works.[3] Their form helped determine their character as biography: they are both historical and didactic. Nothing here compares with Sleidan's interest in the political history of the Empire; Mathesius' vision is concentrated on the church and religious history.[4] Luther is seen on a more than human scale; his teaching is identified with the Word; he was the new Elias, David, Samson, Moses ... Those who deviated from him are judged from these great heights.[5]

Erasmus, it is recognized, contributed to Luther's cause. He knew from his own sojourn there how bad things were in Rome and said so in his dialogue *Julius exclusus*, and in other writings, too, which attacked the sophistries of the theological schools and the unspiritual life of the clergy and helped on the revival of languages and better studies. At the beginning he favoured Luther's writings, as he made clear in a famous interview with Luther's prince, Elector Frederick of Saxony, at Cologne in 1520: Luther had committed two great sins – he had attacked the pope in his crown and the monks in their bellies.[6] The papal legate (Aleander) offered Erasmus a great bishopric if he would write against Luther, but Erasmus replied that he learned more from a fragment of Luther's than from the whole of Aquinas, indeed 'when Luther interpreted scripture, there was more of depth and understanding in one page than in the tomes and tortuous arguments of all the Scotists, Thomists, Albertists, modernists and sophists.' If he was sometimes too violent, the sickness of this last age demanded a stern physician.[7]

Any disciple of Luther's would, however, also have to say Erasmus was an enemy. Mathesius does not refer to the free-will controversy; by contrast, Luther's controversies with the Zwinglians, sacramenta-

2 Cf Luther *Works* (American edition) LIV *Table Talk* 367–8
3 The sermons were delivered from 1562 to 1565 and first published in 1566.
4 Volz *Die Lutherpredigten* 8–9
5 Ibid 62–70; Zeeden *Martin Luther* 41–3
6 Johannes Mathesius *Ausgewählte Werke* III (*Luthers Leben in Predigten*). Cf Allen's note on this interview, IV 370. It was reported by Spalatin, Frederick's secretary, who was present. Erasmus' *Axiomata* on the Luther affair prepared for Spalatin at this time were available to Mathesius in the Wittenberg Latin edition II. They are to be found in *Erasmi opuscula: A Supplement to the Opera omnia* 336–7, with an introduction 329–33. Cf *Table Talk* No 131, Luther *Works* LIV 19.
7 Mathesius *Ausgewählte Werke* III 49, 392. On the offer of the bishopric, cf Allen IV 340.

rians, and radicals bulk large in the sermons. That reflects Mathesius'
situation in Joachimsthal, where, as in other turbulent mining towns,
radical ideas were at work.[8] But Luther's savage expressions were taken
over – those, for example, in a famous letter to Amsdorf where Luther
warned all and sundry against the writings of this unsound and
dangerous individual.[9] Mathesius himself had heard Luther tell at
table the story of Duke George of Albertine Saxony – a Catholic prince
– who had sought Erasmus' advice on a religious question: 'When the
slippery man had given an equivocal and twisted answer, blowing
neither hot nor cold, the wise Duke said: "Dear Erasmus, you wash
without making clean. I prefer the men of Wittenberg who are not
mealy-mouthed but say freely and honestly what they think." '[1]
There is Luther's testimony and legacy.

Mathesius was a friend and associate of Melanchthon. It has been
said that as an interpreter of Luther he stood closest to Melanchthon
while heightening the dramatic or catastrophic in history.[2] But as an
interpreter of Erasmus he stood closer to Luther than to Melanchthon.
Melanchthon's relation to Erasmus and Luther or, more abstractly put,
to humanism and Reformation is very complex. But one may simply
say: in holding to Luther, he did not abandon Erasmus; he brought
humanist preoccupations to the heart of the Reformation.[3] Erasmus
was the revered master of his early studies; once he came within
Luther's field of force that old relationship had to change, but it was not
destroyed. The bitterness between the two men was an agony to him;
his conscience – like many consciences in that desperate age – had to
hold a perilous course between two principles, neither of which he
wanted to deny. One might ask what traces of this anguish are to be
found in his declamation on Erasmus first published twenty years after
the great humanist's death.[4]

8 Volz *Die Lutherpredigten* 50
9 Mathesius *Ausgewählte Werke* III 235–6. Luther to Amsdorf, 11 March
   1534 *D. Martin Luthers Werke: Kritische Gesamtausgabe (Weimarer
   Ausgabe), Briefwechsel* VII 27–40
1 Mathesius *Ausgewählte Werke* III 168; cf *Table Talk* No 4899, *Weimarer
   Ausgabe, Tischreden* IV 573.
2 Zeeden *Martin Luther* 37–40
3 For a survey of recent discussion and a bibliography, see Peter Fraenkel and
   Martin Greschat *Zwanzig Jahre Melanchthonstudium: Sechs Literaturberichte (1945–1965)*, especially 14–17, 46–7, 72–4, 110–11.
4 In the name of Bartholemew Calkreuter, Wittenberg 1557. On Melanchthon's declamations, see introduction to *Philippus Melanchthon, declamationes*.

Philippus Melanchthon
Woodcut in Theodore Beza *Icones*. After Lucas Cranach the Elder
By permission of the Houghton Library, Harvard University

The tone may be sensed immediately. God be praised, the declamation begins, for preserving among us groups of teachers and scholars. Such benefits are not scattered by chance but are gifts of God. The custom in declamations like this is to commend good and useful examples. Erasmus is such an example.[5] The tone then is didactic, the search is for useful guidance to contemporary students, the underlying theme is the providential recovery of learning and good letters in Erasmus' time. The speaker urges the young people who are listening to read Erasmus' works and reflect on his great virtues as writer and scholar – his breadth of mind, his penetration, his judgment, his wit and eloquence, his command of words and figures of speech. His life, too, is a model of many virtues, of application, of patience in work, of moderation and well-doing.[6]

The biography here owes something to Beatus Rhenanus, but the force is weakened by errors and confusions and (as we might think) absurdities. Of the last, suffice it to mention Erasmus' horoscope;[7] among the first, the prophecy of Synthen at Deventer, so shortly and effectively told by Rhenanus, is inexplicably attributed to Rodolphus Agricola, the pioneering German humanist. Chronology is uncertain throughout.[8] In this biography much is made of Erasmus' youthful reputation among the learned and influential, first in Paris and then at the Burgundian court and in England; of his visit to Italy where he heard and consorted with savants, doctors, theologians, and jurists but – an exaggeration of Rhenanus – found no Latinist worthy of the name; of his relations with the great, the friendship of princes and bishops (though he always wisely fled the court), and the anger of Pope Julius II at his complaint against the Italian wars.[9] The climax came when Erasmus, after a life of travel and observation, considering the enormity of the wounds of the church and confident now in his own judgment, decided to edit the New Testament. By this work two great things would be accomplished: studies would be corrected and (in the characteristic imagery of the Protestant Reformation) 'with the rising little by little of the light of truth, darkness would vanish away and the emptiness of many errors be laid bare.' 'I believe,' the speaker adds,

5 *Corpus reformatorum: Philippi Melanchthonis opera quae supersunt omnia* XII col 265
6 Ibid cols 265–6
7 'Suntque in positu stellarum significationes ingenii, Eloquentiae et leporis non obscurae' (ibid col 266). On Melanchthon's belief in astrology, see C.L. Manschreck *Melanchthon: The Quiet Reformer* 102–5.
8 Including a second undated trip to Italy. *Corpus Reformatorum* XII col 268.
9 Ibid cols 267–9

'that divine Providence directed his studies and counsels to this work.'
But men of darkness, all kinds of hypocritical monks, 'fearing for their
authority and their belly, strove to extinguish these new studies and to
undo their author himself,' denouncing him in every possible arena.
'But God armed Erasmus with his shield, namely eloquence, with
which he powerfully drove off his enemies.'[1]

Post tenebras lux. Erasmus came with the first appearance of the
dawn. Later Luther made clear again the whole doctrine of the church.
Thus this declamation confronts its great problem, comes to the corner
it has somehow to turn: how were the two men related? The declamation stresses the positive tones. Erasmus prepared for Luther's appearance and approved of it. It was preparation enough that 'the apostolic
books and old histories were now in men's hands.'[2] There is no doubt
that Erasmus was pleased at that whole side of the Reformation which
condemns the falsity of human institutions in the church. He thought
Luther the superior of all ancient and modern interpreters of scripture.
In conversation with the Elector at Cologne his light-hearted reference
to the bellies of the monks and so on was less important than the
serious deliberation which followed: the essence of Luther's doctrine
was pious but would that he might avoid rough and unnecessary
questions and dispute more calmly. If the Cologne interview was to
become a commonplace of 'Protestant' interpretations more or less
favourable to Erasmus, the handling of the circumstances of his death
was a sure register of the tone of any account: for Melanchthon,
'Erasmus died calling upon God. And he wished to be a member of the
[Protestant] Church of Basel.'[3]

But what of the bitter controversy between Erasmus and Luther? It
is not to be wondered at, the declamation mildly declares, that in so
many controversies even among men of good will there should be
differences of judgment. But these will be passed over. So the declamation skirts the issue and returns to the congenial path of its main
theme: since in Erasmus there were great powers of mind and many
excellent virtues and since the study of languages is necessary to the
church and to civil life, we should keep his memory fresh and read his
books with grateful minds.[4]

About this conclusion there is a blandness appropriate to the horta-
tory genre but uncommunicative about deeper feelings and personal

1 Ibid col 269
2 Ibid
3 Ibid col 270
4 Ibid cols 270–1. The *Adagia* especially are mentioned; they should be read
'much and often.'

commitments. The anguish, candour, and hard-won confidence of the last correspondence between Melanchthon and Erasmus (which certainly contains anticipations of the language of the declamation) is in contrast with this reticence about the conflicts in which the two men had been caught.[5] Melanchthon wishes now to speak of Erasmus with plain affirmation.

In late September 1557 two travellers awaiting dinner at the inn 'Zum wilden Mann' in Basel found an audience gathering and let their tongues run away with them. They were passing through the city on their way to Germany, where they hoped to persuade Protestants to come to the aid of their hard-pressed fellows in France: one was Theodore Beza (1519–1605), already a leading figure of the Reformation in Geneva and its vicinity, the other Guillaume Farel (1489–1565), years before a stormy herald of the Reformation in Switzerland and an avowed enemy of Erasmus.[6] Perhaps they were exasperated by the tolerant Basel atmosphere, so unresponsive to Genevan rigour and dynamism and single-mindedness. Erasmus, Farel ranted, was the lowest of creatures, a wicked and vile miscreant; Beza chimed in to dub him an Arian.

The Basel heirs of Erasmus did not take this provocation in silence. Three, led by Bonifacius Amerbach (1495–1562), Erasmus' younger friend and executor, returned a firm rebuke: this was sheer calumny – no honourable person could or should be scarified and defamed by lies and insults of such a kind. We are reminded even by the civil laws of our duty to protect the reputation of the worthy dead.[7]

This contretemps reveals the difference of temper between Erasmian Basel and the Geneva of Calvin. There was no open break or flat contradiction.[8] But from the beginnings of the Servetus case influential

---

5 Melanchthon to Erasmus, 12 May 1536; Erasmus to Melanchthon, 6 June 1536 (Allen Epp 3120, 3127, XI 322–4, 332–4). Melanchthon speaks of Erasmus' powers of mind, excellent learning, and virtues: 'Etenim non solum veneror te propter vim ingenii, excellentem doctrinam et virtutes tuas, sed etiam in plerisque controversiis iudicandis meam opinionem ad tuam sententiam libenter adiungo?' (ibid 323).

6 Erasmus and Farel met in 1524 and proclaimed a hearty mutual dislike thereafter. See, eg, Erasmus to Melanchthon, 6 September 1524, Allen Ep 1496, V 544–50, at 548–9. Cf ibid 378.

7 *Correspondance de Théodore de Bèze* II (1556–8) no 113, page 114. Cf Paul F. Geisendorf *Théodore de Bèze* 89.

8 Cf Peter G. Bietenholz *Basle and France in the Sixteenth Century: The Basle Humanists and Printers in their Contacts with Francophone Culture* 95.

and vocal circles in the Rhine city did not hide their disapproval of what was happening in Geneva.[9] Even official Basel listened sympathetically to pleas for toleration by Calvin's *bête noire*, Sebastian Castellio. Beza himself pursued Castellio with determined hatred and did not hide his suspicion of Basel itself, a place of various lurking monsters of the same type.[1] Years later Beza, in once again warning the pastors of Basel against Castellio, expressed his distrust of Erasmus, whom Castellio claimed to follow.[2]

Beza returned to Erasmus a number of times. In his juvenilia, the *Poemata* of 1548, offspring of the golden years of his youth amid a circle of Parisian humanists – young and free and unburdened like himself – he paid tribute to Erasmus' greatness in two elegant epigrams.[3] One reads:

> On a half-portrait of Erasmus
> This picture half portrays
> Erasmus about whom the whole world now resounds.
> But why not all? Cease to wonder, reader,
> All the world cannot capture the whole man.

The second, perhaps recalling the Ciceronian controversy, carries a barb. Philaenus, its target, is accused of stupidly heaping on Erasmus whatever calumnies he can put together, holding as dull one whom most consider more learned than any other has been or is likely to be:

> Bark, Philaenus, as long and as much as you like.
> Surely he knows more things than you are ignorant of.[4]

These are the judgments of a literary circle: Erasmus is vaunted as a

9 See Uwe Plath *Calvin und Basel in den Jahren 1552–1556*.
1 Castellio's *De haereticis an sint persequendi* was published ostensibly in Magdeburg but, Beza wrote to Bullinger, this Magdeburg was on the Rhine: ' … sed hoc Magdeburgum, ni fallor, ad Rhenum situm est, ubi haec monstra jamdiu delitescere sciebam' (Beza to Bullinger, 29 March 1554, *Correspondance* I (1539–55) 123).
2 Preface to *Responsio ad defensiones et reprehensiones Sebastiani Castellionis* … (Geneva 1563), addressed to Basel pastors in *Correspondance* IV (1562–3) 190
3 Cf Geisendorf on this circle: 'Tout ce petit monde rit, cause, écrit des vers, chante ses amis ou ses amies … Jours joyeux et ensoleillés, années délicates et frivoles de jeunesse, où le plaisir de vivre n'est pas qu'un mot' (*Théodore de Bèze* 17). See also F. Aubert, J. Boussard, H. Meylan 'Un premier recueil de poésies latines de Théodore de Bèze.'
4 *Theodori Bezae Vezelii poemata* 69, 74–5

great master of studies, but of any inner understanding of his spirit there is no trace.

After his flight to Geneva (1548) and his adherence to the Reformation, Beza handles Erasmus with something of the zeal of the convert, casually at 'Zum wilden Mann' in the autumn of 1557, more formally in his biblical writings. In the preface to his edition of the New Testament (Geneva 1556), Beza reiterates his admiration for Erasmus' study and diligence, certainly, but also criticizes the reliance in his New Testament work on poorer texts and his careless collation of texts. Far from putting Origen ahead of all other ancient commentators as Erasmus does, Beza considers no writer 'magis impurum.'[5] On important questions Erasmus speaks so variously and ambiguously that it is hard to determine what he thinks.[6] The unmistakable impression is of a certain wantonness in the handling of divine things.[7]

In the depths of the civil wars in the late 1570s Beza began looking back on the work of Reformation and collecting portraits of the men engaged in it. The historiographical standpoint of his *Icones*, finally published in 1580, is indicated clearly enough by the selection of figures – in part 1, the 'martyrs' of Christian restoration, Wyclif, Hus, Jerome of Prague and Savonarola, in part 2, 'the main instruments for restoring the Christian faith among the Germans,' Reuchlin, Erasmus, Luther, Melanchthon ...[8] This is the Protestant apostolical succession. Erasmus is included but, as we would expect, with hesitation. (The woodcut portrait – appropriately perhaps – is based on the Holbein portrait of 1532, with its drawn features and tired eyes.)

> Although unexhausted richness of mind and eloquence raised Desiderius Erasmus of Rotterdam to the peak of glory, I nevertheless had some scruple about placing him here on the threshold of the sanctuary. He was one who in religion as in so much else followed his own judgment and, content to deride and

5 *Correspondance* II 226–9
6 From Beza's preface to [Antoine Du Pinet] *Exposition sur l'Apocalypse de Sainct Jean* ... (Geneva 1557) (ibid 231).
7 Cf Anthony Cooke to Beza, London, 17 August 1565 (Cooke was tutor to Edward VI, spent the Marian years at Strasbourg, and was MP for Essex 1558–9): ' ... I would that your judgments on Erasmus and Origen had been more just ... Erasmus in translating the New Testament so advanced the cause of the gospel that I think the authority of his work should not be lessened like this' (ibid VI 138).
8 *Icones, id est verae imagines virorum doctrina simul et pietate illustrium* ...

Erasmus
Woodcut in Beza *Icones*. After Hans Holbein the Younger
Unlike some portraits in *Icones*, which are synthetic
rather than authentic, this and the portrait of Melanchthon (above, 90)
are recognizably based on their respective models
By permission of the Houghton Library, Harvard University

carp at superstition, so refused to learn the truth, either for himself or through others, that he took on the defence of the worst cause. Yet since the rebirth of letters owes more to him than to anyone else in that time he deserves a place in this vestibule ...

There follows the epigram of 1548.[9] That is revealing in itself. The context has changed, but Beza's appreciation of Erasmus is constant between 1548 and 1580: his achievement was purely literary and scholarly. At no time does Beza show an appreciation of Erasmus' mind or distinctive piety. Thus it is easy for him concisely to formulate one of the classic Protestant interpretations of Erasmus: he refused to face the light, turned his back on the truth, and left only a literary fame behind him.[1]

Beza was a towering figure among the Reformed; his judgments carried authority. Two other Reformed writers were much read and quoted, less because of any personal authority they enjoyed or deserved than because what they had to say was offered in readily digested capsules. They were Jean-Jacques Boissard (1528–1602) and Melchior Adam (d 1622), authors of two popular biographical dictionaries. Boissard came from Besançon; he studied in Germany and at Louvain and was first attracted to the Reformation by Melanchthon.[2] After a sojourn in Rome and extensive (as he claimed) Mediterranean travels, he settled again in the Rhine borderland, serving as tutor to various aristocratic families. His best-known work was in Roman antiquities, where, so it is said, he did not hesitate to fabricate and interpolate. 'If he has been thought a great antiquary, he was certainly a great impostor.'[3] Myth-maker about his own life and travels, as about Roman antiquities, he was no less a propagator of myths about Erasmus. The few pages on the humanist in Boissard's *Icones quinquaginta virorum illustrium* ... contain much confused biography and far-fetched anecdotes which, once put into the record, were not easily erased from it.[4]

Erasmus' early studies after Hegius at Deventer – it might have

9 Ibid ciii; French tr *Les vrais pourtraits des hommes illustres en piété et doctrine, traduits du Latin de Th. de Bèze* ... 135–6
1 Budé is treated on the same pattern as Erasmus, Reuchlin somewhat more warmly (T.iiii, c.ii).
2 DBF VI cols 833–4
3 Ibid
4 222–31

surprised even a contemporary to read – were at Louvain, Cambridge, and Bologna! He did not long persevere in the monastic life but visited universities throughout Europe; his erudition, eloquence, and pleasantness of manner carried his fame far and wide. Sought by popes and kings he chose to remain free and to serve posterity by his writings. His refusal of a cardinalate caused a stir among those who sought such honours with much labour.[5] Finally he was attracted to Basel by the companionship of many learned men living there.[6] Boissard claimed to have heard from his uncle and tutor, Hugues Babet (1474–1556), a friend of Erasmus, that Erasmus had been made rector of the University of Basel; exasperated by the indiscipline of the students he tore up the deed of their privileges, which had the effect of bringing them to their senses. This incredible piece of apocrypha was repeated in a work as serious as Samuel Knight's *Life of Erasmus* of the early eighteenth century.[7] Boissard follows with a travesty of Erasmus' unhappy encounter with the Dover Customs in 1500, which cost him nearly all his savings: on this account he hastened back to King Henry VIII (here the chronological confusion is complete) who, laughing, had him returned double – a fiction which combined a happy ending with the graciousness of a royal personage.[8]

Adam's work is more serious, though he offers Boissard's version of the Dover story as an alternative.[9] Mostly Adam's work is a pastiche of earlier accounts – Erasmus' own brief *Compendium vitae*, which became known during Adam's lifetime,[1] Beatus Rhenanus, Melanchthon, and some of the more famous letters, that of 1514, for example, to Erasmus' monastic superior, Servatius Rogerus.[2] The scholarly conscience of the time allowed Adam to follow these masters in their own words; careless omissions in doing so sometimes created bizarre effects.[3] Changes to his sources betrayed Adam's personal position.

5 Ibid 222
6 Ibid 223. Boissard himself had Basel associations. Cf E. Droz 'Les étudiants français de Bâle' 116.
7 316
8 *Icones* 227–31 (pages 223–7 list the contents of the nine volumes of the Basel edition of Erasmus' *Opera omnia*). Cf Erasmus to Jacob Batt, February 1500 CWE 1 118–19.
9 *Dignorum laude virorum* ... 41 (1st ed, Heidelberg 1615)
1 See below, 125–7.
2 CWE II 294–303
3 The *Compendium*, speaking of Erasmus' visit to the monastery at Steyn, says: 'Ibi reperit Cornelium quem Daventriae habuerat sodalem in eodem cubiculo. Is nondum acceperat sacrum illum cultum; viderat Italiam, sed

For a start, Erasmus is included among the German philosophers. Adam was born in Silesia and died in Heidelberg in 1622, the year the city fell to the Catholic forces in that first phase of the Thirty Years War so triumphant for the Catholic Habsburg cause, so catastrophic for German Protestantism.[4] It is not surprising that a servant of the Calvinist Palatinate – Adam belonged to those east European Protestant circles attracted to western Calvinism – should, while following Beatus Rhenanus' life of Erasmus and despite his German patriotism, omit all reference to Erasmus' devotion to the House of Austria. The same goes, of course, for Erasmus' relation to the popes. Adam gives to the death-scene, borrowed essentially from Beatus Rhenanus, a Protestant twist: giving clear proofs of Christian patience and his religious spirit, Erasmus 'witnessed that he put all his hope in Christ.'[5] There is a particular savagery to Adam's handling of Erasmus' envious enemies among the monks: they gnawed at him like bugs and lice; hidden like owls in their cloisters, they could not bear the light of letters reborn.[6]

A Protestant aura seems cast about this Erasmus. But the theme unequivocally stated by Beza is repeated here: Erasmus knew better what he was against than what he was for. Adam elaborates in this way Beatus Rhenanus' account of Erasmus' criticism of scholastic theology and the condition of the church, adding: 'He was too timid and fearful of giving offence; and he sought this especially in his life – to gather the good will of all and sundry.'[7] It was to be the continuing Protestant Reformed grievance against Erasmus – he saw the right road but was too fearful to follow it.

In the disturbed Germany, in the hard-pressed Strasbourg of 1531 (a year of scarcity), Sebastian Franck (1499–1542) published his remarkable *Geschichtsbibel*.[8] It may be the best place to begin a consideration of what Erasmus meant in retrospect to reformers beyond the official 'magisterial' Reformations of Luther and Calvin. The book was to have

redierat parum doctus' (Allen I 50). Adam has the incomprehensible: 'Ibi reperit dum acceperat sacrum illum cultum; viderat Italiam: sed redierat parum doctus.'
4 NDB I 53; ADB I 45–6
5 *Dignorum laude virorum* 44
6 Ibid 45–6
7 Ibid 45: 'Et meticulosior fuit, ac timens offensionum: atque hoc unice in vita studuit: ut omnium ordinum & generum benevolentiam colligeret.'
8 On the Strasbourg background, see Jean Lebeau 'Erasme, Sebastian Franck et la tolérance' 124–5.

a continuing influence and make a strong appeal to pietism and the Enlightenment.

Franck represented one of the many strands in the 'radical reformation,' one of many, for that matter, which owed a debt to the ideas of Erasmus.[9] The crucial phase in his intellectual development had come in the late 1520s with his disenchantment with the Lutheran Reformation and his attraction to a spiritualizing kind of religion.[1] He was moving in south German radical circles, but Erasmus was not a negligible influence; the passage on Erasmus in the *Geschichtsbibel* itself makes clear the workings of that influence.

Franck's philosophy of history as it is revealed in that vast book is an expression of his spiritual religion. God's free spirit works in contradiction to human error and falsehood sitting enthroned in church and state and in all established institutions.[2] In this way history offers a revelation equal to scripture's. The same conflict between the tyranny of outer things and the inward divine working goes on in the individual human spirit – here indeed is a mirror image of the historical process.[3] There is a hope of victory only for a few, but in them the divine light burns. Franck's view of history is generally sombre – in this last age the power of evil grows, and the world heads for catastrophe.

The *Geschichtsbibel* has been called 'a weapon of war directed against the papacy and the Roman Church on one side and the whole temporal hierarchy on the other.'[4] Erasmus is treated in the catalogue of 'heretics' attached to the chronicle of the popes (part 3) but he is also pressed into service elsewhere. In his foreword to the chronicle of the emperors (part 2), for example, Franck makes use of two adages (from

9 Williams *Radical Reformation* 8–11 describes Erasmus as 'a patron of the Radical Reformation,' referring in particular to his questioning of the Trinitarian texts, his pacifism, and 'his insistence on the practical freedom of the will,' though all this is unhappily associated with the idea of Erasmus as spokesman for a 'Third Church.'

1 Rudolf Kommoss *Sebastian Franck und Erasmus von Rotterdam*, 9–12. Justified praise of this study must be qualified, as Flitner (*Erasmus im Urteil seiner Nachwelt* 72) rightly sees, because of its overstating of the rationalist side of Erasmus' thought.

2 See H. Oncken 'Sebastian Franck als Historiker' 275–319; R. Stadelmann *Vom Geist des ausgehenden Mittelalters* 246–66; A. Koyré *Sébastien Franck*; W.-E. Peuckert *Sebastian Franck: Ein deutscher Sucher*; K. Räber *Studien zur Geschichtsbibel Sebastian Francks*. On Franck historiography, see Räber 5–6.

3 Räber says that Franck's history is in fact an assembling of individual examples (10).

4 Lebeau 'Erasme' 127

the 1515 edition of the *Adagia*) critical of the behaviour of princes; indeed he goes further: his rejection of worldly authority is consistent with a hope looking for a remnant only to be saved and leaves behind the moral realism of an Erasmus.[5] The catalogue of heretics is a kind of parody of the Roman catalogues; Franck lists those considered heretics in Rome but, as he himself puts it, he reverses the play and canonizes where Rome condemns.[6] He chooses to include Erasmus.

Franck begins the entry with a reference to Erasmus' influence and reputation, especially in learning and studies. He was born at a time when literature was again raising its head from the dust. Between 1510 and 1531 (when the passage was composed) he became an ornament of the German nation and was called light or phoenix of this world, father and prince of the Latin tongue, a new Cicero, and (in Greek studies) a new Demosthenes. Though slight, even weak of build, he was in his time without equal in studies. He banished barbarism, restored the Latin muses to Italy as well as to Germany, and helped bring back the old Ciceronian world. Even to list his books and editions (many of them intended for the training of youth in the liberal arts) would be a burdensome task.[7] After brief descriptions of the more important works, Franck comes to his central concern: the articles of Erasmus' supposed heresies drawn up by the inquisitors were the offspring more of envy and want of understanding than love of truth.[8]

Franck's plan, so he says, is to place these quotations from Erasmus in context; there they will appear like jewels set in fine gold.[9] Franck characteristically assembles from Erasmus' writings (and especially from his *Apologia ad monachos quosdam Hispanos* of 1528) teachings condemned by his enemies; Franck's own mind is revealed only in marginal summaries.[1] Erasmus is in this way unobtrusively associated with Franck's own radical positions. Thus on Erasmus' handling of the Trinitarian texts, Franck comments marginally: 'The Father alone is called God in the gospel' and 'Prayer should be directed to the Father.'[2] Erasmus' use in his Matthew paraphrase of the parable of the wheat

5 Cf ibid 128–9; Räber *Studien* 12–13, 23–4.
6 The Roman model was the *Catalogus haereticorum* of the Dominican prior, Bernhard of Luxembourg (Cologne 1522). See Oncken 'Sebastian Franck als Historiker' 290–4. Cf Peuckert *Sebastian Franck* 116–17.
7 *Chronick: Geschichte und Zeitbuch* ... cccl
8 Ibid cccli
9 Ibid
1 Cf Räber *Studien* 45: 'One must infer Franck's own views from the way in which he brings forward his material.' The *Apologia* is at LB IX 1015–94.
2 *Chronick* ccclii–iii

and the tares in favour of religious tolerance is summarized drastically: 'No one is to be forced to believe.' Erasmus, Franck says, taught rebaptism, considered aural confession to be a human law and the sacrifice of the mass not to be an article of faith.[3] He is made into a spiritualist: 'He counted all external things as ceremonies and included fasts and sacraments under this name – these achieve nothing for salvation.'[4] Scripture without allegory, Franck summarizes, is a dead letter. Erasmus defended free will, if not as decisively as many others.[5] Towards the authorities of the past and the Fathers he showed a free and critical spirit: 'The best service of the saints, he believed, was to imitate their lives.' The church in his teaching was built not on Peter but on Christ; he questioned the power of the keys – Franck's gloss on this is revealing: 'Without the Holy Spirit the power of the church is nothing.'[6]

Franck takes up the moral and social criticisms of Erasmus and radicalizes them.[7] Erasmus, he says, put marriage above virginity. The New Testament teachings on political obedience had meaning only in the old pagan kingdoms; between Christians now there could be no other bond than brotherly love.[8] He thought servitude indefensible among Christians: 'Since baptism makes us all equal and brothers one to another, how does it tally that one calls his brother a serf?'[9]

It is not surprising that Franck's book angered Erasmus: it took his own words, yet made him speak with an unfamiliar accent. He was associated with an unbridled attack on authorities to whom he looked for the reform of Christendom. He complained bitterly, and on this complaint the Strasbourg government acted sharply against Franck.[1] This turn to the affair does not affect the importance of the *Geschichtsbibel* in the history of Erasmus' reputation: it began that tradition which made Erasmus' writings the seed-bed of religious radicalism and of various forms of radical reappraisal in both church and state. Franck, unabashed by the Strasbourg débâcle, did not back down from his appropriation of Erasmus. Two years before Erasmus' death he

---

3 Ibid cccliiii
4 Ibid ccclv
5 Ibid ccclvi
6 Ibid ccclvii–iii
7 Koyré emphasizes the ethical foundation to Franck's religion (*Sébastien Franck* 7).
8 *Chronick* ccclvii
9 Ibid ccclix
1 The affair is beautifully discussed by Lebeau ('Erasme' 130–5).

published the first German translation of the *Moriae encomium*, interpreting it as a demonstration of the utter vanity before God of the
world and of all things human;[2] three years later he produced a
collection (in German translation) of Erasmus' writings against war.[3]
So he stubbornly wrote the radical Erasmus into the record.

A radicalism of a kind very different from Franck's – a radical
ambiguity, even uncertainty – catches up Erasmus in the strange work
of the late Italian humanist Ortensio Lando, *In Des. Erasmi
Roterodami funus, dialogus lepidissimus* (Basel 1540). Before con-
fronting Lando himself and speculating on how he came to his judgments on Erasmus, let us seek some pattern in the work itself.

One of two interlocutors, the German, Arnoldus, has recently
returned from Strasbourg. His companion, an Italian called Ananias,
asks if he brings any new writings of Erasmus for he knows 'his fertile
mind and perfect learning.'[4] Arnoldus bewails a catastrophe that has
befallen Germany. Immediately a certain characterization of the
speakers appears: Arnoldus is rather stolid and humourless (the
calamity, it is said, must be great to draw tears from this stoic temperament); Ananias tends to the flippant (as in a sally at drunken Germany). Arnoldus is beside himself with grief; like Fridericus Nausea
(of whom this performance may be an exaggerated echo) he is bereft of
speech.[5] To the impatient Ananias, he finally confesses that Erasmus is
dead. Ananias seeks the whole story – he has read some of Erasmus'
writings, but diffidently since rumour has it that he is the source of
Luther's condemned teachings.[6] Arnoldus begins a sober panegyric of
Erasmus: he was a man 'admirable in piety and learning and – what is
not often found in learned men – of great urbanity.' Soon he adds more
extravagant tones: Erasmus has taken the place among the saints
prepared for him from the beginning of the world.[7] The devout
death-scene is treated impartially in colours Catholic (Erasmus confessed and received the sacrament) and Protestant (he called on Christ
alone).[8] There follows a long, apocryphal dying speech which ends in

2 *Das teur und künstlich Büechlin Morie Encomion das ist ein lob der torheit
   von Erasmo Roterodamo ... verteutscht durch Sebastianum Franken von
   Wörd* 1. Götzinger makes clear that the translation is far from perfect
   (xviii).
3 *Das Kriegbüchlin des Friedes*
4 *Funus* A2^v–A3^r
5 Ibid A4^v
6 Ibid A5^r
7 Ibid A5^v
8 Ibid A6^v

an appeal for tolerance ('he exhorted all to tolerance') – a radical phrase dropped into what appears otherwise as an exercise in conventional piety.[9]

In this death-scene is posed the whole problem of Lando's work. The standpoint shifts constantly; to define a tone is impossible – sobriety and exaggeration intermingle; the observer is denied recognizable landmarks. Arnoldus' study of Erasmus' funeral enhances the sense of strangeness and unreality. The monks pursued the dead Erasmus with abuse. Even the cool Ananias is shaken by Arnoldus' report of their turning the funeral service into a riot.[1] They provided a *sotto voce* antiphony to the orator's eulogy on Erasmus, denying every virtue attributed to him. A Gothic scene follows: in the depths of night the monks desecrated the grave and mutilated and dismembered the body of the dead man.[2] They threw down his monument and put the blame on demons. Their agitation, Arnoldus explains, arose from Erasmus' criticisms – his aim was to restore them to the right way, but they would brook no correction.[3]

The dialogue now changes character – indeed it *becomes* a dialogue, bringing together a case for and a case against. Arnoldus sums up his encomium of Erasmus ('serious but not proud, modest but not dull'), not without extravagances: in old age, Erasmus' temper, he says unconvincingly, became sweeter, not sharper.[4] Ananias, who has been making his own commentary on the behaviour of the monks, now speaks for the opposition. 'Beware, I ask you, Arnoldus, of attributing more to him in your fervent speech than he himself while living (because of his modesty) would acknowledge or be able to sustain. For many have reported to me that his nature was hard, implacable, and irascible ... This anyone may gather without much trouble by reading his writings, for his pages are full of rage, hatred, disagreements and insults.'[5] There follows a discussion about how the learned of Italy view Erasmus, some, it is agreed, respecting and encouraging him, many others – on Ananias' assertion – hating rather than loving him.[6]

Arnoldus cuts this short, and the piece changes character again. It becomes a kind of hagiography (or the parody of a hagiography):

9 Ibid A7^v
1 Ibid A8^{r-v}
2 Ibid B1^r, B2^r
3 Ibid B3^r–4^r
4 Ibid B4^{r-v}
5 Ibid B5^r
6 Ibid B5^v–6^v

miracles after Erasmus' death are said to show God's favour towards him and, in the vision of an old hermit, Erasmus' celestial triumph is depicted. Even the damned appeal to Erasmus for succour, among them those who have written unworthily against him including a German speaker (Ulrich von Hutten) and a nobleman (Alberto Pio).[7] What, Arnoldus asks, will be the fate of living anti-Erasmians, Scaliger and Dolet, the Spanish monks, the Sorbonne, Bucer, and the theologians of Strasbourg?[8]

Then Ananias returns to the case against Erasmus, and the dialogue resumes. Erasmus, he says, does not deserve the high place accorded him. Reliable witnesses judge him a bad man, which is not surprising since (an echo of Scaliger?) he was born illegitimate. Germany has many who outdo Erasmus in learning and piety; in France he is thought to lack discrimination, inappropriately mixing the grave and the frivolous.[9]

After these sallies the dialogue settles into bland exchanges between the two men and finishes with a reasoned statement on the condition of monasticism: not all have degenerated; some sparks remain and will burst into new flame.[1] At the end there is a seemingly out-of-character word from Ananias: 'Ask the good God to bring it about that we might come to him by following the same path as Erasmus and treading in his steps.'[2]

How are we to judge this strangely fractured work? Some contemporaries had no doubts. In 1542 there was published in Basel with the encouragement of the civic and academic authorities an oration against Lando's work by Johannes Herold (1511–c 1580).[3] To Herold the work was the outpouring of a mind poisoned against Erasmus and the Basel Reformation; he associates the author with the Ciceronians. He takes everything in the dialogue with the utmost seriousness. This naturally makes difficult any understanding of its strange turns and paradoxes

---

7 Ibid B6^v–C1^r
8 Ibid C1$^{r–v}$
9 Ibid C2^v–3^r
1 Ibid C4^r
2 Ibid C5^v
3 *Philopseudes, sive pro Desiderio Erasmo Roterodamo V.C. contra dialogum famosum anonymi cujusdam declamatio.* Herold mistakenly thought the author was Bassiano Lando (d 1563), a physician who taught at Padua and wrote on medicine. See Paul F. Grendler *Critics of the Italian World (1530–1560): Anton Francesco Doni, Nicolo Franco and Ortensio Lando,* 28. Cf 648E, where Herold says: Erasmus praised physicians; this one in return assails him.

and hyperboles. Herold attributes to the author himself the unflattering judgments reported of Erasmus.[4] He senses the contradictions in the work but finds in them only the two-faced nature of their author. At one and the same time he rejects as fabrication the story of monks rioting at Erasmus' funeral (for there were no monks left at Basel) and criticizes the assertions attributed to those monks. The desecration of Erasmus' body (in the manner of Cicero's) is, he says, a piece of wishful thinking by the author, but he attacks the perpetrators as though the story were true. He is outraged by the claim that Erasmus was illegitimate, which, so he believes, no enemy has asserted before.[5]

The value of Herold's oration in its time lay not in its hysterical attack on Lando's dialogue but in its own presentation of Erasmus' life. Erasmus, speaking in the first person, gives thanks for his birth among the Dutch – a people without deceit – at a time when good literature was reviving.[6] He recounts his own efforts to draw young people to purer studies and says of his satirical works that they were meant not to bite but to admonish, though this will not save him from envy and ill will.[7] Finally he came to Basel, which was congenial to him in every way; under the protection of its rulers he produced much of his work.[8] In the end it is the Erasmus of the Basel tradition which Herold opposes to the denigration he reads into Lando's dialogue: he was urbane, tolerant, charitable, fitly combining the grave and the gay, simple, modest, judicious, pointing others to amendment of life and himself relying on Christ alone.[9] Herold appeals to the luminaries of Basel and beyond them to the emperor himself to vindicate Erasmus' reputation.[1] Basel patriotism and (as in Beatus Rhenanus) German patriotism run as undertones through the whole oration.

No decisive clue to Lando's dialogue can, then, be found in Herold's attack. It has been the subject of important essays by Myron P. Gilmore and Silvana Seidel Menchi.[2] Both certainly see the piece as hostile to Erasmus. Gilmore seeks clues primarily in the names

4 'Rogo, est-ne haec audita referre, an propria pronuntiare?' (ibid 622C).
5 Ibid 627C, 615D–F, 618E–619A, 627F
6 Ibid 636B–D
7 Ibid 638B, 639C
8 Ibid 639D–640A
9 See ibid 612B, 612F, 617E, 620A.
1 Ibid 644E–646B
2 'Anti-Erasmianism in Italy: The Dialogue of Ortensio Lando on Erasmus' Funeral'; 'Sulla fortuna di Erasmo in Italia: Ortensio Lando e altri eterodossi della prima metà del Cinquecento.' For identification of speakers in the dialogue, see Gilmore 13 and Menchi 576.

brought forward from Italian literary and theological circles as favouring Erasmus or opposing him and concludes that the dominant tone of the piece is set by those who 'labored for reform within the framework of the Church.' Lando is anticipating the Catholic Reformation; one of his purposes is 'the advocacy through the figure of Ananias of a tempered reform of monasticism.'[3] Menchi, by contrast, sees in the work a radical Protestant attack on Erasmus. The key to understanding is the reference to Hutten, who is Lando's model. As with Curione (and perhaps anticipating him) Erasmus is left separated from Christ.[4] There may be danger in finding in the work a coherence which it does not possess. Even in the confused religious circumstances of 1540 there are unmistakable contradictions in the names offered for praise. The German list, for example, includes both committed Reformers and those firm in their attachment to the old church. Putting the point positively, this list has a very ecumenical flavour.[5]

The incoherence and ambiguity are genuine and presumably deliberate. 'Lando says yes and no, introduces promising themes and then leaves them in the air.'[6] He is savage with Erasmus but still recognizes an intellectual debt to him. Is Lando placing himself outside the orthodoxies – Rome or Strasbourg or Basel – at times sensing in himself a drift towards scepticism and despair, at times feeling his way towards a form of Christianity alternative to both the Catholic and the Protestant forms? Lando (c 1512–c 1554) belonged to a restless, disenchanted post-humanist generation in Italy. For that generation the promise of the Renaissance remained unrealized and unrealizable.[7] After humanist studies Lando entered a monastery of the Augustinian Eremites; even there he may have encountered heterodox ideas. He was in touch with a reformist group at Bologna whose most dynamic figure was Giovanni Angelo Odini (Odonne) and who followed first Erasmus and then Bucer.[8] In 1534, having presumably abandoned the cloister, he was in Lyon and said to be associated with Dolet, 'a kindred spirit.'[9] The next year he visited Lucca and its dissenting communities,

3 Gilmore 'Anti-Erasmianism' 11–12
4 Menchi 'Sulla fortuna di Erasmo' 584–7
5 The list is at c3^r.
6 Menchi 'Sulla fortuna di Erasmo' 584. Gilmore, quoting Conor Fahy, emphasizes the element of parody in both the pro-Erasmus and anti-Erasmus cases ('Italian Reactions to Erasmian Humanism' 96).
7 Grendler *Critics* passim
8 Menchi 'Sulla fortuna di Erasmo' 549–55
9 Grendler *Critics* 26, 118–19

to which Curione belonged. In 1540 it was Basel's turn, as Lando moved into an uneasy relationship with the Swiss Reformation. Enough has been said to suggest a restless searching. Lando described himself as 'full of anger and scorn, ambitious, impatient, haughty, frenzied, and inconstant.' In his works of the 1540s there was a taste for paradox; of one such, Grendler says: 'Both sides did not receive equal space or eloquence, and he sometimes turned the argument around.'[1] Is not this the feeling one brings away from the *Funus* itself? Discontinuity, sudden reversal has become a principle. Later perhaps, Lando achieved a more coherent identification with a recognizable form of religious radicalism, the Venetian anabaptist community.[2] At the time of the *Funus*, he but suggested possibilities, showed the attraction of one religious solution and then of another, and left all at last uncertain and ill-defined. One cannot look for a completely straightforward judgment of Erasmus in that work.

A straightforward judgment can be found in *De falsa et vera ... cognitione ...* a work belonging in a later time (1567) to the radical reformation in eastern Europe. Religious transformations succeeded one another rapidly there; new ideas coming in waves from the west found openings amid much political uncertainty. In Hungary the Reformation occurred under the shadow of Turkish invasion and political division. In the mountainous eastern reaches of the kingdom, in Transylvania, which from 1556 enjoyed virtual independence, religious division accompanied ethnic complexity and constitutional particularism. Lutheranism had a quick conquest in the 1530s; in the 1550s it lost ground to Calvinism, especially among non-German, Hungarian-speaking sections; by the 1560s, in a tolerant atmosphere unusual for the time, radicalism in its antitrinitarian form was beginning to win converts from both.[3]

The two authors of the *De falsa et vera ... cognitione ...* represented the forces shaping the character of Transylvanian radicalism. One was an outsider bringing the critical and searching spirit that had arisen among the exiles of the second generation of the Reformation; the other was a native who lived through, in a sense embodied, the successive stages of the Transylvanian Reformation. Giorgio Biandrata (1515–c 1590) was Piedmontese.[4] His skill as a doctor won him a

1 Ibid 36–7
2 See Menchi's study of Lando's works 1550–2, 'Spiritualismo radicale nelle opere di Ortensio Lando attorno ad 1550.'
3 See Williams *Radical Reformation* ch 28, and E.M. Wilbur *A History of Unitarianism: In Transylvania, England and America* chs 1–4.
4 See also Cantimori *Italienische Haeretiker* passim.

reputation in the courts of eastern Europe, where he lived between 1540 and 1552. In the mid-1550s he was in Switzerland but, like other religious refugees from Italy (think, for example, of Curione), he could not reconcile himself to Calvinist orthodoxy. He returned to Poland, where he used his standing with the magnates and his diplomatic and intellectual skills to spread heterodox, in particular antitrinitarian, ideas. By the mid-1560s he was a man of quality in his own right at the court of neighbouring Transylvania and a privy councillor of the king, John Sigismund Zapolya (1540–71). The distinguishing marks of his religion were a humanist concern with the ethical and practical, humanitarianism towards the lowly and oppressed, distinguishing between the 'rich Christ' of popes and lords and the poor, true Christ,[5] and a distaste for all that was scholastic and involved, which for him included the Nicene language on the Trinity. In Biandrata were combined the radical and the gradualist, the daring and the prudent.

His co-author, Ferenc David (c 1510–79), was on the radical and daring side. Of comparatively modest origins, he studied at Wittenberg at the very end of Luther's life and became a leader among the Transylvanian Lutherans. 'While indefatigable and persistent in following a course once chosen of whose final triumph he felt assured, ambitious to exercise leadership, self-confident and even headstrong in action, he was yet by temperament open-minded, and ever ready to abandon an old position in favour of a new one that seemed less open to attack.'[6] He moved on to Calvinism but already offered fertile soil for Biandrata's carefully planted teachings. In 1566 the question of the Trinity came to debate in a synod of the Transylvanian churches summoned by the king. David was by then preaching openly against the orthodox doctrine. This was the historical setting of the *De falsa et vera ... cognitione ...*

The work offers an antitrinitarian version of Christian history: indeed, it has been called the first attempt by antitrinitarians at an historical exposition.[7] An individual like Erasmus is fitted into a kind of apostolic succession. The Trinitarian controversies of the early church, it is said, were the occasion of persecution and suffering; they helped consolidate the usurped powers of the papacy; with the intervention of the emperors they brought on wars and devastation. The root of the error lay in the philosophical speculations of the Greeks.[8]

5 See *Antithesis pseudochristi cum vero illo ex Maria nato.*
6 Wilbur *Unitarianism* 29
7 Cantimori *Italienische Haeretiker* 303
8 *De falsa et vera* 104–5

Around AD 1000 these old controversies died down, but Satan devised a new stratagem – the sophistries of the Sorbonne. Still, holy and learned men rose against this intellectual tyranny; through the Middle Ages they wrote against the doctrine of the Trinity as the seed-bed of quarrels, hatreds, and seditions.[9] 'Indeed in our own time did not Erasmus of Rotterdam, a most learned man, neglect nothing to uncover the vanity of this teaching about God, as readers may see in his annotations?'[1] If Erasmus and the early reformers remained in the wilderness and did not enter the promised land, there have since come leaders in a full recovery of truth, a full restoration of the primitive purity of the church: Servetus, Ochino, Socinus ... The axe is now laid to the root of the tree.[2]

The book made an impression in its own setting and elsewhere. This was the book and Biandrata and David were the Transylvanian ministers[3] attacked by Possevino and Bellarmine. Of course, in their judgment of Erasmus the extremes met – for both, he belonged in the Arian tradition. Biandrata and David had given him an honoured place in a book heralding the noontide of antitrinitarianism in Transylvania. Darker hours were to follow. With the advance of the Counter-Reformation in eastern Europe and the death of John Sigismund in 1571, the atmosphere was less tolerant, and at the same time more radical strains appeared in the antitrinitarian (or unitarian) church. David and Biandrata were themselves to become bitter enemies. The historical situation which threw up the *De falsa et vera ... cognitione ...* passed away; the judgment of Erasmus it enshrined – Erasmus as heir to Arius and forerunner of Servetus – was to endure down to the Enlightenment and beyond.

Craig R. Thompson has written a long and beautiful essay on the reception of Erasmus in Tudor England.[4] Beyond the mutual attraction of Erasmus and England (he owed more to her, he thought, than to his native land) and the English friendships which were the most serious of his life, there was the continuing influence of his books on English education, scholarship, religion, and public life. Thomas Cromwell, the architect of the English Reformation, was receptive to Erasmian

9 Ibid 106–8
1 Ibid 109
2 Ibid 109–10
3 The authorship was ascribed: 'Authoribus Ministris Ecclesiarum consentientium in Sarmatia et Transylvania.'
4 'Erasmus and Tudor England'

ideas and promoted those writings that served his public purposes. At the end of Henry VIII's reign his queen, Katherine Parr, sponsored the English translation of Erasmus' paraphrases as an item in a program of reform, part Erasmian and part Protestant.[5] In the next reign, by injunctions of King Edward VI of July 1547, the paraphrases of the gospels in English were ordered to be placed in all churches beside the English Bible, and the clergy were commanded to possess 'the New Testament – both in Latin and in English, with the paraphrase upon the same of Erasmus, and diligently study the same, conferring the one with the other.'[6] Under Elizabeth the Anglican divines drew on Erasmus in shaping their case against Rome.

Rather than recapitulate this story – to pursue what Thompson rightly considers a *desideratum* of future research, an understanding of the influence of Erasmus at different levels of English society, is beyond the scope of this study[7] – discussion here takes one representative figure who may stand, among the different patterns of Reformation, for the English Reformation experience. We are coming to appreciate how representative a figure John Foxe the martyrologist (1516–87) was.[8] His early convictions were determined above all by Protestant friendships and associations – that is, the 'Protestantism' of the last years of Henry VIII's reign, which was penetrated deeply by the values of Christian humanism. Foxe was conscious of a personal debt to Erasmus.[9] He was one of the exiles in Mary's reign – his travels began with a pilgrimage to Erasmus' birthplace at Rotterdam and included four years (1555–9) working with the Basel printers. It was important for his future attitudes that his exile was spent in Basel rather than in Frankfurt or Geneva. In the new reign (while enjoying the patronage of some of its influential figures)[1] he occupied and held middle ground, ideologically speaking. He has been described as 'a mirror of Elizabethan Anglican Puritanism';[2] he shared, that is, the aspirations of the moderate Puritans for the pure preaching of Christ (so continu-

5 Cf James K. McConica *English Humanists and Reformation Politics under Henry VIII and Edward VI.*
6 Thompson 'Erasmus and Tudor England' 53
7 Ibid 30–1
8 J.F. Mozley *John Foxe and His Book*; William Haller *Foxe's Book of Martyrs and the Elect Nation*; Helen C. White *Tudor Books of Saints and Martyrs*; V. Norskov Olsen *John Foxe and the Elizabethan Church*
9 Norskov Olsen *John Foxe* 4–6
1 Haller *Foxe's Book of Martyrs* 117
2 Norskov Olsen *John Foxe* 16

ing the main thrust of the Reformation) but in the setting of episcopacy and the royal supremacy. The extremists, he said, 'hate me because I prefer to follow moderation and public tranquillity.'[3]

Foxe held a view of history in common with the magisterial, mainline Reformers. The church had suffered two periods of intense persecution, one in the first centuries, the other in recent times; this latter indeed heralded the end of the world. Between lay an age of comparative tranquillity beginning with the conversion of Constantine. Though it may be simply stated thus, this interpretation depended on a complex tradition, going back to Eusebius and Augustine, in the understanding of the apocalyptic texts.[4] The times of persecution were times of confrontation between the true church and the false church. In these last days there stands on one side the despised church, the spiritual church, in a sense the invisible church, on the other 'the great and visible ecclesiastical structure of Rome, called Antichrist or the Babylonian harlot.'[5]

Foxe's martyrology, the *Actes and Monuments*, stems from the developing Protestant historiography of continental Europe and also expresses the emerging self-consciousness of English Protestantism. It is suggestive that in 1556 Foxe was working for Oporinus, the Basel printer, when the latter published the martyrology *Catalogus testium veritatis* by Flacius Illyricus, whose Magdeburg *Centuries* were later (1561–74) to be the classic formulation of the Protestant view of history as a conflict under the divine ordering between the true church and the false church.[6] Foxe saw his task as in part transmitting to English readers the witness of the European martyrs. But the Marian exiles wished also to assert a particular English service to the revival of truth in this last age – John Bale, who had gone ahead of them in Henry VIII's time, had pioneered this path.[7] Thus the first version of Foxe's work, the *Commentarii rerum in ecclesia gestarum* (Strasbourg 1554), made Wyclif the first herald of the coming day. The second version – still in Latin (Basel 1559) – recorded what was always to be the heart of Foxe's martyrology, the story of the Marian persecutions, which Foxe hoped to burn into the consciousness of his fellow-countrymen.[8] The early English versions (1563, 1570) belonged to critical years in the

3 Ibid 159
4 Haller *Foxe's Book of Martyrs* 67; Norskov Olsen *John Foxe* 22–32
5 Norskov Olsen *John Foxe* 63
6 Ibid 20
7 Haller *Foxe's Book of Martyrs* 60–3 and Leslie P. Fairfield 'John Bale and the Development of Protestant Historiography in England'
8 Mozley *John Foxe and His Book* 129

establishing of the new regime – the second, for example, was published in the aftermath of the northern rebellion and when Alva was
riding high across the Channel.[9] Foxe's allegiance was clear from his
book itself; he compared Elizabeth to Constantine and in one illustra-
tion (actually set in the capital c of 'Constantine') showed her enthroned with the pope prostrate beneath her feet.[1] In 1571 the upper
house of convocation determined that a copy of *Actes and Monuments*
should be placed in every cathedral church and that bishops, arch-
deacons, deans, and canons should possess copies.[2] Foxe had become a
pillar of the new order in England.

For Foxe the Reformation represents the final crisis of history. As
the last days approach, with Satan let loose in the world, the believing
remnant challenges the power of Antichrist. Wyclif, Hus, Luther –
these are the great milestones. By the sixteenth century the whole of
civilization is alert and resistant: 'all over Europe your foes,' he tells
the papists, 'grow in strength; the pope's borrowed feathers are being
plucked from him; universities and schools spring up; printing alone
will subvert your doings.'[3]

Erasmus appears to Foxe as a pioneer of this revival. 'About this
present tyme [1516],' he writes in the 1570 edition, 'when D. Martin
Luther first began to write, after that Picus Mirandula, and Laurentius
Valla, and laste of all Erasmus Roterodamus, had somewhat broken the
waye before, and had shaken the monkes houses. But Luther gave the
stroke and pluckt down the foundation ...'[4] Foxe belonged to that
Protestant school which saw no sharp break between Renaissance and
Reformation: 'Many were provoked by *Erasmus* learned workes, to
study the Greeke and Latine tongues, who perceivyng a more gentle &
ready order of teachyng than before, began to have in contempt the
Monkes barbarous and sophisticall doctrine: and specially such as were
of a liberall nature and good disposition.'[5] When the crisis came on,
Erasmus supported the challenger to the authority of pope and monks,
as the famous encounter with the pious and prudent Elector Frederick
at Cologne revealed:

> *Erasmus* thus beyng entreated of the Duke, began thus iestyngly
> and merely to aunswere the Dukes request, saying: that in

9 Haller *Foxe's Book of Martyrs* 128
1 Frances A. Yates *Astraea: The Imperial Theme in the Sixteenth Century*
   42–3
2 Mozley *John Foxe and His Book* 147
3 Quoted ibid 186
4 *The Second Volume of the Ecclesiasticall history ...* 969
5 Ibid 970

Luther were ii. great faultes: first, that hee would touch the belyes of Monkes: the second, that he would touche the Popes crowne: whych ii. matters in no case are to bee dealte withall. Then openyng hys mynde plainely to the duke, thus he said, that Luther did well in detectyng errours, & that reformation was to be wished, & very necessarye in the church: and added moreover, that the effect of his doctrine was true, But onely that he wyshed in him, a more temperate moderation and maner of writyng and handlyng. Whereupon Duke *Fridericke* shortly after wrote to *Luther* seriously, exhortyng him to temperate the vehemencie of his stile.[6]

The adoption of this story, its implicit binding of Erasmus to Luther's cause, and the acceptance of a plea for moderation link Foxe to the Melanchthonian tradition about Luther and Erasmus.

The English significance of Erasmus is demonstrated by the enemy's resentment at his paraphrases and the place accorded them in the English church. Stephen Gardiner, who had been one of the apologists of the Henrician Reformation but was then as lord chancellor and bishop of Winchester a servant of Catholic restoration under Mary, had expressed his disquiet at the adoption of the paraphrases in the time of Edward VI, seeing them as covert propaganda for the Protestantism he condemned. To Foxe Gardiner was 'the perfect image of the proud, overbearing, interfering, time-serving, lordly prelate,' his 'favorite villain.'[7] He makes some sport of Gardiner's expressions against the paraphrases. Gardiner wrote that he had never read the book before and now did not sleep until he had finished. Perhaps in so rapid and restless a reading, says Foxe, his judgment was asleep![8]

On the larger canvas Foxe belongs with those Protestant writers who hailed Erasmus as a forerunner and furtherer of the great renovation of Christianity. But he also claims him – as did the Edwardian Reformers – for the peculiarly English pattern of reformation.

6 Ibid 971
7 Haller *Foxe's Book of Martyrs* 184–5; White *Tudor Books* 152. Cf Thompson 'Erasmus and Tudor England' 55–6.
8 *Second Volume* 1524. In the 1563 edition, 740–4, Foxe extensively quoted Gardiner's letters to Protector Somerset.

FOUR

Erasmus in the
Arminian Controversy

❧

AVERSION AND AFFECTION STRUGGLED in Erasmus' regard for his fatherland. It is possible to show – despite his uncommitted life and his distaste for national conceit – a deepening attachment to both Holland and the whole Burgundian Netherlands.[1] That a special relationship existed and indeed continued after Erasmus' death has long been recognized. Modern writers have seen in Erasmus the source of distinctive Netherlandish traditions, especially in religion. Before the dominance of Calvinism, even in the midst of the civil war, there existed, says Johan Lindeboom, a Netherlandish reforming movement striving for apostolic simplicity, condemning dogmatic exclusiveness, seeking reconciliation, and – in all – looking back to Erasmus.[2] Here was a kind of great centre party. Another writer has associated Erasmus more particularly with a 'liberal' strain in Netherlandish piety and pointed to his influence on D.V. Coornheert: he was the master of Coornheert's spiritualism (resembling Franck's) and moral perfectionism; above all he was the source of his (and others') pleas for religious toleration.[3]

That affiliation must not be overlooked, but the reality is more complex, as one would expect. Different parties and traditions each sought their distinctive identification with Erasmus.[4] In the Southern Netherlands there was, as we have seen, a characteristic mitigation of

1 See Alois Gerlo 'Erasme, homo batavus.'
2 'Erasmus' Bedeutung für die Entwicklung des geistigen Lebens in den Niederlanden'
3 Oene Noordenbos *In het voetspoor van Erasmus*; on Coornheert, cf G.H. Williams *The Radical Reformation* 774–5.
4 Cf Noordenbos' remark: 'Erasmus is a spring from which many wells are drawn' (*In het voetspoor* 37).

'View of Leiden' by Jan van Goyen, 1643
Alte Pinakothek, Munich

the harsh judgments on Erasmus otherwise universal among Catholic writers in the last part of the sixteenth century. Although as always he was to have enemies enough, a certain Netherlandish fellowship for Erasmus reached out across the factional and confessional struggles. He was a national possession.

This is demonstrated by the *Batavia* of Hadrianus Junius (Adrian de Jonghe, 1511–75), a versatile polymath who, after studying and living in various parts of Europe, settled in 1563 as town doctor and rector of the Latin School at Haarlem. The book was drafted between 1566 and 1570 before Junius lost his library in the Spanish siege and sack of Haarlem and had to flee to Middelburg (1573).[5] The scholars of Holland, says Junius, have felicitous and fertile minds; they would be able to rival the ancients if they had not been distracted by business and money making. The greatest and most brilliant of them was Erasmus of Rotterdam. 'Certainly by the testimony of the whole world he deserved the crown for universal and especially for sacred learning, though not without arousing envy, the constant companion of eminence.' He overshadowed others by his own clarity of mind; as streams have their beginnings in great oceans, young scholars may turn to him as the first source of their learning.[6]

Calm possession of a national heritage was not given to the Netherlands in the second half of the sixteenth century. The country was consumed by civil war, and recollections of Erasmus were troubled by the passions of the time. More lurid colours were touched into his portraits. Jacob Verheiden (fl c 1590) was the brother of a Netherlands war hero. He studied law at the University of Leiden, founded to commemorate one victory in the long struggle against Spain, and was later rector of a Latin School at Nijmegen.[7] The burden of his book *Praestantium aliquot theologorum ... effigies ...* is all too apparent from its title. The opening words of its preface state the themes: piety (in the Protestant sense) and liberty (in the sense of the Netherlands revolt).[8] These goods attract enemies, especially the hideous tyrannies of Rome and Madrid. But there are enemies closer at hand.[9] Verheiden writes at a time of war-weariness when moderate statesmanship is seeking accommodation and the taut discipline of the hard years is being relaxed. He rejects the idea of a truce, holds to strict Calvinist orthodoxy, scorns those who do not fight Antichrist openly.

5 NNBW VII cols 692–4
6 *Hadriani Junii Hornani, medici, Batavia ...* 234
7 NNBW IX cols 1189–91
8 *2ʳ
9 Ibid *2ᵛ–*3ʳ

In Verheiden's collection of portraits Erasmus comes between Wyclif, Hus, and Savonarola on the one hand and Luther and Melanchthon on the other. Papists, says Verheiden, reject him; Protestants claim him only uncertainly, but he deserves his place as one who fought openly and perseveringly against the Roman Antichrist by his attacks on scholasticism, superstition, and the monks. He was the first of those who by underminings and skirmishings attacked the defenders of the kingdom of darkness and confusion. The hatred that the latter had for him was revealed in Alva's time by the incitement of a Spanish monk to the garrison at Rotterdam to throw down the stone statue of Erasmus there. But the Rotterdam government, once free of Alva's tyranny, erected a new statue to 'their Erasmus,' commemorating his incomparable learning.[1] Erasmus brought more renown to Rotterdam than the great voyagers. 'Today,' Verheiden goes on, 'we must honour Erasmus more because we see the Jesuits, the craftiest kind of sophists, everywhere defaming his name and writings'; in fact, he would be the first from whom those ungrateful calumniators would draw their learning. They seek a reputation by pushing forward against Erasmus their own (like Possevino) and denigrating his work on the Fathers carried through with incredible Herculean labours.[2] Some Catholics, for example the authors of the Index of 1571, have not identified all his antipapal expressions for fear of seeming to have rejected so great a man. The Jesuits have no such scruples – they would get rid of him completely as a pestilence greater than Luther or Calvin.[3]

The warrior spirit of Verheiden thus claims Erasmus. But the Protestant reserve towards Erasmus in the manner of Beza, whom Verheiden quotes, also comes through. 'Would, great Erasmus, that you had remained the sure and constant ally of the followers of the gospel and that neither friends nor enemies had had your doubtful faith for censure.' Erasmus wished to be loved by all, but none in consequence felt really sure of him. He dealt too lightly with the serious business of religion.[4] This is a standard Protestant picture. What distinguishes Verheiden's treatment is the whiff of gunpowder, the sense of real and not just literary wars – Erasmus is called to the barricades and used against the enemies of the Netherlandish intransigents, Spain and Rome, of course, but also against the compromisers or peacelovers in the Netherlands themselves.

1 Ibid 19. On the history of the statues, see N. Van der Blom 'The Erasmus statues in Rotterdam.'
2 *Praestantium aliquot theologorum ... effigies* 20
3 Ibid 21. On the Antwerp Index of 1571, cf above, 41, n6.
4 Ibid *Praestantium aliquot theologorum ... effigies* 20

It was possible for a Netherlandish Protestant to claim Erasmus in a quite straightforward way. The Melanchthonian tradition persisted. Martin Lydius (1539/40–1601) was as a preacher in Amsterdam (1580) and the first rector of the University of Franeker in Friesland (1586), an influential figure in the church affairs of the new republic.[5] He was a prudent man accustomed to playing a mediating role. It was in character that he read diligently the letters and apologies of Erasmus and felt the injustice of criticisms made by his enemies who (as Lydius' son, John, said) were as active after his death as during his life. Lydius wrote an *Apologia pro D. Erasmo Roterodamo*, which John published in 1606 at a time of rising interest in Erasmus among Dutch intellectuals and with a dedication to the magistrates of Rotterdam who showed (it declared) a continuing regard for Erasmus.[6] The work begins with a brief essay by Lydius on the historical role of Erasmus: he was 'God's instrument for restoring the study of languages and good letters in Germany' and strove to cleanse religion of superstitions.[7] His writings testify to the wounds he inflicted on the papal religion while they also cleared the way for Luther.[8] The charges made against him distressed Lydius: that he was drawn to Arianism, that he was a scoffer at religion. In fact, he held to the doctrine of the Trinity although he recognized the flimsiness of some of the texts used to support it.[9] Luther blamed him for not adhering openly and completely to his cause, but Luther's vehemence and exaggeration did not appeal to him. He preferred to take the middle way.[1] In this he was not blameless; he 'was by nature too fearful and too anxious for peace.'[2] In fact he had much in common with Luther, as the papalists ('Pontificii') recognized.[3] He feared for the fate of good letters in the Lutheran tumult and was put off by the way of life – unworthy of their profession – of some of the 'evangelicals.' The failings of individuals should not have daunted him, and inwardly he was not daunted; he helped the Reformers as best he could, secretly.[4] He not only praised Luther and excused him but opposed his persecution; he 'argued strongly against

5 NNBW VIII cols 1088–9
6 LB X 1759–80, John's dedication at 1759
7 Ibid 1761A
8 Ibid 1761D
9 Ibid 1761A–C
1 Ibid 1761DE, 1762C
2 Ibid 1762E
3 Ibid 1763B
4 Ibid 1764C, 1763F–1764A

the use of force or exercise of cruelty against those who professed the [Protestant] gospel.'[5] Lydius is impatient with those who accuse Erasmus of frivolity. His writings affirm his dedication to Christ and the church. He should not be rejected because of his weaknesses 'lest we fail to acknowledge the remarkable gifts of God in him and how great were the benefits God conferred through him on humanity.'[6]

This portrait is the work of a serious-minded Protestant who had read and responded to Erasmus. There are critical questions, but the tone is close to Melanchthon's. At the end of the essay Lydius relates Erasmus to his own troubled age. No one, he says, ought now to imitate Erasmus' 'neutrality'; times have changed and the light of the gospel has shone for sixty years. What was then dubious or in dispute has become clear, and Lydius does not doubt that, were he living now, Erasmus would not be neutral.[7] By God's help, Protestantism has survived wars and dangers and remains resilient in France and Germany and England. This would have convinced Erasmus himself if he had been able to see it.[8] The doctrine of Erasmus, who would have been a supporter of the Reformation if he had but lived long enough to see its true meaning, is constant among sympathetic Protestants in the Netherlands and elsewhere.

Lydius completes his work with a set of chapters culling Erasmus' works and demonstrating his essential orthodoxy (in the Reformed sense): he was completely sound on the Trinity; his critical awareness of textual difficulties did not qualify his acceptance of scripture's authority; he rejected extreme papalist positions and a Judaizing trust in works; he had doubts about indulgences, the devotion paid to saints, to Mary and images, confession, ceremonies; he held that transubstantiation was not certain doctrine and he was really convinced by the eucharistic teaching of Oecolampadius (advancing further towards Protestant positions at the end of his life).[9]

In another connection Erasmus' name was honoured in a straightforward way. During the sixteenth century classical scholar-

5 Ibid 1763D, 1764EF
6 Ibid 1764DE, 1765BC
7 Ibid 1765CD
8 Ibid 1765DE
9 Ibid 1766B–1780F. Erasmus did indeed see the force of Oecolampadius' spiritual understanding of the sacrament but he held nevertheless – as he says, on the clear authority of the church – to the doctrine of the real presence, while remaining uncommitted on transubstantiation. See J.B. Payne *Erasmus: His Theology of the Sacraments* 138–54 and K.H. Oelrich *Der späte Erasmus und die Reformation.*

Joseph Scaliger
A portrait by Paullus Merula, 1597
This is the only known painting by Merula
University of Leiden

ship may have separated itself from the kind of journalism which Erasmus touched with genius, a running commentary – not only in epistles, tracts, and treatises but also in more scholarly works – on current affairs in church and state. It became more specialist and professional, drawing away from other subjects and using 'its established techniques to put its own house in ever finer order.'[1] To a later generation Erasmus could appear utilitarian, even amateur. Yet, despite professional criticism, he remained in honour. This is apparent at the University of Leiden, which, founded in 1575 as a symbol of resistance and victory, quickly became a leader in classical studies. The greatest scholar of the age, Joseph Scaliger (1540–1609), spent his last years (from 1593) at Leiden. After wanderings enforced by the wars of religion – he had embraced the Reformed faith in the 1560s – and a time of retreat and obscurity in a French noble household when he produced his major works, especially *De emendatione temporum* (1583), a first attempt at a science of chronology or universal history, he at Leiden 'tasted for the first time his own fame, and, what is better than fame, the silent recognition of superior knowledge' and was in turn hailed by his colleagues as in scholarship 'without competitor or rival ... our prodigy of nature.'[2]

To Scaliger Erasmus was a man of the acutest mind but, like Giovio, Scaliger would have preferred a more classical restraint (we might say less journalistic verve) in his writing. Like the Germans he was too voluble, even in his best work, the *Adagia*. He might be compared with Melanchthon and Conrad Gesner, the author of the encyclopaedic *Bibliotheca universalis* (1545–9). All three 'were great as gatherers of other men's wisdom rather than as original scholars, a fault they have in common with all the Germans.'[3] Yet, although open to a higher criticism, Erasmus was a very great man.

A personal poignancy enters into Scaliger's consideration of Erasmus. His father, as we know, had savaged Erasmus mercilessly. Scaliger had acted as his father's amanuensis and learned his command of Latin from him.[4] His attachment to his father led him into tragic

1   R.R. Bolgar *The Classical Heritage and its Beneficiaries: From the Carolingian Age to the End of the Renaissance* 377
2   Mark Pattison 'Joseph Scaliger' 183; Baudius in his funeral oration on Scaliger in *Autobiography of Joseph Scaliger* 91–116, at 98–9. On Scaliger, cf Jacob Bernays *Joseph Justus Scaliger*; R.C. Christie 'The Scaligers' 209–22.
3   *Scaligerana ou bons mots, rencontres agreables, et remarques judicieuses et scavantes de J. Scaliger* 139–40
4   Pattison 'Joseph Scaliger' 134–5

VITA
DES. ERASMI
ROTERODAMI.

ex ipſius manu fideliter repræſentata;
comitantibus, quæ ad eandem, alijs.

Additi ſunt

EPISTOLARVM,

quæ nondum lucem aſpexerunt;

Libri duo:

QVAS

conquiſivit, edidit, dedicavit

S. P. Q. ROTERODAMO

PAVLLVS G. F. P. N. MERVLA.

LVGDVNI BATAVORVM,
In officina typographica Thomæ Baſſon.
cIↃ. IↃ CVII.

Ex libris Valery Bartouts ex dono
D. Paule Merula cognati

Title page of Merula's edition of the *Compendium vitae* and other works
The letters G.F.P.N. stand for Gulielmi Filius Pauli Nepos
(son of William, grandson of Paul)
By permission of the Houghton Library, Harvard University
Photo by Barry Donahue

controversies late in his life – he trusted too much in the family claim to princely descent and suffered a galling exposure.[5] Scaliger did not deny his pride in his father but he was embarrassed by the attack on Erasmus. Indeed Julius Caesar Scaliger himself was embarrassed by it: 'My father later saw the folly he had committed in writing against Erasmus.' Joseph Scaliger bought up and suppressed printed copies of letters attacking Erasmus; they cost him '72 escus d'or, 36 doubles pistolets.'[6] He recognized that his father wrote in anger, hastily, without understanding or perhaps reading Erasmus. Certainly Erasmus made a mistake in producing his *Ciceronianus*, but Scaliger's father understood him differently when he read his other works.[7] Here Scaliger moves from a somewhat Olympian judgment on Erasmus as a classical scholar to a warmer approach, characteristic of circles in which he moved at Leiden, of Erasmus as writer and teacher: 'No Papist or Lutheran or Calvinist has written a better book or a more elegant one than Erasmus' paraphrase of the New Testament.'[8]

In 1607 a book was published in Leiden which expressed the feelings of those circles.[9] Along with introductory and commemorative material and familiar pieces like Beatus Rhenanus' life, there were treasures of Erasmus biography, a *Compendium vitae* said to be by Erasmus himself, and unpublished letters. For the first time since considering the Basel circle of his friends and heirs one senses, in this gathering and publication of personal materials about him, an affection for Erasmus going beyond intellectual respect. The associations in the south Holland towns of those concerned suggest a living connection with Erasmus' origins or at least local recollections and a kind of folk memory.

The two leading figures were Paul Merula (1558–1607) and Dominicus Baudius (1561–1613), and the reputation of neither of them is without ambiguity. Merula's family was connected with the leading families of Dordrecht, where he was born.[1] He studied Latin and history at Leiden with the great Justus Lipsius; on his *peregrinatio*

5 Scaliger had taken over from his father claims to belong to the Della Scala family of Verona. He retailed them in his *Epistola de vetustate et splendore gentis Scaligerae et J.C. Scaligeri vita* (1594) and was viciously attacked by the Catholic controversialist Gaspar Scioppius (1607). Pattison 'Joseph Scaliger' 193; Christie 'The Scaligers' 221. Cf Vernon Hall Jr *Life of Julius Caesar Scaliger* (1484–1558) 87–8.

6 *Scaligerana* 140

7 Ibid 142.

8 Ibid 141.

9 *Vita Des. Erasmi Roterodami ...*

1 See S.P. Haak *Paullus Merula 1558–1607*; NNBW II cols 902–4.

academica he met luminaries like Ronsard, Baïf, and Bodin in Paris, studied law at Bourges, and visited the Protestant communities of Geneva, Basel, and Strasbourg as well as Italy and England. In 1587 he was entered as an advocate of the Court of Holland at the Hague, but his preference was probably for the scholarly vocation over legal practice, and in 1592 he was appointed professor extraordinarius at Leiden (Lipsius' departure for Liège and later Louvain opened the way for the appointments of both Scaliger and Merula). Merula was a versatile man – classicist, geographer, historian – though in no field did he enjoy a singular eminence; probably his best work was historical – he was named historiographer to the States-General in 1599, but that cautious body declined to publish his *Historia tumultuum belgicarum.* Scaliger characteristically said of him: 'C'est un pauvre esprit et jugement, comme tous les Hollandais, au reste bon homme.'[2]

Controversy has surrounded Merula's scholarly work and not least his production of the *Compendium vitae* of Erasmus. As is well known, that text has a number of baffling features: it purports to be the life sent by Erasmus to Conradus Goclenius at a time of illness and depression in 1524[3] and deals particularly with the sensitive problem of his illegitimate birth, but lacunae and stylistic oddities have provoked severe challenges to its authenticity. In the nineteenth century, Merula was accused of forging it, although the most unfriendly critic could not now hold to that accusation.[4] Even if it were a later fabrication which Merula's critical method failed to penetrate, it would represent a concern for Erasmus' reputation and a desire to dissipate scandal about him in intellectual circles in Leiden, Gouda, and Rotterdam. Merula claimed to have seen the original manuscript in the possession of Otho Werckmann of Leiden, but copies had also been long available.[5] Of the authenticity of the letters of Erasmus published by Merula there can be no doubt, and in any case there are good grounds for accepting the *Compendium vitae* itself.[6] Merula emerges as a character worthy of respect and as a foremost worker in the

2 Quoted Haak *Paullus Merula*
3 2 April 1524, Allen Ep 1437, V 431. This letter was also printed for the first time in Merula's volume.
4 Cf Roland Crahay 'Recherches sur le "Compendium vitae" attribué à Erasme.'
5 Verheiden had said that a life of Erasmus could be expected from Werckmann, who possessed an autobiography of Erasmus written in his own hand and never published 'ut pretiosum thesaurum' (*Praestantium aliquot theologorum ... effigies ...* 19–20).
6 See the appendices in Allen I 575–8, 597–8, 609–13.

recovery of Erasmus' reputation after its burial in the ash of the great eruptions of the sixteenth century.

What Merula himself writes in dedicating his volume to Rotterdam is in similar terms to those of Lydius, whose work he compliments in passing.[7] He sums up all the praises bestowed on Erasmus: 'Phoenix of his age, father of literary taste reborn, light of the republic of letters, prince of the company of the learned, their glory and crown, God's instrument for restoring languages and sciences to Germany.'[8] He had enemies in his time, and there is no lack today of those who attack a man deserving the gratitude of all. A cabal dares to accuse him of Arianism, calls him a scoffer at religion, a Lucian recalled from the shades.[9] How can Erasmus be an Arian when he expresses the Trinitarian doctrine so plainly in his writings? He was far removed from Lucian and sighed over the corrupt state of the church. What did he not do in seeking for cures?[1] One may see with midday clarity how he applied himself to purifying religion from the abominable squalor of superstition, 'with what great ardour he strove to recall to the ancient sources a world too far fallen into scholastic quibblings and to excite to the study of true piety a world trusting too much in legalistic ceremonies.'[2] On the matters in hand, Merula praises the letters as a source for Erasmus' mind and way of life and, in a letter of address to Werckmann, evaluates the biographical materials not uncritically.[3] Merula could claim to have made a unique scholarly contribution which assembled new sources, especially for Erasmus' early life, and advanced the interpretation of familiar ones.[4]

Baudius was a more colourful personality.[5] Born at Lille, he was still

7 *Vita* *iii[r]
8 Ibid *ii[r]
9 Ibid *ii[v]
1 Ibid *iii[v]
2 Ibid *iv[r]
3 Ibid **i[r]. For example, he recognizes the existence of Erasmus' older brother, Pieter, a recognition based, like Opmeer's, on a true appreciation of the character of the famous letter to Grunnius. Allen Ep 447, II 291–312; CWE 4 6–32 Cf. Baudius' more romantic version below.
4 For an excellent analysis, see A. Flitner *Erasmus in Urteil seiner Nachwelt* 101–3. Some letters had been supplied by Petrus Scriverius (Schrijver), who later reissued Merula's volume with additions including the pieces on Erasmus by Giovio and Boissard and further correspondence, especially with Willibald Pirckheimer (Leiden 1615).
5 The essential source is the *vita* at the head of *Dominici Baudii epistolae semicenturia auctae* ... See also NNBW VI cols 81–2; V.-L. Saulnier 'Les dix années françaises de Dominique Baudier (1591–1601): Étude sur la condi-

Dominicus Baudius
Copperplate engraving by Jacob Matham
University of Leiden

a child when his family sought refuge in the north in Alva's time. He studied at Leiden in its first year or so and then at Geneva, where he was associated with Beza but did not imbibe the sober Calvinist spirit. In 1585 he took a law degree at Leiden and had his first experience of diplomacy with a delegation from the States to England where, on his own account, he enjoyed the patronage of Sir Philip Sidney, sadly ended by that hero's death. For two years he practised advocacy at the Hague, but, like Merula's, his heart was not in it: his passions, it would seem, were for poetry and for women. Probably in the wake of some scandal, he took himself off to France in 1591 and stayed there for ten years. He met Joseph Scaliger and de Thou; above all he moved in the circle of the great *parlementaire* families, among those seeking at that desperate time for a way out of the civil wars by a compromise on religion and a restoration of political authority. Baudius was by temperament sympathetic to these *politiques*. In 1592 he was named advocate of the king in the Parlement of Tours, but in other ambitions he was disappointed – in becoming historiographer of France, for example. He remained through these French years, says Saulnier, a humanist in search of a patron.[6] Yet his *politique* views attracted him to moderates in Holland who were hoping for a truce with Spain. He was a staunch defender of the truce of 1609 and an advocate of the reunion of churches.[7] In 1602 he had returned to Leiden and been appointed professor of rhetoric four years later. He, too, was a versatile scholar, a stylist, who might have achieved more if he had lived a more ordered life.[8] He was – colloquially – a character: voluble, familiar, ingratiating, gregarious, a tippler and a womanizer, always in need of cash, naive and large hearted but with a touch of truculence – 'Sharpsighted enough,' says Mark Pattison, 'in reading the weaknesses of others, so laughably ignorant of his own ...'[9] He belonged to the circle of Erasmus' admirers at Leiden but coloured his own appreciation of the great humanist with traits from his own romantic personality.

A letter from Baudius to Merula in the 1607 volume is preoccupied first with the titillating problem of Erasmus' birth. Baudius rejoices

tion humaniste au temps des Guerres civiles'; P.L.M. Grootens, SJ *Dominicus Baudius: Een Levensschets uit Leidse Humanistenmilieu.*

6 'Les dix années françaises'
7 See Grootens *Dominicus Baudius* 168ff and 192. Bayle emphasizes this aspect of Baudius in the article in his *Dictionnaire historique et critique* III 172–91, at 173–4.
8 L. Miller *Geschichte der klassischen Philologie in den Niederlanden* 38
9 'Joseph Scaliger' 178

that Merula has overcome his hesitations (arising from a fear of damaging Erasmus' reputation) and published the *Compendium*; after all, this is no betrayal of a secret which Erasmus himself wished to keep – on the contrary, he wanted posterity to share his fearful secret and 'the things which offered perverse occasion of calumny to the wrongheaded would if rightly understood serve singularly to light up his fame and honour.'[1] The misfortune of his illegitimate birth and the difficulties of his adolescence only enhanced what he later achieved by his own great abilities. Erasmus appears here as the model of the self-made man. Those like him who are, so to speak, the artisans of their own fortunes are worthy of the highest praise. But Baudius does not see why Erasmus should be ashamed of his origins, for his mother, like Dido (a romantic touch), 'did but to this one fault perchance succumb.'[2] Otherwise she was a woman of model character. The father was of good family, not ignorant of the humane disciplines as understood in his time, witty and urbane in manner. Since the two were joined by an 'inner affection and union of hearts,' only the solemn rite was lacking.[3] The family was from Gouda, which has – a burst of local patriotism here – by its pleasant location, its encouragement of studies, the humane outlook of its people, and the distinction and honesty of its government won no small fame among the chief towns of Holland.

Merula has not rescued Erasmus from oblivion but he has brought him back into the theatre of fame to receive the applause of those who know his virtues and are disgusted by the malice which denigrates so great a man. Disgracefully his books have been replaced in the hands of scholars by the 'abortive offspring of those who in great labour produce only trivialities and whose highest achievement is to gather wisdom from indexes and tables of contents.'[4] (One may see how Baudius endeared himself to his colleagues.) Some have criticized Erasmus' style, and some, more seriously, have accused him of scoffing at all religion and favouring the horrible heresy of the Arians. The first arrogate to themselves the right of determining who may speak or write. Erasmus followed his natural bent, which alone ensures consistency in style; in him there was an admirable correspondence between words and thoughts. As for the second, 'Many fine works, breathing a spirit of true and lively piety, clear him from the disgrace of irreligion.'[5] Baudius repeats a familiar point: Erasmus should not be

1 *Vita* 2* ii[r]
2 Cf *Aeneid* IV 19.
3 *Vita* 2* ii[v]. There is no reference to the father's clerical status.
4 Ibid 2* iii[r]
5 Ibid

accused of Arianism because he demonstrated the inappropriateness of certain texts. Those truly familiar with the Fathers' writings know that occasionally their zeal is not according to knowledge. Erasmus should not come under suspicion for his more acute and accurate interpretations.

His works, Baudius admits, are full of sarcasms aimed at gross error and superstition, but that does not make him a despiser of religion. Perhaps he knew better what he wanted to avoid than what he adhered to; one man could not see into everything; he achieved something great amid the darkness of ignorance by lifting men's eyes in the search for truth. He was fearful of giving offence and so held back from exposing all the mystery of iniquity. Yet posterity's debt to him cannot be measured, and his detractors would have nothing to say if his own honesty had not offered them evidence.[6] The romantic gloom surrounding Erasmus' birth, the charge of Arianism and its rebuttal, Erasmus' role in Renaissance and Reformation: these are the main elements of Baudius' letter to Merula.

It is time to sum up this group of Erasmus' admirers and their work. They are Protestant, not free thinking, but they are out of sympathy with the superorthodox who are too ready to accuse others of heresy. They are not strait-laced – there is something unbuttoned about Baudius at least – and they have no patience with humourless persons who treat every frivolity as a demeaning of religion.[7] They are *politiques* and against the bellicose and intransigent. Their Erasmus brought clarity in learning and enlightenment in religion. He had a light touch. He was an orthodox believer, not Protestant, certainly, but looking towards Reformation. In this area one senses a certain defensiveness: the charge of Arianism especially seems to nettle these writers. That is a storm signal of controversies blowing up in the church in the Netherlands when they wrote.

Troubled consciences and intellectual doubts over the doctrine of predestination had appeared among the Calvinist ministers of the Netherlands. Arminius, appointed pastor at Amsterdam in 1588 after studies at Leiden, Geneva, and Basel, was posing his difficulties by the

---

6 Ibid 2*iii^v
7 One may add two footnotes. In 1638 (Amsterdam) Scriverius edited Baudius *Amores*, which included Erasmus' *suasoria* and *dissuasoria* to marriage. In an accompanying poem Scriverius advises a friend to heed the former and not the latter (243–4). A century later Baudius was used for a treatment of Erasmus in a book on great bastards (Chr. Weise *Dissertationem de spuriis in ecclesia et re litteraria claris: Von gelehrten Huren Kindern ...* (actually arising from a disputation in 1693)).

1590s; already, too, some were accusing him of Pelagianism and Socinianism.[8] Early in the new century division was at the heart of the University of Leiden, where Arminius was appointed professor of theology in 1603. Arminius was no polemicist, but the temperature in the church in the Netherlands began to rise around 1607, and the trend was irreversible. A party rallying to Arminius appeared among the ministers, with Uytenbogaert, minister at the Hague, as its most distinguished spokesman. In 1610 he prepared for a meeting of forty-six preachers a Remonstrance rejecting troublesome or offensive points in Calvinist orthodoxy and making an *apologia* for Arminius who had died in the previous year, and his supporters. The States of Holland representing the oligarchies of the towns of this, the most wealthy and influential of the seven United Provinces which over two agonizing generations had fought free of Spain, passed a resolution that ministers adhering to the Remonstrance should not be subject to censure. That meant that the storm would shake not only the church but also the commonwealth.

Political eddies and currents were there from the beginning. The affinities of Uytenbogaert and his friends were with the oligarchy, and they believed that the disputes in church and university should be settled by the political authority. Uytenbogaert's ideal was a comprehensive church where a mutual toleration was imposed on the parties by the state, whose sovereignty could not be qualified or abrogated. To the orthodox, whose theological leader was Gomarus, professor of theology at Leiden and later at the University of Groningen, which was founded in 1614 in the orthodox interest as a rival to Leiden, such Erastianism was a denial of the liberty of the church to compose its own confessions. This was the issue which above all fired their anger. The controversy threatened to shatter the precarious unity of the new republic. Oldenbarnevelt, the advocate of Holland from 1586, whose political skills had contributed more than any man's to the founding of the republic, shared the Remonstrant preference for theological comprehension guaranteed by the state.[9] In his own religious outlook he was impatient of disputatiousness and party spirit; he was out of sympathy with younger, more zealous ministers who had not shared the perils and rigours of the revolt but who now wanted – as

8 See A.W. Harrison *The Beginnings of Arminianism to the Synod of Dort*; D. Nobbs *Theocracy and Toleration: A Study of the Disputes in Dutch Calvinism from 1600 to 1650*.
9 Jan den Tex *Oldenbarnevelt*, especially ch 12–14

he saw it – to create a theocracy. Politically he was anxious to keep the dominance of the oligarchy of Holland in the political system. The Arminian controversy in fact opened dangerous cracks in the whole structure. The Arminians (Remonstrants) were strong in Utrecht, Oldenbarnevelt's province and the smallest and poorest of the seven, and in the south Holland towns, the Erasmus towns – Gouda, Rotterdam, Leiden: a signal of the interest of these controversies to us. The outlying provinces, the rural provinces of Friesland and Groningen, for example, were Contra-Remonstrant. Even international politics added to the danger: James I indulged his taste for meddling in other people's affairs, especially their theological squabbles, and encouraged the zeal of the orthodox.

Finally, the cleft ran into the very foundations of the Dutch commonwealth. The Contra-Remonstrants wanted a national synod to determine the issues; the Remonstrants appeared more and more as the defenders of the special position of the Holland oligarchy in the republic, but even Holland was divided, for Amsterdam – always conscious of its distinctiveness – was Contra-Remonstrant. The pamphlet war was fierce, and looming behind it came the threat of violence. The stadtholder, Maurice of Nassau, who represented a counterweight in the political system to the republican oligarchy and who commanded the armed forces, was won to the Contra-Remonstrant side. By 1617 the States of Holland were left isolated in the face of most of the other provinces, the standtholder, and Amsterdam. From that time the outcome of the tragedy was sure. Oldenbarnevelt was arrested, tried, and condemned; the Remonstrants were rejected by the National Synod at Dordrecht (1618–19), and their congregations suppressed and dispersed.

The specifically theological differences between the parties may seem small to us. On the other hand, everything suggests the seriousness of the conflict for the political system; yet even there the effects of the Contra-Remonstrant victory were not permanent. The dominance of the temporal authority, for which in a sense Oldenbarnevelt died, was not abridged, and a degree of religious toleration unique in seventeenth-century Europe returned within fifteen or twenty years of the great convulsion – it was essential to a society as open and cosmopolitan as this one and to a political system so grounded in compromise. What was of lasting interest in the struggle was the confrontation of two moralities, two mental sets – the orthodox looking for precise definition and credal loyalty, the others feeling, with Arminius, 'The most learned man, and he who is conversant with the

Scriptures is ignorant of many things ... It is better for him to speak somewhat doubtfully than dogmatically about those things of which he has no certain knowledge.'[1] It was natural that in this country and in this atmosphere Erasmus should be brought into the controversy. I have already suggested the uneasiness of his friends like Merula and Baudius and their suspicions of the orthodox.

How easily he could be brought in is indicated by the strange case of the expatriate Englishman Matthew Slade (1589–1628?).[2] Slade was an Oxford graduate and a learned man. He come to Amsterdam about 1597 and had been an elder in the English separatist congregation there. But by 1610 his associations were more with the high Calvinists of the Dutch Reformed Church. A few years later he was rector of the Latin School on de Oude Zijde at Amsterdam. Slade threw himself into one of the more bizarre controversies sparked off by the Arminian affair. When Arminius died in 1609 there was bound to be a battle over the filling of his chair. The authorities in Leiden and Holland chose an outsider, Conrad Vorstius, who had been trained at Heidelberg and was then teaching at Steinfurt. It was an extraordinary appointment in the circumstances, for Vorstius had written treatises that could be given a Socinian interpretation. The storm broke from various sides. In particular, the royal theologian in England, working himself into a fine fury, came out against Vorstius. His confirmation had become impossible, and a curious, almost farcical, solution was found to the problem. Vorstius drew his pay but never taught at Leiden; the work of the chair was done by Simon Episcopius (Bischop), a young and able spokesman for the Remonstrant party, which had suffered badly from the affair and its undeserved association with Vorstius' unusual opinions.

Slade, whose letters had encouraged an English intervention as early as 1611, followed his king into the fray, as is clear from the title of his work *Cum Conrado Vorstio ... de blasphemiis, haeresibus et atheismis a ... Jacobo ... primo ... in ... Vorstii de Deo tractatu ... notatis scholastica disceptatio*. In a second part, which appeared in 1614, he chose to drag in Erasmus as a progenitor of Vorstius and the Remonstrants.[3] He attacked Vorstius and the Socinians for their handling of scripture, especially Paul, and went on:

I am not sure whether Erasmus of Rotterdam, who did not hide

1 Quoted in Harrison *Beginnings* 115
2 DNB LII 365. Cf G.J. Hoendedaarl 'The Debate about Arminius outside the Netherlands' at 149; Frederick Shriver 'Orthodoxy and Diplomacy: James I and the Vorstius Affair.'
3 *Matthaei Sladi Anglo-Britanni disceptationis ...*

his support for the antitrinitarians and the Pelagians and is therefore dear to the partisans of Vorstius, shrank from this crime; for in a letter to Peter Barbirius he said ... that he did not wish to be so bound to either Jerome or Augustine that he would defend or approve of their writings – and scarcely even to Paul himself [*vix etiam ipsi Paulo*]. But, God be thanked, the blessed apostle does not need such a defender who was often in collusion with his ostensible enemies ... as the Romanists contend and we not deny.[4]

In support of these judgments on Erasmus, Slade quotes Bellarmine and Luther: so the extremes meet! Erasmus is presented as the spiritual ancestor of Socinians and Arminians, who are treated as one and the same. The argument is that, despite their insistence on scripture as the sole authority, they handle it as they please.

Slade's attacks caused a furore among the Remonstrants. In September 1614 Hugo Grotius was just over thirty and had recently been appointed pensionary of Rotterdam; he had long been an associate of the Arminians and was a political protégé of Oldenbarnevelt and publicist for the States of Holland. He wrote to his friend, the scholar G.J. Vossius, then rector of the Latin School at Dordrecht but soon, on Grotius' recommendation, to become regent of the States (Theological) College at Leiden, that Slade's book against Vorstius was no less against Holland and was aimed at destroying the reputation of the whole people: 'He so treated Erasmus that the Jesuits themselves who wish ill to him as much as to Luther (and deservedly so) could not be more cruel ...'[5] In his reply Vossius worried at some length Erasmus' expression 'vix etiam ipsi Paulo.'[6] Erasmus was here referring to the purely human matters touched on by Paul about which, being human, he could err. Slade has misunderstood Erasmus' use of hyperbole: wishing to refute the claim that Luther wrote everything by divine inspiration, he preferred to agree with those of the Fathers who said that even the Apostles' writings contained human frailty. Vossius took up other expressions of Erasmus that were used against him by his critics. Erasmus had said that he could agree with the Arians or Pelagians if the church so taught. Vossius comments: Erasmus is saying no more than that the safest thing is to follow the unanimous opinion of the Catholic church. Erasmus had said that Christian faith is

4 Ibid, appendix 8–9. Cf Erasmus to Barbirius, 13 August 1521, Allen Ep 1225, IV, 554–64 at 563.
5 8 September 1614, *Briefwisseling van Hugo Grotius* I 349–50
6 Vossius to Grotius, 16 September 1614, ibid 353–9

a kind of divine folly. Vossius adds: this is, as Erasmus explained to Maarten Dorp, foolishness in the eyes of men and of Folly, not in truth. So Vossius enters a rather solemn and literal-minded defence of Erasmus and misses the subtleties of the last pages of the *Moria*.

Vossius had been in conversation with a defender of Slade's book, Balthasar Lydius, a son of Martin, a preacher at Dordrecht and a Contra-Remonstrant, whose remark about Luther showed how far the atmosphere had deteriorated since his father's time: '[Luther] who on his death bed left his followers a legacy of hatred towards Erasmus, no less than towards the pope, and who saw that Erasmus was a scoffer at religion ...' 'Erasmus,' Vossius replied, 'aroused hatred because he would not commit himself to every judgment of the Protestant doctors (who in any case disagreed among themselves) against the consensus of the ancients.'[7] Slade, says Grotius in another comment to his friend, traduced both Erasmus and Luther; his purpose was to show that Calvin alone remained orthodox.[8]

The most sustained of the Remonstrant attacks on Slade came from Caspar Barlaeus (Kaspar van Baerle, 1584–1648), vice-regent of the States (Theological) College of Leiden, as part of an onslaught on Contra-Remonstrant critics of Grotius' defence of the States of Holland, his *Pietas ordinum Hollandiae* (1613).[9] That Slade goes on, says Barlaeus, from Vorstius, the States of Holland, the university, and Grotius to Erasmus shows that he has read Quintilian: lying cannot be done more safely than against the dead. Barlaeus takes up the particulars already treated by Vossius: if, instead of taking a single phrase out of context, Slade had read Erasmus' many praises of the dignity of scripture, he would have recognized how reverently he thought about it. Learned and pious men accept Erasmus' expression, for they know that minor errors appear in the prophetic and apostolic writings. Erasmus acknowledged the authority of scripture simple and piously; divinely inspired, it was for him the rule of faith and life. He was devoted to Paul, the teacher of the mysteries of the faith and of

7 Ibid 357–8
8 Grotius to Vossius, 11 October 1614, ibid 361
9 *Casparis Barlaei Bogermannus ... In quo etiam crimina a Matthaeo Slado impacta Erasmo Roterodamo diluuntur.* The work is a reply to Bogerman's criticisms of Grotius' *Pietas*. Bogerman was minister at Leeuwarden, an intransigent Contra-Remonstrant and later president of the synod at Dordrecht. The digression on Erasmus is at 46–67. On Barlaeus, a Latin poet and scholar of great reputation and an attractive personality, NNBW II cols 67–70. For the more tragic side to Barlaeus' life, see F.F. Blok *Caspar Barlaeus, From the Correspondence of a Melancholic.*

salvation. The charges of Arianism and Pelagianism were fabricated by enemies of Erasmus and have been sufficiently answered by Merula and Martin Lydius. Erasmus was among the pioneers of reformation, as Bucer and Beza recognized. Indeed, the Reformation would be in strange case if he who first undertook the work was an Arian or unsure of the authority of scripture.[1]

Slade's mind is poisoned against Erasmus because he is valued by the Remonstrants for his sound and moderate theology. Barlaeus compares the controversies that plagued Erasmus with the Arminian controversy of his day:

> There now return the times in which Erasmus fought with ignorant monks and censorious theologians. It is the same cause, to reform some dogmas and rites which, by long custom, have lost their force. Then there were those renowned for calumnies and noisy agitations, Lee, Stunica, Sutor etc ... Today we have such men – in them you might see evil speaking or impudence with ignorance combined. Erasmus appealed to his superiors and the monks were indignant; now we appeal to the States of Holland and our opponents likewise are indignant.[2]

Erasmus was said to be overthrowing the old faith, the Remonstrants the doctrine received in the church in the Netherlands for forty years. With such charges the Contra-Remonstrants know how to frighten the multitude.

So Barlaeus suggests across a century his fellowship with Erasmus. The embattled quality of Erasmus' life is movingly recalled by the Remonstrants on the eve of the final crisis of their cause. But the one who was most aware of the bond with Erasmus and most convinced of the identity of the two struggles was Hugo Grotius (1583–1645). From his precocious boyhood he was in an environment rich in Erasmian associations. At the age of eleven he entered the University of Leiden, where his father was curator and at a time when an uncle was rector magnificus, to be greeted by a Latin poem of address from another of the curators, Janus Dousa, who had led Leiden during the great siege and was one of the founders of the university: it praised his parentage and talents, adding that the greatness of such spirits can be seen in their beginnings. 'Am I deceived? Was not our Erasmus such? I believe so. The portents do not deceive me: for nothing childish finds expression

1 *Bogermannus* 46, 49–50, 51–2, 57, 60, 65
2 Ibid 79

Hugo Grotius
Portrait by Jan van Ravesteijn, c 1613
University of Leiden

in your heart or speech.' Grotius, who has begun so precociously, will in the end be seen to rival the ancients and outstrip the moderns.[3]

The comparison with Erasmus was there from the very beginning of Grotius' scholarly and public career, tempting him to emulation, haunting his own struggles with recollections of another age. He was a student of Scaliger's and entered into the humanist inheritance. The other side of the Erasmian tradition, a piety sure but unscholastic, was also opened to him early. He lived for a time in the house of Franciscus Junius, professor of theology at Leiden, whose Calvinism was tempered by an Erasmian tolerance.[4] It is possible to say that Grotius' other commitment from his youth, to Holland and her political system, distinguished him from his great predecessor; yet that would be to overlook the complexity of Erasmus' relation with his fatherland, which had many positive traits.[5] In any case in an early work characteristically suggesting parallels between the Dutch and the ancient republics, *Parallelon rerumpublicarum liber tertius* ..., he gave Erasmus an honoured place.[6]

Foreigners, Grotius says, scarcely believe that among the Dutch living beside distant seas and amid the sounds of war and commerce there could be a place for humane studies. But in philosophy they compare well with the ancients. The Athenians did not treat their philosophers kindly, and Roman philosophy was undistinguished. The first part of philosophy is theology, not the myths of the ancients but philosophy illumined by divine grace.[7] So Grotius leads into a great apostrophe to Erasmus:

> How could I wickedly stay silent, Erasmus, greatest glory of Holland? Or with what words might I describe your remarkable learning, your heavenly genius, your incomparable diligence?

3 Quoted in Axel Nelson 'Hugo Grotius: Quelques observations sur ses débuts comme philologue, sur ses études de droit romain et sur ses relations relations avec J.-A. de Thou, historien et président au Parlement de Paris' 35. Cf G.J. de Voogd *Erasmus en Grotius: Twee grote Nederlanders en hun boodschap aan onze tijd* 91–2; W.J.M. van Eysinga *Huigh de Groot: Een Schets*; Denis van Berchem 'Grotius à l'Université de Leyde.'

4 Voogd *Erasmus en Grotius* 93

5 Cf ibid 133. On the 'Burgundian' element in Erasmus' political thought, see, eg, G. Ritter *Erasmus und der deutsche Humanistenkreis am Oberrhein* 29–31.

6 Of the work only this third book survived in manuscript. It was first published by Johann Meerman (Haarlem 1801–3). The section on Erasmus is in vol 3 (1802).

7 Ibid 32–3

For I do not now call to mind your goodness and constancy, your loftiness of spirit capable of all things. On a world filled with a Cimmerian darkness 800 years long, on minds covered by the thickest veil your sun first began to shine. And when in Italy or France there were scarcely one or two who had the boldness to think, you, born in this far corner of the earth, led learning and letters into the light, letters fouled by long inactivity and a flood of barbarism. You cleansed again holy theology more polluted than the Augean stable with foul quibblings and cavillings and, with liberating hand, set it free from the cruel tyranny of the sophists. You first separated what is required of us by the divine law from human institutions; you dared to condemn as errors opinions long accepted and to pierce deceptions with stinging thrusts. You were admired by all, and most justly, for, while you yourself yielded to none, sceptres submitted themselves to you, and kings and princes revered you, a private man. You opened the way of truth to us and taught with such prudence, such moderation and strength of character that the supreme pontiff, then the master of sacred things, feared you, but you were not afraid of him. You are he of whom we wonder either how in writing so much he found time to read or in reading so much he had leisure to write; thus you have shown yourself the Christian Varro. Beside your own writings filled with learning of every kind, how many ancient writings have you published, how many authors have you interpreted? Hail, father of letters and – by the presage of your name – desire of the human race ...[8]

All the praises of Erasmus by liberal-minded Dutch protestants are summed up here. There is passion, too, and not least a passionate pride in Erasmus as a Hollander. But the gift is offered to mankind: 'Erasmus is the possession of the whole world.'[9]

Grotius was drawn to Arminius after hearing him debate with Gomarus in 1608.[1] Increasingly, the Arminian positions attracted him because they corresponded with his personal religion – unscholastic,

8 Ibid 33–5. Note the reference to Erasmus' motto 'Concedo nulli'; but the words belong not to Erasmus himself but to the god Terminus. See James K. McConica 'The Riddle of ''Terminus.''' The last sentence of the quoted passage reads: 'Salve literarum parens, &, nominis praesagio, Amor Desideriumque generis humani ...'
9 *Parallelon* 35
1 Harrison *Beginnings* 104

unpolemical, orthodox in a comprehensive sense (on the primacy of grace or the authority of scripture, for example), and, in the Erasmian tradition, more devoted to purity of life than to the niceties of dogma.[2] Through Christian history true spirituality has been threatened by turbulent spirits hot to subject others to convictions of their own. That was so in the Reformation, on which Grotius cast a cold eye – he sympathized with Erasmus in his debates with the Reformers and characteristically found Melanchthon the most congenial Reformer.[3] In the Remonstrant affair the ferocity of the Reformation controversies had returned. 'Now indeed,' he wrote to the great Protestant scholar Isaac Casaubon in 1612, 'the sane simplicity of Erasmus and the agreeable spirit of Melanchthon so lack imitators that the public fury of all parties assails them most cruelly. It has become a hateful thing to write without hatred.'[4] Grotius will, he declares, devote what time he can find from duties of his office to putting an end to the controversies of the church.

The hope was vain, for Grotius' public offices tied him more and more to the Remonstrant cause. By 1612 he was the leading publicist of the States of Holland and Oldenbarnevelt's right-hand man in politics: in 1601 Oldenbarnevelt had had him appointed historiographer of Holland, in 1607 public prosecutor, and now in 1612 pensionary of Rotterdam in succession to Oldenbarnevelt's brother, Elias. Grotius was a great publicist but not always an effective administrator or politician – he showed the weaknesses and suffered the fate of the intellectual in politics.[5] In 1615 he explained his role to de Thou, whose outlook in many ways he shared; he had been drawn into controversial writing not by love of it but 'to help first the fatherland, then the church and indeed the church more than the fatherland.' Like Melanchthon he believed that extreme teachings about predestination or divine omnipotence should be brought back to 'the golden mean.' Melanchthon himself had at first been carried away by Luther but he saw the danger and with Erasmus' advice corrected his course.[6]

2 Cf Henri Meylan 'Grotius théologien'; Johannes Spörl 'Hugo Grotius und der Humanismus des 17. Jahrhunderts'; Joachim Schlüter *Die Theologie des Hugo Grotius* (which interprets the Érasmian tradition too much in an Enlightenment sense).
3 Cf Schlüter *Die Theologie* 52; Erich Seeberg *Gottfried Arnold: Die Wissenschaft und die Mystik seiner Zeit* 319–20.
4 9 May 1612 *Briefwisseling* I 207
5 Den Tex *Oldenbarnevelt* 545–6, 566, and passim
6 Grotius to de Thou, 5 June 1615, *Briefwisseling* I 395

By 1616 the crisis had unhappily passed beyond the reach of Melanchthonian wisdom and the golden mean. In the terrible dénouement Grotius fell with his chief and was condemned to perpetual imprisonment. His spectacular escape from the castle of Louvestein in a book chest cleverly provided by his wife (1621) opened the way not for rehabilitation but for exile. In the years of exile he enhanced his great European reputation, especially of course by the publication of his magisterial works on international law, themselves enriched by Erasmian undertones. But he also reflected publicly on the crisis which had destroyed his friends and pondered again parallels with Erasmus and the bond between them. In 1622 in Paris he published a new defence of the States of Holland and a critical review of the judgment against him, *Apologeticus eorum qui Hollandiae Westfrisiaeque et vicinis quibusdam nationibus ex legibus praefuerunt ante mutationem qui evenit anno 1618.*[7]

Difficulties arose, he wrote, over how religious affairs should be handled between the secular and ecclesiastical authorities, the former (as long as divine law remained inviolate) seeking to maintain civil peace through mutual concessions.[8] This difference went back to the beginnings of the Netherlands revolt, for William of Orange and the regents of Holland did not want the issues to be so narrowly defined as to introduce divisions among those seeking the church reforms which they, too, earnestly desired, while the ministers wanted to define teachings authoritatively. 'This difference in aim was greatly increased because many of the regents owed their knowledge of the errors which had crept into the church to the writings of Erasmus of Rotterdam, who aimed wholly at peace and equality. The ministers on the other hand drew their instruction mostly from the writings of Calvin and other zealous defenders of his opinions.'[9] As a result the regents and the ministers understood the Reformation differently, the latter staying in line with their teachers on doctrinal questions, the former seeking to cleanse the worship of God of corruption and free it from too narrow a dogmatism. The regents preferred to speak of the evangelical faith and so tied everything back to the gospel teaching and avoided conflicts among human interpreters.[1] They did not believe that a difference of opinion over points in dispute among the learned made for heresy. The

7 Cf Eysinga *Huigh de Groot* 91–2
8 *Apologeticus* 50
9 Ibid 51
1 Ibid 51–2

doctrine of predestination did not deserve the prominence it had been given:

> Although the greater part of the ministers of our country adopted from their teachers the doctrine of absolute predestination, it is certain nevertheless that from the very beginning of the revolt there were some ministers, many regents, and countless of the common people who accepted the other opinion. It could hardly be otherwise since here so much weight was given to the books of Erasmus ... and to the commonplaces of Melanchthon ...[2]

That is a remarkable and, from its own standpoint, perceptive account of the Reformation in the Netherlands. Grotius is conscious of an Erasmian tradition to which he himself belongs; but beyond personal attachment there is an alternative theology, an alternative historiography, and Erasmus is central to both.

In 1631 Grotius returned to Holland. He sought restoration and trusted in the justice of his cause. The reality betrayed him: Delft, his birthplace, Rotterdam, and Amsterdam, where the mood had changed since 1618, sought an amnesty; Maurice's successor as stadtholder, Frederick Henry, supported it, but his enemies could not be persuaded. From this sad, abortive journey one striking picture survives. Grotius wrote to Uytenbogaert, who had himself returned in 1626: 'My first visit to Rotterdam was to show my affection for the memory of Erasmus. I went to see the statue of the man who had so well shown us the way to a measured reformation, never binding himself on disputable questions to one side or the other. We Hollanders cannot thank this man enough, and I hold myself fortunate that I can from afar understand his virtue.'[3] There is a weight of sadness in that 'from afar'; but there is also a firm reiteration of the Erasmian/Remonstrant tradition and a spirit of pride in 'we Hollanders.' The statue itself, the elegant bronze figure by Hendrik de Keyzer, had been erected in 1622 on the morrow of the Contra-Remonstrant victory and gave new vent to the rancours of which Grotius had been the most distinguished victim.[4]

There was one last stage in Grotius' long dialogue with Erasmus. From 1635 he was in official life the ambassador of the queen of Sweden in Paris, but his passion was for Christian reunion. That arose natur-

2 Ibid 55–6
3 26 January 1632, *Briefwisseling* v 15
4 Van der Blom 'The Erasmus Statues' 7

ally from a theology which stressed peace and tolerance, the search for common foundations, especially in the first age of the church, and the demands of the Christian ethic above doctrinal exactitude. 'Through my whole life have I longed with burning desire for the reunion of the Christian world.'[5] At the end he freed himself from every confessional commitment and left even his Remonstrant friends behind.[6] Here, too, Erasmus was lodestar. In January 1641 Grotius commented in a letter to his brother on a work on which he had been engaged, probably his book on the papacy (1641). The essentials of the Reformation and peace with the papacy, he argued, were compatible so long as the latter was not exasperated by abuse. He referred to those in whom he placed hopes, Richelieu and Laud. As for the troubles in England, the prospering of seditions ought not to dissuade us from the care for peace. 'Such tumults did not frighten Erasmus, Cassander, Melanchthon, from devoting their prayers and counsels to the cause of truth and peace. To know the times belongs to God; our duty is to act and to live or die in longing for the good.'[7] The words are an epitaph for this life where mingle achievements and defeats, greatnesses and frustrations, glories and miseries. It is not to be wondered at that Grotius' mind returned again and again to Erasmus.

The view of history sketched out by Barlaeus and Grotius was elaborated in a later, more tranquil generation by the Remonstrant pastor Gerard Brandt (1626–85).[8] The worst of the persecution had ceased by 1630, and Vossius and Barlaeus were installed in 1631 as the first professors in a Remonstrant college in Amsterdam, the Athenaeum Illustre, which in a later century was to become the University of Amsterdam. The winking at heterodoxy, whatever the law might say, characteristic of Dutch society offered the substance of toleration. Brandt enjoyed the benefits as teacher and minister in Amsterdam. His view of the Reformation is coloured by the Remonstrant experience. The good beginnings, he wrote, were speedily corrupted: 'Piety yields to subtil learning, a virtue very different from

5 Quoted in Schlüter *Die Theologie* 48
6 See D. Wolf *Die Irenik des Hugo Grotius nach ihrem Prinzipien und biographischgeistesgeschichtlichen Perspektiven*, especially 116.
7 19 January 1641, *Hugo Grotii reginae, regnique sueciae consiliarii … epistolae quotquot reperiri potuerunt … 911*
8 *Historie der Reformatie* 4 vols (Amsterdam 1671–1704), Eng tr *The History of the Reformation & Other Ecclesiastical Transactions in and about the Low-Countries …* The bulk of this history, which was prepared at the request of the Remonstrant community, concerns the Remonstrant controversy. On Brandt, who was Barlaeus' son-in-law, see NNBW VI cols 184–7.

it.'[9] Men turn to force in religious affairs, and the majority lords it over the minority. Such an outcome was indeed feared from the beginning. Erasmus was among those 'who interposed between both sides, that they might correct their mutual Faults, moderate their Disputes, and promote Peace.' The purpose of studying Reformation history is to test the claims of party and get behind appearances, to promote unity among Christians and not least between Calvinists and Remonstrants.[1]

Erasmus, 'that great miracle of Wit & Learning,' is introduced by the words of the letter to Uytenbogaert of January 1632 from Grotius, who was 'so like him in many things, that fell short of him in very few & in some exceeded him.'[2] The world at the beginning of the sixteenth century was dominated by monkery and ignorance. Erasmus chastised the monks 'with great liberty,' though he adhered to the old church 'which he thought might & ought to reform itself, when admonished by him and others, without Schism or Separation.' He began by thinking well of Luther, 'believing that God had sent him to reform Mankind ... but wishing that he had shewn a little more temper.' He did what he could to hinder the oppression of Luther 'by a Faction of raging Zealots'; he saw how the fury of both sides threatened tumults and insurrections; by interposing between them he drew the ill will of both.[3] Some Reformers criticized him for remaining loyal to Rome despite its errors and abuses, but there were others who praised his impartiality and 'were more particularly pleased with his distinguishing between Error, Heresie and Sedition.'[4] He opposed persecution, which was 'the work of Hangmen, and not of Divines.'[5] He advised the Roman authorities with '*Dutch* plainness and freedom of speaking.'[6] When he wrote against Luther on free will it was 'with great temper,' but Luther replied with a 'furious Book.' Still, Erasmus made his mark, for the more reasonable and moderate, especially Melanchthon, withdrew from the more rigorous doctrine of predestination. Always Erasmus is presented as the apostle of a 'measured reformation,' recommending to both sides 'the great medicine of mutual Toleration' and

9 *History of the Reformation* i ii
1 Ibid iv, vi. The historian, Brandt said, should enquire 'whether he that relates [events] has seen or heard them himself, or whether he has received them from others at the first, second, or third hand; whether from Friends or Enemies; or from such as are wholly free from the suspicion of *Partiship* ...' For Erasmus he relies most on the epistles.
2 Ibid 29–30
3 Ibid 37–8
4 Ibid 39
5 Ibid 46
6 Ibid 48

CHRISTO SERVATORI S.

DES. ERASMO ROTERODAMO VIRO OMNIBVS MODIS
MAXIMO, CVIVS INCOMPARABILEM IN OMNI DISCI-
PLINARVM GENERE ERVDITIONEM PARI CONIVNC
TAM PRVDENTIA POSTERI ET ADMIRABVNTVR ET
PRÆDICABVNT. BONIFACIVS AMERBACHIVS. HIE:
FROBENNIVS. NIC. EPISCOPIVS. HEREDES ET NVNC
PATI SVPREMÆ SVÆ .VOLVNTATIS VINDICES, PATRO
NO OPTIMO, NON MEMORIÆ QVAM IMMORTALEM SIBI
AEDITIS LVCVBRATIONIBVS COMPARAVIT, IIS TANTIS,
PER DVM ORBIS TERRARVM STABIT SVPERFVTVRO
AC ERVDITIS VBIQVE GENTIVM COLLOQVVTVRO
SED CORPORIS MORTALIS QVO RECONDITVM SIT
ERGO, HOC SAXVM POSVERE

MORTVVS EST · 4 · EIDVS   IVL·
IAM SEPTVAGENARIVS ANN· A CHRISTO NATO
· M · D · XXXVI ·

Erasmus' monument at Basel
From Boxhorn's *Monumenta illustrium virorum, et elogia*
Courtesy of the British Library Board

endeavouring 'to reform the Reformers, and the Reformation itself.'[7] He anticipated the positions of the Remonstrants, by his denunciation of tumult and sedition, by his preaching of peace and charity, but, above all, by his advocacy of a 'publick Reformation of the Church,' based on an inner reformation of conscience and a recognition of the rights of the public authorities. This and the advice quietly to leave an established church whose practice was unacceptable to conscience and join one's self 'to other private Christians, or Christian assemblies that are more godly, reasonable and moderate,' but even then not in a way to break the 'band of spiritual brotherhood,' was thoroughly Remonstrant.[8]

Erasmus could then be presented as a Remonstrant before his time. Yet he remained a national possession. M.-Z. Boxhorn (1612–53) was appointed in his twentieth year to the chair of eloquence at Leiden; he also published at Amsterdam in the same year (1632) a compilation, *Theatrum sive Hollandiae comitatis et urbium nova descriptio*, in which he presented Erasmus as one of the glories of Holland. In a dedicatory epistle to the States of Holland he thus addressed Rotterdam: 'You bore the great Erasmus whom Gouda conceived. I need say nothing more. That is greatness enough.'[9] Those who have striven to lessen his reputation have but buried their own. Boxhorn's work offered a brief biography and a statement of Erasmus' universal reputation: 'His learning and diligence were inexhaustible.' But what especially links this modest account to the Holland of the Golden Age is its rare recollection of Erasmus' early efforts in painting – a crucifix which he painted was known in Delft.[1]

Erasmus remained in honour in the Golden Age of the Netherlands. To trace the Erasmian echoes in the Dutch literature of the seventeenth century is beyond the scope of this discussion.[2] The great poet Vondel drew for his own works on the *Enchiridion*, the *Adagia*, the *Colloquia*, and the *Moriae encomium*. He also intervened in the controversy over the Rotterdam statue with two poems depicting Erasmus as the purifier of Christendom and honouring his struggle for peace among Christians.[3] The more homely verses of Jacob Cats, especially his work on

7 Ibid 73
8 Ibid, Annotations 11. Cf ibid II x–xiii.
9 *Theatrum* 3^v
1 Ibid 284–5. The passage on Erasmus is repeated in Boxhorn's beautiful volume published in Amsterdam in 1638, *Monumenta illustrium virorum, et elogia* 26. On Erasmus as painter, see A. Hyma *The Youth of Erasmus* 166. The tradition, however, remains very uncertain.
2 Cf G. Degroote 'Erasmiaanse Echo's in de Gouden Eeuw in Nederland.'
3 Ibid 392–7

marriage, were inspired by Erasmus.[4] In the family of Constantine Huygens admiration of Erasmus was a tradition.[5] These are but peaks in the long Erasmian range which runs through the Dutch seventeenth century. Our subject has been the controversial treatments and presentations of Erasmus as an historical figure among his countrymen in the period between the running down of the revolt and the calm that slowly settled after the crisis of 1618–19, but we need reminding constantly that in this country especially there was a more diffuse, less tangible appreciation of Erasmus belonging to the very texture of the common life, 'rooted in a popular tradition at once national, humanist and religious.'[6]

As Grotius saw, however, the appearance of the Remonstrant party in the Netherlands had a wider European significance. It represented a reaction from the fierce dogmatism of the confessional age, in part a return to Erasmian irenicism, in part a *politique* appreciation of civil authority as the alternative to religious war. The new, more tolerant mood did not triumph quickly – after all, the Remonstrant defeat coincided with the start of the Thirty Years War and was soon followed by England's drift into revolution and civil war; but the longer future was on its side. Even in the mid-century crises Erasmian voices were sometimes heard and Erasmus himself sometimes recalled with pleasure. In England in the 1630s the name 'Arminian' was, of course, associated with William Laud and his particular program for the Church of England, a clerical, High Church, and authoritarian program; but the common ground between Laudians and Remonstrants was less the tolerance and irenicism which drew the latter to the memory of Erasmus than a shared hatred of the determined Calvinists. To see the recovery in England of the Remonstrant appreciation of Erasmus one must look in a somewhat different direction.

Lucius Cary, Viscount Falkland (1610–43), had his own experience of the tensions of the confessional age.[7] His father was lord deputy of Ireland, and from Trinity College, Dublin, he received strong Calvinist influences. His wife was staunchly Protestant. On the other hand, his mother became Catholic; indeed on one occasion she abducted his two

4 Jean-Claude Margolin 'L'inspiration érasmienne de Jacob Cats'
5 Degroote 'Erasmiaanse Echo's' 392
6 Margolin 'L'inspiration érasmienne' 140
7 DNB III 1155–60 (S.R. Gardiner); Kurt Weber *Lucius Cary Second Viscount Falkland*; K.B. Murdock *The Sun at Noon: Three Biographical Sketches*; J.A.R. Marriott *The Life and Times of Lucius Cary Viscount Falkland*. H.R. Trevor-Roper referred to Falkland's admiration of Erasmus in his famous essay 'Desiderius Erasmus.'

younger brothers for Catholic education abroad. Quickly, however, the extremes repelled him; he had no taste for Laudian solutions, while on doctrinal issues preferring Arminianism to high Calvinism. He was the classic type of the moderate, 'a man of the most delicate discrimination, of the utmost restraint and mental balance';[8] but he was not insipid: 'For him the study of the Church Fathers and the varieties of doctrine was no escape from reality, but a coming to grips with problems of great personal moment. In no other way could he hope to make order out of the warring intellectual and emotional elements which underlay his whole relation to the world.'[9]

In the 1630s on his estate of Great Tew near Oxford, Falkland was the centre of a circle which recreated as near as was possible in that ominous time the atmosphere of the *Symposium* and Erasmus' *Convivium religiosum*. His house, said Clarendon, 'looked like the University itselfe, by the company that was always founde there.'[1] The Great Tew circle sought an accommodation of warring doctrines within a broadly based national church. But they could not avoid controversial encounters with their opponents and especially the Church of Rome. 'The studies in fashion in those dayes (in England) were poetry, and controversie with the church of Rome,' said John Aubrey.[2] Falkland and his theological companions John Hales and William Chillingworth were preoccupied especially with the problems of tradition, authority, and infallibility. Falkland wrote a *Discourse of Infallibility* and then a much longer *Reply* to a Catholic answer to it.[3]

In the *Reply* Falkland makes clear his own fundamental positions and from time to time cites Erasmus, who – it was said – he never tired of reading,[4] in comment or support. Thus the claim to a verbal tradition come down unbroken from the Apostles may be false. Piety may sanctify traditions which are in themselves dubious, 'as we saw *Erasmus*, who beleeved your confession, not to have been instituted by the Apostles, yet would not reprehend them that said so, thinking it an error, that would increase Piety ...'[5] Again, there are sharp and serious differences among the Catholic doctors. Erasmus on one occasion said

8 W.K. Jordan *The Development of Religious Toleration in England from the Accession of James I to the Convention of the Long Parliament (1603–1640)* 371
9 Murdock *The Sun at Noon* 103
1 Quoted in Weber *Lucius Cary* 77
2 *Brief Lives and Other Selected Writings* 356
3 *A Discourse of Infallibility, with Mr Thomas White's Answer to it, and a Reply to him*. The first edition was published posthumously in 1651.
4 Ibid, Triplet's dedication, n.p.
5 Ibid 64

that what was heresy among the Thomists was orthodox among the Scotists. 'Religion,' he remarked on another occasion, 'is come down to Sophistry, and a Miriad of Articles are broken out.'[6] Falkland states as his own the Reformation principle: 'The Bookes of the Evangelists, and the Apostles, and the Oracles of the Ancient Prophets teach us clearly what we are to think of the Divinity.'[7] But here is no simple assertion of the all-sufficiency of scripture. Truth must also be sought by reason, not to deny the grace of God, which is like the sun to our sight, but because grace works through reason as its minister. Truth is not a simple thing; why should it not lie sometimes with one party, sometimes with another, sometimes midway between, sometimes with no party? Let there be liberty to follow truth where it leads and more irenic spirits; unity with charity will follow.[8] What cannot be sustained is unity resting on the historic claims of the Roman Church. The case of Erasmus and the fate of his reputation among Catholics, Falkland says to his critic, in themselves disprove the claim to unanimity and untroubled authority:

> And for the same reason, it were wholly impossible, that at the same time the Popes, and most notable, and most pious, and most learned Papists living, should have justified, and applauded *Erasmus* for the same workes (the one by his printed *Diplomas*, and the rest by their Letters) for which, at the same instant, the greatest part of the Monkes counted and proclaimed him a more pestilent Heretick than *Luther*, if they had all weighed heresie in the same ballance, and more impossible if in yours; which the learned will yet lesse approve of, when they see how soon the worse opinion, and lesser authoritie may prevaile, as how that of the Monkes hath done against that of the Popes, and Bishops, and that so much, that *Erasmus* is now generallie disavowed as no Catholicke and given to us (whom wee accept as a great present) that *Bellarmine* will allow him to be but halfe a Christian ...[9]

So Falkland claims Erasmus, 'who thought himself no Martyr, yet one who may passe for a Confessor, having suffered, and long by the Bigotts of both Parties,'[1] for his own tolerant, eclectic, rationalizing version of Protestant Christianity.

6   Ibid 111
7   Ibid 79
8   Ibid 139
9   Ibid 161
1   Ibid 187–8

Falkland grieved deeply over England's descent into civil war. Like Grotius, whom he addressed as 'our Ages Wonder, by thy birth, the Fame of *Belgia;* by thy Banishment, the Shame,'[2] he bore his own measure of suffering for his country's troubles. He felt heavily the burden of political responsibility. He became despondent, perhaps despairing; observers saw his death on the royalist side at Newbury Fight in 1643 as a kind of suicide.

It is fitting that we should end this part of the volume with Falkland. Great Tew might be seen as a last attempt to recover the irenic vision of Erasmus. In one sense it was a dying echo of the vigorous Christian humanism of a century and a half before. As Falkland himself recognized, the confessional struggles had emaciated Christian humanism and the reputation of Erasmus which had supported it – this has been the burden of these three chapters. Yet Falkland (and the Remonstrant movement too in its later stages) was a beginning as well as an end. He looked forward to a religion of private judgment, of critical temper, civil discourse, and enlightened sensibilities.[3] How the reputation of Erasmus was to fare with the strong flowing in of that kind of religion is the main theme of the second part of this volume.[4]

2 Quoted in Weber *Lucius Cary* 192
3 For how the Tew circle thus pointed forward see, eg, R. Orr 'Chillingworth versus Hooker: A Criticism of Natural Law Theory.'
4 The moderate Anglican/royalist standpoint was not the only one from which favourable judgments of Erasmus were made during the English crisis. John Milton's prose writings include a number of references to Erasmus. In particular he quotes him in support of his – for the time – unusual opinion that divorce is justified by mutual incompatibility of temper. Erasmus pioneered a more truthful reading of the biblical texts on divorce, eg, in recognizing that they allow other grounds for divorce than adultery. Further, Erasmus, 'who for learning was the wonder of his age,' defended his opinion with vigour and feared not 'to ingage all his fame on the Argument.' The references are to Erasmus' annotations on Matthew and 1 Corinthians and his *Responsio ad disputationem cuiusdam Phimostomi de divortio* and are to be found in Milton's *Tetrachordon: Expositions upon the foure chief places in Scripture, which treat of Mariage or nullities in Mariage* 620, 709. Cf Milton's 'Post-Script' to *The Judgment of Martin Bucer, concerning Divorce* ... 478–9. Erasmus, like Bucer, addressed his 'eloquent and right Christian discours' on divorce primarily to English needs, as now did Milton himself in face of a suspicious Presbyterian Parliament. Cf V. Norskov Olsen *The New Testament Logia on Divorce: A Study of their Interpretation from Erasmus to Milton.*

PART TWO

ERASMUS AND 'THE EUROPEAN MIND

1680–1715'

FIVE

Introduction to Part Two

❧

THE REPUTATION OF ERASMUS SUFFERED BADLY in the confessional age. Belligerents called him a neutral, and neutrality was a crime; worse, his detachment cloaked more corrosive or destructive designs – antitrinitarianism, for example. The recovery of Erasmus' reputation depended on changes in the moral and intellectual climate, a decline in exclusiveness and partisanship and dogmatism and the recovery of more personal and even sentimental strains in religion.

We must of course avoid gross contrasts. We know of corners in the confessional age itself where the reverent scepticism of Erasmus was understood – among the Basel Protestants or in the sombre reflections of de Thou, for example. The Arminian appeal for mutual toleration was a sharp if ineffective reaction against the prevailing mood.

In some quarters a more thoroughgoing scepticism had already been anticipated, or at least a detachment from prevailing orthodoxies and commitments and an uneasy quest for spiritual freedom. Garasse, as we know, had made much of the so-called *beaux esprits*. He was dealing with those in France – scholars, lawyers, medical men – who were in revulsion against the fanaticism and excesses of the Catholic League and who were left untouched by the religious revival of the reign of Louis XIII. A characteristic figure was Guy Patin, dean of the faculty of medicine at Paris. He was devoted to the classical writers but also to the humanist writers of the previous century. He did not break with the traditional faith or deny a religious attachment but he could, as Pintard puts it, hang over the abyss of unbelief and demonstrate his spiritual independence.[1] He had a particular hatred of the Jesuits.

Patin did not write an extended piece on Erasmus but often referred

1 René Pintard *Le Libertinage érudit dans la première moitié du xviie siècle* 1

317

to him in his correspondence and conversation.[2] The Erasmus that Patin and his friends, such as Gabriel Naudé, the celebrated custodian of the Mazarin Library, admired was not the editor of the New Testament or of St Augustine but the ironic correspondent and the author of the *Adagia* and the *Colloquia*, understood in a certain sense.[3] Erasmus was a free spirit whose great service was to expose the monks and abuses of power, ecclesiastical and to an extent political. From sentiments like these it may seem no great step to Voltaire, though the different historical settings give different meanings to the same words. A French edition of the *Colloquia*, said Patin on one occasion, would be 'marvellously well received in this age so curious of novelties ...'[4] The very irony suggests the tone – curious, questioning, critical (despite Patin's inflexible conservatism on some matters, including medicine). Patin and his friends, not least in their way of understanding and appreciating Erasmus, signalled ahead of time a change in the intellectual atmosphere.[5]

A new mood had set in by the last decades of the seventeenth century. There was no sudden or complete change. Much Erasmus literature persisted in the preoccupations of the previous age – the security of his hold on Catholic dogma or the sincerity of his support for Luther. Old controversies burst again into flame with the revocation of the Edict of Nantes. But they lacked staying power, and there was an intermixture of new questions: ever more insistent was the question of toleration and the individual conscience.[6]

2 Erasmus' portrait had a place of honour in his house: its companions included portraits of the Scaligers, Montaigne, de Thou, Rabelais, and Grotius (ibid 312). Patin knew Grotius during his Paris ambassadorship and discussed Erasmus with him.

3 Jean-Claude Margolin 'Guy Patin, lecteur d'Erasme' 326. Margolin's very full study is the basis of this passage.

4 Ibid 331

5 Patin's son, Charles, also a physician and antiquarian, was forced into exile under suspicion of heresy and political opposition. From Basel he published an edition of the *Moriae encomium*, with the title *Moriae encomium stultitiae laus, Des Erasmi Rot. declamatio. Cum commentariis Ger. Listrii, & figuris Jo. Holbenii* (1676). It is prefaced by a life of Erasmus which is a pastiche of Beatus Rhenanus, Melanchthon, Melchior Adam, and the *Compendium*. It was dedicated to the great minister, Colbert, who was said to be the cause of Patin's exile. Patin's description of Erasmus' purpose in the book could accord with Colbert's wish for the husbanding and frugal use of resources: 'ut detecta opinionum morumque perversitate, ad frugalem & meliorem vitam eos instigaret.' See *Bibliotheca Belgica* II 887–90.

6 The classic study is Paul Hazard *La Crise de la conscience européenne 1680–1715*, Eng tr *The European Mind (1680–1715)*. There are warnings

Critical scholarship was winning its victories too – in classical and biblical studies. But the new mood advanced above all through the widening and formalizing of contacts among the learned throughout Europe and among the educated generally. The 'republic of letters' was seen as an established institution. It was especially conspicuous in a new creation, the journal, offering in regular numbers summaries, extracts, or reviews of a large number of books over a range of intellectual interests.

The major journals appeared first between the 1660s and 1700, the *Journal des Sçavans* in Paris in 1665, the Royal Society's *Philosophical Transactions* in London in the same year, *Acta eruditorum* in Leipzig in 1682, Bayle's *Nouvelles de la République des lettres* in Holland in 1684 and Le Clerc's *Bibliothèque universelle et historique* also in Holland two years later.[7] At the end of the century Bayle could mention twenty journals in different countries,[8] though the more tolerant atmosphere of Holland was especially congenial to them. The journals were a natural response to the growth of the reading public and to the consequent proliferation of books – Bayle spoke of a 'fever' of publication.[9] Those who conducted them were intellectually restless, with minds wide-ranging if perhaps at times limited in thrust or penetration; the pervading tone was critical and rationalistic, not necessarily profound, certainly not destructive, but seeking clarity, directness, openness in learning, sacred and profane.[1] Typically the purpose of the *Observationum selectarum ad rem litterarium spectantium* in Halle, to which Christian Thomasius contributed and in which a striking essay on Erasmus appeared in 1701, was 'to refute common errors, destroy widely held myths, defend those falsely accused, expound the lives of illustrious men ...'[2]

In this atmosphere, despite the many vestiges of the past, the reputation of Erasmus was bound to enter on a new stage of its history.

against overstating the sharpness or suddenness of the changes of this period. I refer to the inaugural lecture by John McManners 'Paul Hazard and the "Crisis of the European Conscience."'
7 On the journals, see, eg, Hendrika J. Reesink *L'Angleterre et la littérature anglaise dans les trois plus anciens périodiques français de Hollande de 1684 à 1709*; Elizabeth R. Labrousse 'Les coulisses du journal de Bayle'; Hanns Freydank 'Christian Thomasius der Journalist'; Samuel A. Golden *Jean Le Clerc* 32–3, 41–2.
8 Reesink *L'Angleterre* 67
9 Ibid 102
1 Cf Annie Barnes *Jean Le Clerc (1657–1736) et la République des Lettres* 10–12.
2 Quoted in Freydank 'Christian Thomasius' 363

SIX

France:
Jesuits, Jansenists, Gallicans,
Irenicists

꫞

IN THE AFTERMATH OF THE COUNTER-REFORMATION, in the time of the confessional struggles and the exhaustion and disenchantment which followed, the norm was the hostile Catholic judgment of Erasmus expounded especially by the Jesuits and taken to a point of hysteria by Garasse, as we have seen. This judgment, which is the foil against which to set any fresh interpretations, was savagely enunciated once again on the eve of the period we are now considering by the celebrated French Jesuit Théophile Raynaud (1583 or 1587–1663).

Raynaud himself was a turbulent character with a developed taste for ferocity in literary encounters.[1] Ordained priest in the Society of Jesus in 1613 he spent most of his life in Lyon, with brief and stormy passages in Rome and in Paris, where his refusal to write against a Spanish theologian in support of Richelieu's foreign policy earned him the displeasure of the mighty cardinal. Two of his pieces were placed on the Index, and the work in which he manhandled Erasmus was an exposition of his own views on the censorship of books and was itself placed on the Index until changes were made. Ellies Du Pin, who was later to write about Erasmus in a very different spirit, accused Raynaud of lack of discrimination and said: 'He had an extremely satirical and biting pen and his works are full of bitterness and injuries.'[2] On the other hand, his learning and industry were prodigious, and Guy Patin called him 'un grand maître' in theology.[3] He was a perfect representative of a Catholicism wounded by the Reformation and the religious wars, still lacking in serenity and unable to judge men and events

---

1 On Raynaud, see DTC XIII 2 cols 1823–9; *New Cath Enc* XII 107; Michaud XXXV 267–8; Hoefer XL cols 766–9; Pierre Bayle *Dictionnaire historique et critique* XII 429–43.
2 Quoted in DTC XIII 2 col 1825
3 Ibid col 1824

with equanimity. The bizarre style on which his critics commented frequently accords well, one must assume, with his troubled personality.

The passage on Erasmus in Raynaud's *Erotemata de malis ac bonis libris deque iusta aut iniusta eorundem confixione* (Lyon 1653) comes in the first section, where the most damnable books are treated. Headings account for books heretical, magical, and obscene; Erasmus is included among the atheist authors. There is a list of Erasmus' depredations on Catholic doctrine, at which he gnawed like a mouse ('huiusce muris arrosiones'). Some charges, if they could be proved, would be serious: Arianism, iconoclasm, doubts about the power of God ('De Dei immensitate dubitavit ...') and about the sacrament of penance. Others seem ridiculous: while challenging the power of the pope to canonize saints, Erasmus arrogated such a power to himself by placing Reuchlin among the saints for his skill in languages.[4] Proof is, however, not attempted – this is no more than a culling of charges from earlier writers, a gathering of every possible condemnation.[5]

The accusation in chief is developed at more length, namely the irreverent wit of Erasmus. He belonged, with Rabelais, to the class of scurrilous jesters. As Lucian with perhaps some justification derided the pagan gods, Erasmus turned the most sacred mysteries of the Christian religion to sport and ridicule. His licentious jesting, as Canisius saw, opened a window for Luther, though what he did equivocally Luther, being of another temperament, did boldly and openly. It is astonishing that some have failed to condemn the blasphemous jeering of the Dutch buffoon.[6] This portrait confirms how maiming the confessional struggles were to a sense of humour. Erasmus' playfulness and his truly reverent jesting were impenetrable to a mind like Raynaud's. Does such playfulness, shimmering like light but never fully giving up its secret, belong to times of confidence and expansion, not to times of contraction like the middle years of the seventeenth century? Certainly it reappears in Bayle at the end of the century.

What else, Raynaud concludes, than this intolerable jesting could be expected from one born of an adulterous, nay a sacrilegious, union and apostate from his religious order? Here Raynaud attempts a joke of his own, but it is nasty and poor: Erasmus was not a king's son but he was fathered by a crowned head – a wretched reference to the priestly status

4 *Erotemata* 23–4
5 Cf A. Flitner *Erasmus im Urteil seiner Nachwelt* 89.
6 *Erotemata* 22–3

of Erasmus' father. In his second entry into the world, his departure from the monastery, he became the model for all apostates and atheists.[7]

A still more celebrated and less eccentric work was Lous Maimbourg's history of Lutheranism.[8] It too belonged to the Jesuit tradition, Maimbourg (1610–86) himself being a Jesuit father educated at Rome and teaching in the Jesuit college at Rouen.[9] However, his defence of Gallican positions (revealed in the flattering dedication to Louis xiv who, while paying the Holy See the obedience due under the apostolic constitutions, had also protected the rights and privileges of the Gallican church) forced a break with the order, and a certain lightening in his attitude towards Erasmus at least may have followed from that. He had the fluency, elegance, and taste for the striking formulations, not to mention the topical allusions, of the popular historian.

Luther, Maimbourg says, had the sympathy of the bad churchmen of his time and also of the partisans of *belles lettres* who formed a kind of cabal to back him up in the interests of their own freedom. To the fore was Erasmus, who had a fine mind and fortunate disposition distorted by his upbringing and education. Maimbourg does not call Erasmus an apostate but says that he entered the monastery 'much more by necessity than devotion' and left it again after nine years, 'one doesn't exactly know by what door.'[1] He had a high reputation for capacity of mind, for moderation and decency and a polished style, but one cannot tell from his writings what he believed; he was neither Lutheran nor Catholic, always ready to hold the *pro* and the *contra* out of 'a false love of peace.' In the early days his sympathy and support were of inestimable benefit to Luther.[2]

Yet Luther's pleasure was turned to chagrin when he was attacked by him who 'of all his friends had done him the most useful service at the beginning of his revolt.' Erasmus made his attack on a capital point of Luther's doctrine, his rejection of free will. For Maimbourg Erasmus' 'learned and eloquent treatise' had the best of the argument, and for a time – here Maimbourg follows the account of Cochlaeus – Luther was shaken by it, though before long he published his *De servo arbitrio* which exposed his necessitarian doctrine with complete clarity. So

7 Ibid 25
8 *Histoire du Lutheranisme*
9 Hoefer xxxii cols 891–3
1 A studied ignorance. It was perfectly well known to Erasmus' biographers how he came to leave the monastery.
2 *Histoire* 54–6

SENTIMENS
D'ERASME
DE ROTERDAM,

CONFORMES à CEUX DE
L'EGLISE CATHOLIQUE,

Sur tous les points Controverſez.

DEDIE'ES

AU ROI DE LA GRANDE
BRETAGNE.

L'abbé Jean Richard

*Auris audiens beatificabat me, & oculus videns teſtimonium
reddebat mihi. Eo quod liberaſſem pauperem vociferantem.
& pupillum, cui non eſſet adjutor. Job. 29. 11.*

A C·OLOGNE,
Chez ADRIAN LE JEUNE,
1688.

Title page of Jean Richard
*Sentimens d'Erasme de Roterdam
conformes à ceux de l'Eglise Catholique*
Harvard University Library

Erasmus, for all his ambiguity in religion, played a part in the earliest controversies of the Reformation.[3]

Maimbourg's book makes a serviceable landmark, and from it one may follow two distinct trails. In itself it was lightweight, as later generations recognized – Voltaire said that Maimbourg was too much praised in his lifetime and too much neglected later[4] – but the massive reply by Seckendorf from the Lutheran side leads the discussion naturally into the historiography of Lutheran orthodoxy and pietism.[5] The other trail runs through the Erasmus debate in French Catholicism; the Jesuit tradition remains in full vigour but refinements, qualifications, challenges come from writers associated with Jansenist, Gallican, or irenicist positions.

Maimbourg struck a couple of glancing blows at the Jansenists, towards whom, as was well known, he had great hostility: in the dedication, where Louis XIV was praised, not only for turning back heresy but also for checking the new kind of Calvinism which had arisen in the Gallican church, and in his long digression on the free-will question, where he condemns the misuse by heretics of Augustine, the favourite of the Jansenists.

As it happens, the work which first indicated a new wave of interest in Erasmus was by a Jansenist – Jean Richard's *Sentimens d'Erasme de Roterdam, conformes à ceux de l'Eglise Catholique, sur tous les points de controversez* (Cologne 1688). Richard was born in Paris in December 1615 and did his theology at the Sorbonne.[6] When parish priest of Triel near Pontoise in the 1660s he refused to sign the anti-Jansenist formulary of Alexander VII and suffered harassment aggravated by ill health. He reflected on a Christian's life of persecution: Paul's example was instructive to those 'unjustly persecuted,' truth demanding of its professors not only patience and mildness but also a courage which was God's gift.[7] In 1663 he was arrested and imprisoned by the archbishop of Rouen, de Harlay, a bitter opponent of Jansenism who had presided at the Assembly of the Clergy at Pontoise in 1660 when the enforcement of the formulary was decided on; according to a Jansenist chronicler, Richard, 'one of the wisest and most charitable pastors in the whole district of Rouen,' was carried off like a criminal – his parishion-

3 Ibid 104–8
4 Hoefer XXXII col 892
5 See next chapter.
6 Christian G. Jöcher ed *Allgemeines Gelehrten-Lexicon* col 2078
7 Letter of 29 October 1662, in A. Gazier ed *Mémoires de Godefroi Hermant sur l'histoire ecclésiastique du XVIIe siècle (1630–1663)* v 610–12

ers indeed resisted, but Richard calmed them, for he 'knew that the church has no other arms than those of sweetness, obedience, and justice.'[8] During this personal crisis he published two works in defence of his Jansenist belief and behaviour. As we shall see, there are grounds for believing that his *Sentimens d'Erasme* was meant, in part at least, to achieve the same end. Nevertheless mysteries surround the work: it was published posthumously (Richard died in 1686, having been prior of Beaulieu Saint-Avoie since 1673); what we have is the first part, and we may only guess at how seriously the promise of a second part was intended. As it stands this is an ill-organized book, repetitive, with many digressions, but filled with a naive enthusiasm and fascinating partly because of the evidences of a sound judgment about Erasmus, partly because of the tantalizing but insoluble problem of the author's aims.

The avowed aim was proselytism. The book is dedicated – on the eve of the Revolution of 1688 – to James II of England, a new Theodosius, who is hazarding three kingdoms for the sake of the kingdom of heaven. May it help the English people to follow the king's example (in conversion to Catholicism) by showing them the true character of Erasmus' religion:

> He lived in a century and in a country where the pope's name was in aversion and his authority disdained; nevertheless he roundly declared – and on every occasion – that nothing would ever separate him from the respect which he owed to the Church of Rome and that he would be the enemy of the enemies of the primacy of the pope. And because excess is always blameworthy when it comes to declaring one's views on religion, as Erasmus opposed all those who assailed the primacy of the pope, so he resisted those who flattered him and gave him a temporal authority over kings which he has not received from Jesus Christ.[9]

Thus for a Jansenist, facing by the 1680s the hostility of both pope and king, a nice balance is struck.[1] In his preface Richard turns from the Channel to the Rhine and speaks of German Protestants held back from looking more closely into Catholicism by their belief that Erasmus – the most learned man of the Reformation period – was in effect a Lutheran. That Erasmus had such credit with Richard's Protestant

---

8 Ibid VI 560–1. Cf DTC VIII 1 cols 504–11.
9 *Sentimens d'Erasme* *6ʳ
1 This dedication has been described as 'guileful' (Margaret Mann Phillips 'Erasmus and Propaganda: A Study of the Translations of Erasmus in England and France' 8)

contemporaries was sceptically received in the Protestant journals. John Locke ingeniously turned Richard's own sympathies against him: how can the Protestants be persuaded to return to the church when – on Richard's own showing – laxists and casuists are still master there and her most faithful servants (the Jansenists) are persecuted and excluded from office and influence, that is, when the church has taken so little to heart the criticisms of Erasmus, whose faithfulness is offered for emulation?[2] Yet there is no reason for doubting the sincerity of Richard's proselytizing purpose; at the end he naively has Erasmus in heaven praying for those gone astray because they have misunderstood his attachment to the Church![3] To this extent his work may be related to the attempts at church reunion in the later seventeenth century;[4] here too is a link between Richard and the Erasmus sympathizers of the next generation, the Du Pins and Le Courayers.

The Jansenist reference of the book is more sure. Notice, for example, the clear statement of Jansenist preferences where Richard touches on Erasmus' editing of St Augustine, the avowed master of the Jansenists, and his criticism of Aristotle, the philosopher of the scholastics and their Jesuit successors. The Jansenists contrasted the costly grace of their teaching with the human philosophy and relaxed morality with which they charged the Jesuits. So, according to Richard, Erasmus deserves praise 'for giving the church invincible arms against all heretics, who corrupt the faith by human reasonings, and against casuists who change the purity of her morality out of favour or complaisance towards the wickedness of sinners.' Augustine's works printed under Erasmus' care at Basel will be a stronghold of faith until the end of the world. As for Aristotle, there is no philosophy more contrary to the religion of Christ than his.[5] Clearly Richard sees Augustinianism as a bond between Erasmus' struggle and his own.[6]

2   Review of Richard in *Bibliothèque universelle et historique*. See below, 250. Cf *Acta eruditorum* 267–70; W.E. Tentzel in *Monatliche Unterredungen einiger guten Freunde von allerhand Büchern und andern annemlichen Geschichten* 780.
3   *Sentimens d'Erasme* 412
4   Cf André Stegmann 'La réhabilitation de l'orthodoxie chez Erasme par Jean Richard (1688)' 867.
5   *Sentimens d'Erasme* 64–70. A more precise Jansenist reference is to the strict enforcement of the unjust condemnation of certain propositions attributed (in the Jansenist view falsely) to the Jansenists (the five propositions) and the lenient treatment by contrast accorded non-Jansenist, probably Jesuit, works containing condemned propositions (the sixty-five propositions condemned by Innocent XI, 1679) (321–2).
6   Ibid 104. Cf Stegmann 'La réhabilitation' 872.

The main theme of the book which we have (the first part deals with Erasmus himself; the missing second part was to expound his teachings systematically) is the undeserved calumny suffered by Erasmus, to which a parallel is constantly made with the persecution of the Jansenists during the reign of Louis XIV. His enemies in the old church smeared the reputation of Erasmus, they wanted to make a heretic of him and push him outside the circle of salvation; his adherence to Luther would have given them the pleasure of undoing him completely.[7] One catches echoes more than once of Richard's sad letter of 1662 under his own persecution: Erasmus' experience conformed to the teaching of the gospels; he was slandered and persecuted because he spoke the truth; false teachers by contrast were flattered and honoured; it is ever so. Erasmus' persecutors were hypocritical, self-regarding, deceitful, implacable; so are the enemies of the Jansenists. The tactics of these 'faux devots' in every generation is to cover their own failings (in Richard's time, their casuistical corruption of Christian morality, their lack of devotion to the sacrament) by accusing of heresy those who are truly devoted to the faith of scripture, the Councils, and the Fathers. How can hearts so implacable against a Christian brother receive the Eucharist? These people are set stubbornly in the spiritual sins of pride, envy, malice.[8]

A root of the evil is in the *esprit de corps* of the religious orders, of the mendicants of Erasmus' time, who browbeat popes and bishops and kings and formed a conspiracy against him, and of the Jesuits of Richard's time, who hound those seeking to restore Christian morality and true devotion to the sacrament. It is for bishops and kings to take notice.[9]

It would not then be too strong to call Richard's book on Erasmus a weapon of war against the enemies of the Jansenists.[1] The title-page quotation from a letter of Cyprian applies to both Erasmians and Jansenists: 'This is always the devil's work, to destroy with lies the servants of God and defame their glorious name with false opinions.' Erasmus, not his diabolical enemies, was the true upholder of the church; such is the case also with the Jansenists. At the same time we may find in this book much sound appreciation of Erasmus' ideas, based on a study of the correspondence and works of piety. The case for his undeviating orthodoxy is of course overstated, partly out of anxiety

7 *Sentimens d'Erasme* 59
8 Ibid 81, 158, 194–8
9 Ibid 150–2
1 Contrary to the view of Stegmann ('La réhabilitation' 867)

to protect the Jansenist claim to orthodoxy: he had a perfect submission to the church, as the Jansenists claimed to have; he had a sincere faith in the sacrament of the altar to which the Jansenists were especially devoted – indeed, since the high scholastics no Catholic doctor had spoken 'as distinctly, as learnedly, as divinely, as soundly of the mysteries of our altars.'[2] Erasmus' criticism of an essentially external religion, his treasuring of the Christian lay life, his distinction between doctrines and abuses, his acceptance of the monastic state but criticism of monastic disorders, his skilful reminding of rulers of their Christian responsibilities, his teaching on peace – all these points made only in passing in this volume could have formed a persuasive picture (by the standards of that time) in the second part which never appeared. In this part Richard could fairly claim to have destroyed the alternative picture of Erasmus as libertine and free thinker.[3]

The historical arguments of the book are interesting if not completely compelling. Erasmus' position in the German Reformation was critical. He recognized the evils from which the church suffered and condemned them candidly. This was a service to the church. It also drew correctly the battle-lines against Luther, who had to be opposed not for his criticisms of corruptions in the church but for his false doctrines. Not to make this distinction or to excuse or hide the corrupt state of the church would be to arouse suspicion that the doctrine itself was corrupt. So it worked out to the ruin of the church's position in Germany. Erasmus was left under attack by both sides, by Luther for his faithfulness to Catholic doctrine, by the fanatical monks for his honesty in criticism and urging of reforms.[4] Yet the church saved something from the German wreck, and that was essentially Erasmus' doing. All Germany recognized in him the first scholar of the age and a man of irreproachable life; his defection would have brought on a rout. Luther's temperament was imperious, violent, and immoderate, Erasmus' by contrast sweet, modest, and honourable. Erasmus' support of Luther would have made his cause more attractive; Erasmus would have been 'le plus consideré de tous les Lutheriens.' But he was not seduced; he was held by the fear of God and love of his church.[5] In turn he helped to hold many. Indeed the church would have held more ground and averted the loss of millions of souls if Erasmus' advice had

2 *Sentimens d'Erasme* 410
3 Ibid 411
4 Ibid 360–5
5 Ibid 210–22

Bossuet
Painted by Hyacinthe Rigaud, November 1701
The stance and setting express the grandeurs of the age
and the expression perhaps the strains of 'that tormented end of century'
Musée du Louvre, Paris. Cliché des Musées Nationaux

been followed.[6] Instead, the issues were debated at large by ignorant and turbulent friars who made more Lutherans the more they preached. Small sparks were thus blown into a great conflagration, and obvious measures like meeting the request of the German princes for church reform were not taken. 'Never was heresy easier to cure; never did heresy become more incurable. Never was heresy more combatted by fire and steel; never did heresy spread more widely.'[7] So Erasmus is presented as the apostle, if not of a 'third church,' then at least of an alternative Reformation, Catholic and moderate.

With Richard as point of departure one may trace out the wide circle of French interpretations in the last critical decades of Louis xiv's reign, a time of fierce and debilitating conflicts within and around the French church and of the first warnings of a new and corrosive scepticism. The great Bossuet, eloquent and embattled defender of throne and altar, used Erasmus' correspondence as a source in his *Histoire des variations des églises protestantes* and included an account of Erasmus which, though brief, was more subtle and serene than has sometimes been realized.[8] It would be unlikely for Bossuet to owe anything to Richard; this would anyhow be impossible for the two books were published in the same year (1688). But they have an affinity; both are concerned with the witness of Erasmus in face of the Protestants. Bossuet calls it a strong witness. Erasmus did not leave the communion of the church but in the Reformation controversies he kept a distinctive stance 'which made the Protestants grant him credence in facts of which he was a witness.'[9] At first he favoured Luther but without any wish to leave the church. When schism appeared he at once separated himself from Luther and wrote against him, but still with moderation.[1] Later he exposed the unhappy moral consequences of Luther's Reformation, not to flatter the Catholics, whose own failings he had criticized freely enough, but from a need to distinguish between the neglect of good works out of frailty and a dogmatic rejection of them.[2] In this account of Erasmus one may glimpse both Bossuet, defender of the faith, and Bossuet, irenicist.

6 Ibid 121–4
7 Ibid 284
8 A. Rébelliau in his *Bossuet, historien du Protestantisme* seems to me to overstate Bossuet's critical judgment of Erasmus as a supporter of Luther (195–203).
9 *Histoire des variations des églises protestantes* 26
1 Ibid 31
2 Ibid 84

For indeed, at that tormented end of century, one of the abortive strivings was for a reunion of the churches, and Bossuet himself had a hand there. That Erasmus entered into these strivings was not surprising. There had been a prologue many years before. In 1656 Nicholas Mercier had published in Paris an expurgated edition of the *Colloquia*.[3] It represented a kind of return by Erasmus to the University of Paris, where he had been a mature undergraduate and where later he had been roughly handled by his conservative scholastic critics. Then according to Mercier he had been forgotten, to be revived first in the classroom of Pierre Le Venier, a teacher of grammar who expounded his *De copia*. Mercier, vice-principal of the College of Navarre, dedicated his work to Le Venier. He was making the *Colloquia* available to the youth of the university and similar academies after a prudent expurgation in the spirit of the Council of Trent and with the advice of doctors of the Sorbonne, so ensuring that no snake would lurk still in this grass.[4] The work would benefit not only the style and expression but also the piety of the young men – in one colloquy they would find a summing-up of the orthodox faith, in another many things conducive to true and genuine piety.[5] The university may here be seen claiming Erasmus as one of the more illustrious writers of France, as zealous French humanists had done in his own lifetime.[6] In the biography attached to this edition Mercier gives an account of Erasmus' life, appearance, and disposition following familiar sources – the correspondence, especially the letters to Grunnius and Servatius, the lives of Beatus Rhenanus and Melchior Adam (he used Guy Patin's remarkable library).

Erasmus – so Mercier – may have been too free in those expressions which earned the censure of the theologians of Paris but, whatever several may have said, he was not a heretic, having no bad intention and recognizing in himself the possibility of error. From this summary solution to the problem which preoccupied most Catholic writers, Mercier passes to the matter which – surprisingly early, at the time of the Fronde and the English Commonwealth and with the Peace of Westphalia less than ten years old – makes his treatment distinctive: ' ... as he wished to see nothing so much as a perfect union and concord

---

3 *Desiderii Erasmi Roterodami colloquia familiaria* ... I have used the 3rd ed of 1661.
4 Ibid, Dedication iii–v
5 Ibid, Preface to Reader, n.p.
6 ' ... quem inter illustres nostros scriptores possumus non temerè recensere' (ibid 32–3).

between the Catholics and the heretics, he believed that it would not be pointless to make them some concession, especially in matters not touching the mysteries of our religion or conflicting with articles of faith.[7] There follows a compendium of such matters which owes something to Erasmus' own list in his *Liber de sarcienda ecclesiae concordia* (1533): the invocation of the saints, holy relics, prayers for the dead, proliferation of masses. At the end Mercier leaves things in delicate balance: Erasmus advised making 'human constitutions,' to whose presence in the church the heretics staunchly objected, a matter of counsel rather than of obligation; Erasmus always submitted his judgments to the authority of the church.[8]

Another luminary of the Sorbonne (doctor, 1684) and a more avowed irenicist, Louis Ellies Du Pin (1657–1719), was born the year after Mercier's edition first appeared. His irenic endeavours belonged to a new and more likely time, the early years of the eighteenth century, when the revocation of the Edict of Nantes had exposed the bankruptcy of traditional principles of uniformity, and Christians in all camps were becoming aware of differences of opinion – between belief and unbelief, for example – more serious than the old confessional ones. Du Pin had other associations: he was strongly Gallican and anti-Roman; he criticized the Jesuits and defended the Jansenists – in the end he was one of the signatories of the famous apology for Jansenism, *Histoire du cas de conscience signé par quarante docteurs de Sorbonne ...* (Nancy 1705). Despite his willingness to submit after the work had been condemned at Rome, he had won the displeasure of both the papal nuncio and Louis XIV and lost his chair of philosophy at the Collège royale.[9] He may certainly be called 'théologien aventureux,' though 'moderniste avant la lettre' raises more delicate problems.[1] Looking towards a union of the Gallican and Anglican churches, he entered into a long correspondence with William Wake, archbishop of Canterbury, who at his death called him 'the principal man for learning, and probity in the Gallican church.'[2]

Du Pin's scholarly labours were prodigious, and the scale of his work must to an extent excuse the weaknesses in accuracy and organization

7   Ibid 40–1
8   Ibid 46–7
9   DBF XII cols 366–9; DTC XII 2 cols 2111–15; Charles Jourdain *Histoire de l'Université de Paris, au xviie et au xviiie siècle* II 70–1
1   DBF XII col 367; E. Préclin and E. Jarry *Les Luttes politiques et doctrinales aux xviie et xviiie siècles* 675
2   Quoted in Norman Sykes *William Wake Archbishop of Canterbury* I 295

of which he was frequently accused. His *Nouvelle Bibliothèque des auteurs ecclésiastiques*, which began to appear in 1686, ran finally to forty-seven volumes. The first volumes raised trouble – they were criticized by Bossuet and both condemned by the archbishop of Paris and placed on the Index. Du Pin submitted and went on his way; between 1701 and 1703 appeared the *Histoire de l'église et des auteurs ecclésiastiques du XVIᵉ siècle*, which included a long essay on Erasmus.[3]

Du Pin's was a moderate Catholic judgment of Erasmus coloured here there by some personal predilections. His objective was to demonstrate the Catholic acceptabiilty of Erasmus. Certain tell-tale features distinguished the sympathetic from the unsympathetic Catholic biography: Erasmus left the monastery not as a renegade but with the consent of his bishop and superiors; he had the pope's approval for his work on the New Testament and the favour of the popes generally; his death was serene, and no issue need be made of his dying in a Protestant town. He was a great enemy of Luther and the sacramentarians.[4] Indeed, in the preliminary historical section of his work Du Pin takes over Richard's arguments: Erasmus' reputation was so great that, if he had declared for Luther, he would have carried most of Germany with him; at first, when Luther's doctrine was unclear to him, he kept a wise reserve; later he held firm in the faith and condemned both Luther's doctrine and his passion. His writing against him won many in Germany away from Luther because of the respect in which Erasmus was held there.[5] On the other hand, Erasmus was no friend to Luther's enemies, the ignorant or half-learned monks and theologians. This was consistent with his earlier achievement: not only was the rebirth of good letters due chiefly to him; he was also among the first (in the eighteenth-century language of the translation) to treat theology 'in a genteel way, disengaged from the Sophistry and Chicanery of the Schools.'[6] In all this, one might note, there was a certain saving of the position of the Sorbonne: Erasmus was grieved that he had so many enemies at the Sorbonne because of his esteem for that body and for the French nation as a whole; he would do all he could to meet its censures; in any case, the Spanish monks were 'more virulent, and more unrea-

3 Eng tr *A New Ecclesiastical History of the Sixteenth Century: Containing an Impartial Account of the Reformation of Religion, and other ecclesiastical affairs* ... 263–51. I have used this translation.
4 Ibid 264, 266, 269
5 Ibid 45, 101
6 Ibid 269

sonable' in their handling of Erasmus than the Paris theologians.[7] He may sometimes have spoken too freely and replied to his enemies too tartly, but generally – in life as in doctrine – he was sound, without ambition, devoted to study, sober, constant, and sincere.

Long summaries of Erasmus' letters and works make up the bulk of this essay. From the summaries of the letters a characteristic picture emerges: Erasmus' positive services to the church in his works of erudition and his call to true piety; his defence of the beliefs and practices of the church, divorced from all superstition and triviality; the folly and injustice of his opponents within the church but the respect in which he was held by the popes; his condemnation of Luther's lack of restraint; his search nevertheless for a moderate solution to the deepening crisis. But what distinguishes Du Pin's essay most is its feeling and understanding for Erasmus' works of piety; works hardly noticed by previous writers (including the *Ratio, Paraclesis*, and *Ecclesiastes*) are given faithful summary. In the *Enchiridion* he found, despite the lack of unction felt by both Loyola and St Cyran, 'very wholesome Instructions which for the most part are taken out of Holy Scriptures,' in the *De immensa Dei misericordia* 'Reflections and Exhortations full of Life and Solidity.' Erasmus' treatise on the creed was 'not like the greatest part of Catechisms, which are barren of useful Thoughts; but tho' it be plain, yet it is Learned, Instructive, full of Knowledge and elegantly written.'[8]

Du Pin refers to Erasmus' efforts for reconciliation. He sought a settlement though he mistrusted meetings which would not 'allow him to speak his Thoughts with that Freedom he desired to do.' The whole portrait is informed with Du Pin's own irenic spirit; in a letter to Wake he appealed to his writings to show 'that in religious matters I speak and write with as much fairness and moderation as I can.'[9] His English translator recognized this but slyly turned it to his own advantage: 'Such an Account from a Doctor of the Sorbonne, (in a Country where the Protestant Religion has been lately rooted out) as we ought to bless God for, and of which admirable Use may be made.'[1] Du Pin's work lacked art; a close scrutiny would certainly reveal carelessness as to facts; he made no attempt to resolve chronological confusions in Erasmus' letters or works; but the spirit is heartening and attractive. Pierre-François Le Courayer, a later and more spectacular irenicist who

7 Ibid 334–44
8 Ibid 312, 321, 328
9 Ibid 267; Sykes *William Wake* I 258
1 *New Ecclesiastical History* translator's 'Advertisement'

is also to appear in this story, wrote of another work of Du Pin's words which might well be applied to this: 'It is always the same rapidity in composition, the same lightness in style, the same moderation in views, the same discerning judgments, the same precipitateness in researches, the same inexactness in the facts – it is always M. Du Pin.'[2]

Du Pin's massive if unpolished publications were representative of the age of polymathic scholarship. In some other writers of the time there were signs of a scholarship more specialist and more professional; the beginnings of modern biblical criticism have been traced to this period. Erasmus, editor of the New Testament, was bound to call for the attention of workers in that field. The erudite and versatile P.-D. Huet (1630–1721), whose scholarly zeal when bishop of Avranches led his flock – so it was said – to declare that the king should send them a bishop who had completed his studies, and who at the end came paradoxically to a philosophic doubt about all human knowledge, devoted his first book to problems of biblical translation, *De interpretatione libri duo; quorum prior est, de optimo genere interpretandi: alter, de claris interpretibus* (1661).[3] It was directed against those who offered mere paraphrase instead of exact translation and especially those who were too free with the sacred books.[4] Erasmus was presented as the chief ('princeps') of those who had devoted themselves only to the interpretation of the New Testament – his work revealed his perspicacity, his sense of fitness, the integrity of his faith.[5] He was 'truly the Phoenix of his age.' Who could compare with him in learning, in memory, in style, above all in the capacities required in the translator or interpreter? 'He examines meanings acutely and explains them clearly; everything is genuine and sound, dry but without aridity, well defined but without thinness, open but without extravagance ...'[6]

The judgment on Erasmus by Richard Simon, the great progenitor of modern criticism (1638–1712), is more problematical. The explana-

2 *L'Europe sçavante* VII 35, quoted in Jean Pierre Nicéron *Mémoires pour servir à l'histoire des hommes illustres dans la république des lettres* 47–8
3 Hoefer XXV cols 380–90. Cf DTC VII 1 cols 199–201; RE 3, VIII 427–9.
4 Léon Tolmer *Pierre-Daniel Huet (1630–1721), Humaniste-physicien*, 220
5 *De interpretatione* 118
6 Ibid 173–4. In his *Origeniana* (1180, 1274–5) Huet praises Erasmus' services to Origen studies while criticizing his too precipitate judgment at some places. On one question of authorship Huet is much more severe: Erasmus is accused of gross temerity in mixing up the writings of the Fathers with his own vain conjectures, so endangering posterity's understanding of the early church.

tion lies partly in Simon's cast of mind, his temperament, and his personal situation. Despite a marked conservative strain which is quite apparent in his writing on Erasmus, Simon's critical method, fully deployed for the first time in his *Histoire critique du Vieux Testament* (1678), was a challenge to received positions well capable of inducing anxiety, if not panic.[7] This book and its successors were attacked from various sides; in return Simon displayed a certain even-handed astringency. His controversial style was mordant. He quarrelled with his own order, the Oratory, with the Jansenists, the Jesuits, the Benedictines, the Sorbonne, the Protestants. Although he criticized Erasmus for needlessly mixing theological controversies with scholarly work, he did much the same by criticisms of Augustine which offended the strong Augustinianism of the Oratory and Bossuet, not to mention the Jansenists. In the end he was isolated and fearful of ever more severe persecution, yet he pursued his way, cleaving his own furrow with a courage and dedication reminiscent of Erasmus himself. Strangely, he gives no sign of fellow-feeling for Erasmus, also savagely attacked from many sides. There is perhaps a coldness, a reserve in Simon that forbids any such betrayal of feeling. In Simon's religious position, too, there seems much of Erasmus: here is a loyal Catholicism which yet finds no inconsistency in the application of a sound method to the explanation of the sacred texts, a preference for the original pattern in the life and piety of the church over later elaborations. Once again there is no warmth of recognition in Simon's judgment of any of this in Erasmus. He is strictly the scholar putting to the test an often wayward predecessor.

Simon discusses Erasmus in many places but principally in his *Histoire critique des principaux commentateurs du Nouveau Testament depuis le commencement du Christianisme jusques à notre tems* (1693), a work on a larger scale than any that he had published before. He also offered a critique of Du Pin's too unqualified praise of Erasmus as part of an assessment of Du Pin's whole work which was published long after the deaths of both writers and opened with the characteristic declaration 'However great Du Pin's capacities may be, he often falls into gross errors which ought to be removed; he could have corrected them himself if he had wished to take the trouble, but he seems to have

---

7 On Simon, DTC XIV 2 cols 2094–118; Jean Steinmann *Richard Simon et les origines de l'exégèse biblique*; Henri Margival *Essai sur Richard Simon et la critique biblique au XVIIᵉ siècle*; Paul Hazard *La Crise de la conscience européenne 1680–1715*

had no other aim than to multiply the number of his books without troubling himself to be exact.'[8]

Erasmus, says Simon, was one of the great critics of his time; he brought much enlightenment ('il a fourni de grandes lumieres') to those who worked after him, and his researches cannot be too highly praised. Yet at once, for he can leave no praise unqualified, Simon adds that Erasmus read the Fathers too precipitately, did not reflect long enough, and had too many works going forward at the one time.[9] In the meeting between Erasmus and Simon there is something of a confrontation between the scholar and the publicist. Erasmus turned his critical notes into commentaries and ranged far and wide, assailing monks and scholastic theologians – so he played the part of a declaimer rather than a critic in the strict sense. A monk of good sense could have complained that Erasmus carried the spirit of his *Colloquia* over into his notes on the New Testament. A critic should stick to his last.[1] On one argument of Erasmus' Simon says: 'He would have done much better to stick to grammar and the literal sense of his text rather than to argue so pitifully.'[2] There is an unmistakable echo here of a contention dear to hostile Catholic writers: Erasmus should have kept to literature and not strayed into theology. And, going back to the aphorism of Erasmus' relentless enemy, J.C. Scaliger, which Simon actually uses, he would have been greater if he had wished to be less.[3] One is perhaps reminded that amid all the conflict and disturbance of his career Simon had an association with and even a friendship for the Jesuits.[4]

Simon does not doubt the essential orthodoxy of Erasmus. Du Pin went too far in taking Richard as his guide, but Erasmus' writings demonstrate his inviolable attachment to the Roman church, and the Protestants bore witness that they had no greater adversary than he. Yet he was too free in his handling of sacred things, too inclined to raillery and satire, too enamoured of 'fausses plaisanteries.'[5] Here a difference of temperament again appears: Simon's sense of humour is a

8 *Critique de la bibliotèque des auteurs ecclesiastiques* ... iv. Other works of Simon's to be referred to are *Histoire critique des versions du Nouveau Testament* ... (Eng tr *The Critical History of the Versions of the New Testament*) and *Nouvelles Observations sur le texte et les versions du Nouveau Testament*.
9 *Commentateurs* 516
1 Ibid 504–5
2 Ibid 510
3 *Critique* 581–2
4 DTC XIV 2 col 2112
5 *Critique* 579–80

thin gruel compared with the more robust draughts of which Erasmus was capable. Erasmus was orthodox. Nevertheless, Simon does not forbear to reopen the charge of Arianism arising from expressions in the notes on the New Testament but he gives it a new and more sophisticated twist: Erasmus treated the charge lightly because he believed Arianism a defunct heresy; he did not foresee its revival in his own time, the new Arians using his more incautious notes to their advantage.[6]

Erasmus was also too free in his critical work itself. The strain of conservatism in Simon may be traced here. A reasoned and not merely an authoritarian defence of the Sorbonne's treatment of Erasmus is offered, perhaps for the first time. Erasmus should have been more respectful of the scholastic traditions: 'He did not sufficiently consider that, when once theology was reduced to a skill [un fois réduite en art], it became necessary to submit oneself to certain received rules.' He believed it enough to quote some ancient Father who had spoken pretty much as he did, but that way of arguing was inconclusive because the Fathers did not always speak with the one voice. 'Thus Erasmus was to be reprehended whenever he opposed in an opinionated way the teaching received in the theological schools in his time.'[7] Similarly he did not need to go as far as he did in altering the language of the Vulgate; indeed, he would have done enough if he had supplied some notes to the Vulgate and not made a completely new Latin version. In the strictly scholarly sphere he relied too much on imperfect Greek manuscripts, and his own command of Greek was not absolutely sure.[8] The Vulgate deserved more respect – so, by an interesting analogy, did Cicero: Erasmus was justified in his attack on the Ciceronian 'malady' but he spoke of Cicero with too much freedom.[9] In sum, the Sorbonne had a case against Erasmus: his favour for vernacular versions was injudicious in a time when these were a menace to both church and state, and the Sorbonne wisely condemned him on this matter.[1] Wherever the issues were theological Erasmus made a poor showing; if he had stayed with points of grammar he would have held a tactical advantage, for the doctors of the Sorbonne urged some ill-founded

---

6 Ibid 607; *Commentateurs* 513. For a contemporary Unitarian claim to Erasmus (and Grotius), see [John Biddle] *A Brief History of the Unitarians, Called also Socinians: In Four Letters to a Friend* 31.
7 *Critique* 590–1; *Commentateurs* 535
8 *Critical History of the Versions* 180–7
9 *Lettres choisies de M. Simon* 133, 136
1 *Nouvelles Observations* 486

grammatical points and absurdly made a heresy out of Erasmus' reference to the Greek.[2]

To us Simon often seems reserved and conservative; to Bossuet he was dangerous and destructive through and through – that is an indication of how tightly the ancient ground in theology and biblical scholarship was being contested. Bossuet's last great work, *Défense de la tradition et des Saints Peres*, written in the last years of his life but published only posthumously (Paris 1763), was a massive attempt at the demolition of Simon. Erasmus receives his mention there. Indeed, Simon's very defence of scholastic method against Erasmus is turned against him: to speak of theology reduced to a method is to demean it, as though there were here a decline from an original purity and simplicity; theology is not an 'art' but the most sublime of sciences. Particularly venomous is Simon's insinuation that nothing certain can be drawn from the Fathers because of their disagreements among themselves. The outcome of that would be the destruction of theology: 'Tout sera réduit à la critique.'[3]

More fundamental was the great issue of Augustinianism. In the controversy about grace which dominated French Catholic theology in the seventeenth century, Simon was Molinist and anti-Augustinian. He preferred the Greek Fathers to Augustine and indeed declared that Augustine imperfectly understood elements in the earlier Christian tradition.[4] By contrast Bossuet saw Augustine as the very foundation of the Christian tradition; his *Défense* was 'a very complete exposition of Augustinian and thomist theology' on sin, grace, and predestination.[5] Simon could with an easy conscience exculpate Erasmus from the charge of Pelagianism.[6] Further, he shared Erasmus' stated preference for St Jerome over St Augustine. Before the revival of letters and criticism (in the Renaissance), the works of Augustine alone were in the hands of theologians; he is still 'their oracle' because few of them read any language other than Latin. Most also follow St Thomas without taking care that he lived in 'un siecle barbare.'[7] On all this, Bossuet penned this stern sentence:

In truth no one can help laughing who sees an Erasmus and a

2 *Commentateurs* 520–1
3 *Défense* I 220
4 DTC XIV 2 col 2111; Steinmann *Richard Simon* 281, 285–6; Margival *Richard Simon* 297–303
5 Steinmann *Richard Simon* 402
6 *Commentateurs* 513
7 Ibid 531

Simon, on the strength of some superiority that they have in *belles lettres* and knowledge of languages, taking it upon themselves to pronounce between St Jerome and St Augustine and to adjudicate which of the two deserve the prize for solid knowledge of sacred things.[8]

Thus two centuries later Erasmus is drawn again into controversies familiar in his own time, indeed central to the whole history of the Christian West, but whose resonance and urgency have subtly changed, whose context is quite different. Thus is he used and ill-used.

Jansenism, Gallicanism, irenicism, biblical criticism, all the various and conflicting concerns of the religious life of seventeenth-century France affected contemporaries' judgments of Erasmus. Another influence seems more surprising – the Fronde.

Claude Joly (1607–1700) came from a legal family; his mother's father was a celebrated advocate and legal writer, and he himself studied the law.[9] Then he turned to the church and was ordained, becoming in 1631 a canon of the cathedral of Paris. Yet he did not altogether abandon public life; in 1646 he accompanied the party of the Duc de Longueville to the protracted negotiations at Münster that were to end the Thirty Years War. More than one experience of that journey aroused his interest in Erasmus, as we shall see. It was natural that Joly should side with the *Parlements* in their challenge to Mazarin: 'Come from old *parlementaire* families, *frondeur* in temperament, royalist but given also to making remonstrances, he was the very opposite of a courtier.'[1] He wrote a book in defence of the Fronde which was condemned to be burned.[2] He has been described as 'the great theorist of the Fronde,' but his writing in fact reveals the hesitations and confusions of that movement.[3] He insisted on his loyalty – 'ny factieux, ny Republiquain' – and on that of his family, which had opposed the Catholic League during the religious wars and rallied to Henry IV.[4] At the same time he argued for a limited monarchy based on the franchises of the past; he believed that that view of the French monarchy could be validated from the constitutional writers of the Middle

8 *Défense* 222
9 Hoefer xxvi cols 856–8; Michaud xxi 118–19; Jean Brissaud *Un Libéral au xvii*^e *siècle, Claude Joly (1607–1700)*
1 Brissaud *Claude Joly* 10
2 *Recueil de maximes veritables et importantes pour l'institution du roy* ...
3 Cf Paul Doolin *The Fronde* 121–34 and Ernst H. Kossmann *La Fronde* 11.
4 *Recueil* preface

Ages and Renaissance. The Erasmian spirit still breathes in Joly's book. The conflict between Mazarin and his opponents is seen as a conflict over the education of the young king, Louis XIV. Mazarin is presented as a teacher of false maxims from which great evils will arise in the monarchy. Joly's book is an alternative instruction for the king, and the Erasmian tone is revealed in a sentence like this: 'It is a very great error, which Kings ought to be warned against, to believe that politics and Christian piety are incompatible, and that it is impossible to reconcile the laws of the State with those of the Gospel.'[5] But the strong patriotic strain in Joly's work, his Gallicanism, his reliance on legal and historical arguments do not carry the mark of Erasmus.

Later, Joly republished a sixteenth-century French abridgement of Erasmus' *Institutio principis christiani*.[6] France, he says in his introduction, is distinguished among kingdoms less by arms than by faith and justice; between king and people there is mutual affection; yet all kings need instruction when young. A long line of writers has given such instruction but none is to be preferred to Erasmus, who knew how to advise and make remonstrance with mildness ('douceur') and respect but also with liberty.

Meantime in these years of political writing Joly had also become interested in the biography of Erasmus. His journey to Münster took him to Rotterdam, where he saw in the market Hendrik de Keyzer's statue of Erasmus, 'this famous person of whom so much good and ill has been spoken,' and in a neighbouring street the house where he was born. The fame of Erasmus made these two spots, 'though small, the most considerable of the town.'[7] In Münster itself, Joly was much in the company of the dean of the cathedral, Bernard von Malinckrodt (1591–1664), among whose considerable literary labours, supported by a remarkable library of over five thousand volumes, was a projected life of Erasmus; there, Malinckrodt said, every safeguard taken of faith and morals, he would work to show that Erasmus could with a good conscience be esteemed by Catholics.[8] This predecessor of Richard's

5 Quoted in Doolin *The Fronde* 122; *Recueil* 63
6 *Codicille d'or, ou petit recueil tiré de l'Institution du prince chrestien composée par Erasme*
7 *Voyage fait à Munster en Westphalie et autres lieux voisins, en 1646 & 1647* 143–6
8 Quoted in ibid 82–3. The passage occurs in the preface to the reader of Malinckrodt's *De ortu ac progressu artis typographicae dissertatio historica* ... The projected biography is mentioned also in Malinckrodt's autobiography of 1635 under the title 'De vita et scriptis Erasmi Roterodami contra obtrectatores et calumniatores eius assertio catholica.' It is one

book was never published. How much was thus lost? One's curiosity is aroused by the fact that Malinckrodt's conversion from Protestantism as a young man (1616) was influenced by writers not at all sympathetic to Erasmus, Canisius and Bellarmine.[9] In his prime Malinckrodt was a scholar of stature, but his was also a strangely *frondeur* spirit.[1] Failing in 1650 to win election to the see of Münster he at once refused obedience to his successful rival. Excommunication, arrest, escape in the midst of tumult, and reimprisonment followed over the years. In 1664 he died in prison, and his book died with him. Joly, stimulated – one must assume – by Malinckrodt to attempt his own life of Erasmus, survived into years of serenity and comparative obscurity more suitable perhaps for biographical reflections than the disturbed years of the Fronde or of Malinckrodt's turbulent proceedings at Münster.

Joly wrote his biography and an accompanying history of the revival of letters around 1667–8. It was known then to Guy Patin, who pressed Joly to publish. Joly has said of his long silence only that he did not wish to provoke controversy. One may well imagine that he did not consider the early splendid years of the reign of Louis XIV congenial to the publication of a life of Erasmus. In the 1690s, amid the bitter fruits of glory and war and intolerance, he returned to the work. He had, he said in his preface, the encouragement of a doctor of the Sorbonne. It became a point of honour for him that the faculty of theology, whose predecessors had treated Erasmus so cruelly, should now approve his life. He willingly submitted the work to scrutiny (1698) since his purpose was to build up, not to pull down. The faculty's decision was, he believed, a late vindication of Erasmus and a goad for himself. But others remained suspicious; the archbishop of Paris, de Noailles, stopped the printing to examine the manuscript for himself. The aged Joly began (like some famous contemporaries) to seek a publisher in Holland, but death intervened.[2]

among a large number of works, philological and historical, to be completed 'si Deo placuerit et operae pretium fuerit' (*Die Autobiographie des Münsterchen Domdechanten Bernhardt v. Mallinckrodt, 1635* 15). According to Keussen the manuscript was preserved in the cathedral library at Münster, but Flitner reported that it could no longer be found (*Erasmus* 110).

9 *Autobiographie* 11

1 ADB XX 143

2 For the above, Bayle *Dictionnaire historique* VI, 'Erasme,' note P, 234–5; J. Lévesque de Burigny *Vie d'Erasme* I xi–xiv; J. Le Clerc 'Candido lectori' LB III *2; and Joly himself (below). For a fuller discussion of the known history of Joly's work, see Flitner *Erasmus* 111–14. Flitner was the first to

A

Monseigneur le Duc de Bourgogne.

(4626)

Monseigneur.

La réputation dans laquelle vous estes d'aymer les bonnes lettres m'a fait enfin resoudre de donner au public un ouvrage qui est dans mon cabinet depuis plusieurs années, et de vous le dédier; parce que j'ay cru qu'il vous seroit agréable, estant fort propre à former les princes Chrestiens; et sur tout un fils de France. C'est l'Histoire de la renaissance des Lettres dans la fin du quinzieme Siècle, et dans les commencements du seizieme.

Cette Histoire contient les éloges de plusieurs Scavans hommes de ces temps là, et particulierement la vie d'Erasme de Roterdam, qui de tous a le plus contribué à cette nouvelle vie des belles lettres, lesquelles avoient esté quasi esteintes par la barbarie et l'ignorance des Siecles precedents.

Aussi, Monseigneur, c'est cette grande entreprise d'Erasme, et son succès, qui l'ont fait rechercher en son temps, par les premieres Puissances de l'Europe, pour venir demeurer dans leurs Estats; et notamment par le Roi François I, lorsqu'il voulut establir à Paris les leçons publiques, qui font encore à present, ce qu'on appelle le College Royal. Mais Erasme (*) ne peut se resoudre de quitter l'Empereur Charles quint, son prince naturel, qui l'avoit mis au nombre de ses Conseillers d'Estat.

Il y a desja longtemps que le corps d'Erasme est dans le tombeau: mais son esprit vit encore aujourd'huy dans les bibliotheques, et son nom va y devenir dans peu plus fameux que jamais par

Glimpses of Joly the *frondeur*, or at least the political pamphleteer, are to be had in this work. Joly echoed Erasmus' praise of More's *Utopia* as an exposure of political evils; he saw in Erasmus' panegyric of Philip of Burgundy an oblique attack on those who taught princes that they were above the law and could do as they liked.[3] Joly himself, writing in the time of 'respite' after the Peace of Ryswick (1697), likewise gave instruction under the mask of praise: in making peace, Louis xiv had followed the Christian counsel of Erasmus.[4] Most indicative is Joly's dedication of his work to the young Duke of Burgundy, grandson of the king, around whom had gathered a circle of reformers whose plans were aristocratic and devout and in some ways backward-looking but who made searching criticisms of the absolutist régime none the less. Joly commended Erasmus' writings on the duties of princes to the duke and his advisers.[5]

What are the main themes of Joly's work? An emphatic, if minor, theme is that Erasmus was a Frenchman and a Gallican. France and especially Paris had the glory of being more hospitable than other places to good letters when they first came north from Italy.[6] She could also claim the greatest of the northern scholars. Chapter 4 of book 2 is entitled 'How Erasmus, though a Dutchman, has been included among the renowned Frenchmen.' Caesar had associated Holland with the Gauls rather than the Germans, and Erasmus accepted this association. He wished to be considered French rather than German.[7]

The great themes are Erasmus' place in the revival of letters and the nature of his Catholicism. The first book – about one hundred pages in the transcription – is concerned with the death and resurrection of

make a study of the manuscript. See his extended note (113–14) on its later history. The first section (a general history of the revival of letters and Erasmus' life to his Italian visit of 1506) is available in a good nineteenth-century transcription; the original manuscript is extant but badly damaged by water (in a shipwreck at the time of the Belgian revolution of 1830). Both original and transcription are in the Bibliothèque de l'Arsenal, Paris (respectively MS 4625 and MS 4626). I have used microfilm copies obtained by the Macquarie University Library. I thank Monsieur F.B. Py, Conservateur. References unless otherwise stated are to MS 4626. Joly's preface, on the history of his work, 11–13.

3 'Histoire de la renaissance des lettres dans la fin du quinzième siècle, et dans les commencemens du seizième ...' 312, 365–7
4 Ibid 3. Pierre Goubert calls the years 1697–1701 'the respite' (*Louis xiv and Twenty Million Frenchmen* 223).
5 'Histoire' 5
6 Ibid 117
7 Ibid 132–4

literature. Its design is simple: there was light, darkness fell, there was light again. Letters flourished in the early days of the church, eloquence was the servant of wisdom, sacred and profane. The long decline into barbarism was checked only by exceptional individuals like Bede, Bernard, Thomas, or Bonaventure. True revival began with Petrarch, though honour was also due to Dante and Boccaccio. The pace quickened in the fifteenth century with the Greek migration to Italy before and after the fall of Constantinople, the invention of printing (recounted by Malinckrodt), the patronage of the popes Nicholas v and Pius II and of the Medici, and the 'esprit libre' of Valla. In the North the first commanding figure was Rodolphus Agricola, a Netherlander.[8] So comes a chapter (20) entitled 'How letters began to flourish again everywhere at the beginning of the sixteenth century.'[9] Tributaries, brooks, channels were flowing together in a mighty stream. To this movement at its height Erasmus contributed more than any man. Joly's long work is intended as a demonstration of that assertion.

But Joly also wished to show, as he said in his preface and against the prejudices of some people, that Erasmus was a good Catholic and an enemy of Luther and of other false evangelicals.[1] Sustaining these two propositions without inconsistency required Joly to give a particular character to Erasmus' devotion to letters. In chapter 14 of book 2 Joly explains how Erasmus read the pagan poets. He loved them from his youth but was aware of the dangers and did not think that young people should make them all their study. On the other hand, he saw that much in ancient poetry could serve the praise of God and advance the loving ethic of Jesus. The ignorant reproaches of some on this score provoked Erasmus to his *Antibarbari*.[2] Later Joly adds that Erasmus' devotion to the works of Jerome should stop the mouths of those who accused him of being too devoted to humane letters.[3] Other indications of the

8 Ancient eloquence and the decline into barbarism, ch 1, 29–31; Dante, ch 2, 32–40; Petrarch, ch 4, 45–55; Boccaccio, ch 5, 56–60; Greek scholars, ch 6, 60–8; Nicholas v and Pius II, ch 9, 73–80; Valla and printing, ch 15, 92–6; Medici circle, ch 17, 99–105; Agricola, ch 19, 113–15. This pattern of interpretation was an established one by the later seventeenth century. See W.K. Ferguson *The Renaissance in Historical Thought: Five Centuries of Interpretation* 68–70. It is sad nevertheless that his failure or inability to publish his work deprived Joly of his place in the succession of writers on the Renaissance.

9 'Histoire' 115

1 Ibid 15

2 Ibid 161–2

3 Ibid 166

essentially sacred rather than profane direction of his studies were his defence of the study of Greek – it was 'pour la Theologie, et la piété Chrestienne' – and his way of reading Lucian: Erasmus had no sympathy for his raillery at religion and left his obscene dialogues untranslated but thought other translations justified because of the good style and the morality Lucian taught underneath his laughter.[4] In the language of modern scholarship Joly is presenting the portrait of a Christian humanist.

Erasmus had a Catholic destiny. That he overcame great obstacles revealed the hand of God, who often uses the humble and despised to fulfil his purposes.[5] One obstacle was the illegitimacy of which he himself was ashamed.[6] Another was the grossness of the education he received even at Deventer. Yet his natural taste and ability and his natural aversion to the gross and confused asserted themselves, the providential ordering of his talents enabled him not only to raise himself but also to banish barbarism from France and Germany.[7]

The monastic phase is handled in a way that demonstrates Erasmus' Catholic character. As the letters to Grunnius and Servatius make clear, all his inclinations, his temperament and physical disposition, were against the monastic life. Those like Giovio who have accused him of inconsistency have not understood that he did not enter the cloister voluntarily.[8] But while there he showed a truly Catholic spirit, docile and anxious to avoid reproach. He modestly gave in to menaces and exhortations. Unlike his brother, who broke from the monastery and threw himself into a disorderly life, Erasmus was determined to accommodate himself as best he could and to give no occasion to scandal. Studies were his consolation.[9] His *De contemptu mundi* was a sincere appreciation of monastic piety, for one cannot persuade others of what is not in one's own heart.[1] Erasmus' departure from the monastery was

4 Ibid 351, 354–6
5 Ibid 123
6 Ibid 135–7. Joly contests the more hostile Catholic tradition represented by Giovio, Possevino, and Raynaud: Erasmus' mother was the daughter of a physician, not a servant; his father was not a priest when he was conceived. Joly settles the year as 1467 and the place as Rotterdam (in the house near the great church which he himself had visited) (125–9).
7 Ibid 125, 140–1
8 Ibid 158; account of tutors' pressure 144–6
9 Ibid 159–60. This account of his brother, Pieter, owes something to Erasmus' own harsh expressions (letter to Lambertus Grunnius, August 1516, Allen Ep 447, II 298). They are probably unjust. Cf CWE 1 4.
1 'Histoire' 166–7

in the same spirit. It was no apostasy. Certainly he seized an opportunity of freedom offered to him but he left with the consent and good will
of his community and without offence to others. He was not seeking a
wholly secular life.[2]

By the time he came to study in Paris under the patronage of the
bishop of Cambrai, to whom Joly devotes a sympathetic chapter
(chapter 2 of book 3), Erasmus' greatest affection was for theology.
That is why Paris, the seat of theological learning, attracted him. The
kind of theology in vogue there did not attract him, for he 'was not
made for the disputes of the schools and had no mind for syllogisms.'
Yet he did not reject scholastic theology outright; it could be useful if
made purer and more serious. The true theology had all his esteem; its
character was defined by his preaching at Paris – the expression of a
simple faith, beyond disputing and content to listen to scripture.[3]

Erasmus was a Catholic, but a certain kind of Catholic. The tones are
as significant as the bold outline; Joly anticipates a Catholicism touched
by enlightenment and sensibility. Take Erasmus' prayers to Ste-
Geneviève for a cure to the quatrain fever. He was devoted to this saint.
'But one should note that while Erasmus had much faith in the prayers
of Ste-Geneviève, nevertheless as he was well instructed on the way to
receive the graces God bestows through the saints, he gives God all the
glory for his cure as the author of it.' Joly's interest – to the extent of a
long digression – in Vitrier, a spiritual but independent figure, exposes
the character of his religiosity.[5] His treatment of Loyola's rejection of
Erasmus' *Enchiridion* is a touchstone. He is, he says, writing a life and
not a panegyric; hence he reports the ill sometimes said of Erasmus and
his writings. But we should ask about the motives of those so speaking.
Without disrespect to Loyola, whom the church has placed among the
saints, we ought not to be surprised at his judgment – all men are not
touched by the spirit of God in the same way. Many have had a
different experience of the book from Loyola's – they have been edified
by it, filled with a love for God and converted to a better life.[6] Joly
identifies himself with the alternative to the Jesuit tradition about
Erasmus. He insists on the legitimacy of Erasmus' understanding of

2 Ibid 167, 176–7
3 Ibid 187–90
4 Ibid 202
5 Ibid, book 3, chs 16–18, 207–17. There are corresponding sections on Colet
   (book 4, chs 8–10, 255–68) and More (book 5, chs 1–3 and 5–9, 285–93 and
   299–313).
6 Ibid 220–2

the Catholic faith and reiterates his defence against the grosser calumnies. When Erasmus spoke of the cult of the saints in his *Moriae encomium*, he was criticizing only the superstitious.[7] He was not partial to heresy, as his defence of More's actions against heretics when chancellor reveals.[8] Joly accepts Richard's argument that the perseverance of the Catholics in Germany against the onrush of heresy was due more to Erasmus than to any other.[9] Through all, as a pointer to the foundations of his faith and of Joly's, is Erasmus' love of and reliance on the ancient Fathers of the church.[1]

If it had been published, Joly's massive work would have been counted the first approach to a biography of Erasmus of the modern kind. It would have taken the place now occupied by Burigny's biography of the 1750s. It also had characteristics of its own time: its ample scale, its annalistic form, its disorder, its lack of scruple about digressions of all kinds – biographical, anecdotal, anthropological, scholarly.[2] In our discussion its importance lies in its definition and defence of Erasmus' faith and of his allegiance to the church and the Catholic tradition.

Joly had praised Erasmus' services to literature and criticism and defended the character of his Catholicism. In Paris in the first two decades of the eighteenth century there was a little spate of publication also aimed at a revival of both his reputation and his kind of piety. One finds no work of any great substance, but all had a certain warmth and charm. Most important was the *Apologie, ou justification d'Erasme* published by François Babuty in 1713. Little is known of its author, Abbé Jacques Marsollier (1647–1724), who from a good legal family became a canon regular of Ste-Geneviève and later canon and provost of the cathedral of Uzès.[3] The other publications were translations with introductions of Erasmus' works, including the *Enchiridion*, the *De*

7 Ibid, book 7, ch 2, MS 4625, f154^r
8 MS 4626, 299–302
9 Some examples: little biographies scattered through the work of friends, associates, and contemporaries, eg, on Grocyn, Linacre, Latimer, and Tunstall, book 4, ch 7, 248–54; an account of the Turks in book 1, chs 6–7, 60–71; the debate between John Fisher and Lefèvre d'Etaples on the three Magdalens, book 5, chs 11–16, 318–49; a story of demon possession in a convent, admittedly based on an account by Erasmus, book 3, ch 5, 185–7
1 Ibid 4
2 Eg, 352, MS 4625 ff174^r, 218^r
3 Hoefer XXXIII cols 982–3; Phillips 'Erasmus and Propaganda' 9–10

APOLOGIE,

O U

JUSTIFICATION

D'ERASME.

Par Monsieur l'Abbé MARSOLLIER,
Chanoine & ancien Prevôt de l'Eglise
Cathedrale d'Usez.

A PARIS,

Chez FRANÇOIS BABUTY, ruë saint
Jâques , au-deſſus de la ruë des
Mathurins , à S. Chryſoſtome.

M. DCC. XIII.

Avec Approbation & Privilege.

Title page of Jacques Marsollier
Apologie, ou justification d'Erasme
Gemeentebibliotheek, Rotterdam

contemptu mundi epistola, and the *Institutio christiani matrimonii*.[4] Among the printers of these books was François Babuty, who published Marsollier; of their editor even less is known than of Marsollier. The royal censor in approving his work described him as an 'illustre et pieux Magistrat' who, despite poor health, devoted his leisure to translating the best of Erasmus.[5] He was Claude du Bosc de Montandré, councillor of state.[6] He is witness to the devout dispositions still to be found within the parliamentary class. In some of the translation Marsollier himself probably had a hand.[7]

The main argument of Marsollier's *Apologie* is an external one. He would not defend Erasmus by following him in every point of controversy; that would fail to make a book for the great public. Rather he would report the high opinions held of him by those whose judgments must silence his critics, by popes and Catholic kings and princes. This way of justifying him, Marsollier declares, is short and easy but decisive.[8] It is an exercise in recovering Erasmus for the Catholic side against the false Protestant claim to him. Erasmus lived in the public eye. If he had erred on a matter as important, let us say, as the Trinity, the Catholic élite would certainly have disowned him.[9] In times so dangerous for the church, would a prince like Ferdinand of Austria write of him as he did if his warm expressions were not sincerely meant?[1] Why did not the Protestant princes use the same expressions when his defection would have been so valuable to them? They recognized his unbreakable attachment to the old church.[2] Would Pope Adrian VI have encouraged Erasmus to take up the defence of the faith if his doctrine had been suspect?[3] Princes and prelates disapproved the

4 *Le Manuel du soldat chrétien* ... (1711); *Du Mépris du monde, et de la pureté de l'église chrétienne* ... (1713); *Le Mariage chrétien* ... (1714)
5 *Le Mariage chrétien* xxv–vi; *Mépris du monde* x–xi
6 Cf F. Vander Haeghen et al *Bibliotheca Belgica* II 474–5; J.-M. Quérard *La France littéraire* III 27–8; A.-A. Barbier *Dictionnaire des ouvrages anonymes* III cols 64–5. Pierre Mesnard associates Du Bosc with Jesuit piety; the series in which the *Manuel du soldat chrétien* appeared also included various Jesuit ascetical and spiritual writers (printer, E. Couterot). Thus, he says, was Erasmus' own orthodoxy guaranteed ('La dernière traduction française de l'Enchiridion'). But, as we shall see, the main (hostile) Jesuit tradition about Erasmus remained in full strength.
7 So says Quérard of *Du Mépris du monde* (*La France littéraire*).
8 *Apologie* xxii–vii
9 Ibid 10–11
1 Ibid 22–9
2 Ibid 59–60
3 Ibid 86

irrational and outrageous attacks of his Catholic enemies, who were moved above all by envy – merit always appears an injury to certain kinds of men. Erasmus fought for the church when it had fewer defenders and helpers than it has had since.[4]

This is a fair sampling of the main part of Marsollier's argument. It is not especially compelling. Yet there is more to Marsollier than this; he seems genuinely to respond to the appeal of the warmer strains in the Erasmian piety. Erasmus freed theology from the thorns of sophistry and sowed the seeds of piety; his books have an unusual elegance certainly, but also a solidity and an unction which inspires love of the gospel.[5] More interesting to us are the touches already apparent in these expressions of the reasonable, sentimental, common-sense religion of the eighteenth century. In reading Marsollier we know that we are in the borderlands of the Enlightenment. Erasmus was the morning-star of a religion which both enlightened the mind and moved the heart. Everywhere in his works there is 'une piété éclairée, solide, tendre, affective, qui persuade, & qui gagne les cœurs.'[6] Marsollier takes a utilitarian line. Erasmus' writings are useful to society – that is one reason why society owes him at least the protection of his reputation.[7] He cultivated his talents for the service of the public. He instructed the young in all that made the good Christian and the good citizen useful to religion and the state. He wrote for all conditions of society, overlooking nothing that could contribute to the happiness of families (the works on marriage) and teaching men to live 'heureusement, chrétiennement, saintement' – for him these three went together.[8] One senses here a recovery of that bourgeois strain in Erasmus of which his first interpreters – those at least who belonged to the Basel circle – had been unselfconsciously aware, an awareness lost in the time of the confessional struggles when Erasmus was seen by and large out of social context, a disembodied representative of heretical or reforming ideas.

Marsollier is not wholly a stranger to the emergent religious boldness of his age. Prejudice against Erasmus arose in part from an excessive credulity. He condemned those who wanted to keep the people in credulity by pious frauds. One should be convinced by solid proofs, not held by prejudice, habit, or deceit. Erasmus was teaching

4 Ibid 97–8, 102–3
5 Ibid 241–2
6 Ibid xviii
7 Ibid iv
8 Ibid vi, ix, x–xii

men to distinguish true from false. The church needs such critical intelligences: will the gospel suffer if it is shown against popular belief that St James never went to Spain? The essentials of faith and morals (to bear one's cross, to love one's neighbour) are unaffected. Erasmus recognized that the Protestants could use 'fables, human traditions, and ill-conceived legends' to discredit the church; he preferred the 'sage sobriété' taught by St Paul.[9] As for his criticism of the institution, the church has never denied that abuses can arise or treated as an enemy those who wish for reform so long as they speak with respect and love. The reforming work of Trent showed how justified he was.[1] The apology finishes with positive praises of Erasmus' services to the church. He was the principal restorer of good letters and so gave her arms against the heretics.[2]

There is no trace of heterodoxy in Marsollier's own writing, of course; there is no partisan angle as in Richard's work; for all the Erasmian moderation of his attitude to the Protestants, there is no irenicist program as in Du Pin. Marsollier is unpolemical; he enters into no controversy with contemporaries. He may even be a little naive. His warm praises of the Jesuits[3] seem strangely out of line with the long Jesuit tradition of hostility towards the subject of Marsollier's apology, a tradition soon to be renewed in a devastating assault on the apology itself. Its sentimental tones and rhetorical style are evidence enough that its purpose was indeed the avowed one – to convince the educated public of the soundness of Erasmus, of the 'unction' of his work for 'this enlightened age.'

Du Bosc's prefaces are miniature versions of Marsollier's apology. There is the same validation of Erasmus' piety through the witness of popes, kings, and bishops.[4] The same praise, too, of his services to the church, including (decidedly) his services as theologian; he was 'one of the greatest men God has given to his church,' capable of stemming heresy and recalling those who had strayed.[5] Above all, the same account of the character of his religion: if he was unsure on some disputed theological questions, he remained an exemplary Christian moralist, bent on 'producing true Christians, worthy men, good citizens, equally useful to their families, religion and the state' and not at

9 Ibid 156–68, 172–6, 185
1 Ibid 198, 209–10
2 Ibid 234–5
3 Ibid 267
4 *Manuel* aiiii[v]
5 Ibid aiiii[r]

all to the taste of the libertines of the time.[6] Here is a solid piety gracefully expressed and drawn from the purest sources in scripture and the Fathers. In his discourse on the child Jesus, for example, he notes all that would give us the highest idea of Jesus Christ, encourage us to love and imitate him, and make us grateful for what he has done for us.[7] In Du Bosc as in Marsollier Erasmus is attached to the religion of an enlightened age: his work on Christian marriage is based not only on the biblical and patristic literature but also on 'good sense and the soundest reason enlightened by revelation.'[8] All is useful and full of unction. Occasionally indeed the editor sweetens and purifies that unction: the strong expressions against monasticism at the end of the *Enchiridion* are much abbreviated – Erasmus would have written thus, says Du Bosc, if he had lived in these better times; the famous twelfth chapter of the *De contemptu mundi*, where Erasmus dissuaded anyone from hastening into a monastery, is transformed into advice for choosing one monastery rather than another.[9] Thus is Erasmus made what he is said to be.

Du Bosc de Montandré's happy presumption that Erasmus' orthodoxy and piety were now beyond dispute was sanguine and premature. A formidable sortie was mounted against his and Marsollier's interpretation from within the old hostile Jesuit tradition. The vehicle of assault was the Jesuit *Journal de Trévoux*.[1] For the Jesuits in France had learned the lesson of the journals of Holland, the need to appeal to the widening educated public of the early eighteenth century. The idea of a new journal was conceived by two Jesuit Fathers, Jacques-Philippe Lallement and Michel Le Tellier.[2] They sought and readily obtained the support of the Duc de Maine, natural son of Louis XIV, who wished to associate his tiny but independent principality of Dombes with intellectual pursuits and in particular with the intellectual defence of the traditional faith. Already he had established in Trévoux, its capital, an important printery; now he would make that little centre famous throughout Europe by the publication of a journal to rival those of

6 Ibid av^r; *Mariage chrétien* xvii
7 *Mépris du monde* vi
8 *Mariage chrétien* vii–viii
9 *Manuel* 334; *Mépris du monde* 115–18
1 *Mémoires pour l'histoire des sciences et des beaux arts* (1701–62). See DTC xv 1 cols 1510–16; Gustave Dumas *Histoire du Journal de Trévoux depuis 1701 jusqu'en 1762*; Alfred R. Desautels *Les Mémoires de Trévoux et le mouvement des idées au XVIIIᵉ siècle 1701–1734*
2 Jean Faux 'La fondation et les premiers redacteurs des Mémoires de Trévoux (1701–1739) d'après quelques documents inédits'

Amsterdam and Leipzig. The editorial effort was concentrated in the Jesuit Collège Louis-Le-Grand with its great library and lively intellectual life. The *Journal de Trévoux* had much in common with the other great journals of the period: its primary purpose was the review of current literature, but it aimed generally at promoting the discussion of literary and scientific questions. Not all its contributors by any means were from the Jesuit ranks; it was well and widely received. Its discussions, especially of biblical questions, were often open and critical, and its handling of non-Catholic or anti-Catholic writers often surprisingly restrained.[3] An analysis has revealed the genuine responsiveness of the journal to changes in public taste over the sixty-odd years of its life.[4] Yet there was an important proviso: the journal would maintain a strict neutrality except 'where the interests of religion, good morals and the state are concerned; in these it is not permitted to be neutral.'[5] Marsollier's defence of Erasmus was to be condemned under that rubric.

The apologetic purpose of the journal had been present from the beginning but expressed itself more definitely, even more aggressively, in time. The directing spirit between 1701 and 1719 was René-Joseph de Tournemine (1661–1739), the teacher of Voltaire in his days at Louis-le-Grand. Tournemine was well equipped for his role of journalist in the eighteenth-century sense: 'Une mémoire heureuse, une imagination vive, féconde, un goût également sûr et delicat, un esprit étendu et pénétrant ... Un style aisé, naturel, noble, nerveux, sans rudesse, brillant sans affectation, varié sans être inégal, l'ordre, la netteté avec laquelle il exposait ses idées ...'[6] Yet where the faith was in question he was belligerent and polemical. He represented well the Jesuit cast of mind at that time; for all its openness to the literary and scientific debates of the age, its hold on the faith was narrow and traditional and it was strongly fideist: '... God had spoken, the church had the text which gave it authority to govern; it was necessary to believe.'[7]

Tournemine was the author of *Trévoux*'s sharp attack on Marsollier's *Apologie*.[8] Marsollier's skill and candour were worthy of a better

---

3 Dumas *Histoire* 43–6. On *Trévoux*'s relation to Bayle, see Desautels *Les Mémoires* 192–9.
4 Robert R. Palmer 'The French Jesuits in the Age of Enlightenment'
5 Quoted in Dumas *Histoire* 33
6 *Trévoux* 1739, quoted in ibid 78–9
7 Desautels *Les Mémoires* 174
8 'Refutation de l'Apologie d'Erasme.' Desautels confirms Tournemine's authorship (*Les Mémoires* 218).

cause – that is the burden of Tournemine's piece: 'The more doubtful the cause, the more necessary an able advocate.'[9] Richard, the Jansenist, had neither the authority to silence Erasmus' critics nor the skill to overcome them. The ingenious and attractive Marsollier will have more effect; that is why a sharp refutation is necessary – to uncover the poison hidden in flowers, to turn the flock of Jesus Christ from diseased pastures, to unmask wolves in sheep's clothing.[1] Marsollier may go to great lengths to justify Erasmus, persons of rank and virtue may issue his spiritual works (Du Bosc); the fact remains that Catholic writers have rejected him because he derided the religious orders and the ceremonies of the church, overthrew sure doctrine and (being little versed in theology and too full of his own ideas) altered dogmas in purporting to explain them, hazarded new and dangerous explanations of scripture, and – an echo of writers from Bellarmine to Simon – furnished arms to the 'new Arians.'[2] Certainly there are some subjects for praise, especially in the sphere of letters and criticism, but the essential thing is indicated by his way of entering the world and his way of leaving it: he entered it through apostasy; he was a vagabond, a deserter, an excommunicate monk; he died in a heretical town, among heretics, without priest or sacrament. Was this a doctor of the church, was this a master of the spiritual life? A very singular one indeed.[3]

The key to his character and career was his indifference to religion. By inclination he loved novelty but, regarding his freedom and repose as the greatest goods, he feared the controversies which novelty brought. Hence his 'moderation,' his swinging between two inclinations, love of novelty and timidity. He did not adhere to any sect but he founded a very numerous one, 'la secte des Tolerans.' He boasted of holding the middle ground between the Lutherans and the Catholic church – very well, do not then make an orthodox doctor out of him; leave him on the middle ground he has chosen.[4] Tournemine admits the praises accorded him by popes and bishops and orthodox princes. How are they to be explained? Popes and kings feared Erasmus, or rather they feared the consequences of his defection (here is an argument of Richard's but in negative form). So they flattered him, they ran after the wandering sheep. Yet there were limits to their indulgence: in the end his works were condemned. His replies to criti-

9 'Refutation' 935
1 Ibid 936, 954
2 Ibid 940–1, 955
3 Ibid 956–8
4 Ibid 957, 959

cism were 'frivoles, artificieuses'; Tournemine will not go into them unless – a threat of continuing controversy – Erasmus is obstinately defended and his books circulated. The piece ends in passionate invective: from Erasmus, unlike other doubtful writers, the Origens and Tertullians, the Catholic faithful can learn nothing; he is not a Christian, he is a *philosophe*.[5] Then in its dying breath, testimony to the Jesuit obsession with Jansenism, a final swipe at Richard: what possible interest can the Jansenists – with their exaltation of grace – have in Erasmus, whose most respectable work defended the freedom of the will?[6]

Tournemine's piece, written with a rhetorical verve which Erasmus himself would not have disdained, represented the Jesuit tradition in its most uncompromising form; it was a reiteration of Garasse and Raynaud, a draught of pure bile. It called forth equally rhetorical replies. In the *Journal literaire* of the Hague in 1715 a writer signing himself 'Cleral' took Tournemine's points one by one.[7] Erasmus left the monastery responsibly, after serious reflection and with permission; he died in Basel preparing an edition of his works that would bring enlightenment to the church.[8] Where he opposed received dogmas it was because he believed them false or ill supported; where he held to them it was not out of hypocrisy or to save appearances but from a genuine adherence of mind and heart. He cannot be accused of abandoning Catholicism because he criticized abuses which had encrusted themselves on the church like moss on a tree and rust on metal and could be removed without doing harm to tree or metal. He cannot be accused of indifference in religion because he, like the Fathers and from missionary concern, questioned the need for scholastic formulae when speaking of Christ. 'Erasmus struck with a masterly hand not at the truths and mysteries (he believed them, he revered them) but at the rubbish, the froth stirred up by empty disputes. And for that he is accused of indifference to the essential truths! What morality! What logic!'[9] In his criticism of superstitions Erasmus was in the position of Paul facing the silversmiths at Ephesus.[1] According to this author, the whole episode showed that, despite the best efforts of an attractive

5 Ibid 964–8, 970
6 Ibid 971–2
7 'Replique sur la Réfutation inserée aux Mémoires de Trevoux Juin 1714 de l'Apologie d'Erasme, faite par M. Marsollier'
8 Ibid 374, 381
9 Ibid 375–8
1 Ibid 379–80; Acts 19

apologist like Marsollier, Erasmus – 'above popular opinions, the enemy of superstition, inclined to moderate dogmas, instructed by antiquity' – could not be made to please those who took a quite contrary view of religion.[2]

A similar moderate Catholic view, assessing the sixteenth century from the standpoint of a more enlightened age, but longer and – because of the personal history of its author – more interesting, was published in another short-lived journal, the *Mémoires litteraires* of Hyacinthe Cordonnier (called Thémiseul de Saint Hyacinthe, 1684–1746), a representative of the more bohemian element in the journalistic world of the time who, in the midst of travels, of adventures amorous and otherwise, and of literary quarrels, edited or assisted in editing more than one of the journals of Holland.[3] This 'Réponse à la Réfutation de l'Apologie d'Erasme,' like so much in contemporary journalism, appeared anonymously. A consideration of the piece might precede reflection on its author.

The critic of Marsollier had claimed to write in the interests of the church. 'But what new kind of zeal is this, to force men to be heretics in spite of themselves?' If Erasmus had been portrayed as weak in faith, unwilling to preach the truth from the roof-tops or to sacrifice his life for it, there could be no quarrel. But to speak of him as 'apostate,' 'atheist,' 'c'est agir ou en insensé ou en calumniateur impudent ...' There is an infinite difference between a weak man and a man without religion. Erasmus' avowal of his unwillingness for martyrdom at least showed a wish to avoid temerity and presumption. Besides, in criticizing his weakness one should beware of exposing one's own.[4] But the censurer (Tournemine, who is not named) has a suspicious mind and a malignant heart and turns everything to Erasmus' disadvantage.[5]

The familiar responses are given – on Erasmus' departure from the monastery, on the honours paid him by popes and princes, on his criticism of abuses and of the scholastic elaboration of theology (' ... Erasmus feared with good grounds that faith would finally degenerate into a vain and criminal curiosity ...'),[6] on his death in a Protestant city. Naturally, however, the main defence is against the charge of religious indifference. Tournemine may quote Loyola's criticism of Erasmus' piety 'but is it surprising that this great saint, who carried the

2 'Replique' 374
3 Hoefer XLIII cols 36–8; Michaud XXXVII 332–5
4 'Réponse' 356–7, 381–2
5 Ibid 384
6 Ibid 377

taste for chivalry even into his devotions, did not find congenial Erasmus' devotional treatises, where neither enthusiasm nor the supernatural [*surnaturalité*] are to be found?' One may find overtones or undertones in that almost to taste. Then a more positive line is taken: the Erasmian piety is always within the reach of the most simple; it is distant equally from superstition and free thought; it is drawn only from the purest sources, 'pleine de lumière & de vérité, pleine de douceur & de modestie.' Good sense rules there: 'L'esprit y regne par-tout, mais jamais sans le cœur.' It is expressed in an eloquence worthy of the majesty of the gospel with power to convince of the truth.[7]

Erasmus' love of peace was the result not of indifference but of 'une sage œconomie' which always preferred moderation to force. He did not disapprove Luther's criticism of abuses and cry for church reform but when he saw him go to excess and bring on a schism he rejected him. If Tournemine had not been so inflamed by that pharisaic zeal which knows no other way of dealing with error than by fire and sword, would he have been able to condemn Erasmus' reasonable and Christian expressions? The rhetorical question is characteristic of the manner and the enlightened tone of the matter of this author. Erasmus, he concludes, justifies himself before the tribunal of public opinion: '... pour justifier *Erasme* il suffit presque de le lire.'[8]

There is a certain journalistic boldness in this essay. It has an attacking thrust but also an air of sweet reason and good sense: no thinking man could be expected to disagree with it. Animus against the Jesuits informs it, as is clear from various references to the Jansenist controversy in its later stages, a generation or more after the affairs in which Richard was involved. The actors may be different, but the scene is the same as in Erasmus' time – the persecuting ecclesiastics still hold sway.[9] Perhaps Tournemine's violence against Erasmus is due to the fact that his first apologist was a Jansenist (Richard): one falls into these excesses when the judgment is swayed by interest or passion. Erasmus and the Jansenists have this in common: they were both victims of irregular procedures, of the manipulation of the Holy See by ignorant cabals, of the dishonesty of their enemies. Again, perhaps Tournemine's heat against Erasmus' questioning of Pope Leo x's bull against Luther arises from fear of a like questioning of the bulls

7 Ibid 363–4
8 Ibid 369–70, 380–1, 387
9 Ibid 389–90

Pierre-François Le Courayer
Portrait painted by an unknown artist and
given to Bishop Atterbury, 1727
Reproduced by permission of the Curators of the
Bodleian Library, Oxford

produced against the Jansenists in suspicious circumstances. It was Erasmus' misfortune that the Jesuits did not become his defenders – then he would have been cried up as the first man of his century.[1]

One ought not to be deceived: the author of this piece was not a Jansenist, but by temperament and to an extent by association he was drawn to the defence of the Jansenist minority. He was Pierre-François Le Courayer (1681–1776).[2] His family belonged to the professional bourgeoisie of Rouen. He joined the order of Ste-Geneviève in Paris and was ordained priest and canon regular in 1706. He studied Cartesian philosophy and Thomist theology in an intellectually unconstrained and eclectic atmosphere. It is strange but indicative that when he began teaching at Ste-Geneviève he was set to expound the *Ars critica* of Jean Le Clerc, the great journalist of Holland, an Arminian in faith and the editor of Erasmus. Le Courayer entered into a correspondence with Le Clerc, and one must assume that Erasmus had a place in their exchanges.[3] By 1717 he was the librarian of Ste-Geneviève. He sympathized with the appeal of his order against the anti-Jansenist bull, *Unigenitus*, though he did not share the Augustinianism of the order; he tended to the Molinist side and like Simon he was critical of Augustine's handling of scripture.[4] The Jansenists attracted him because they were the opposition and above all because they were at daggers drawn with the Jesuits. Erasmus as he understood him had a similar attraction: strange partners though they were theologically speaking, as Tournemine rightly saw, Erasmus and the Jansenists stood together in Le Courayer's mind because their respective struggles promised an opening up of the church, the moderating of its more authoritarian traditions, and a more sceptical and eclectic atmosphere. At the time of his essay on Erasmus Le Courayer was a Catholic tinged with the early Enlightenment. The tone is unmistakable in his correspondence of 1722–3 with Archbishop Wake about the more elaborate apology of Erasmus he was preparing against – as he put it – the clamours and calumnies of monks; these were inimical to religion itself

1 Ibid 365, 378–9, 391–2
2 See above all E. Préclin *L'Union des églises gallicane et anglicane: Une Tentative au temps de Louis xv: Pierre-François Le Courayer (de 1681 à 1732) et Guillaume Wake.* Préclin corrects standard works like Michaud ix 353–4; Eugène and Emile Haag *La France protestante* vi 484. Cf Hoefer xxx col 243; dtc ix 1 cols 112–16. It is strange that both *Bibliotheca Erasmiana* and dtc attribute Tournemine's article to Le Courayer, which is obviously absurd.
3 Préclin *L'Union* 25–6
4 Ibid 42–3

because they carried with them a defence of ignorance and superstition. With the work almost complete, Le Courayer was persuaded to transform it into a life of Erasmus: there was as yet, so it was represented to him, no adequate biography, and his easy narrative and lack of prejudice would fit him better than many others for the task. So he began to reread the letters of Erasmus.[5] He hoped to finish in a year or fifteen months, but a letter to Wake of 4 October 1723 already betrayed a certain pessimism about the work's completion.[6] Le Courayer was on the eve of a spectacular change in his fortunes which put the Erasmus project out of mind.

In 1723 Le Courayer published anonymously a defence of Anglican orders. The book was quickly attacked, not least, as one would expect, in the *Journal de Trévoux*. Later he revealed his authorship and published a further defence, but in 1727 thirty-two propositions were condemned by an assembly of bishops, and his books were suppressed by decree of the royal council. In the early 1730s he fled to England, where he was warmly received. Le Courayer was then Du Pin's successor in the attempt at a reunion of the Anglican and Gallican churches; for him, however, events took a more dangerous turn than for his predecessor, perhaps because he was bolder in temperament and more lively and more opinionated in mind. The question of interest to us is this: was the Le Courayer of the controversy over Anglican orders, of the years of exile (one should add, of happy exile) when he translated Sarpi's history of the Council of Trent and added tendentious notes of his own and when he edited Sleidan's Protestant history of the Reformation, already apparent in the essay on Erasmus? There is reason to answer in the affirmative: his approval of Erasmus' call for more simplicity in theology, his hostility to everything exclusive, authoritarian, and extreme in his own time or Erasmus' pointed towards his later irenic endeavours. The picture he gives of Erasmus is in fact distorted: he seems too moderate, too bland, almost too insipid, though Le Courayer did insist that his essay was a reply to Tournemine, not a full study, or even a full defence.

How heterodox is Le Courayer's Erasmus? How heterodox was Le Courayer himself? Perhaps a nineteenth-century Tractarian author speaking from his own very particular standpoint struck the right note:

5   Le Courayer to Wake, 25 October 1722, 12 June 1723 (Wake correspondence, MS 244, Christ Church Library, Oxford, nos 21, 23). Cf Préclin *L'Union* 44; Sykes *William Wake* I 318–19. Le Courayer wanted to place Wake's picture side by side with those of Erasmus and Grotius! (Le Courayer to Wake, 12 December 1721, ibid no 11).
6   Wake correspondence no 24

To a power of mind and clearness of head rarely surpassed, [Le Courayer] added a vast extent of systematically arranged Ecclesiastical learning; he had no party interest or blind prejudice to warp his judgment; – on the contrary, the very object of his life appeared to be the discovery of truth ... Nor was he by any means the man to maintain paradoxes, an affecter of singularity, or otherwise of a peculiar turn of mind; unless indeed a very uncommon freedom from prejudice and sincere love for the truth, together with that high and straightforward tone of mind, which, in spite of an extensive knowledge of the world, made him above availing himself of its arts and intrigues, might justly intitle him to be considered as such ... But alas! ... there was one thing wanting ... He had learnt unhappily to *defer*, instead of to *submit*, to the authority of the Church.[7]

From the same standpoint this would do as a summary of Le Courayer's account of Erasmus.

The most substantial contribution to the exchanges which began with Marsollier's apology was written from a quite different and very conservative point of view – a series of fourteen letters ostensibly directed to a 'Monsieur l'Abbé de Guyon, Prévôt d'Orange' and composed in 1715 before Le Courayer's reply to Tournemine but, because of its author's absence abroad, published only four years later.[8] The tone is established by this remark on Erasmus' efforts for the reunion of the churches (and, one must assume, on the corresponding efforts of Du Pin and Le Courayer and those like them): 'What reunion can there be between light and darkness, truth and lies? Who is not with Jesus Christ is against him; the faith is one and indivisible, and all neutrality is odious and horrible in matters of faith.' Erasmus is, so to speak, for ever imprisoned in the middle.[9] The writing has neither the verve nor the bitterness of Tournemine (it would be 'sans aigreur & sans passion') but the judgments are as extreme. The author took up his task reluctantly since it required much reading on a subject 'au fonds presque inutile,' but the interests of truth constrained him.[1] What standard of judgment should be applied? A critic should follow his

---

7 Introduction to Le Courayer's *A Dissertation on the Validity of the Ordinations of the English, and of the Succession of Bishops of the Anglican Church* lxi–lxii
8 Gabriel de Toulon *Critique de l'Apologie d'Erasme de M. l'Abbé Marsolier.* See the 'Avis' and the approbation and royal privilege which declares the critique to be well founded!
9 Ibid 85–6
1 Ibid 2

subject carefully, comparing him with himself and with his contemporaries, abstaining from all hurtful comment (Scaliger's defamation
of Erasmus is condemned) but above all he should have in view only the
good of the church.[2] The mind of the author is revealed by the
theological tests he sets for Erasmus: tradition is 'the principal column
of the Catholic church'; scholasticism should be seen as 'the dogmas of
the faith, disposed in that beautiful order in which St Thomas put
them, supported by all the force of reasoning to which the faith may be
susceptible'; the monastic orders are the glory of the church.[3] Here is a
world of thought, or at least an intellectual tone, quite distant from Le
Courayer's. Otherwise we know virtually nothing of this author; he
was said to be an Augustinian friar called Father Gabriel de Toulon with
the family name of Vieilh.[4]

Father Gabriel makes no attack on Marsollier himself: he was a 'wise
priest applied to study and his duties.' His apology, however, was a
failure. Its main argument – that 'Erasmus is irreproachable because
the great of the earth have praised him' – did not come off. 'What can
all these marks of distinction do to establish the catholicity of Erasmus?' The latter is the concern, not of princes, but of theologians in
their exacting discipline where truth and error often rub shoulders.[5]
There are, says Father Gabriel, two traditions about Erasmus. The one
on which Marsollier sought to build is weak and poorly supported.
Scarcely a Catholic author of repute can be found to defend Erasmus.
The other tradition includes the great doctors Canisius, Bellarmine,
Stapleton, Gretser, Raynaud, Possevino. Can these be written off as
ignorant or half-learned?[6] 'Thus has a tradition bestowing little honour on the memory of Erasmus continued to our time; it subsists now
and will always subsist ...'[7] This method is simply Marsollier's in-
verted, with a selectivity and exaggeration even less defensible than
his. Furthermore a tongue-in-cheek demonstration is offered of a
Protestant tradition about Erasmus, going back to Luther himself,
which confirms the main Catholic tradition: the Protestants too have
recognized his talents but have portrayed him as 'variable, douteux,
inconstant' in religion.[8]

2 Ibid 4, 9
3 Ibid 125, 149, 160
4 Burigny *Vie d'Erasme* II 550; A.-A. Barbier *Dictionnaire des ouvrages
   anonymes* I cols 820–1
5 *Critique* 11–13, 255–7
6 Ibid 24–45
7 Ibid 47
8 Ibid 75–6

Biographical questions are handled in the expected manner:[9] Erasmus' desertion of the monastery was an apostasy; his claim to have been forced there unwillingly is dismissed as the refrain of all bad monks; his was the case of a good beginning and then a turning back to the world; he was moved by 'le démon de l'inquiétude & de la liberté.'[1] At the end of his life there were rumours that he was to be offered a cardinalate, but that may not be used to establish his catholicity. Here Father Gabriel, like Tournemine, uses an argument that seems to do little for the moral credit of the Holy See: it was the practice to dangle such honours before suspect scholars to silence them.[2]

What of Erasmus' writings, of whose unction Marsollier and Du Bosc had made so much? The *Colloquia* are condemned as wounding to modesty and religion, fit only to destroy the innocence of youth and seduce it from the faith.[3] Folly's praise of the higher foolishness of the saints is treated in the solemn, unimaginative way characteristic of this whole tradition about Erasmus: 'In the saints there is neither madness nor folly; their state is the perfection of reason, the height of wisdom ...'[4] Words which were edifying to Marsollier are for Father Gabriel a subject of scandal, lacking true devotion, 'dry and arid.' Indeed he finds in the *Enchiridion* the anachronistic design of bringing in 'la spiritualité des Protestans.' Erasmus' writings were the expression of a bitter, vain, and licentious spirit.[5]

On the recurrent charge of Arianism Father Gabriel shows some cunning (his ploy is not far from Simon's). Erasmus was not an Arian but he eased the path for the Arians by weakening the force of the texts which the Fathers had used against them. See, Father Gabriel might say, how discriminating is my judgment of Erasmus. In fact, however, this judgment is destructive of Erasmus' work on scripture: certain readings of scripture are held to be inviolable because of the dogmas they are used to support.[6]

9 Father Gabriel does not accept the assertion that Erasmus' father was a priest at the time of his conception (ibid 52–3).
1 Erasmus' early *De contemptu mundi* is used to prove his satisfaction with the monastic life. Apparent contradictions within it are interpreted as one would expect from the summary in the text: while a good monk Erasmus wrote favourably of the life; later he added derogatory sections (ibid 305–6). All this is still a subject of controversy. Cf R.H. Bainton 'The Continuity of Thought of Erasmus' and A. Hyma *The Life of Desiderius Erasmus* 22–30.
2 *Critique* 277–80
3 Ibid 88–110
4 Ibid 117
5 Ibid 286–90
6 Ibid 182–3

Father Gabriel's main concern is with Erasmus' position in the Luther affair. He was 'the dawn before Luther's day' – there is the essence of the argument.[7] At one point it is taken to extremes: Luther read Erasmus constantly and 'drew from his books all his teaching' ('il y puisa toute sa doctrine').[8] The selection of the matters on which Erasmus prepared the way for the heresiarch is interesting in itself:[9] on tradition, on the visibility and infallibility of the church, on sacerdotal celibacy (of the *Encomium matrimonii*: 'The most open libertine would not have said more ...'),[1] on confession, on abstinence, on scholasticism, on the invocation of saints, on the Blessed Virgin, on the monasteries. He encouraged Luther and 'defended his interests at a critical moment for the salvation of Germany and the welfare of the Catholic church ...'[2] Richard's argument is reversed: that so much of Germany remained Catholic was for him to Erasmus' credit; for Father Gabriel that so much was lost was to Erasmus' discredit. By another answer to the Elector Frederick at a critical moment in 1520 he might have saved everything. But he observed the desolation of the church with dry eyes.[3] His final writing against Luther was more from self-regard than good faith.[4]

None of this says much for Father Gabriel's historical sense. In fact a historical sense is missing throughout the book. Of Erasmus' criticisms of monks and priests it asks not 'What is the evidence, for and against?' but 'How could one claiming to be a true Catholic say such things of the clergy of the church?' Yet, one must add, Father Gabriel is not sparing in his own use of evidence; his work is not mere polemic: Erasmus is quoted at length over a range of his works. There is a sharpness in the argument lacking in most of the anti-Erasmian writings: how could Richard and Marsollier think to persuade the Protestants of Erasmus' authority for them by quoting the resounding praises given him by the *popes*?[5] This is an ordered and sustained piece of advocacy, a credit to its author's powers, but still advocacy fired by a determination to hang the prisoner, without balance or moderation, far short of the understanding looked for in a historian, let alone the sympathy of a biographer.

7 Ibid 82
8 Ibid 122
9 Ibid 124–59
1 Ibid 131
2 Ibid 195–6
3 Ibid 217–18, 232
4 Ibid 251
5 Ibid 17

Naturally it won the praise of the journalists of Trévoux. In a review of the whole controversy since the appearance of Marsollier's book, the journal – on the strength of Father Gabriel's work – reversed Le Courayer's aphorism: 'Whoever reads Erasmus can no longer justify him.'[6] As for Le Courayer's 'pretended defence,' it was refuted in advanced by Tournemine's essay, to which it purported to be a reply, and had now been demolished by Father Gabriel. It was one of those pieces which prepared the way for the flight of their authors into Holland.[7] Chance or foresight? This was 1723, and Le Courayer's work on Anglican orders was to appear in that year.

The last word seemed then to rest with the enemies of Erasmus. A case had meantime been put for the other side but it was not a strong one – Michel David de La Bizardière's *Histoire d'Erasme, sa vie, ses mœurs, sa mort et sa religion.*[8] La Bizardière was the author of some well-regarded histories of Poland and a church history of the sixteenth century.[9] His book on Erasmus was dedicated to Louis-François-Armand du Plessis, Duc de Richelieu et de Fronsac. This duke was twenty-five years old at the time of the dedication.[1] Mme de Maintenon described his first appearance at court in 1710: '... il danse très bien, il joue honnêtement; il est à cheval à merveille, il est poli ...'. By 1721 he had been in the Bastille three times after various amorous and political intrigues. Admitted to the Academy founded by his great ancestor he offered in his discourse of acceptance a pastiche of pieces taken from distinguished authors and simplified. In him a nineteenth-century biographer saw the epitome of the court aristocracy of the eighteenth century, 'in his frivolity, his taste for intrigue, his gallantry without scruples, his immorality without remorse, his elegant ignorance, his superstitious incredulity and, over all, his imperturbable good humour and his scornful courage.'[2] This then was the Erasmian young man to whose discernment, already revealed in his discourse to the Academy, La Bizardière offered his Erasmus. It revealed a sad lack of judgment which runs in fact through the whole work.

La Bizardière begins with the aphorism that 'great men are always subject to envy.' Have not those who wrote against Erasmus exceeded

---

6 March 1723, article XXXIII, 507–26, at 509
7 Ibid 508
8 It was printed by Claude Jombert, who also printed Father Gabriel's work!
9 Michaud IV 379
1 The following from Hoefer XLII, cols 221–8
2 Ibid col 221

the limits set by the gospel?[3] He must be judged by his own writings, on scripture, on the Fathers, against the heretics of his time. His enemies have not used such sources but, like bad workmen, have gone to poor materials, the testimonies of false witnesses like those who accused Susanna.[4] This is a fair beginning, but La Bizardière does not heed his own advice: despite his insistence on knowing Erasmus only in his works, there is no real consideration of them. Erasmus' life is sketched from the familiar sources and with an occasional aside: his scrupulous care to obtain dispensations from the monastic rules, for example, should be a model for 'religious of our own time who solicit dispensations and translations from one order to another under different pretexts, when the true reason is often only libertinage.'[5] Strange discrepancies of judgment appear. Erasmus' role in the church crisis of his time was apostolic (' ... la Providence le choisit comme un Apôtre ...').[6] On the other hand, his advice on reunion elicits this comment: 'This way of uniting different religions has always appeared easy to those who have much presumption and impossible to true theologians.'[7] (Did La Bizardière know of the irenic efforts of Du Pin? It is impossible to tell.) La Bizardière seems to want to have it both ways. The purpose, the conception of his work remain obscure: it is possibly Gallican, it is certainly anti-Protestant. A long digression on Luther's marriage is indebted to Cochlaeus. Luther, piqued by his critics, 'discharged his rage on Erasmus, and made him suffer all that the cruelty of a barbarian could suggest to him; he did it without spilling blood, as the first persecutors of the church did, but rather like Julian the Apostate.'[8] However, by its chronological arrangements Providence spared Erasmus, 'son fidele serviteur,' from encounter with the 'monstre' John Calvin.[9]

La Bizardière finishes with a positive appreciation – as a man, Erasmus was without dissimulation or ambition, faithful to his friends, not vengeful towards his enemies, free in word, irreproachable in conduct. He also makes a strong and – for his time – unusual point: Erasmus must be judged in the light of times and circumstances; he died before the meetings of the Council of Trent, he lived among

3 *Histoire d'Erasme* 1, 7
4 Ibid 8–11
5 Ibid 25–6
6 Ibid 13
7 Ibid 34
8 Ibid 74–5
9 Ibid 48

Lutherans, Anabaptists, and Zwinglians, 'like the fish of the sea which does not take on the bitterness of the element in which it lives.'[1] But like so much else in his brief work the point is not taken very far. La Bizardière's defence is light-weight. Something on an altogether different scale was required: in Joly's absence one must await the great biography of Burigny.

Is there a pattern in the French writings of the early eighteenth century on Erasmus or at least in the attachments of the writers? That he was attractive to those primarily interested in personal piety is understandable so long as his works of devotion are read aright, as with Marsollier and Du Bosc. Nor is it difficult to explain the interest in him of irenicists like Du Pin and Le Courayer: his own work for reunion, the whole moderate and accommodating cast of his mind are part of any such explanation. On the other side, the virulence of a Tournemine belongs to a tradition whose course we have traced. The role of Jansenism in the whole controversy is more problematic for – despite Richard's assumption of a common Augustinianism – the defenders of a high doctrine of grace seem strangely drawn to the author of the *Diatribe on Free Will*: here there is less an affinity of ideas than a comparability of position, the beleaguered and controversial positions of Erasmus and the Jansenists in their respective times.

1   Ibid 103

SEVEN

Germany:
Orthodoxy and Pietism

⁂

MAIMBOURG HAD PROVOKED THE JANSENISTS; his small-arms
volley also called up a great bombardment from the Lutheran lines.
Veit Ludwig von Seckendorf (1626–92) read the *Histoire du
lutheranisme* in his retirement after years of service to Saxon governments.[1] He believed that it needed a reply. These were not, however,
his first thoughts about composing a history of the Reformation. One
of his duties on entering the service of Duke Ernest the Pious of
Saxe-Gotha had been to cull from books useful or entertaining matter
for reading to the duke at suitable times; thus began his collection of
historiographical material. The duke also drew his attention to the
unused sources for the history of the Reformation in the Saxon archives, as Seckendorf recalls in the *Praeloquium* to his history. Retirement made it possible to fulfil these two aims: a retort to Maimbourg
and a history of the Reformation based on manuscript as well as printed
sources. For the form of the work the first objective was determining:
Seckendorf translated Maimbourg's book into Latin and added diverse
commentary – some of the pieces substantial essays in their own right.
This performance far outstripped Maimbourg's – Seckendorf had
taken a sledgehammer to a nut. Besides he had written a book for
savants and in the language of scholarship; connected reading would be
difficult, if not impossible. In form the book has more in common with
the encyclopaedias and biographical dictionaries which were still the
commonest kinds of historical writing than with modern historiography.[2] Its first version (1688) covered only book 1 of Maimbourg (the

---

1 ADB XXXIII 519–21; RE3 XVIII 110–14; RGG V cols 1629–30
2 Eduard Fueter (*Geschichte der neueren Historiographie* 309) says that
  seventeenth-century historians had the accuracy of the lexicographer as
  their ideal rather than the sense of style of their humanist predecessors.

years 1517 to 1525); the second added a treatment of books 2 and 3 but was also a supplementation and reworking of the first – now could be seen the fruits of Seckendorf's harvesting of the Saxon archives at Weimar.[3] Though in form uncreative, the work made an epoch because of its serious encounter with the sources[4] – it was, said Bayle, the best thing of its kind.[5]

Its attitude also marked an advance. Seckendorf belongs to the historiographical tradition of Lutheran orthodoxy. His piety was deep and personal.[6] In his political writings he reiterated against its critics the traditional view of secular authority. His history then must be 'an arsenal for the defense of the Reformation.' At the same time he is 'more ready to conciliate than to offend.'[7] His purpose is confessional, but he pursues that purpose with charity, sobriety, reason, and common sense. Though neither pietist nor rationalist his mind seems somehow touched by the impulses that were to produce on the one hand pietism and on the other rationalism in the following generations.

Seckendorf does not waste on Maimbourg many of the words he has to devote to Erasmus. The Jesuit's sources are inadequate, he says, and his prejudice is too apparent.[8] By contrast Seckendorf is scrupulous and ample in quoting from the sources and is never carried away by bile. One finds, in fact, a certain strain in Seckendorf's Erasmus interpretation, a tension between his loyal adherence to Luther's judgments and his own natural sympathy for Erasmus. He is indeed embarrassed by Luther's more extravagant expressions: 'When controversies concern personalities more than articles of faith I do not wish to waste time in recounting them.'[9] He shows signs of wanting to stay within the confines of the orthodox interpretation as defined by Luther's words. Erasmus has been praised for preparing the way for the Reformation; but, says Seckendorf, 'I would not wish to see such praise extended

3 *Commentarius historicus et apologeticus de Lutheranismo* ...
4 L.W. Spitz 'Seckendorf as a Church Historian'
5 Quoted in RE3 XVIII 114
6 Owed to his mother. His father served with the Swedes in the Thirty Years War and indeed was condemned to death by them for correspondence with the imperial side.
7 Spitz 'Seckendorf' 171
8 *Commentarius* book 1 140–1. Other sources for Erasmus' life which should have been used include the *Compendium vitae*, the letters to Servatius and Grunnius, and Beatus Rhenanus' introduction to the Origen edition of 1536.
9 Ibid book 3 77 (in reference to Luther's charge of atheism)

beyond the great assistance he gave to the understanding of sacred letters through a more refined study [*exquisitiora studia*] of languages, especially Greek.'[1] Yet there are more positive flashes, and the restrained tone through his whole discussion puts Seckendorf at a great distance from the more rabid elements in the Lutheran tradition. Erasmus ought not to be blamed by Maimbourg (or for that matter, one might add, by Luther) for his persuasions to peace, arising as they did from the kindness of his nature or his sensitivity of conscience since all bloodthirsty counsels were abhorrent to him.[2]

In general Seckendorf adopts the classical Protestant position: Erasmus recognized the corruption of the church; he wished to see it reformed, but the methods he preferred were hopelessly inadequate for the task: 'That sickness of the church could not be cured by the plasters applied by Erasmus.'[3] He failed to do what he could and should, though (here Seckendorf's left hand checks the right) he certainly had more excuse if he was moved by love of peace and hatred of tumult:

> I confess that I have often considered [it is Seckendorf speaking] nay grieved over what might have kept a man so great in learning and moderation, at a time and stage in life when he could have found an honoured position anywhere in the world, from openly supporting the truth, abandoning hope of correcting the abuses in the Roman curia and, as he was able, helping on the work of reformation seriously and frankly.[4]

Erasmus closed his eyes to the truth; it was a needless blindness. Yet Seckendorf will not attribute base motives; he will not adopt Hutten's calumny that Erasmus prostituted his conscience to his greed for honours and awards: 'nolui meo judicio Hutteni fervori subscribere.'[5] The essential thing is that the situation required Luther's perseverance and harshness; from Erasmus' mildness Rome – corrupt and unreformed – had nothing to fear. This is the mainline Protestant apology for the violence of the Reformation; it is also an argument from

1 Ibid 137. The words are reminiscent of Luther's in a famous letter to Oecolampadius, 20 June 1523: 'He has accomplished what he was called to do: he has introduced among us [the knowledge of] languages, and he has called us away from the sacrilegious studies. Perhaps he himself will die with Moses in the plains of Moab, for he does not advance to the better studies (which pertain to piety)' (*Works* XLIX *Letters* 44).
2 *Commentarius* book 2 196
3 Ibid book 1 93
4 Ibid 140
5 Ibid

circumstances, and Seckendorf is willing to carry it through: today, he says, in a Germany of diverse religious opinions, where peace is written into the laws so that hatreds might be moderated and abuses corrected, Erasmus' admonitions are to be read with profit.[6]

There are places where Seckendorf takes a higher line. Erasmus failed to see the divine power in Luther's words and actions: no weakness of Luther's could 'stand in the way of the power of the Holy Spirit by which he proclaimed the truth of the Gospel.'[7] From that standpoint the whole discussion is abruptly closed off, but Seckendorf has not abandoned more historical arguments: Erasmus was not so valuable a supporter of Luther in the early days as Maimbourg claimed nor so dangerous an enemy later; if he was far above Luther's cruder adversaries, he was yet too subtle and vacillating.[8] His contention about the decline of learning under the Reformation was mistaken; letters flourished more than ever. On the breakdown of morality he had a better case, but he incautiously attributed it to Luther's doctrine; he failed to distinguish the fanatics and hypocrites from believers or to acknowledge the same difficulties on the Catholic side, though earlier he more than anybody had deplored the decline of morals and discipline in the church.[9]

Seckendorf seems to be entering into controversy with Erasmus but in a brotherly spirit; the latter is what distinguishes his from almost all other writing of a confessional kind in the sixteenth and seventeenth centuries. This is apparent in his treatment of Erasmus' last great effort at religious concord, his book on mending the peace of the church (1533).[1] Erasmus' commentary on Psalm 83 which is the foundation of the work is, says Seckendorf, pious and learned. On the issue of grace and free will Erasmus has drawn close to Luther (how misconceived then, Seckendorf goes on, is Richard's attempt to appropriate Erasmus for the Roman Church). Even Luther's more striking formulations ('quod homo nihil aliud agat, quam peccet') he now approaches sympathetically. On the other hand, he is too ready to excuse superstitious practices, and what he says of the Mass does not remove its objectionable character for Lutherans. All this is friendly and courteous exchange. Then the compass-point jerks and steadies on Luther's words: Erasmus may not be followed with a good conscience. Seckendorf sums

6 Ibid 262
7 Ibid book 2 88
8 Ibid book 1, 173, 309–10
9 Ibid 70; Ibid book 2 57
1 Ibid book 3 49–52

up with the authoritative but – for judging Erasmus as an historical figure – largely irrelevant dictum: scriptural truth alone should be followed, what lies outside it should be set aside.[2]

In Seckendorf then there is an incoherence: on the one side the restrained judgment of the historian and even the sympathy of the friend of the first pietists, on the other side the formidable authority of Luther and the orthodox tradition. In the end this incoherence prevents him from ever deciding what led Erasmus to choose and so pertinaciously to hold the middle way.

Seckendorf's uncertainty arises from an uncommon sensitivity. By contrast, there were spokesmen for the raw Lutheran tradition in his time. W.E. Tentzel (1659–1707), also a servant of the Saxon states as well as a wide-ranging 'Polyhistor,'[3] published a commentary on Seckendorf's book in a journal he edited at Leipzig between 1689 and 1698, the *Monatliche Unterredungen einiger guten Freunde von allerhand Büchern und andern annemlichen Geschichten.*[4] Its spirit may be seen in this description of the work's significance for Protestants: '... with it they will in the future be able to protect themselves against all lies and calumnies and know that the Reformation is the work not of any man but of God.'[5] Erasmus is handled coldly. He was 'ein *Proteus in der Religion'*; he trimmed his sails to the wind; he was 'neither a good Catholic nor a good Lutheran but an arch-syncretist [*Ertz-Syncretist*] since he wanted to keep to the middle way.'[6] So lived on (as it still lives) the spirit of Luther's table-talk.

As we know, there were other Protestant traditions, and in pietism there was to be a new departure. The special relationship between

2 Ibid 53–4
3 ADB XXXVII 571–2. He was numismatist at Gotha for seventeen years and later historiographer of the Ernestine line of Saxony and from 1702 to 1703 archivist at Dresden, a position he lost in mysterious circumstances.
4 762–82, 901–10, 995–1024
5 Ibid 763
6 Ibid 780. Compare the somewhat different view of another Lutheran historian and polemicist, Christian Kortholt (1632–94), professor of theology and pro-chancellor at Kiel (ADB XVI 725–6; RE3 XI 47–8; RGG IV col 25). Erasmus was essentially Luther's precursor: 'And although afterwards – for fear of losing the benefits that he enjoyed in the Roman church – he wished to appear to oppose Luther, even by writing against him, he did this so timidly that it was all the more apparent how he favoured his cause' (*Historia ecclesiastica Novi Testamenti* ... 719). The titles of two of Kortholt's polemical works perhaps deserve recollection: *Coal-black Papacy or Proof that the Papacy at Rome was founded by the Devil* and *Roman Beelzebub or Proof that the Pope at Rome is the Devil* (1660).

Zwingli and Erasmus had consequences historiographically. Johann Heinrich Hottinger (1620–67) was a Zürich man, offspring of a burgher family, married to the daughter of a Zürich pastor, professor of oriental languages, church history, rhetoric, and catechetics at the university, pride of his fellow-townsmen.[7] Between 1655 and 1661 he was at Heidelberg assisting in the reconstruction of the university after the disasters of the Thirty Years War, but that activity itself was indicative of the bond between Zürich and the German Protestants – the city used Hottinger during that time for diplomatic missions in the Empire. His fame, which would in the end have taken him to Leiden but for his tragic death by drowning, rested on his work in oriental languages, but his church history – admittedly polemical in purpose and scholastic rather than analytical in method – showed a knowledge of sources and sound judgment.[8]

Hottinger's history of the sixteenth century is written from Zürich's standpoint and Zwingli's: 'Zwinglii reformandi conatus & Priores ex tempore, & puriores eventu, Reformatione Luth.'[9] Zwingli's Reformation had both temporal and moral priority. Undoubtedly his vantage-point affected Hottinger's judgment of Erasmus. Luther's stubborn hatred after the free-will controversy was neither authoritative nor decisive. Erasmus and the other literati of the time prepared the way for the Reformation by exposing scholastic trickery, promoting erudition, and rebuking abuses. Some doubt that Erasmus should be enrolled among the pre-Reformers? 'Read,' Hottinger replies,

the preface to his New Testament Paraphrases and you will conclude that the neglect of scripture which had crept into the church at that time had to be corrected. Scan the introduction to his Jerome and you will see how monasticism had utterly deteriorated. Turn over the pages of his *Adagia* and the *Moriae encomium* and you will note how church and university were corrupted by ignorance and superstition: they had therefore to be cleansed and their splendour restored. Look into his famous *Enchiridion* and you will judge that ministers of the church then were apostate ... rather than apostolic.[1]

7 RE3 VIII 399–401; RGG III col 460; Peter Meinhold *Geschichte der kirch-lichen Historiographie* I 388–95; R. Feller and E. Bonjour *Geschichts-schreibung der Schweiz vom Spätmittelalter zur Neuzeit* 408–10; O.F. Fritzsche 'Johann Heinrich Hottinger,' especially 251–5.
8 *Historiae ecclesiasticae Novi Testamenti ...*
9 Ibid 8
1 Ibid 23

Erasmus is a supreme witness of that utter depravity in the church which required and justified Zwingli's Reformation.

Certainly weaknesses are to be admitted. Erasmus recognized the gross errors of the church better than the more subtle ones, seeking the correction of abuses rather than the abolition of dangerous and new-fangled doctrine. He was equivocal, unwilling to call a spade a spade in the deeper mysteries of faith. On the pretext of peace or from love of tranquillity he was frightened to adopt necessary and drastic remedies. He was held back by the awe and magnificence of Rome.[2]

Yet there is a case for Erasmus, and Hottinger develops it at some length. It is, of course, a Zwinglian Reformed case. Erasmus first broke the ice.[3] By his biblical and patristic learning and by his personal stance he helped on the Reformation.[4] He could not be rushed – be it by argument or threat or blandishment – into writing against the Reformers, though he did not fail to counsel Rome on the handling of the Luther affair. He thought well of Zwingli.[5] The Reformers themselves recognized his value to them: 'Good God,' said Ambrosius Blaurer, the Reformer of Constance, 'what could not Luther and Erasmus achieve if they agreed together.'[6] If he failed in the end to adhere to the Reformation that was not through solidarity with Rome but from a failure of understanding and enlightenment or from human weakness.[7] He never ceased to call for reform in the church – whence the ceaseless reproaches of the papists against Erasmus, living or dead.[8]

Hottinger's is on the whole a sympathetic judgment. But his depiction of the historical context is conventional: the Reformation was a providential work; Erasmus did much more for it than he did against it; for that reason he deserves much more praise than blame. To turn to Gottfried Arnold (1666–1714) is to enter another spiritual world and to confront a radically different historiography.

Arnold's significant encounter with Erasmus is in his *Unparteyische Kirchen- und Ketzer-Historie, vom Anfang des Neuen Testaments bis auf das Jahr 1688*. That book came at a critical point in Arnold's life. He was early in reaction from Lutheran orthodoxy, under the influence of the burgeoning pietist movement and connected

2 Ibid 23–5
3 Ibid 36
4 Ibid 25
5 Ibid 27–8
6 Ibid 32
7 Ibid 34
8 Ibid 43

Gottfried Arnold
Copperplate engraving by G.P. Busch, 1716
Staatliche Kunstsammlungen Dresden
Kupferstich-Kabinett

with spiritualist groups.[9] Already in his first book, *Die erste Liebe der Gemeinen Jesu Christi* ... (1696), typically pietist notions appear, especially that of the fall of the church. This book led to a call to a chair at Giessen from the pietistically inclined Landgrave of Hesse. But in the very time of his writing the *Unparteyische Kirchen- und Ketzer-Historie* (1697–1700) Arnold abandoned his chair, an act symbolic of his rejection of the security and standing offered by the world and expressive of his understanding of the radical contradiction between God and the world, to which also the worldly church belonged. The work itself, great in scale and conception, in its use of sources, in its freedom from conventional ideas, shows the progressive radicalizing of Arnold's thought. It is possible to demonstrate a development between the *Vorworte* and the *Nachworte*.[1] The reader – so Arnold concludes – will in the course of the work have seen for himself the utter emptiness of so-called Christendom. The contemptuous *so-called* is used again and again. The so-called church was divided into parties and sects from the beginning – there were as many religions as there were heads; from the fall of the church (which goes back almost to the beginning) the words and deeds of the so-called Christians proved how few were truly united to Christ Jesus and to one another. Those who were so united and who held themselves in lowliness of spirit were condemned as heretics and sectarians by those in authority – but it is not difficult to determine where the true church lay.[2] This conclusion was in fact the extreme point of Arnold's development. After that – with his marriage in 1701, his pastoral and literary work, including his appointment by the Prussian king as superintendent at Perleberg in 1707 – he found his way back to some reconciliation of faith and world. He wrote his interpretation of Erasmus as he was approaching that extremity.

One may say (of course, putting aside any suggestion of presumption) that Arnold's history is written from the vantage-point of the

9 ADB I 587–8; NDB I 385–6; RGG I cols 633–4; Meinhold *Geschichte* I 430–42; F.Ch. Baur *Die Epochen der kirchlichen Geschichtsschreibung* 84–107; W. Nigg *Die Kirchengeschichtsschreibung: Grundzüge ihrer historischen Entwicklung* 76–97; E. Hirsch *Geschichte der neuern evangelischen Theologie im Zusammenhang mit den allgemeinen Bewegungen des europäischen Denkens* 260–74; above all, E. Seeberg *Gottfried Arnold: Die Wissenschaft und die Mystik seiner Zeit: Studien zur Historiographie und die Mystik*; H. Dörries *Geist und Geschichte bei Gottfried Arnold*; I. Büchsel *Gottfried Arnold: Sein Verständnis von Kirche und Wiedergeburt*
1 Büchsel *Gottfried Arnold* 104–5
2 *Kirchen- und Ketzer-Historie* 1200

God who sees into all hearts. It is not an elaborate case for the sects against the established church, or even for the individual against authority or against the mass.[3] The matter should rather be put like this: great institutions, established hierarchies, opinionated teachers, and rigid creeds are all in their different ways barriers to the working of the Holy Spirit; the Spirit indeed breaks free in individuals and in small groups who are responsive to its leading. The teachers, hierarchies, and institutions which have appropriated the names of truth and orthodoxy for themselves treat these groups and individuals as heretics and condemn and persecute them. A revaluation has then taken place: if one looks not to externals but to the spirit that is in them the 'heretics' are the true children of God, the orthodox are the true heretics. Such things are tested not by the phrasing of creeds but by men's actions and inner dispositions – how close is this at least to the mind of Erasmus!

These then are the key ideas of Arnold's history. First, the fall of the church: from the time when dogma and liturgy were securely instituted, from the time when the 'Clerisey' (Arnold bequeathed the word to the Enlightenment)[4] separated itself from the people, from the time when fellow-believers first suffered abuse and violence for divergences of belief, the apostolic church was in decay, and that decay has continued to the present time. Secondly, 'Unparteilichkeit': this is a spirit at once independent and irenic, best understood as the opposite of 'party spirit'; the seed of the church's decay lay precisely in the confusion of truth and partisanship. Thirdly, personalism, a supreme concern with the inward, the personally experienced, and the personally appropriated in religion: as it affects Arnold's history, this idea has two sides – he is interested in the individual personality so that the history may be seen as 'a book of portraits in religious individualism';[5] he aims not at ecclesiastical history, let alone at confessional history, but rather at religious history, the history of piety.

Arnold's view of the Reformation is determined by these ideas. In the enormous book 16 of part 2 of the history, which deals with the sixteenth century, chapter 13 is crucial: 'von dem verfall der reformation insgemein.' Arnold's summary of one of its paragraphs reads: 'The causes of this decay were the teachers themselves; their perverted gospel, flattery and hypocrisy, and the hypocrisy of the Lutherans generally.' The Reformation, for all the hope it offered momentarily of

3 Dörries *Geist und Geschichte* 26
4 Büchsel *Gottfried Arnold* 86
5 F. Meinecke *Die Entstehung des Historismus* 52. Cf Seeberg *Gottfried Arnold* 145–8

a restoration of the primitive church – the one true church and the only model – belonged to the fall of the church: it developed its own dogmatism, scholasticism, intolerance. Erasmus himself is quoted early in this chapter on the divisions and unevangelical conduct of the 'evangelicals.'[6] Arnold turned the expressions which Luther had used about the papacy against Lutheran confessionalism itself: 'Menschenwerk, Menschenlehre und Gewissenzwang.'[7] In the following chapters the consequences of the rapid fall of the Reformation are drawn out. With chapter 19 comes another turning-point: here the alternative Christianity of the sixteenth century begins to be sketched out, with the 'enthusiasts,' Carlstadt, Schwenckfeld, the Anabaptists, and, at chapter 22, Paracelsus and other individuals 'who committed themselves to no party.'[8] These alone have Arnold's respect, and among them he places Erasmus.

Actually the humanist first appears in the early chapters of book 16 as a witness to the corruption of the papacy. Arnold may seem to have adopted one kind of Protestant view of Erasmus, that of him as Luther's John Baptist. He was one of the instruments in God's hand for the reformation of the church. In an acute, penetrating way he uncovered the folly and cruelty of the monks; he deserved more recognition than many had been prepared to admit for his services to church reform and to Luther himself.[9] His attempts to moderate Luther's passion and party spirit were sound and salutary – to say even that was not to abandon Protestant traditions in interpretation, at least as they were represented by Melanchthon.[1] But then in chapter 22 Arnold's interpretation of Erasmus takes the expected radical turn.

In that chapter Arnold has already dealt with people like Paracelsus, Postel, and Ochino, those who sought the truth not in scholastic books but in God's own revelation, who suffered hate and envy and misrepresentation because they would not adhere to received opinions but followed truth as they saw it.[2] All that was enough to have them accused – falsely – of atheism. There were those, too, like Staupitz and Beatus Rhenanus who, alienated by the corruption of the Roman church, were yet unwilling to attach themselves to another party or

6 Kirchen- und Ketzer-Historie 611
7 E.W. Zeeden Martin Luther und die Reformation im Urteil des deutschen Luthertums I 179
8 Kirchen- und Ketzer-Historie 778
9 Ibid 495
1 Ibid 504
2 Ibid, Postel at 783, Ochino at 786

adopt the exclusive spirit in another form. Such men are scorned as 'neutralists' or 'generalists' because corrupted human nature cannot bear the sight of love and gentleness. Having come so far, Arnold checks himself: 'I had almost forgotten a famous neutralist who was abused and condemned by all sects, namely Erasmus of Rotterdam.'[3]

Erasmus is, Arnold says, so well known for his learning and great gifts that no biography is necessary. Even in his own time he was praised by some because of his great moderation in theological controversy. To others he was an atheist, a Lucian, indeed a heretic because clearly and pointedly he attacked the stupidities of the 'Clerisey,' as schoolboys know through his *Colloquia*. Again he was called an Arian. One thing is sure: in the Reformation controversies he was an 'indifferent' – and for Arnold the term is one of praise. His spirit was irenic and is apparent from his book on mending the peace of the church 'wherein he wished to show both parties, Lutherans and papists, a way to unity, while making it clear that he found a great deal lacking on both sides ...' That he did much for Luther's Reformation – and not only for politic reasons – was confessed by Melanchthon and even by Luther himself.[4] He openly stated the failings of the Protestants, but Luther took no heed. The book on free will was in fact damaging to Luther, and the issue as put by Luther in his reply sowed doubt and discord among his followers. By contrast, 'Erasmus stood consistently by his first understanding of both reform and theology,' and for that he earned the blame of the majority.[5] Erasmus defended himself: he could not adhere to a Reformation which appeared to make men not better but worse.

In this history, then, Erasmus is linked with the so-called 'heretics,' the neutralists and indifferentists – those terms to be read in a positive, approving way. These people made a diverse group, but they had some things in common: they rose above party spirit; they preferred reconciliation to conflict; they were tolerant, charitable, irenic; they saw the old corruptions and perversions continuing in the new churches; they were hounded by the orthodox of all parties and wrongly accused of 'atheism.' Arnold has not really offered a consideration of Erasmus' spirituality, but he has placed him among those in whom the Holy Spirit still moves and speaks.

Arnold's was a positive, if limited, interpretation within a defined, if

3 Ibid 792
4 Ibid
5 Ibid 793

contestable, framework. More impressive is a sympathetic and well-rounded appreciation from inside Lutheranism itself.[6] This carries more weight, too, than the sympathetic interpretations of French Catholicism – those of Marsollier and Du Bosc – where there was much hedging and doctoring, as we have seen.

Johann Albert Fabricius (1668–1736) was one of the most versatile and productive scholars of the early eighteenth century. From 1694 he was settled in Hamburg as a pastor but also as professor of ethics and eloquence at the academic Gymnasium. He was a congenial personality, by temperament large and irenic.[7] It was characteristic that he had one of his students, Johannes Klefeker, celebrate the second centenary of the Reformation by a sympathetic discourse on Erasmus.

First, some reflections on Erasmus' fame. He owed it to the charm and acuteness, the openness and fecundity of his mind, and to his labours for letters and religion. It went beyond erudition to a wise understanding of theology based on the scriptures and church Fathers. Philosophy he followed only so far as it helped in forming and defending sound judgment; of natural science he made no study.[8] He used his great talents not for the pursuit of fame itself or wealth or honours but 'ad communem utilitatem.' He was moved by Providence ('divinitus excitatus') to give all his strength to advancing the great renovation – in the church and in learning – which was then being prepared in Europe. To the evils of the present he offered a salutary alternative – he not only criticized 'perversum studendi, vivendi & docendi morem' but did all he could to show a better way. Against the enemies of the great change he defended himself with skill and dexterity.[9] In sum,

he brought back divine letters and pure theology in place of scholastic quibbling and a labyrinth of fatuous questions; refined eloquence, more humane learning, and useful knowledge in place of the mean and disturbed ignorance which held sway far and wide; virtues worthy of Christians and true piety in place of the observance of innumerable little traditions and pharisaic customs.[1]

This then was his historical importance.

So far we have an account in the Melanchthonian tradition. But

6 Johannes Klefeker 'Exercitatio critica de religione Erasmi ...'
7 ADB VI 518–21; NDB IV 732–3
8 'Exercitatio critica' 361, 365
9 Ibid 366, 368–9
1 Ibid 369

after an analysis of Erasmus' works Klefeker confronts the great question – Luther and Erasmus – and achieves a breakthrough unique in Protestant writing on Erasmus up to that time. The issue must be faced: how could men so enlightened and at first joined in a friendly spirit for the common cause fall in the end into such enmities and maledictions? Here is Klefeker's finely judged answer. Each remained consistent with himself, but they were different in mind and in gifts; what is more, their fates differed, Luther being condemned, Erasmus being praised by the popes. Luther concluded from his situation that he must make a final choice between Christ and Belial; Erasmus concluded that he stood, not between Christ and Belial, but between Scylla and Charybdis (he used these very expressions in a letter to Coelius). If Erasmus had acted other than he did, he would have acted not only against prudence but also against his conscience and against the 'common cause of religion and letters.' We, Klefeker concludes, would have lost 'a great witness to the truth within the church of Rome,' and the cause of good letters would have been much more threatened in those parts of Europe which remained subject to Rome.[2]

For the first time in the Protestant literature – and from this remarkable achievement many later Protestant interpretations down to the twentieth century were to fall far short – recognition was given to the independent validity of Erasmus' conscience.

Certainly more conventional Protestant emphases are also present. Erasmus did much to help Luther. Yet he was mistaken in thinking that mild methods would suffice or that the popes themselves would reform abuses. Here Klefeker agrees with Seckendorf. Erasmus fought by word solidly and powerfully; but the need was rather for someone who would 'attack the monster of superstition with violent deeds' ('apertis armis & plusquam Herculea clava'). But even here – in these rather stale dramatics – Klefeker shows independence of mind. Luther's judgment that Erasmus could point out errors but not teach the truth was not fair – in sacred letters and in piety there was excellent merit in Erasmus.[3] The importance of this remark lies not in its criticism of Luther's judgment, though that is unusual enough, but in its appreciation of Erasmus' piety. It in fact anticipates a full defence against all the main charges levied against Erasmus' religion.

2 Ibid 384–5
3 Ibid 390–1. Klefeker rejects suspicions that Erasmus wrote against Luther from fear of losing his English pensions. He was provoked rather by the false rumours emanating from England (as expressed in a letter from Tunstall) that he was helping Luther with his works (392–3).

It would be tedious – so Klefeker – to recount all the calumnies directed at Erasmus. They can be found in the writings of the Jesuits, Canisius, Possevino, Raynaud, and the journalists of Trévoux (the latter mentioned lest anyone think that modern Jesuits are more just than their predecessors).[4] Atheism? Klefeker does not believe that the charge is made in good faith. Many controversialists use such hyperboles without respect to truth or Christian charity. No one reading his writings or studying his life could seriously believe that Erasmus was an atheist or 'a Christi cultu alienum Deistam.' But to some people anyone is an atheist who does not adopt the whole body of their opinions, even to the most trivial.[5] Pyrrhonism? It is clear from his writings that Erasmus is always consistent with himself unless he has been honestly persuaded to change his mind – that is very different from Pyrrhonism. Three things might have led some to consider him a sceptic: his prudent, scrupulous way of writing about abuses – but one cannot doubt his firm opposition to them; his doubts, not about the dogmas themselves but about the arguments used to advance or defend them; the expectation of the Romanists that he would come to the defence of everything taught and done in the old church – indeed in his consistency to his vision (the reflowering of letters and restoring of piety and the church without a schism) he satisfied neither side.[6] Arianism (of which Catholics and Calvinists accuse him and for which the unitarians claim him)? If Erasmus doubted whether some passages used against the Arians were in fact to the point he nevertheless rejected Arian teachings and plainly professed the doctrine of the Trinity. Pelagianism? Yet he is defended by the Jansenists rather than the Jesuits. On grace he adopted the teaching of the Greek Fathers – it would be a sign of ignorance to apply the hated name 'Pelagian' to that today.[7]

What of Erasmus' character, of the charges – dear to Protestants – of fear and timidity? He is not timid who hesitates to plunge unprotected into a fire or to swim against the torrent when he knows he must drown or who has an equal fear of Scylla and Charybdis. Klefeker finds in Erasmus a large not a fearful spirit, capable of criticizing in fullest liberty but in the end adhering to Rome not from timidity but from

4 Ibid 394. Klefeker will on occasion use other Catholic writers, eg, Raemond, Richard, Marsollier, Le Courayer, against the Jesuits.
5 Ibid 395
6 Ibid 396–7
7 Ibid 402

judgment ('bonum an malum, alia quaestio est').[8] How could he be expected to join Luther when he still sincerely held many doctrines of the old church assailed by Luther – episcopal authority, the Mass, free will, devotion to the saints? He took the middle way, the way of peace and concord. Would Luther himself have made a revolution if the popes and bishops had been so many Erasmuses ('si illa Pontificem & Episcopos totidem Erasmos habuisset ...')?[9]

I repeat: neither from the Catholic nor the Protestant side had there been an interpretation approaching this essay's inner understanding of Erasmus' mind and appreciation of his historical stance. It was written at a time when the religious impulse of the Reformation was still not spent, when a man like Fabricius (and we must look to him as the inspirer of the work) – freed from an exclusive spirit without following Arnold into a root-and-branch renunciation of all but a tiny remnant of the past – could still appreciate the religious preoccupations at the heart of Erasmus' life and thought and his deep and abiding commitments. From this the Enlightenment presentation of Erasmus as jester – not to mention the nineteenth century's obsession with his alleged 'weakness' of character – was a decline into triviality.

But 'Enlightenment' and 'nineteenth century' can be gross simplifications or stereotypes in Erasmus interpretation as in all else. There will be different 'Enlightenment' views of Erasmus as there were different Protestant views and different Catholic views. A little ceremony at Helmstedt for the centenary to which Klefeker addressed his discourse associated Erasmus with one form of Enlightenment historiography, the idea of progress. This ceremony was the work of Hermann von der Hardt (1660–1746).[1]

Like a wide pathway the purer studies of the humanists prepared the way for Luther's Reformation – that is Hardt's theme. It would then be appropriate on the eve of the celebrations for the jubilee of the Reformation to celebrate the jubilee 'humanitatis & fontium sacrorum.'[2] For the occasion Hardt adorned his lecture-room with figures and pictures symbolizing the progress of reformation from Moses to Luther. His oration explained these symbols: for the Old Testament's imperfect understanding the figure of Jacob sleeping, for the abundant light of the New Testament a depiction of Christ's nativity. Yet in Europe, in Germany the penetration of Christianity was shallow, its hold tenu-

8 Ibid 402–3
9 Ibid 404
1 *Jubilaeum humanitatis & fontium sacrorum* ...
2 Ibid 4

ous. The evil condition of religion in the Middle Ages was represented by the figures of Peter Lombard (scholasticism), Tribonianus and Gratian (the civil law and the canon law, both unsuited to the German temperament), Hugo Carrensis and Lyra (an exegesis tied to the Vulgate rather than the original text). There follow the figures of those who prepared the way for a great renovation – Valla, Reuchlin, Erasmus, Hutten, Ximenes – and finally, as a climax, the figure of Luther himself.[3] The oration was accompanied by symbolic actions (in the full seriousness of some of them it is hard to believe): the kissing of the Erasmus and Ximenes editions, the presentation by Hardt himself of a copy of Erasmus' New Testament of 1516 ('magni pretii rarissimum monumentum'), a vow to care unceasingly for humane and biblical studies, the uncovering of a bowl of fruits 'with the prayer that humane and biblical studies will bear fruit a hundredfold.'[4]

The vision of history expressed in this celebration of 29 October 1717 is one of progressive revelation and enlightenment: from the humanists to Luther there was a growing illumination, humane studies were a stepping-stone to Reformation. It is consistent with Hardt's intellectual biography: Hebrew erudition leading to the chair of oriental languages at Helmstedt, a movement in his interpretation of the Old Testament from a pietist (there had been friendships with the pietists August Hermann Francke and Philipp Spener) to a more rationalist approach, an interest in great themes of universal history.[5] Ultimately he saw history moulded to a single curve. In the general preface to his larger contemporaneous work, *Historia literaria reformationis in honorem jubilaei anno* MDCCXVII ... he reiterated his essential idea: historical progress was the work of Providence brooding over human affairs. Civilization slowly fought its way upward; with Christianity ('Christianae disciplinae lumen admirabile') came a new age; yet the peoples were satisfied with the name rather than the reality of Christian virtue; medieval scholasticism and clericalism were in fact a retardation, even a degeneration; the struggle of the temporal authorities to correct these evils was checked. 'But God could do what was beyond human strength. His eternal wisdom proposed to cure the evil fundamentally. Therefore at the beginning of the sixteenth century he roused up Erasmus, who began the general renovation first in letters.'[6]

This is a strange work. Its different parts deal with various literary

3 Ibid 8–11
4 Ibid 6, 12–13
5 ADB X 595–6; NDB VII 668–9
6 'Praefatio' 2

controversies of the Reformation period. Part 1 is primarily concerned with Erasmus' controversy with Alberto Pio, prince of Carpi.[7] There are long quotations from the sources and some whole texts. Hardt's own contribution, however, goes beyond mere commentary on the sources: it is rhetorical and repetitive (favoured phrases occur and recur like a litany, familiar metaphors, for example, the hapless egg laid by Erasmus and hatched by Luther, are worked and reworked).

The place of Erasmus in Hardt's scheme of literary history is clear from the general preface. The Reformation began with the restoration of learning and letters; that was Erasmus' work. No rivalry or envy can deprive him of this glory in the eyes of posterity: he broke the scholastic toils (whose encumbrance he himself felt when a student at Paris), dissipated the shades of ignorance, recalled men to the sacred sources, pointed the way – by a knowledge of Christian things – to a renewal of the commonwealth, all in a mild and humane spirit and as a friend, not an enemy, of the church.

Erasmus' reformation had a distinctive character for Hardt. It could best be described as a 'pre-Enlightenment.' Erasmus represented the party of humanity. Burning for the great renovation, seeking to enrol others in the struggle, he yet recognized that the end must be achieved not by clamour but by humane dealing and the spread of enlightenment: 'Tenebrae non pellendae minis sed luce, nec inhumana barbareis corrigenda clamoribus sed humanitate.'[8] If the methods are characteristically described in this kind of language, so are the ends. Virtue was to be, not forced as in the medieval schools ('all by force and fear'), but spontaneous, lively, free. Men's natures would be changed by the new institutions of learning and education: 'pro barbaris homines, pro rudibus periti, pro incultis politi, pro malis boni.'[9] Studies would have utility for the commonwealth; they would not be sterile, as in scholasticism, but would bear fruit. Erasmus himself was a forerunner of the new kind of man: 'Bold and fearless appearance, honest and open face, fine brow, prompt and upright spirit ...'[1] He was not terrified by the ragings of the barbarians. For naturally those who preferred darkness

---

7 'Historia certaminis inter Erasmum Roterodamum Caroli v. consiliarium, et Albertum Pium, Carporum principem, Caroli v. in Romana curia oratorem, de bonis literis ab Erasmo suscitatis, de Novo imprimis Testamento Graeco, cum nova versione et notis, A. 1516 per Erasmum edito, communis emendationis ac mansuetae reformationis fonte.' On this controversy, see Myron P. Gilmore 'Erasmus and Alberto Pio, Prince of Carpi.'
8 *Historia* 29
9 Ibid 62
1 Ibid 58

to light, constraint to freedom, narrowness to expansion of spirit fought against him. His New Testament – a trumpet to the walls of Jericho – aroused panic in class-room and pulpit.[2] Here in Hardt it is Erasmus who wields the Herculean club![3]

The whole picture is not a subtle one. There was darkness; there came light – mediated by Erasmus. Only in his interest in Erasmus' significance for the commonwealth does Hardt make a distinctive contribution to Erasmus interpretation. He had more to say of the political works than earlier or contemporary writers preoccupied with theological issues. Erasmus' literary labours portended a larger trans-formation than might appear on the surface.[4] He sought not some small change in religious rites and ceremonies but the peace of the commonwealth and a tranquil life for all Christian citizens.[5] One source of renewal was the liberation of the civil power from clerical bonds – to that Erasmus contributed. Social transformation was to follow on reform in education – of that his *Institutio principis christ-iani* was a model.[6] His *Querela pacis*, above all, showed his seriousness of purpose: it was written for a particular situation and can only be understood in the light of that situation – to support the peace party in controversies at the Burgundian court (the court of the later Charles v) over the peace with France in Flanders.[7]

There is in fact an unusual Habsburg dynasticism in Hardt's work and a not so unexpected German patriotism. One of its dedications is to the memory of Emperor Charles v. Through his connection with the Burgundian court and the House of Austria Erasmus had the widest possible sphere of influence. In a sense that dynasty was the midwife of the renewal of letters and consequently of the great renovation in Christendom.[8] If Erasmus had accepted the pressing invitations to move away from the centre of affairs, to settle in England or even in France, Germany would have remained in barbarism; the Reformation – the high-point of renewal – could not have carried the day there.[9]

2 Ibid 20
3 Ibid 53: 'Novum Erasmi in primis Testamentum Graecum illis terribile, tanquam Herculis clava ...'
4 Ibid 100
5 Ibid 92
6 Ibid 15
7 Ibid 89–92
8 Ibid 8–11
9 Ibid 11. Hardt really avoids the issue of Erasmus versus Luther, while emphasizing the consistency of Erasmus' preference for non-violent methods. He could hardly take the issue seriously, since he sees them both working for the one great transformation (103–4, 106–7).

Light breaking out of darkness, new life bursting from barren ground, for corruption purity, for constraint freedom – that is the burden of Hardt's Reformation historiography. It was to have a great future in the eighteenth and nineteenth centuries. Another interest of the coming age – in a determinist kind of psychology – had been anticipated by an essay appearing in a journal edited by the rationalizing jurist Christian Thomasius (1665–1728).[1]

The first part of this essay, a portrait of Erasmus, seems on familiar ground. After regretting the absence of a biography worthy of Erasmus' fame and remarking that the humanist himself might not have cared for a frank portrait (why then did he reveal so much of himself in his letters?), it moves into a catalogue of Erasmus' weaknesses of temperament. First, his timidity. Although he had perceived the truth as well as any, he could never be induced to profess it openly. What others call prudence or moderation the author considers fear of losing his reputation, comfort, or livelihood or of suffering peril or persecution. His intrepidity in fighting the monks was not as serious as it seems since that was a battle of the giant and the pygmy, and with the support of popes and bishops Erasmus had no need to fear the monks' impotent rage.[2] In fact from his timidity arose a distaste for conflict and controversy. Only by playing on his fears and his self-esteem (part and parcel of this kind of personality) could Pope Adrian VI persuade him to write against Luther – and even then he tried to keep in well with both parties.[3] Secondly his love of pleasure ('ad voluptates maxime propensum'), the evidence extraordinarily including Erasmus' playful letter to Faustus Andrelinus about the kissing nymphs of England.[4] Thirdly, a proclivity to jokes and laughter, as in the *Morie encomium*. Time is taken solemnly to defend his too acid style – it was what the age deserved.[5]

All this seems familiar enough, that Protestant view of Erasmus which had him recognizing the truth but failing to follow it because of

1 'Icon Desiderii Erasmi Roterodamensis.' Thomasius himself was not the author. Cf Hanns Freydank 'Christian Thomasius der Journalist.'
2 'Icon Desiderii Erasmi Roterodamensis' 443–4
3 Ibid 445–6
4 Ibid 447–8. Letter to Faustus dated England [summer] 1499, CWE 1 Ep 103: '... there are in England nymphs of divine appearance, both engaging and agreeable, whom you would certainly prefer to your Muses; and there is, besides, one custom which can never be commended too highly. When you arrive anywhere, you are received with kisses on all sides ...'
5 'Icon Desiderii Erasmi Roterodamensis' 443–4

weakness of character. Yet in mid-essay there are considerations to make one pause. Erasmus adhered inwardly to neither party but chose the middle way; thus he attracted the hatred of both, of those who could not tolerate anyone who did not side with them. Thus Bellarmine, Possevino, and Stapleton are accused, but also Luther, whose charge of atheism was without justification.[6] Further, the author is sympathetic to Erasmus' theological writing, tossing quickly aside the oft-repeated contention that he should have stuck to literature and left theology alone. That would be to make words superior to things. Erasmus rightly combined humane and divine letters; his New Testament earned the applause of the learned world in his generation and later.[7] But the author's interest is not here. If one looks back again at the catalogue of weaknesses, one sees that the author's concern is less with making a moral, let alone a theological, judgment than with depicting a certain kind of personality which is all of a piece. From the disposition already described flowed other traits, inevitably: the adulation of the great, hesitation and uncertainty, even inconstancy, a love of personal freedom.[8] This is a determinist psychology or at least a unitary psychology of temperament or disposition, now applied for the first time to Erasmus. The author's assumptions are abundantly apparent in the last section of the essay dealing with Erasmus' virtues. Many err, he says, because they attribute to Erasmus' virtue what arises from his nature: his moderation, for example, and his love of peace.[9] This way of seeing a personality virtually removes it from the realm of praise and blame. There seem inconsistencies: the language of moral judgment is still used, and there is talk of 'vices' and 'virtues.' Nevertheless the interest of this essay is in its enunciation of a certain view of human nature. This may derive ultimately from Galen, but it also anticipates Lavater and all those interested in the typology of character. It was the first 'psychological' study.[1]

6 Ibid 454–5
7 Ibid 455–8. Huet's praise is mentioned.
8 Ibid 450, 452, 459
9 Ibid 460
1 One might associate with this essay the extraordinary piece *Nöthiger historischer Unterredungen*. It is a dialogue in the other world between Erasmus and Diogenes Cynicus on a variety of topics. Its affinity with the Thomasius essay lies in its presentation of Erasmus (his career is discussed at 54–73) as a man who followed his own bent, the leading of his temperament. His was the temperament of an independent man of the world. Thus after leaving the monastery he was beholden to no one but trusted God and followed (Erasmus himself is speaking) 'meinem muntern und auf-

There are obvious differences between the German writers we have been considering and the French Catholic writers discussed earlier. The latter were preoccupied with Erasmus' standing to the scholastics, Fathers, and creeds, the former with his relation to Luther and the Reformation. One is tempted to say that there is more penetration with the German writers, though that may be unfair at least to Joly and Simon. There is less journalistic verve but more solid scholarship. Certainly one finds more variety – not differences of opinion over Erasmus (it is a great distance from Tournemine to Le Courayer) but in approach, in the very fundamentals. The French contestants fight over a familiar and well-defined ground. To travel the triangle from Seckendorf through Arnold to the Thomasius essay is to enter more unfamiliar, more mysterious, and more exciting territory. Is it that in Germany around 1700 the beginnings of historicism – that serious, professional, in the end exclusive preoccupation with history and the historical – have already appeared?

geweckten *naturelle* ...' (57). In a work like the *Ciceronianus*, 'I wrote just as my temperament gave me thoughts and words' (67). The *Adagia* were a gathering of a life of free wandering about the world. Controversy was a pleasure to Erasmus. At the same time certain Christian traits are emphasized: he died as a Christian. For the rest the dialogue is noteworthy for its egregious errors in Erasmus' biography. One example: in Paris in the 1490s Erasmus earned the favour of King Francis I (reigned 1515–47).

EIGHT

In Dictionary and Journal: Bayle and Le Clerc

ERASMUS WAS TREATED OR MISTREATED in various works of theological, historical, and literary polemic from 1680 to 1715. The Erasmuses depicted in the last two chapters – like their predecessors of the confessional age – inhabited a fiercely controversial world. But Erasmus often found a place, too, in works of a more stately or sober kind – biographical dictionaries and national 'encyclopedias' or gazetteers. Such works helped make up the common stock of the European learned community in the sixteenth and seventeenth centuries, as the confident reliance of one on the other makes clear. They continued to be published into the eighteenth century; indeed, in Pierre Bayle's *Dictionnaire historique et critique* this modest genre was raised to the level of genius. Here, too, however, a controversial purpose was more or less always present.

Running debate was easier in the journal, whose early history and place in the republic of letters we have already touched on.[1] The journals created a web of contacts and associations; they were links for the learned, to the tiro in studies they gave guidance and stimulus, to the literate bourgeois a compendium of current information and debate. Theirs was a work of pin-pointing, of culling and clarification and abbreviation, so designed that, in the words of Keble's hymn, he who ran might read. They could also be very polemical, as *Trévoux*'s intervention in the Erasmus debate demonstrates. The piece to be considered here – Jean Le Clerc's biography of Erasmus – was unusually substantial for a journal article. The polymathic journals in fact occupied an intermediate stage in European intellectual history. By the second half of the eighteenth century the reading publics were drawing

---

1 See part 2, introduction, above.

apart, specialization was setting in, and journals of another kind were being called for. In the history of writing about Erasmus the time had then come for the massive biography.

Among the more popular dictionaries was *Le Grand Dictionnaire historique*, which first appeared in Lyon in 1674.[2] Its author, Louis Moreri (1643–80), was an industrious and good-natured priest in that city. He completed the work – begun for his own instruction but published on the insistence of his friends (a not unusual story with this type of work) – in his late twenties. He made a revision for the second edition before his early death at the age of thirty-seven.[3] He wished, he said, to include no useless information but also to omit nothing which would satisfy the legitimate curiosity of his readers. His preface recites the whole prehistory of the dictionary as he conceived it; there have been dictionaries and reference works of all kinds down to that of Anthony Sandere who 'made a collection of all the authors with the name Anthony.'[4]

The biographical outline for the entry on Erasmus was drawn above all from Beatus Rhenanus.[5] Romantic colouring was, however, added to the story of Erasmus' birth: Gerard – his father – took the pregnant Margaret with him in his sudden flight; even the indulgent *Compendium vitae* is outdone by that touch. Moreri is interested especially in Erasmus' relation with Rome, where during his visit (1506–9) cardinals and learned men assisted him and sought to retain him by reputable promises. Pope Paul III, it is added out of sequence, promised him a cardinalate. Kings and popes wished to attract him to themselves, but he would not sacrifice his liberty.[6] Yet his inner commitment was to the church; he dedicated his edition of the New Testament to Pope Leo X; he left Basel for Freiburg when the heretics were creating 'unbelievable disorder' there. He died in Basel, but Moreri hints at no theologically troubling circumstances about his death or burial.

2 The unusual literary dictionary by Thomas Pope Blount (1649–97), *Censura celebriorum authorum* ..., must be relegated to a footnote. Blount, from an old Staffordshire family and a public figure under Charles II and William III, put together the opinions of a large number of writers on six hundred of their more distinguished fellows. Cf DNB II 718–19. On Erasmus, there are a dozen or so extracts and many names familiar to us – Beatus Rhenanus, Baudius, Sweertius, Miraeus, Joseph Scaliger, Huet.

3 Hoefer XXXVI, cols 551–3; foreword by Parayre (added in 1681 edition)

4 *Le Grand Dictionnaire historique* preface

5 I use the 4th edition, *Le Grand Dictionnaire historique, ou le mélange curieux de l'histoire sacrée et profane* ... II (Lyon 1687) 1150–1.

6 'Mais il ne voulut jamais s'attacher.'

Moreri's is a moderate Catholic judgment of Erasmus suggesting no serious ambiguity in his relation with the church.[7] In his associations with popes and cardinals all was honey. The one critical passage is without bitterness or excess:

It is necessary in good faith to avow that Erasmus was a little too free in his discourses, and that he even held some views which were justly censured by the Faculty of Theology at Paris during his lifetime and by the Council of Trent after his death. It is true, as he often says in his books, that, being man, he could err but he never lent will to his errors; which shows that he did not speak under the impulse of that spirit of pride and preconception which is the character of heresy.

His wish to see Christians reunited led him to make concessions to the heretics, but mostly in matters not contrary to the Catholic mysteries. And, of course, he wrote against Luther.

Moreri's Erasmus, untroubled by the contemporary conflicts of Jesuit and Jansenist over that personage, was an Erasmus for the simple faithful, an Erasmus to pique Pierre Bayle, as we shall see.

The *Polyhistor* of Daniel Georg Morhof (1639–91) was a more complex work than Moreri's. Indeed, the scheme was so ambitious that Morhof barely completed the first part (*polyhistor literarius*) before his death, and the remaining two parts (*polyhistor philosophicus* and *polyhistor practicus*) were put together by others. The scale and the thoroughness befit the earnest polymath who was professor of eloquence and poetry and later of history at the newly founded University of Kiel.[8] While still a young teacher he began the work for his students as a methodical categorization of writers of all kinds, an attempt to embrace in a critical system all contemporary knowledge. 'I set sail on an ocean,' Morhof said sombrely, 'where a haven is hard to find and danger threatens of shipwreck from rocks and shoals.' Readers differ in their tastes, and each is both judge and executioner.[9] This combination of confidence and diffidence issued in a work – the Erasmus passages themselves make it clear – of sharper formulations and more secure judgments than are to be found in most of its predecessors of the same type.

---

7 Cf W. Kaegi 'Erasmus im achtzehnten Jahrhundert' 217: Moreri 'versucht, soweit es im Rahmen der kirchlichen Tradition zulässig war, dem besonderen Genius des Erasmus gerecht zu werden.'
8 ADB XXII 236–42
9 *Polyhistor* preface

There are substantial sections on Erasmus in part 1 (*polyhistor literarius*).[1] Erasmus appears as the collector of adages, in the Ciceronian controversy, as a letter-writer, in his works on rhetoric and preaching. 'He was first among the collectors of adages, a very difficult task in his time. I believe that he put more work and care into this than into many other writings ... It is a book which no student of Latin can do without.'[2] In the Ciceronian controversy Erasmus wrote not so much against Cicero as against his bad imitators. He found it unbearable that mere patchwork compilors, whose effusions imitated Cicero as a monkey might, alone boasted the name Ciceronian and accused others of stuttering barbarously. He became carried away and spoke – to his later regret – too freely of Cicero; but that did not justify Julius Caesar Scaliger's bitter attack, later repented of by Scaliger himself and expiated by his son.[3]

Erasmus' eclectic style lacked the purity of those which followed the best models. He rather excused than commended it himself. Yet 'no writings were more agreeable or more acute than his letters. Their Latinity is not bad; no one ought to model himself on it (for here the ancient writers carry the day) but it is natural and extemporary and takes its character from its subject-matter ...' They are full of literary information, of civil and ecclesiastical wisdom and also of light-hearted and jocular things, for he was of a merry disposition. The theological controversies of the time were aired there; Erasmus himself occupied the middle ground, but the student may find in his letters the views of the warring parties. His mind was 'lofty, broad, diverse, fertile, vigorous, ready, born to be the ornament and wonder of his age.' Holland may glory in Erasmus and Grotius; posterity will not see their like.[4]

Of Erasmus' rhetorical works Morhof says that *De copia verborum et rerum* was 'a most useful book, more known by name than frequently used' and the *Ecclesiastes* an application of sound rhetorical rules to preaching. He especially points to what is said about allegory in preaching, for the unhealthy taste for the allegorical rather than the natural sense remains in his own time.[5] Morhof comes no closer than

1 I use the 4th edition (Lübeck 1747; reprint Aalen 1970).
2 I, (bk) 1, (ch) XXI, 67, 69, vol 1, 250
3 I, 1, XXIII, 14–17, vol 1, 274–5. The chapter (XXIII) is concerned 'De epistolarum scriptoribus,' and the Ciceronian controversy arises in a treatment of Cicero as letter-writer. (Further references are to volume and page only.)
4 Vol 1, 279–81
5 Vol 1, 952, 985–6

this to the great theological controversies of the early sixteenth century; brief references in the posthumous *polyhistor practicus* place Erasmus among those 'who laboured to show the truth of the Christian religion with the assistance of natural theology,' although some found traces of Arianism in his paraphrase on John.[6]

If the humanist and Protestant images of liberation and rebirth, of light breaking on darkness are implicit in Morhof's account of Erasmus, he is not directly concerned with the great humanist's relation to the Reformation; Erasmus appears essentially as a figure in literary history.[7]

The shadowy Johann Christoph Rüdiger (Adolphus Clarmundus) returns in his biographical dictionary to typically Protestant preoccupations.[8] Rüdiger wrote his literary biographies to demonstrate to young aspirants to literature that the masters owed their reputations above all to industry. Erasmus, whom the learned called a phoenix, is offered as the first such model. Rüdiger's, too, is a romantic reading of the *Compendium vitae*: Gerard wished to marry Margaret on his return from Italy, though the *Compendium* itself says that he was already by then a priest; he brought back from Italy codices which Erasmus later used in his studies; from the union of Margaret and Gerard there was but one son.[9] One might expect a biographer by Rüdiger's time to be better informed – his ignorance demonstrates perhaps that the day of the quick one-man biographical dictionary had passed.[1]

Rüdiger's picture is of a free scholar unwilling to sacrifice his vocation for ease and comfort. He was supported best by Englishmen, and especially by Thomas More.[2] He might indeed have been more prudent in table conversation against the monks, but he was not politic by nature.[3] As a critic and interpreter he deserves high praise; sometimes he had to work with poor codices, but he did not treat the texts (for example, the famous Trinitarian text in 1 John 5) in bad faith and

---

6 Vol 2, 528, 538
7 Cf Kaegi 'Erasmus' 207.
8 *Vitae clarissimorum in re literaria virorum* ... Erasmus appears at 1–4, 17–31 (break in pagination).
9 Ibid 2–4
1 In another connection a contemporary referred to Clarmundus (Rüdiger) as 'infelicissimus vitarum scriptor' (F.O. Menckenius *Historia vitae et in literas meritorum Angeli Politiani* 423).
2 He lived in England as 'eine *privat Person* gantz honnet' (*Vitae* 19).
3 Ibid 20–2

candidly presented what he found in the codex.[4] What Rüdiger says of his style and of his letters is borrowed from Morhof.[5]

One would expect a Saxon historian to make much of the Luther affair and to begin (as Rüdiger does) with the famous interview between Erasmus and Frederick the Wise. Some say Erasmus turned against Luther for selfish reasons, but Rüdiger does not accept that. Erasmus was a spirited and upright man who made many enemies by telling people the truth beneath his railleries.[6] The conclusion reveals this appreciative, if sketchy, study as a late representative of the sympathetic (Melanchthonian) Wittenberg tradition.

Dictionaries like Moreri's and Rüdiger's, although useful enough in their way, were bland compendia of received information and misinformation. One thinks of the cruel jibe at university extension lecturers:

> Through the land they circulate
> The secondhand and the second rate.

The acumen, astringency, and sheer intelligence they lacked were present in full measure in Bayle's dictionary. How did a Huguenot exile in Holland make of this tired literary form a formidable engine of the critical intelligence? How is Bayle's own position to be defined in his generation and in the 'crisis of the European conscience'? What is the meaning of the entry on Erasmus in the dictionary? What is its bearing on the problem of Bayle himself?

When Andreas Flitner a quarter of a century ago made Bayle with Jean Le Clerc the climax of his admirable study, he interpreted the dictionary article on Erasmus in a particular way – a way consistent with the then established view of Bayle himself: 'Bayle first made Erasmus the church father of the Enlightenment, the pioneer of the modern age.'[7] Earlier Hazard called Bayle's dictionary 'the inspirer of heterodoxy in every land, the sceptic's bible.'[8] So the circle closes: Bayle, the forerunner of modern scepticism, celebrates Erasmus, the forerunner of modern scepticism; past, present, and future mirror one another in an indistinguishable succession. An attentive reading of the Erasmus article might stir doubts about this interpretation; we will return to that. Also, Bayle scholarship is (since 1952) a drastically

4 Ibid 24
5 Ibid 25–6
6 Ibid 27–9
7 *Erasmus im Urteil seiner Nachwelt* 122
8 *The European Mind 1680–1715* 114

changed landscape. Bayle, it suggests, is to be understood in his own setting, not by anticipation of another age and another world.

Bayle was a seventeenth-century provincial Huguenot; the son of a pastor, destined himself to be a pastor, he belonged to a persecuted and self-conscious minority; he must be defined always, says his biographer, by reference to Calvinism.[9] From 1675 to 1681 he was professor of philosophy in the Calvinist academy at Sedan, one of the three principal academies of the kingdom, and the colleague and friend of the redoubtable Pierre Jurieu, who was to be a spokesman for the Huguenots in their hour of trial and the representative of one side of the Huguenot temperament – its intransigence, its powers of resistance. Bayle, as we shall see, spoke for other sides. The suppression of the academy in 1681 and the impending destruction of the Huguenot church forced him to look to England or Holland; already he had been weaving connections in the republic of letters as well as acquiring a knowledge exceptional for one of his age and background. In 1681 he was called to the chair of philosophy and history at the new Ecole Illustre in Rotterdam. He came to Erasmus' town, where he could find the intellectual resources and the contacts he craved.

Here was no break with the Calvinist past; his associations in Rotterdam were with the French-speaking Walloon congregations, undogmatic and unpolemical for seventeenth-century Calvinist congregations but familiar to Bayle in their practical piety.[1] Yet the provincial was becoming an international figure. He published anonymously his *Lettre sur les comètes*, already written before he left Sedan, but his authorship was soon revealed. There quickly followed his reply to Louis Maimbourg's history of Calvinism. This work, like its predecessor, had a great success in the learned world. Bayle's standing in the republic of letters was confirmed by the success of his journal, founded in 1684 on the eve of the revocation of the Edict of Nantes under the auspices of another French refugee, the publisher Henry Desbordes. The web of his connections was much extended as intellectuals throughout Europe sent him books, articles, reviews, and comments.[2]

The cessation of the journal in 1687 freed Bayle for work on the dictionary which was to be his masterpiece and great legacy to posterity

9 Elisabeth Labrousse *Pierre Bayle* I: *Du Pays de Foix à la Cité d'Erasme* 55. What follows is based on this great biography.
1 Ibid 170–1
2 Elisabeth Labrousse 'Les coulisses du journal de Bayle'

Pierre Bayle
Frontispiece to *The Dictionary Historical and Critical*, London 1734
After Carl Vanloo
Reproduced by permission of the Thomas Fisher Rare Book Library
University of Toronto

– a rather too solemn description of so sharp and so curious a work.[3] The dictionary form was admirably suited to Bayle – from his childhood he had been an avid gatherer of knowledge and news and an insatiable reader. But, unlike other editors of dictionaries, he was not satisfied with what came easily to hand. He had a mania for precision which saved him from the superficiality of his fellows, while his relentless curiosity about many things saved him from an arid specialism.[4] The form of his dictionary, to which we will return, conformed to Bayle's personal style and temperament and also to his intended readership; the dictionary was to offer solid nourishment to the general educated reader, but to the initiated in intellectual controversies headier stuff – sharp assaults on established errors, the authoritative settlement of disputed questions, and the ironic, even flippant, upsetting of pompous ignorance. The author of the dictionary displayed still the flair of the journalist, 'a most meticulous ... erudition distilled in the infectious good humour of a writer given over to the inspiration of the moment.'[5] Bayle was dissatisfied with existing dictionaries like Moreri's; he did not accuse Moreri of bad faith but neither did he excuse his naivety, credulity, or haste. The word *critical* in the title of his own work was deliberately chosen; he took up in a more sophisticated age the humanist critical tradition; like his great predecessors he wished to separate the genuine from the spurious. Underlying all was a passionate commitment to certain moral and intellectual positions; defining these brings one to the heart of the problem of Pierre Bayle.

Bayle belonged to seventeenth-century Huguenot history. His biography makes that clear. Only hindsight could simplify his significance to a pioneering of the Enlightenment alone. In the dilemmas of the Huguenot minority, its sense of belonging and yet of not belonging to the French community, he knew tensions which later generations could hardly understand. These tensions were heightened sharply by the experience of exile after the revocation, by the atmosphere of the 'Refuge.'[6] How were the refugees to see their future – assimilation to their new environment, especially to Holland, or return to France? What should be their posture towards France and the great king who had banished them? Bayle was caught up in the controversies

3 First edition, 4 parts in 2 vols (Rotterdam 1697)
4 Labrousse *Bayle* I 46
5 Ibid 243. Cf Labrousse on Bayle's characteristic tone – 'celui du jeu, pris dans son sens le moins pejoratif et le plus plein' (ibid 123).
6 Ibid 202–13

of the Refuge and especially in opposition to his old colleague and protector, Pierre Jurieu. Jurieu was fixed in his hostility towards Louis xiv and worked for the overthrow of the solution of 1685. He fanned the old Huguenot fires and demanded the pristine zeal and the pristine intransigence. Bayle's was another answer to the questions posed by the Refuge. He could not accept the call to resistance and the rejection of absolutism. His solution was a strong civil society, guaranteeing the individual conscience and religious diversity, the solution of general toleration. Articles in the dictionary which later generations saw as striking anticipations of modern scepticism belonged rather to the polemics of the Refuge. The famous article on 'David,' recounting the crimes of the Hebrew king, expressed Bayle's pacifism and his opposition to the politics of revenge.[7]

More generally, Bayle's ideas arose from a wrestling with his Calvinist heritage in the setting of late seventeenth-century French society and culture. Bayle's scepticism was a scepticism about human pretensions, indeed about human nature and human reason. It was rooted (at times, one may think, precariously) in an absolute faith in revelation and in the divine providence and grace.[8] There Bayle was a disciple of Calvin and Augustine; indeed, in the post-Descartes age, he held to fideism with an enhanced logical rigour. There he diverged from the Erasmian line – he could not have written in favour of free will[9] – but in other ways he was Erasmus' disciple, too: in the value he gave to personal piety and morality and in his critical handling of texts and histories.[1] He was Erasmus' disciple, above all, in his distaste for fanaticism and violence. What angered him most was party spirit, the self-serving of sects and factions. Of these crimes the theologians on all sides (but the Roman most of all) stood condemned. Their quarrels became crusades, holy wars quite foreign – how close this is to Erasmus – to the Christian spirit. Princely egoism and the passions of the people

7 Walter Rex 'Bayle's Article on David'
8 Labrousse *Pierre Bayle* II *Heterodoxie et rigorisme* 295–313, 442–6. The 1960s produced a spate of writings on Bayle's religious outlook. See, eg, E.D. James 'Scepticism and Fideism in Bayle's *Dictionnaire*'; H.T. Mason 'Pierre Bayle's Religious Views'; Harry M. Bracken 'Bayle Not a Sceptic?'; Richard H. Popkin 'Pierre Bayle'; cf Popkin, 'Pierre Bayle's Place in 17th Century Scepticism'; Craig R. Bush *Montaigne and Bayle: Variations on the Theme of Skepticism*; Pierre Rétat *Le Dictionnaire de Bayle et la lutte philosophique au xviiie siècle*.
9 Labrousse *Bayle* II 415: 'Mais Bayle est un Erasme qui composerait le traité du Serf-Arbitre ...'
1 Ibid 415, 440

both bring on wars, but most destructive of all are religious tumults.[2] The Reformation might be an exception because it recovered, if but momentarily, the original purity of the church, but Bayle preferred reform without violence or disorder. He broke through to a position which in fact made him the vanguard of a new age – the inviolability of the individual conscience. In civil life there should be mutual toleration and a plurality of confessions, guaranteed by the law and if necessary enforced by the state. Personal experience – the death of a loved brother in prison for his faith in November 1685 – gave poignancy to Bayle's arguments, but beyond that was the matter of broad principle.[3] Bayle did not deny that conscience could err, but it was not for men to presume upon its freedom or set themselves up as inquisitors; that, far more than any error in belief or indeed than heresy itself, was the real affront to the divine Majesty.[4]

Modern scholarship has placed Bayle at a crossroads.[5] He inherited a faith and held to fundamental tenets of that faith. But the more critical atmosphere of the later seventeenth century posed questions which his own critical temper and intellectual courage did not allow him to evade. He was not satisfied with the easier solutions offered, for example, by the natural theologians; for him faith and nature remained in con-tradiction. But the very tensions in his position, the clinging to faith against the stream, the scepticism about all claims, even those of the men of faith, made toleration and freedom of conscience a necessity for him. It was not surprising that he finished his days and did his best work in Holland, which had pioneered a practical toleration in Europe. Bayle rather despised the Arminians of his time because they had taken up a natural theology which he thought facile, but he shared important concerns with them and above all that for intellectual and religious freedom. Bayle's pilgrimage has brought us back to the Holland of Grotius and his friends.

So, recognizing the new visage which contemporary scholarship has given to Bayle, we may turn to the Erasmus article. Everything made the subject congenial to him – his preoccupation with the sixteenth century as a critical moment in the history of civilization and of Christianity, his interest in literary men, their psychological profiles

2 Ibid 416–19, 500–4
3 Ibid 542
4 Ibid 574–5
5 Cf Karl C. Sandberg *At the Crossroads of Faith and Reason: An Essay on Pierre Bayle*. See also Michael Heyd 'A Disguised Atheist or a Sincere Christian? The Enigma of Pierre Bayle.'

and historical roles. The uncertainties in Erasmus' biography, the controversies surrounding his work and career were a happy challenge to his critical skills. And always there was the natural sympathy of outlook between the two men.

The text of the article is brief, no more than two or three pages.[6] It is hardly rounded out and may even seem sketchy. Erasmus' illegitimacy, which cannot be denied (the fact, however, justifies some extended notes, as we shall see), his rapid progress in studies (it is false that he was slow of mind, as the story about Synthen indicates),[7] his orphaning and forced entry to a monastery, his reception in England, where he accommodated himself wonderfully to the learning and other advantages of the country,[8] his life in Flanders where he became counsellor to Charles v and in Basel where he published much but which he abandoned on the abolition of the mass[9] – these are the main stages of his career as Bayle presents it. His significance is quickly gathered up in the remark that it would be superfluous to say that 'he was one of the greatest men ever seen in the Republic of letters.'[1] This is a truth little disputed. Of his many enemies J.C. Scaliger merits most attention and receives a chain of notes. Staccato remarks pick up a variety of points: those who denied the wish at Rome to make Erasmus a cardinal were wrong; the 'Life' promised by Joly has not yet appeared; Erasmus was unwilling to be painted, although the Holbein portrait which Beza adorned with an epigram has been much praised; Barlaeus solidly refuted Slade; the projected complete edition by Le Clerc is very praiseworthy.[2]

A more flowing passage exposes the heart of Bayle's interest in Erasmus:

Because Erasmus did not embrace the reformation of Luther and because he yet condemned many things practised in popery, he drew on himself a thousand injuries, as much from the Catholics as the Protestants. Never has a man been further from the

6 I use the most complete edition, *Dictionnaire historique et critique de Pierre Bayle* 16 vols (Paris 1820) VI 215–46 (text at 215–17, notes at 217–46).
7 Ibid note E, 223–4
8 As Bayle himself might have done if he had taken that way instead of the road to Holland.
9 Note G (ibid 225) accurately renders the circumstances of Erasmus' death in Basel from Beatus Rhenanus' dedication of Erasmus' edition of Origen.
1 Ibid 216
2 Ibid 216–17

impetuous temper of certain theologians who approve violence and like to sound the battle-cry. He loved peace and knew its importance.[3]

There are scattered comments on Erasmus' writings: those printed most often were the *Colloquia* and the *Moriae encomium*; he was too sensitive to lampoons written against him; he was accused of having but a small knowledge of Greek; he wrote too hastily much of what he published. Then, in a change of tone which need never surprise us in Bayle, he deals with the calumny that Erasmus drank too much: 'In the same place where he declares that he had not lived chastely enough, he protests that he had always lived most soberly and been sorry that he could not live without drinking or eating.'[4]

So much for the text, which thus finishes with a characteristically back-handed defence. The elaboration, the bite, the critical reach are in the notes (*Remarques*). Note A settles the date of Erasmus' birth (1467)[5] and those that follow (B–D) deal with the congenial question of its circumstances.

As long as the world endures, Erasmus will be included in the list of illustrious bastards. But he has been wrongly described as the son of an actual priest. Bayle contests the assertion from the *Compendium*, a work admittedly 'composed with the utmost negligence, where is found only a great simplicity without any extended detail.'[6] Baudius wrote well about Erasmus' mother; she fell but once – conduct very different from debauchery – and, in any case, she produced an excellent man and could boast more than the mother of Peter Lombard, Gratian, and Comestor (all reputedly bastards of the one mother) who (it is said) declared that she need not repent of giving such gifts to the church. Merula was afflicted with an ill-founded scruple in fearing to publish the circumstances at the beginning of the seventeenth century. The fact was already well known and indeed aggravated by false assertions about Erasmus' father which publication would dispel. Baudius might very well have pressed that point, in persuading Merula to publish, if he had known what was in Loos and in the *Tractatus de liberâ hominis nativitate, seu de liberis naturalibus* of Pontius Huetérus published in 1600. The first public assertion of the status of Erasmus' father was in

---

3 Ibid 217
4 Ibid
5 Bayle, like Joly (*Voyage fait à Munster*), accepts initially the date on the Rotterdam statue and elaborates from evidence in the letters (ibid 217–19).
6 Ibid 219

Lando's phrase 'ex condemnato concubitu natus,' to which Herold gave a rather embarrassed reply.[7] Catholic writers especially are blamed for propagating the falsity – Raynaud must have had it from Loos – especially after the refutation by Valerius Andreas.[8] As for J.C. Scaliger, why did not he deal with Erasmus' father in his orations against Erasmus rather than in a private letter written not long after the second oration went to press? Bayle is sceptical of his claim not to have used something still uncertain for fear of casting doubt on his justified charges against Erasmus.[9]

That Erasmus' attraction to England – the country of his adoption – corresponded to an attachment of Bayle himself is confirmed by the warm feeling of note F. Learning was in honour there – among the nobility, too, as it still is (Bayle adds) today. How could Bayle let pass the kissing passage in the letter to Andrelinus? 'If he spoke so well of England when he spoke about it seriously, he gave a description not less attractive when he adopted his playful style ... You see that the Englishwomen pleased him not less than the Englishmen.'[1]

Bayle's fascination with the quarrels of intellectuals may explain the seemingly inordinate attention given in the notes to the Scaliger affair, seven pages out of thirty. But as always he has his reasons, the opportunity to comment on human frailty, even (perhaps most of all) among those devoted to learning and the rule of reason. Scaliger's response to Erasmus' *Ciceronianus* was grossly exaggerated; he cried 'murder, parricide, triple parricide.' One would think Erasmus some barbarian captain set on destroying all learning and setting fire to all libraries.[2] Joseph Scaliger's account of the affair in *Scaligerana* is quite untrustworthy, for example the assertion that his father had not read or understood Erasmus. 'After that will you any longer believe what

7 Bayle is here basing himself on remarks of the poet, philologian, and academician Bernard de la Monnoye (1641–1728) (ibid note c, 221). The phrase used in the dispensation of Leo x to Erasmus in 1517 was 'de illicito et, ut timet, incesto damnatoque coitu genitus.' It does not necessarily imply the father's priestly status (CWE 4 188–90, Ep 517 intro). Scaliger's expression in the letter passed over for publication by his son and finally published in the Toulouse edition of 1620 was 'ex incesto natum concubitu, sordidis parentibus, altero sacrificulo, altera prostituta' (Scaliger to Le Ferron, 31 January 1535, *Jul. Caes. Scaligeri epistolae aliquot* ...). As with Loos later, the information purports to come from neighbours of the family.
8 *Dictionnaire historique* note D
9 Ibid note I 226–7
1 Ibid 224–5
2 Ibid note I 226

learned men tell you at their chimney corners? Here is one of the most distinguished who at every turn says and repeats two or three lies concerning his own father which public and original sources manifestly refute.'[3] Bayle's scepticism, his distrust, his historical sense are all in play here. And the judgment of Erasmus himself is fallible. He attributed Scaliger's first attack to Aleander, the humanist cardinal who was his persistent enemy. '... If Erasmus, who was sweetness and modesty itself, has with so much temerity made a wrong attribution, one ought not to place any reliance on what minds proud, assertive by habit and temperament, opinionated and fanatical, can declaim with a magisterial tone on such a subject.'[4]

Note N settles authoritatively the question of Erasmus' cardinalate. The tone is slightly discreditable to the Roman See. 'Undoubtedly' Erasmus would have been a cardinal under Pope Adrian VI if he had wished to court his favour. 'But under Pope Paul III, the affair was taken further: the cardinalate became a ripe fruit for Erasmus; to receive it he needed only to hold out his hand.' Both Richard and Joly understood this, though some of their assertions are not justified by the evidence. 'Nevertheless the thing is certain ...' from the letters and Beatus Rhenanus.[5]

In writing about the *Colloquia* Bayle achieves an ambiguity worthy of Erasmus himself. He recommends Erasmus' defence of the dialogue form. A contrary point, however, is that the author should not choose subjects on which, in following the logic of the dialogue, he is led to say something unedifying. Further, 'whoever puts in the mouths of heretics all that can best be said for their heresy either pleads a cause dear to his heart or falls into a rash and ridiculous judgment.'[6] Is this to be taken with a grain of salt? Is Bayle saying that Erasmus really intended to say more than he avowed? Is it ironical, as the anticlerical writers of the Enlightenment might have thought? Or is Bayle genuinely speaking for stability and orthodoxy? Or is his pen writing out an unresolved tension in his own mind? The disarming phrase which follows – 'However that may be ...' – might suggest that.

In the Reformation Erasmus was attacked by both sides:

It is not a question here of knowing if Erasmus' conduct on religious matters was good; I will say only that he was, it seems to me, one of those witnesses of the truth who longed for the

3 Ibid note K 228
4 Ibid note M 232
5 Ibid 233–4
6 Ibid note Q 235–6

reformation of the church but who did not believe that it was necessary to achieve it by erecting another society which relied at first on conspiracies [*ligues*] and which quickly passed from words to blows [*à verbis ad verbera*]. He had too limited an idea of God's presence and did not sufficiently consider that He leads us to the same end, sometimes by one route and sometimes by another.

With his famous expression 'I do not like seditious truths,' he remained in the slough; he imagined mistakenly that he was siding with the stronger party and that Luther's conduct suggested that the time of deliverance had not yet come. One could not deny that on the whole Erasmus was what is called 'Catholic.' Yet he saw with joy Luther's first proceedings and was much disturbed when Lutheranism seemed lost, for he feared a renewal of the monks' tyranny. He was not in the end unhappy at the stand-off between the parties.[7]

A characteristic ambiguity flickers through this passage, but the main line is clear. Despite the turbulence of its beginnings, which Bayle must disapprove of, the Reformation was a providential deliverance. Erasmus misjudged it, though he was looking for deliverance and actually responded to it, if with a divided mind. He was also sensitive to the party spirit which was to disfigure it. Underlying the passage is not religious relativism but a sense of the providential ordering of history beyond all its obscurities and confusions.

Erasmus loved peace – Bayle stresses it in note U. His *Dulce bellum inexpertis* is 'one of the most beautiful dissertations one could read ...' It showed that he had thought deeply about 'the most important principles of reason and the gospel and the most common causes of wars.' They arise from the wickedness of individuals and the stupidity of peoples.[8] The behaviour of intellectuals is no better. Erasmus made many enemies by the liberty of his pen. In revenge the monks falsely accused him of writing books like Luther's *Babylonian Captivity* which would discredit him. So today, says Bayle in a direct reference to the controversies of the Refuge and his own quarrel with Jurieu, men react to justified ridicule of 'their dangerous dreams' by false accusations.[9]

The last notes clear away some myths about Erasmus' life – Moreri's assertion that Gerard took Margaret with him in his flight, the tales about Henry VIII and Erasmus' mishap at Dover, and his occupancy of

7 Ibid note T 238–9
8 Ibid 239
9 Ibid note Y 240

the Rectorate at Basel University[1] – and throw in a joke or two: that Erasmus reputedly burst an abscess in laughing at the *Epistolae obscurorum virorum*, the notorious satire of 1515 about the Reuchlin affair, demonstrates one of the benefits of reading.[2] At the end, Bayle happily returns to the question of Erasmus' chastity; the passage, says Mme Labrousse, reveals more of Bayle than of Erasmus.[3] He has the celibate's interest in such matters. In a letter, Erasmus said that he had not been the slave of Venus but did not claim perfect chastity. His assertion that his studies left him no leisure for love is worthy of faith. 'A man of much leisure and careful of nourishing his body would be suspected of lying if he spoke in this way; for idleness and good cheer nurture lust.'[4] Bayle offers another argument. Erasmus needed to take care of his reputation; going about a love affair circumspectly takes time and leisure. Since, given all that he wrote, Erasmus had no leisure, he must have been chaste.[5]

The entry in Bayle's dictionary was the most remarkable piece so far written about Erasmus. Much of it was a settling of scholarly questions in Erasmus' biography. It was the graveyard of a number of myths. Its critical manner and implicit plea for religious toleration made it attractive to liberal minds later. But it is a distortion to see this piece only as a forerunner of the Enlightenment view of Erasmus. Erasmus appears to Bayle primarily as a great figure in the republic of letters; his entry has that in common with those of other dictionaries of his generation, Morhof's for example. There are glimpses of the controversies of the Refuge, however, and his Calvinist heritage is apparent in Bayle's understanding of the Reformation and Erasmus' relation to it: *post tenebras lux*. The playful, the serious, the carping, the deeply committed are mixed together here in a tantalizing way; but the mind and character of Pierre Bayle are unmistakably present on every page.

Even more than Bayle's the name of Jean Le Clerc (1657–1736) is a commonplace to students of Erasmus. All must use the *Opera omnia* which he edited at the request of the Leiden publisher Peter van der Aa and which Bayle welcomed. This was a prodigious labour, like Bayle's on his dictionary, but only a fraction of Le Clerc's startling output. Jean Le Clerc was a Genevan. His grandfather was a Huguenot

1 Ibid notes AA, BB, 241–2
2 Ibid note z 241
3 *Bayle* I 150
4 *Dictionnaire historique* note EE 244–5
5 Ibid 245. Cf Erasmus to Servatius Rogerus 1514: 'I have never been a slave to pleasures, though I was once inclined to them' (CWE 2 296, Ep 296).

refugee from Picardy to Geneva after the massacre of St Bartholomew. His father and uncle built on the grandfather's success in establishing himself in the Genevan community; both were important figures in the academic, ecclesiastical, and political life of the city.[6] Seventeenth-century Geneva was no longer the city of Calvin but, despite the agitations set up in the French Calvinist church over the doctrine of grace and repeated there, orthodoxy held the line through the century.[7] The Le Clercs, however, tended to the more universalist, critical, and tolerant side.[8]

Jean, born in 1657, was a precocious student. He had in earliest life, his autobiography says, stamina to endure 'the Fatigue of Reading.'[9] As a student at the Genevan Academy, he followed his family and his favourite teachers in adhering to the minority party in the city and in the Calvinist church and that meant to the teaching of the universality of grace against the strict proponents of double predestination.[1] Although, as he claimed, he came off in his Divinity exams 'with extraordinary Applause'[2] he was already out of sympathy with the dominant spirit in the Genevan church.[3]

While still a student, Le Clerc was in intellectual contact with the Arminians of Holland. He read Grotius. But he was won to contemporary Arminianism, especially to its acceptance of the compatibility between faith and reason, by a book, *Quaternio dissertationum theologicarum adv. Sam. Maresium*, by his great-uncle, Etienne de Courcelles, himself an enemy of the Dordrecht decrees ('a yoke to which foreign Churches ... had no desire to submit'), a refugee in Holland, and a teacher in the Remonstrant college at Amsterdam.[4] In 1680 he went to Saumur, seat of the most famous of the Calvinist academies, where the universalist teaching had had its stronghold, although controversy and the perilous situation of French Protestantism generally on the eve of the revocation brought decline and disarray. There in 1681 the young Le Clerc eagerly but anonymously

6 Annie Barnes *Jean Le Clerc (1657–1736) et la République des Lettres* 28–34
7 Ibid 22–8. On the disputes in French Calvinism, see Brian G. Armstrong *Calvinism and the Amyraut Heresy: Protestant Scholasticism and Humanism in Seventeenth-Century France*. Whether seventeenth-century orthodoxy was true to Calvin is debatable.
8 Barnes *Jean Le Clerc* 36
9 *An Account of the Life and Writings of Mr John Le Clerc ...* 4–5
1 Ibid 5–6
2 Ibid 7
3 Barnes *Jean Le Clerc* 48
4 *Life* 7; Barnes *Jean Le Clerc* 53; Emile G. Léonard *A History of Protestantism* II *The Establishment* 371

published his first book, *Liberii de Sancto Amore epistolae theologicae*. It was meant to be a challenge to old orthodoxies and in the febrile atmosphere of the time provoked an agitated response. Le Clerc concluded that he could no longer live in an orthodox Calvinist country.[5]

From Saumur Le Clerc wrote to Philip van Limborch in Amsterdam, the doyen of the Arminian theologians, and was warmly received. His mind was turning to Holland. In the event he took in London on the way to Amsterdam. Though his hope of becoming minister in the French congregation there was disappointed, he learned English and began to cultivate his interest in English thought. Before leaving London in 1683, he completed a dissertation on Sodom and Gomorrah and the wife of Lot, his beginnings in biblical criticism. It was characteristically rationalist: that Lot's wife was turned to salt was a figure; she actually died petrified of fear.[6]

Le Clerc finally settled in Amsterdam in 1684 after an utterly disenchanting return to Geneva. His friendship with Limborch stood firm, and he was soon appointed to a chair of philosophy at the Remonstrant college. He lived, he declares, a quiet life there for twenty-seven years 'remote from all Ambition,' serving learning and virtue without popular favour or powerful patronage and on meagre pay, 'suffering Envy from several ill-natured Wits, which are so pestilent in the Republic of letters.'[7] His embroilment with the orthodox of Geneva and Saumur had, his biographer says, marked his mind for life and made him a passionate advocate of toleration. Unlike Bayle in Holland he had deliberately forsaken the Calvinist communities. He does not then belong to the Refuge. Already when he came to Holland he was an Arminian and found his own refuge in the Remonstrant community. He shared its critical, tolerant, irenic outlook.[8]

Le Clerc became a major figure in the republic of letters through his journal, the *Bibliothèque universelle et historique* (1686–93). He was a natural journalist, quick, facile, well read, a skilled transmitter of ideas.[9] The journal reviewed current works in science, philosophy,

5 Barnes *Jean Le Clerc* 64
6 Ibid 75
7 *Life* 12–14
8 Barnes *Jean Le Clerc* 86, 94–5
9 Cf Rosalie L. Colie's comparison of Limborch and Le Clerc: 'Limborch was a conventional scholar and theologian in the Erasmian tradition, grave, considerate, philosophical; Le Clerc was an eighteenth-century man of letters, a publicist, eternally active, universal – and in consequence often superficial' (*Light and Enlightenment: A Study of the Cambridge Platonists and the Dutch Arminians* 31).

theology, and scholarship. Above all, it was an intermediary for British writings; Le Clerc helped make Locke, Burnet, and Newton known on the continent.[1] His later journal, contemporary with the Erasmus edition, the *Bibliothèque choisie*, had 'more boldness, more authority, more liveliness, and wider range.'[2] It adopted the more flexible form of the essay and the miscellany with more extended treatments and a deliberately more controversial tone.

John Locke was in exile in Holland from the governments of Charles II and James II between 1683 and 1689. He became a friend of Le Clerc and other Remonstrants and contributed extensively to the *Bibliothèque universelle* from 1685. Indeed, he wrote almost everything in it between July 1687 and February 1688.[3] As we have seen, the books he reviewed included Richard's on Erasmus.[4] Locke saw the purpose behind the work: by reference to the persecutions Erasmus suffered, to show what the Jansenists still endured in the Roman church.[5] But Locke (as we know) turned Richard's own sympathies against him: how can the Protestants be persuaded to return to the church when there is so much evidence that it has not taken to heart the criticisms by Erasmus and others and indeed still excludes its most faithful servants from office and influence?[6] He revised Richard's account of Erasmus' relation to the Reformers: he may have disagreed with particular dogmas and disapproved of the Reformers' methods but he was not against them essentially; 'He speaks out not so much against their opinions as against their way of supporting them and against their behaviour, which was in his view too violent.'[7] Locke's crypto-Protestant is a fair anticipation of the Erasmus of Le Clerc.

Le Clerc had, he said, 'always an Affection for this Second Eye of *Holland* (for *Hugo Grotius* was the other, as he us'd to call him) ...' The praise he gave him was not above his deserts:

Erasmus, in those times, was an extraordinary Genius, and, to

1 Samuel A. Golden *Jean Le Clerc* 38, 60–7
2 Ibid 68
3 Maurice Cranston *John Locke: A Biography* 293. Locke's authorship is established on the basis of Locke's marks in his own copy of the journal. Cf ibid 256 and Barnes *Jean Le Clerc* 156–9.
4 *Bibliothèque universelle* VII (1688) 122–41
5 Ibid 131
6 Ibid 126–7
7 Ibid 136–7. Locke finishes with an undocumented story not, on the face of it, very creditable to Erasmus' character: how – in the matter of pears stolen from the monastery garden – he played a trick on his superior and a fellow-monk. Erasmus, the account concludes, loved a good story so much that he would not take badly one told against himself (141).

his extreme Desire of Learning, and his unwearied Patience in his Studies, by which he did service to his Contemporaries and Posterity, had join'd a piercing and sound Judgment, a pleasant Wit, a wonderful Candor, and, at so young an Age, a singular Love of Truth and Virtue, and an admirable Eloquence.[8]

That is what Erasmus meant to Le Clerc as a citizen of the republic of letters. His more extended treatments are to be found in two places, first in the prefaces to the succeeding volumes of the *Opera omnia* (appearing in Leiden between 1703 and 1706) and the comments in contemporaneous issues of the *Bibliothèque choisie* and, secondly, in a long article 'Vie d'Erasme tirée de ses lettres' in volumes 5 and 6 of that journal.

Between the prefaces and the article there is a marked difference of tone. In one Erasmus appears more in his own right; the other is preoccupied with his relation to the Reformation. The sunnier, more positive presentation was better suited to places where Le Clerc was praising or advancing his great edition. Erasmus, said the preface to volume 1, was one of those rare scholars 'who dared to apply a healing hand to the evils of their age.'[9] Some criticize his Latinity, but he did not claim to model his style completely on that of the Augustan age. It is better to have something to say and to use appropriate words than to imitate a style. He was among the greatest philologians of the age but he was of too noble a mind to grow old in lesser studies. He turned to theology and applied the humane disciplines to a higher purpose. He was, however, not like those who seek the abstruse and controversial in theology.[1] 'But *Erasmus* without neglecting Mysteries & Rites, by which Religion becomes more decent, and Human Imbecillity is assisted, chiefly requir'd the Fear of God, and observation of his most Holy Commandments ...'[2] He sought by his writings to spread this true understanding of theology throughout Europe and so aroused the enmity of the ignorant and the wicked who are always in a majority. He offended both those who wanted him to flatter the vices of the age and those who wanted him to denounce them utterly. He sought amendment courteously and humanely and held a middle course against those who would inflame civil wars. If not all his actions deserve to be defended (though the difficulties of the time should be remembered), the true Erasmus buried in old volumes should, as in Le

8 *Life* 50
9 LB I (1)
1 Ibid (3)–(4)
2 Ibid (4) as repeated in *Life* 52

je l'ai été, en lifant Mr. *Cudworth*, &
en abregeant fes penfées ; je n'aurai pas
perdu ma peine, à l'égard des Lecteurs ;
& j'efpere qu'ils me fauront plus de
gré de cet Extrait, que de celui d'une
douzaine de petits livres plus nouveaux.
Je puis affurer que la fuite ne fera pas
moindre, comme on le verra par les
autres Tomes, fi Dieu me fait la grace
de me conferver la vie & la fanté.

ARTICLE III.

*Des Tomes III, V, & VI. des Oeu-
vres d'ERASME, de l'édition de
Leide, chez P. Vander Aa. Où l'on
donne un Abregé de la vie d'Erafme,
tiré de fes Lettres.*

J'AI parlé affez au long de la Nouvelle Edition des Oeuvres d'*Erafme*,
dans le Tome I. de cette *Bibliotheque
Choifie.* Si les Volumes précedens
d'*Erafme* ont été reçus favorablement,
ceux que l'on va publier ne le feront
pas moins. Je fai qu'il y a de certaines
gens, qui parlent avec quelque forte
de mépris d'*Erafme* ; parce que c'étoit
un génie infiniment au deffus d'eux.
Il n'a pas vieilli dans des vetilles gram-

Tome V.   G   ma-

Clerc's own edition, be brought out again to enlighten even the present fastidious age.[3] Indeed, despite the enmities of his own time, now all 'reasonable and enlightened persons of both parties' can esteem him equally. Every people envied Holland for producing one of such erudition, moderation, and liberty of mind.

In the study in volumes 5 and 6 of the *Bibliothèque choisie* Le Clerc was less bland. Perhaps the strains of the moment had their effect; these volumes appeared in the depths of the War of the Spanish Succession. The 'Avertissement' to volume 5 spoke of the 'great cabal' which sought to dominate Europe, to keep Christians in ignorance so that a few could lord it and live at ease. It is not surprising that the problem of the Reformation bulks largest in this 'life' of Erasmus.

Le Clerc offers not so much a biography as a commentary on the letters of Erasmus, which he was then preparing for his edition, fully aware of the problems of placing and dating which they posed.[4] (The work called for a solid critical performance, if one not so spectacular – or even exhibitionist – as Bayle's.) The presentation is chronological, year by year. Consequently there is much, as there is in the correspondence, about journeys and friends, about money difficulties and problems with printers. The method may be tedious but it brings also a conviction of reality. Where biographical problems arise, Le Clerc turns to the familiar sources – the *Compendium*, whose authenticity he accepts, Beatus Rhenanus, the major letters to Servatius Rogerus (1514) and Grunnius (1516), which give accounts of Erasmus' early life and experiences, and the catalogue of his works prepared for John Botzheim in 1523. On the problems surrounding Erasmus' birth and childhood and youth Le Clerc in fact says little – strangely he refers the reader to the dictionary of his arch-enemy, Pierre Bayle.[5]

Le Clerc's interpretation is in part familiar – it belongs to the Protestant tradition – but also anticipatory: some of its language heralds the Enlightenment. Of course, the image of light breaking from darkness was long established among Protestants. The historic role of Erasmus was to be aware of the darkness, to rail against it, and to give his generation glimpses of the light. 'It cannot be doubted that he has contributed greatly to the enlightenment of his age and to preparing men to accept a day of which he himself has seen only the dawn.'[6] Long before Luther he had criticized the empty devotions into which

3 LB I (5)
4 'Vie d'Erasme tirée de ses lettres ...'
5 Ibid v 150
6 Ibid 147

the people had been led instead of into a true piety which consists in the exercise of the Christian virtues.

Erasmus is seen above all as a critic of the abuses and disorders in the religious life of his time. The *Moriae encomium* is 'plein de sel et de censures ingenieuses des vices de son tems' and especially those of the monks, Le Clerc had said in his commentary in volume 1 of the *Bibliothèque choisie*.[7] His writings against war are mentioned with appreciation (he wrote 'with much spirit, good sense, and eloquence') but too quickly passed over.[8] He is praised for the practical sense shown in his controversy with the Ciceronians: unlike them he had more regard for things than for words.[9] His religious ideas are very moralistically presented: in contrast to the religion of ceremonies, which bad men as well as good can perform, his consisted in things of which only the good are capable – the exercise of the Christian virtues, established in the mind by one's sense of duty and by one's being persuaded of their importance and necessity.[1] If the people had been convinced that the essentials of religion lay in faith in God and in Jesus Christ and in the practice of the precepts of the gospel, there would have been an end to the mendicant friars and mass-priests.[2] This is a religion of strenuous moral endeavour, indeed a religion for a kind of moral aristocracy. Le Clerc goes no further here in developing Erasmus' religious ideas on their own foundations; he is content to assume that he was at heart for the Reformation.

The appearance of Luther made an epoch in Erasmus' life. That is the point on which Le Clerc's whole interpretation swings. Erasmus was forced amid the tumult to deny the best part of himself. Certainly he disapproved of some dogmas of Luther's (those indeed which contemporary Protestants disown) but he was more out of sympathy with the dogmas of the other side, and its more virulent spokesmen were pursuing him with relentless hatred. Above all, he expressed distaste for turbulence and discord and revolution. But these things did not turn out as badly as he feared.[3] The question is: could reform and enlightenment have come without violent proceedings? Le Clerc's answer is negative because of the intransigent malevolence of the Roman party. Erasmus' call for an arbitration of the differences could

7 397
8 'Vie d'Erasme' v 181
9 Ibid 263
1 Ibid 187
2 Ibid 197
3 Ibid vi 103

not be taken seriously. Luther had either to succumb or to resist. Rome would not now – for the first time in its history – make concessions.[4] 'Great benefits though peace and concord are, they ought not to be bought at the price of truth and liberty, which are infinitely more precious than a base tranquillity which one enjoys by submitting to the yoke of lies and tyranny.'[5] Without Luther's rebellion and the Reformation of Calvin Europe would still be in utter darkness. Good letters, over whose fate Erasmus was most troubled, would be more secure amidst the turbulence on the Protestant side than at the mercy of Rome, which was committed to defend the monkish party to the bitter end and recognized that it had more to fear than to hope from intellectual enlightenment.[6] Does not a comparison of the present states of the Protestant lands and of Spain and Italy make this clear?

Why did Erasmus not understand? It was partly a question of character. Le Clerc set a pattern which was to have many followers, especially among biographers of the nineteenth century: the old Erasmus went through a kind of moral decline. The candour and sincerity which were virtues of his youth were much diminished in his old age. Wishing to present himself as a defender of the Roman party, he filled his letters with 'dissimulations and slanders.'[7] It was 'a shameful baseness' to be embarrassed by the praises of those with whom he was really in sympathy (the Reformers) from fear of angering those (popes, cardinals, and Catholic princes) of whom he had a low opinion – and this out of pure self-interest, for the sake of his pensions or his reputation with the great of the world or out of fear for his life.[8] He would have been better advised to take up a professorship in Switzerland and abandon the struggle to reconcile the Roman party![9]

Le Clerc challenges Erasmus' adherence, as he put it in his famous letter to Pirckheimer, to the consent of the church, the consensus of the whole Christian people.[1] If the orthodox faith is to be found in scripture – as Erasmus himself believed – what need is there of the consent of any society? It is not true that there will be arguments without end, for surely 'in reasoning well one arrives at the Truth'; in believing

4 Ibid 21–2
5 Ibid 93
6 Ibid 12
7 Ibid 193
8 Ibid 143–4. Cf ibid 62.
9 As Le Clerc had spited his enemies by taking a professorship in Holland?
1 Erasmus to Pirckheimer, 15 October 1527: 'I call the Church the consensus of the whole Christian people' (Allen Ep 1893, VII 216).

what one is told one is likely to be deceived. False doctrine must be separated from true by the study of church history and the application of reason. Otherwise false religions, where they are dominant, would be able to claim 'consent' and rebut Christian missionaries.[2] So Le Clerc mingles the gospel of the Reformation and the gospel of Reason.

Erasmus' predicament, however, did not arise only from weakness of character. He was the prisoner of the Roman party, whose ill will and intransigence he perhaps did not properly measure. For Le Clerc, the old church is unchanging, monolithic, malevolent. Its attitude to Erasmus is indicated by its placing much in his works on the Index. His faith in reform through the better education of youth was belied by the work of a society, 'a religious order, very hostile to the memory of Erasmus' (the Jesuits, of course), which has taken possession of education in the interests of the old unreformed religion.[3] Erasmus' attachment to the old church was a fearful *contretemps*. If only he had sensed the need to break free as he sensed the folly of settling in Italy, for 'the land of ceremonies and the Inquisition was not a fit land for a man as free and as far from Italian posturing [*grimaces italiennes*] as he.'[4]

Yet at the end Erasmus was able to break free. He died 'in the arms of his best friends who were then disciples of Zwingli and Oecolampadius.' In a Catholic country he might have been obliged to make some recantation or perform some act of monkish religion.[5] Le Clerc has been a sharp critic of Erasmus' attitude to the Reformers, his public disavowal of the truth he saw in them – all that is in harmony with a long Protestant tradition. But his view of his larger significance is wholly positive. There is, he says, a need in many places for a new Erasmus who would censure superstition anew in the Catholic lands and awaken those Christians who are strong in theological speculations but whose actions belie their theology, among them, no doubt, the orthodox Calivinists who had threatened Le Clerc himself.[6]

There are points in common between this Erasmus and Bayle's. Both Bayle and Le Clerc sympathized with Erasmus in his troubles; they too were victims of over-zealous, intolerant theologians. Both wanted toleration and religious liberty and saw Erasmus as a pioneer.

2 'Vie d'Erasme' VI 179–82
3 Ibid 65
4 Ibid V 172
5 Ibid VI 234
6 Ibid V 164–5. In his *Parrhasiana ou pensées diverses sur des matières de critique, d'histoire, de morale et de politique*, I 438, Le Clerc compared his embattled situation with those of Erasmus and Grotius.

But the differences were great. The optimism of Le Clerc's trust in human reasoning and in historical activism (as one might put it) were confronted by Bayle's radical pessimism.

Despite their common refuge in Holland, the two men – the one in Rotterdam, the other in Amsterdam – became more and more embittered. There were personal grievances on one side and the other and a certain rivalry in journalism, but the roots of this enmity ran deeper.[7] Le Clerc's was the more straightforward, Bayle's the more tortured personality; Bayle had the more subtle mind. To Le Clerc Bayle's scepticism was what it appeared to be, the destroyer of all religion and morality: 'Away therefore with those silly Men, who think this Sceptic has favour'd the Patrons of Religion, because he took away all use of Reason; the Method by which they are wont to defend Religion, whereas he plainly ridicul'd both it and them.'[8] To Bayle, Le Clerc's candour about difficulties in biblical exegesis, his preference for the lucid and simple over the complex and the abstruse, his quest for reconciling intellectual positions, his Platonism as revealed in his enthusiasm for Cudworth's *True Intellectual System of the Universe* suggested that he was a Socinian and a pathfinder for atheism (though in fact Le Clerc's theology was not truly radical).[9] The rock on which they split was Le Clerc's repeated assertion that religion and reason were not at odds: all the principles of the gospel may, 'without Danger, be reduc'd to the most severe laws of Right Reason.'[1]

These things are relevant to their studies of Erasmus. As historians and biographers they shared many assumptions; both tried to rise above common prejudices and to avoid fixed judgments (admirable men may commit crimes and unworthy men may do good, said Le Clerc)[2] but both gave history a didactic purpose and believed that the historian must judge men's actions.[3] In their judgments of Erasmus Le Clerc is characteristically the plainer, Bayle the more ambiguous. Bayle did not deny that the Reformation was a liberation, a providential ordering, but he saw also its ambiguities and contradictions. In the onward thrust of history which it represented for Le Clerc the Reformation brought turbulence and disorder; Erasmus was wrong to con-

7 See Barnes *Jean Le Clerc* 228–37. Cf Labrousse *Bayle* II 330–1.
8 *Life* 45
9 On Le Clerc's religion, see Barnes *Jean Le Clerc* 237–44, Colie *Light and Enlightenment* 113–18
1 *Life* 22
2 *Parrhasiana* 165
3 Ibid 183; Labrousse *Bayle* II 33

demn it for that reason: 'Great benefits though peace and concord are, they ought not to be bought at the price of truth and liberty ...' Bayle's comment on the same issue was the laconic 'he loved peace and knew its importance.' Here are two views of history and its perils, one bright, the other dark.

Attached though it was to an old Protestant interpretation, Le Clerc's understanding of Erasmus was to have a great future. Erasmus helped bring in the light; to a degree he turned his back upon it when the powers of darkness resisted; that may be a reflection on his character or an indication of the difficulties of his personal position, but nothing detracts from his significance as a pioneer of reason and enlightenment. To Falkland half a century before that cause could be given up in near despair; to Le Clerc at the beginning of the eighteenth century, despite the cavillings and buffetings, it was making irresistible headway.

NINE

The First Biographies

꿏

THE GREAT ERASMIAN PIERRE MESNARD once said that the 'age of objectivity' in the study of Erasmus opened with the publication of Le Clerc's edition in 1703–6; henceforth the need was to interpret a figure 'whose features seem set since the beginning of the eighteenth century.'[1] The claim is optimistic: Erasmuses with very different features continue to inhabit the literature in the eighteenth and nineteenth centuries, and some of them are painfully familiar: the Erasmuses of Luther and Canisius for example. Nevertheless Le Clerc's edition and biography are a landmark; they signal the appearance of studies on a larger scale than had been possible or even wished for before. Critical work on the correspondence prepared the way for the first full-length biographies. First of all was the work of an Englishman, Samuel Knight.

We have noted more than once how well Erasmus' reputation had taken root in English soil. With Foxe he had been taken into the main Protestant tradition in England. All parties, other than the Catholic recusants anxious to keep him at arm's length from a Thomas More increasingly depicted as a Counter-Reformation saint, accepted him. A liberal Anglican like Falkland, a religious radical like Milton, even the Caroline divines appealed to him for their own purposes, the last in support of their idea of moderation and comprehensiveness.[2]

Knight's biography was then no rediscovery of Erasmus after a time of neglect. He continued to be noticed in the two generations between

1 In a review article on Flitner's book, 'La tradition érasmienne' 365
2 Jeremy Taylor included him among the 'very wise men' who sought peace among the contending sects (sermon 'Via Intelligentiae,' quoted in L.O. Frappell 'Interpretations of the Continental Reformation in Great Britain during the Nineteenth Century' 5).

the Restoration and the Hanoverian settlement. John Aubrey included his among the 'brief lives,' a two-page fragment not noticeably accurate[3] but with some characteristically memorable phrasing: 'He was a tender chitt ... He loved not fish, though borne in a fish towne ... His deepest divinity is where a man would least expect it: viz. in his Colloquies in a Dialogue between a Butcher and a Fishmonger, *Ichthyophagia.*' He had a chamber over the water in Queen's College, Cambridge, and did not like the beer there, on which another unhappy drinker had observed: 'sicut erat in principio.' He had a controversy with Julius Scaliger who 'gott nothing by it, for as Fuller sayth, he was like a badger, that never bitt but he made his teeth meet.' On the larger stage Erasmus was 'the man that made the rough and untrodden wayes smooth and passable.'[4]

That was in line with the main English tradition about Erasmus – he was the restorer of learning and religion. Gilbert Burnet, Whig churchman and writer, associate of Locke and Le Clerc, and after the Revolution of 1688 bishop of Salisbury, said in his substantial *History of the Reformation of the Church of England* written in King Charles II's reign to demonstrate that truth and legitimacy were on the side of the reformed Church of England:

> The monks being thus settled in most cathedrals of England, gave themselves up to idleness and pleasure, which had been long complained of; but now that learning began to be restored, they, being everywhere possessed of the best church benefices, were looked upon by all learned men with an evil eye, as having in their hands the chief encouragements of learning, and yet doing nothing towards it ... And the restorers of learning such as Erasmus, Vives, and others, did not spare them, but did expose their ignorance and ill manners to the world.[5]

Similarly, the scholastics

> had little other learning but a sleight of tossing some arguments from hand to hand, with a gibberish kind of language, that sounded like somewhat that was sublime; but had really nothing under it. By constant practice they were very nimble at this sort of legerdemain, of which both Erasmus and sir Thomas More,

3 Thus he went to school at Düsseldorf (Deventer) and changed his habit when it was confused with the plague doctor's at Pisa (Bologna).
4 *Brief Lives and Other Selected Writings* 92–3
5 *History* I 54

with the other learned men of that age, had made such sport, that it was become sufficiently ridiculous: and the Protestants laid hold on that advantage which such great authorities gave them to disparage it.[6]

Erasmus was a familiar part of the English Protestant polemic against Rome. That was recognized in the curious preface of Roger L'Estrange's edition of twenty of the *Colloquia* published in London in 1680, a year after Burnet's first volume. It was a moment of high tension in the country and of acute peril for L'Estrange himself. He had made a reputation as a rather scurrilous pamphleteer on the royalist side both before and after the Restoration. In the political controversies of Charles II's reign he was vigorous against the Whigs but he also pleaded for more tender treatment of Catholics. He thought it prudent to flee the country during the murderous panic over the Popish plot and was burnt in effigy in London.[7] His preface touches on these circumstances and uses the moderation of Erasmus for his own advantage. 'The Fanatiques will have him,' the translator says of himself, 'to be a Favourer of the Plot, or (as all Episcopal men are accounted nowadays) a Papist in Masquerade ... so that with Erasmus himself, he is crush'd betwixt the Two Extremes. Upon the sense of these Unkindnesses, he has now made English of These Colloquies, as an Apology on the One hand, and a Revenge, on the Other.' As for Erasmus, an eminent member of the Roman communion, his Colloquies make clear the great need for reform in that church. One will find in them 'Reason also (from the Candour and Moderation of our Learned Author) to distinguish betwixt the Romish Doctors themselves; and not to involve All Papists under the same Condemnation.' May they 'mollifie the Evil Spirit,' turning 'some Part of the Rage and Bitterness that is now in course, into Pitty, and Laughter.'[8]

In a later edition of the *Colloquia* Erasmus is used as an instrument of the English domination and the Protestant ascendancy in Ireland. Its author, Guillaume Binauld (Gulielmus Binaldus), dedicated it to the Anglican archbishop of Dublin and to Binauld's pupil, friend, and patron, Samuel Molyneux (1689–1728), the politician and scientist.

6 Ibid II 195–6
7 DNB XI 997–1007
8 *Twenty Select Colloquies, Out of Erasmus Roterodamus* ... 3. Cf Margaret Mann Phillips 'Erasmus and Propaganda: A Study of the Translations of Erasmus in England and France' 7–8. Dr Phillips considers L'Estrange's translations among the best ever made.

Molyneux was the son of William Molyneux, a distinguished philosopher and engineer and the apologist of the Glorious Revolution in Ireland, who educated his son on Locke's principles.[9] Nowhere, said Binauld in his preface, could the *Colloquia* be more useful than in 'our whole British Empire' because, if the Erasmian spirit which inhabits them lived in us, those who still adhere to the Roman side would at once defect, seeing on our side not only truth but peace, concord, and respect of public authority.[1] In an Ireland crushed by the Penal Code, a 'machine as well fitted,' said Edmund Burke, 'for the oppression, impoverishment and degradation of a people, and the debasement in them of human nature itself as ever proceeded from the perverted ingenuity of man,'[2] that must seem a cruel joke and no kindness to the 'Erasmian spirit.' Binauld's Erasmus is Le Clerc's Protestant Erasmus with the more tolerant traits removed. No book, he said, was better fitted than the *Colloquia* to overthrow papal opinions and superstitions and replace them with 'pure Protestant ideas.' Erasmus taught the supremacy, indeed the infallibility, of scripture and rejected saints, ceremonies, purgatory, auricular confession, masses for the dead, and the whole monastic system. In rejecting also the absolute authority and infallibility of the pope or council Erasmus removed the chief foundation of popery. To an objection that Erasmus worked by derision rather than by serious argument the reply is given: there is much in popery that deserves only laughter. Why did he not attack directly transsubstantiation, the greatest monster of all? Perhaps he believed that it would die of its own accord. There are reasons for believing that he did not speak his whole mind on this question and that he had lost faith in the doctrine of a corporal presence. He did not abandon the Roman side for a variety of reasons – fear of schism and tumult, love of peace, distaste for Luther and his followers, natural timidity and fear. But it can be said (as Le Clerc has shown) that, had he seen the schism effected and Protestant communities established, he would have deserted Rome and become an open defender of Protestantism. The love of peace which led him in a time of uncertainty to hold to a communion full of abuses would have made him adhere in more stable times to purer communities. As it was Erasmus died a Protestant without recalling papal superstitions and relying on the mercy of God alone.

9 DNB XIII 583–4. Cf Sir George Clark *The Later Stuarts 1660–1714* 320; Edith Mary Johnston *Ireland in the Eighteenth Century* 60–1.
1 *Desid. Erasmi Roterodami colloquia familiaria* ...
2 Quoted in Johnston *Ireland* 17

That is the crude, one might say brutal, form of the Protestant interpretation of Erasmus. But in these years, as we have seen, Protestant thought itself was undergoing a transformation, and not least in England. As early as 1672 Sir Charles Wolseley had published a book with the title *The Reasonableness of Scripture Belief* and Mark Pattison summed up the changes in the sweeping sentence: 'The title of Locke's treatise, *The Reasonabless of Christianity*, may be said to have been the solitary thesis of Christian theology in England for the greater part of a century.'[3] It was not difficult to fit Erasmus into an apologetic built on that foundation. Edward Stillingfleet (1635–99), who became dean of St Paul's in 1678 and bishop of Worcester after the Revolution, was one of the most attractive apologists of Anglican latitude and the *via media*. Pepys said that the bishops believed him as a London preacher 'the ablest young man to preach the Gospel of any since the Apostles' and his nickname 'the beauty of holiness' suggested a charm both physical and spiritual. His controversial activity was 'prodigious' but without excessive bitterness or bigotry: his purpose was to demonstrate the reasonableness of Christianity and the validity of natural religion.[4] In one of his 'Several Conferences between a Romish Priest, a Fanatick-Chaplain, and a Divine of the Church of England, concerning the Idolatry of the Church of Rome,' he gave its final form to a moderate Anglican interpretation of Erasmus:

It was not *Luther*, or *Zwinglius* that contributed so to the Reformation, as *Erasmus*; especially among us in *England*. For *Erasmus* was the Man who awakened Mens Understandings, and brought them from the *Friars Divinity* to a Relish of general Learning: He by his Wit laughed down the imperious Ignorance of the Monks, and made them the Scorn of *Christendom*: And by his Learning he brought most of the *Latin* Fathers to Light, and published them with excellent Editions, and useful Notes; by which Means Men of Parts set themselves to consider the Ancient Church from the Writings of the *Fathers* themselves, and not from the *Canonists* and *Schoolmen*. So that most learned and impartial Men were prepared for the *Doctrines* of the Reformation before it broke forth. For it is a foolish thing to imagine that a Quarrel between Two *Monks at Wittemberg* should make such

---

3 'Tendencies of Religious Thought in England, 1688–1750' in *Essays* vol 2, quoted in Frappell 'Interpretations' 7
4 DNB XVIII 1262–5. Cf Robert Todd Carroll *The Common-Sense Philosophy of Religion of Bishop Edward Stillingfleet 1635–1699*.

an Alteration in the State of *Christendom*. But things had been
tending that way a good while before, by the gradual Restoration
of Learning in these Western Parts.[5]

Greek refugees from Constantinople, Italian humanists, Reuchlin and
others in Germany prepared the way for Erasmus' New Testament
which 'infinitely took among all pious and learned Men and as much
enraged the Monks and Friars and all the fast Friends to their Dulness
and Superstition.'[6]

Wise men saw, Stillingfleet goes on, that a violent Reformation, a
sudden purging, would do more harm than good: 'Although such
Persons saw the Corruptions, and wished them Reformed; yet considering the Hazard of a sudden Change, they thought it best for particular Persons to inform the World better, and so by Degrees bring it
about, than to make any violent Disturbance in the Church.' The
impudence of the indulgence preachers brought things to a head – they
were challenged by the bold monk of Wittenberg. 'But when *Reformation* begins below, it is not to be expected that no Disorders and
Heats should happen in the Management of it; which gave Distastes to
such Persons as *Erasmus* was, which made him like so ill the *Wittemberg Reformation*, and whatever was carried on by popular Tumults.'
The true enduring Reformation was indeed Erasmus'; when the English Reformation was under Edward VI and Elizabeth

> settled on the Principles it now stands, there was no such regard
> had to *Luther*, or *Calvin*, as to *Erasmus* and *Melanchthon*,
> whose Learning and Moderation were in greater Esteem here,
> than the Fiery Spirits of the other. From hence, things were
> carry'd with greater Temper, the Church settled with a Succes-
> sion of *Bishops*; the *Liturgy* reformed according to the Ancient
> *Models*; some decent Ceremonies retained, without the Follies
> and Superstitions which were before practised: And to prevent
> the Extravagancies of the People in the Interpreting of Scripture,
> the most excellent *Paraphrase* of *Erasmus* was translated into
> *English*, and set up in *Churches*; and to this Day, Erasmus is in
> far greater Esteem among the Divines of our *Church*, than either
> *Luther* or *Calvin*.[7]

Erasmus has become the church father of Anglican moderation, the

5 *Works* VI 38–9
6 Ibid 39
7 Ibid 39–40

pioneer of reasonable religion as well as the patron of the patristic and scriptural revival.

Before coming to Knight's biography, where Stillingfleet is quoted, we should here find a place for the appreciation of Erasmus by an undogmatic Roman Catholic who also in his own way was an advocate of reasonable religion against Gothic superstition. These lines from the *Essay on Criticism* of the young Alexander Pope[8] are famous:

> With *Tyranny*, then *Superstition* join'd,
> As that the *Body*, this enslav'd the *Mind*;
> Much was *Believ'd*, but little *understood*,
> And to be *dull* was constru'd to be *good*;
> A *second* Deluge Learning thus o'er-run,
> And the *Monks* finish'd what the *Goths* begun.
>   At length, *Erasmus*, that *great injur'd* Name,
> (The *Glory* of the *Priesthood*, and the *Shame!*)
> *Stemm'd* the *wild Torrent* of a *barb'rous* Age,
> And drove those *Holy Vandals* off the Stage.[9]

It is not necessary to seek a particular source for Pope's expressions.[1] An *Essay* which identified classical rules with the wisdom of nature[2] was, not surprisingly, cool towards scholasticism and medieval culture and compared the Renaissance with starting from a trance.[3] These were commonplaces, and Pope had moved in circles where they might be repeated; in the London round he met the 'good-natured deistic toler-

8 On Pope's account the *Essay*, published in 1711, was largely written in 1709, when he was twenty-one (George Sherburn *The Early Career of Alexander Pope* 86).
9 Lines 687–96
1 James King has suggested a derivation from Thomas Brown's remarks in *Seven New Colloquies Translated out of Erasmus Roterodamus: As also the Life of Erasmus* (London 1699): 'He carried on a Reformation in Learning, at the same time as he advanced that of Religion, and promoted a Purity and Simplicity of Stile as well as of Worship. This drew upon him the Hatred of the Ecclesiastics, who were no less Bigotted to their Barbarisms in Language and Philosophy, than they were to their unjust innovations in the Church ...' ('Pope and Erasmus' "*Great, Injur'd* Name"'). But these were familiar views, and one might as easily hear the voice of Burnet. Indeed, Sherburn wonders whether Pope had read the books of polemic divinity which had belonged to his Anglican grandparents (*Alexander Pope* 95).
2 Those Rules of old, *discover'd*, not *devis'd*,
Are *Nature* still, but *Nature Methodized* (lines 88–9).
3 But see! each *Muse* in *Leo's* Golden Days
Starts from her *Trance*, and trims her wither'd Bays (lines 697–8).

ance' of Sir Samuel Garth, the author of the popular *Dispensary*, and the practical moralism of Steele and Addison.[4] But Pope inhabited a second world alongside that of the London coffee-houses; he belonged to a Catholic community 'uneasy and fretful' in the days of William and Mary and Queen Anne:

> Hopes after hopes of pious Papists fail'd
> While mighty William's thund'ring arm prevail'd.[5]

His parents were both Catholics, his father by conversion. The family lived at Binfield in Windsor Forest among a circle of Catholic families. Here the expressions of the *Essay* about the monks and Erasmus aroused suspicion and dismay.

Pope was told of these agitations by his friend John Caryll. The Carylls were a cultivated Catholic landowning family also living in Windsor Forest; an uncle of John Caryll was secretary to the exiled James II and Jacobite, although not extremist, as Pope's epitaph indicates:

> Honour unchang'd; a Principle profest;
> Fix'd to one side, but mod'rate to the rest.[6]

Caryll had an informed interest in literature, and through him Pope came in contact with the writers of an older generation, Dryden, Wycherley, and L'Estrange.[7] The correspondence of Caryll and Pope in 1711 shows how deeply the poet was affected by the case of Erasmus, how the lines from the *Essay* were far from a witty commonplace and ran roots down into his surest convictions.

'If the heat of these disputants,' Pope wrote on 18 June 1711, who I'm afraid, being bred up to wrangle in the schools, cannot get rid of the humour all their lives, should proceed so far as to personal reflections upon me, I do assure you notwithstanding, I will do or say nothing, however provoked (for some people can no more provoke than oblige), that is unbecoming the character of a true Catholic. I will set before me that excellent example of that great saint, Erasmus, who in the midst of calumny proceeded with all the calmness of innocence, the unrevenging spirit of primitive Christianity![8]

4 Sherburn *Alexander Pope* 61, 64
5 Ibid 35
6 Quoted in Howard Erskine-Hill *The Social Milieu of Alexander Pope: Lives, Example and the Poetic Response* 52. On the Carylls generally see 42–102.
7 Ibid 58
8 *The Correspondence of Alexander Pope* 118

Pope advises his critics to pass unregarded the mention of Erasmus lest he do for that reputation what he would not do for his own, vindicate in no uncertain language 'so great a light of our Church from the malice of past times and the ignorance of the present.'[9] Pope must have known the strength of the prejudice against Erasmus in the Catholic literature since the sixteenth century. Writing again to Caryll a month later he explained the virulence of his critics thus: 'What these people in their own opinion are really angry at is that a man whom their tribe oppressed and persecuted (Erasmus by name) should be vindicated after a whole age of obloquy, by one of their own people who is free and bold enough to utter a generous truth in behalf of the dead, whom no man sure will flatter, and few do justice to.' He would ever be guilty of 'this sort of liberty and latitude of principle' which speaks well of those oppressed by envy even after they are dead.[1]

These letters reveal how Pope believed the English Catholics should behave in their peculiar situation. His expressions in the *Essay* could only help his co-religionists 'in a nation and time, wherein we are the smaller party' and therefore the victims of misrepresentation.[2] Silence might lead their adversaries to think that Catholics persisted in bigotries 'which in reality all good and sensible men despise ...' But Pope was also stating an alternative to the Counter-Reformation Catholicism which, among other things, had so distorted the portrait of Erasmus. 'I've ever thought the best piece of service one could do to our religion was openly to expose our detestation and scorn of all artifices and *piae fraudes* which it stands so little in need of ...' The culprit was the spirit of exclusiveness and partisanship. Nothing was so much a scarecrow to the opponents of Catholicism

> as the too peremptory and seemingly uncharitable assertion of an utter impossibility of salvation to all but ourselves, invincible ignorance excepted, which indeed some people define under so great limitations and with such exclusions, that it seems as if that word were rather invented as a salvo or expedient, not to be thought too bold with the thunderbolts of God (which are hurled about so freely almost on all mankind by the hands of the ecclesiastics) than as a real exceptive to almost universal damnation.[3]

9 Ibid 119
1 19 July 1711, ibid 128
2 Cf Pope's description of the status of the papist, 'when one is obnoxious to four parts in five as being so too much, and to the fifth part as being so too little' (quoted in Erskine-Hill *Alexander Pope* 66).
3 *Correspondence* 126–7. Cf Erskine-Hill *Alexander Pope* 93. Pope wrote to

Faith must be accompanied by charity, tolerance, moderation; it would be no less faith and no weaker a faith for these companions. So Pope defined a Catholicism for the age of reason; Erasmus was the key to that Catholicism.

Pope broke deliberately with the interpretation of Erasmus which had been dominant in Catholicism since the 1550s. He also expressed the new European sensibility – not the passionate and intense but the moderate and restrained deserved admiration. The biographies, beginning with Samuel Knight's, were touched by the same sensibility.

Samuel Knight (1675–1746) was a clergyman and antiquary. 'A very black and thin man' with much 'the look of a Frenchman,'[4] he was, according to one bilious observer, exceedingly active and ambitious. 'Yesterday,' wrote William Warburton from Cambridge in 1737,

> Dr Knight shot through the town on the spur ... He seems to think there is no way of overtaking Fame, that is oft shy, and flies the pursuer, but on horseback. He is today searching her in the fogs of Ely, and tomorrow in the smoke of London. He now hopes to win her in the character of Gentleman-Usher to Erasmus; and now again as Patron to *Alderman* Peck.[5]

A more favourable and no doubt more truthful picture has him not only a studious antiquary and a patron of excellence in learning (as witnessed by his life of Erasmus itself) but also a dutiful preacher and a diligent friend and servant of the church.[6] His circumstances were comfortable; his father had been 'free of the Mercers' Company' and

---

Francis Atterbury in 1717: 'I am not a Papist, for I renounce the temporal invasions of the Papal power ... I am a Catholick, in the strictest sense of the word ...' Between Pope and Caryll there was later a certain reserve because Pope feared the ultramontane associations of a family where the second son became a Jesuit priest (1711) (ibid 93–4).

4 DNB XI 261
5 'Original letters of Mr Warburton (afterwards Bp. of Gloucester) to Dr Stukeley, when both were young' in John Nichols *Illustrations of the Literary History of the Eighteenth Century* II 1–54, at 44. Warburton was, of course, an impossible person. Hume spoke of 'the illiberal petulance, arrogance, and scurrility which distinguish the Warburtonian school' (quoted in DNB XX 764).
6 From the 'neat monument of white marble' in the chancel of Bluntisham church, an inscription composed 'by his friend Mr Castle, dean of Hereford, who knew him well, and has given him a character, which all who remember Dr Knight will readily allow to be a just one' (John Nichols *Literary Anecdotes of the Eighteenth Century* V 356).

Knight himself left an ample fortune to his son.[7] Knight's strong Protestantism led some to believe that he had been brought up a dissenter. Actually his career followed a regular enough pattern for a successful Anglican clergyman: St Paul's School and Trinity College, Cambridge (BA 1702, MA 1706), presentation to various livings in Cambridgeshire, collation in 1714 to a prebendal chair in Ely, and in 1717 a Cambridge DD. Certainly he was at the Protestant end of the Anglican spectrum. Strype tried to persuade him to write a life of Archbishop Bancroft but, said Knight, 'I have not stomach to it, having no great opinion of him on more accounts than one. He had a greater inveteracy against the Puritans than any of his predecessors.'[8] He was also a defender of the Hanoverian succession. He became chaplain to George II in 1730, and his two best known works, the lives of Colet and Erasmus, were dedicated to Spencer Compton, speaker of the House of Commons from 1715 to 1727 and a favourite of that monarch. A sermon of 1725 at once commemorated the Restoration of 1660, condemned Jacobitism, and expressed a Whig satisfaction in the Hanoverian settlement: 'We enjoy our religion, and our liberties, under the most excellent laws adapted to a free people ... there are but few, comparatively speaking, that do not think themselves easy under the present administration.'[9]

Knight's literary labours carried on from those of White Kennett, who became bishop of Peterborough after the Hanoverian succession and was among a generation of productive scholars and antiquaries developing a critical historiography in England. As a young man Kennett had made one of the most popular translations of the *Moriae encomium* – his *Witt against Wisdom* (1683).[1] He later collected materials for a life of Dean Colet which he passed to Knight to digest and publish.[2] Knight fulfilled the assignment; he also supported Kennett in his great controversies with the 'High Church' party.

A literary expression of the High Church outlook was Richard

7 Ibid 354, 363
8 Knight to Rev Dr Z. Grey, 24 March 1733/4, ibid 360
9 *The great Happiness of a lawful Government* ... 25
1 H.H. Hudson 'Current English Translations of "The Praise of Folly" ';
   Hudson considers preferable the translation by the contemporary playwright John Wilson (1668). Kennett was lively in the humorous sections but 'either flat or unbecomingly vivacious' in the poetic or deeply religious ones.
2 DNB XI 2–6, at 6; G.V. Bennett *White Kennett, 1660–1728, Bishop of Peterborough: A Study in the Political and Ecclesiastical History of the Early Eighteenth Century* 174

Fiddes' *Life of Wolsey*. It offered a view 'less unfavourable to the medieval church than that of most protestant writers' and showed a sympathetic insight into Wolsey's character. The English Reformation, according to Fiddes, was not introduced 'with certain *German*, and other foreign Sectaries, without any Authority, either from God or Man.' It rested on regular ecclesiastical procedure and was consistent with 'the Primitive Constitution and true *Rights* of the Christian Church ...' The deeper purpose of his work was to assert the unity and authority of the church, 'the Dignity, and especially the Succession of the Christian Priesthood.'[3] A final tribute to Atterbury, who had begun by asserting the historic independence of the church through its convocation and finished in a Jacobite exile, led his enemies, including Knight, to accuse Fiddes of Jacobitism and popery. Erasmus was drawn into this controversy. Fiddes attacked Erasmus for changing his mind about Wolsey after his fall and when he could hope for nothing more from him. Beforehand Wolsey was liberal and humane, afterwards ungenerous and failing in his promises. But even if Erasmus were ill-used, which was not the case, 'he had no Occasion, in order to gratify that Passion, to contradict his former Elogies upon the Cardinal, or to ascribe to him what was not only irreconcileable to his own Testimony, but to Truth ...' To this Knight entered a spirited defence and counter-attacked against the *Wolsey*, written, so he claimed, under the auspices of Atterbury, in contradiction to Archbishop Wake, who had criticized Wolsey, and in the interests of popery and 'a Popish Pretender.'[4]

Knight's *Colet* is a fair introduction to his *Erasmus*.[5] The author intended in that book to say more of Erasmus, but as the work proceeded he decided on the second biography.[6] Knight's account of the comradeship of Colet, Erasmus, and More anticipates Seebohm's famous study of their 'fellow-work': they were 'the happy Triumvirate'; Colet and Erasmus were 'the most familiar Friends imaginable, to the very End of their Lives.'[7] The Protestant interpretation of Erasmus is here applied to Colet: he cannot be called a Protestant but he did great service towards the Reformation; in an age when men loved darkness rather than light, he 'was as a Light shining in that Darkness.' He was

3 *The Life of Cardinal Wolsey* iii–viii
4 *The Life of Erasmus* ... 370–82
5 *The Life of Dr John Colet* ...
6 Ibid xii
7 Ibid 11, 40. Cf Frederic Seebohm *The Oxford Reformers of 1498: A History of the Fellow-work of John Colet, Erasmus and Thomas More.*

'a happy Forerunner and Promoter of the Reformation, and alarm'd
this Nation first toward the throwing off the Yoke of Superstition and
Popery.'⁸ He attacked 'the Cob-web Divinity of the Schools' and was
'wholly wrapt up' in the Pauline epistles which, he believed, contained
the fundamental doctrines of salvation.⁹

In his *Erasmus* Knight sought to do justice to Erasmus, 'as an
English-man, a *Protestant*, and an *Antiquary*.'¹ The dedication and
introduction spell out the themes implicit in that avowal. The Englishman is naively parochial. Even if Joly had completed his work –
aborted in the end because he pondered and sought perfection too long
– the need for Knight's work, with its interest in England and English
authors, would have remained. Equally to consider Erasmus' relations
with other countries would be 'nauseous to the *English* Reader, since
the Characters of his Foreign Friends though highly Deserving, would
have been accounted an Entertainment not very agreeable, we being
more affected with Things and Persons of our own growth.' Knight
suggests that foreigners parcel out among themselves studies of Erasmus' relations with their respective countries. He has been told by 'a
most Reverend Prelate' – this must be Wake speaking of Le Courayer –
that a very learned Frenchman is engaged on such a task, 'but who
knows not the Difficulty of Speaking Truth in a Popish Country?'²
England was in the last resort Erasmus' 'admired Place'; most of his
best productions 'were, in a great measure, owing to the Suggestion &
Advice of some of the most considerable Persons in this Kingdom.'³

Knight the Protestant takes a middle position like Le Clerc's among
the various options offered by the Protestant controversialists of two
centuries. Erasmus was a Protestant at heart though he did not carry
through. He continued in the Roman pale, 'yet at the same time he
sapp'd the very Foundation of it, by the bold advances he made towards
a Reformation.' He gave the world 'a true Tast of the rational &
genuine use of Religion' and denounced its greatest enemy, the *opus
operatum*.⁴ He supported Luther as far as was 'Consistent with his own
safety in a Persecuting Church.' The need in those times was for a bold
temperament like Luther's rather than for Erasmus' delight in 'a
Studious Ease and Safety.' He was, however, no good Catholic, as

8 *Colet* v, vii
9 Ibid 52, 71
1 *Erasmus* xxx
2 Ibid ii–v
3 Ibid xxv–vi
4 Ibid xix–xxi

Marsollier claims; the latter's *Trévoux* assailant was right in this at least. We Protestants on the other hand are 'willing to take him in amongst us Hereticks.'[5] To the charge of Arianism Baudius has given reply and recent controversies have shown his faithfulness and sincerity in handling the biblical record on the Trinitarian question.[6]

Erasmus was a moderate, 'in the modest sense of the word a Freethinker, & wou'd *call no Man Master*, but judge for himself. A noble Vein of Freedom runs through all his massy volumes.'[7] As a reviewer of Knight put it, he was 'a very great Latitudinarian.'[8] Here is the authentic voice of the early eighteenth century. Like Le Clerc, Knight is relying on the main Protestant tradition about Erasmus but he is also anticipating the Protestantism of the age of reason.

The antiquarian in Knight appears in the main body of his work: he is interested in Erasmus as writer and scholar; he recognizes the problems in Erasmus biography and attempts to solve them, although his success in these attempts is partial at best. The book lacks structure and may thus faithfully represent Knight's mind. The conception, birth, childhood, and education of Erasmus are told as in Beatus Rhenanus or the *Compendium*, 'said to be composed by himself.'[9] The familiar stories are touched by the charm of Knight's phrasing: Erasmus had many misfortunes as a student in Paris, 'yet his sprightly Genius surmounted them all.'[1]

The peculiarly invertebrate character of Knight's book is due to his distracting interest in Erasmus' English friends and the English universities. Erasmus had enemies in England, too, as Knight recognizes: the opposition of certain bigots helped drive him from England; the virulence of Edward Lee, later archbishop of York, towards him was inexcusable, though Erasmus himself lost his temper in that case.[2]

---

5 Ibid x–xiii
6 Ibid xxii–xxiv. Cf Thomas Emlyn *An Answer to Mr Martin's Critical Dissertation on 1 John v.7* ... Knight also questioned Le Clerc's criticism of Erasmus' biblical scholarship (ibid xvi). He referred to the confutation of this criticism in the *Reflections upon Learning* (London 1714) by his 'very Learned Friend,' Thomas Baker. Cf DNB I 938–40.
7 *Erasmus* xxv
8 *New Memoirs of Literature* ... 89. After quoting Stillingfleet on Erasmus' significance for the English Reformation, the reviewer writes: 'Whereupon I shall observe that most of *Erasmus'* Works are still worth reading; which can hardly be said of those of Luther and Calvin' (88).
9 *Erasmus* 5
1 Ibid 12
2 Ibid 267–89

Each English character is given his own biography and some of these run to many pages. To Mountjoy, Erasmus' first English patron, England owed all the advantages she received from Erasmus' sojourn; Erasmus acknowledged John Fisher as 'the greatest favorer of Learning and Learned Men'; Thomas More, Erasmus' dearest English friend, cautioned him lest he be accused of heresy, but Erasmus would not prevaricate.[3] As for the English universities, both were conscious of their debt to the great scholar and were rivals as to 'who should have most of his company.'[4] Oxford brought love of Greek and perhaps some proficiency in it; Cambridge gave him many friends.[5] Erasmus was also a 'great admirer of the constitution of the *English* Church,' even in its unreformed state. No English bishop or abbot exercised political or military authority, and Erasmus commended the country for 'guarding against so preposterous a Practice, too much used in other Nations ...'[6] Knight does not hide his regret that Erasmus did not return to England in the 1520s, though he recognizes the bond between the humanist and Basel.[7] There he died, his last expressions free of superstition, 'trusting only in the merits of his Saviour ... so that the Church of *Rome* has little reason to value herself upon his dying in her Communion ...'[8]

It is odd that of the fables introduced into the Erasmus literature by Boissard, one concerning England and the other Basel, Knight saw through the first but credulously accepted the second: there was no restitution by Henry VIII of losses at the Dover customs, but Erasmus is made to tear up the privileges of the students at Basel University when, as rector, he failed to restrain their licence.[9] Knight recognized that the problems of dating Erasmus' letters had not been solved by the Leiden edition but he could hardly be expected to overcome them himself; chronological confusions remain – in the dates of the English visits, for example; they were, of course, long to remain in the Erasmus literature.[1]

Knight's judgments of the major works are those to be expected

3 Ibid 17, 136, 334–8
4 Ibid 29
5 Ibid 22, 90, 92, 142–7
6 Ibid 244. The reference is to Erasmus' *Consultatio de bello Turcico*, LB V 362. Knight continues, however, as unsympathetic to Wolsey as to his biographer.
7 *Erasmus* 333–4
8 Ibid 349
9 Ibid 55–6, 316
1 Ibid xviii, 61–2

JOANNES JORTIN.
MORTALIS ESSE DESIIT
ANNO SALUTIS, MDCCLXX.
ÆTATIS, LXXII.

John Jortin
Engraving by John Hall from a painting by E. Penny
Frontispiece to *Tracts, Philological, Critical, and Miscellaneous*
By permission of the Houghton Library, Harvard University

from one of his outlook. The *Enchiridion* was an 'excellent Manual of Piety and good Morals ... inconsistent with the common Religion of the Church of Rome'; the whole design of the *Moriae encomium* was to express his disdain of Rome, sparing neither the papal court nor the pope himself – never after was he 'look'd upon as a true Son of that Church'; his edition of the New Testament raised 'more Opposition from the snarling Divines of that Age' than any other work; the *Colloquia* were 'a Treasure of Wit and good Sense,' ostensibly a schoolbook but 'not unworthy the perusal, of the most advanced in Knowledge'; the work against the Ciceronians exposed the 'Superstition and Folly [and] Pedantick Humour' of that sect; the work finally extracted from him against Luther was 'upon a Subject that least concerned the Reformation, some speculative Points about the *Servitude* or *Freedom* of the Will.'[2] For his services to the 'Republick of Learning' Knight has unqualified praise. His natural endowments were 'very uncommon,' but he united to them amazing industry and application. He was essentially self-taught, needing nothing from Italy and lacking the encouragement he deserved from France and even from England.[3] He achieved a restoration of learning under disabilities that others would have felt crippling – bodily infirmity, an unsettled life, useless controversies; but in this sphere even the controversies of the Reformation did not bring a 'chasm in his Life' or discourage 'his noble Designs of promoting the publick Good.'[4] For all the boastings of others, it was Erasmus who 'broke the Ice' and opened learning to many.[5]

The worlds of Pierre Bayle and Samuel Knight were, broadly speaking, mingled in the beginnings of the second of the three biographers discussed in this chapter, John Jortin (1698–1770). His father, Renatus, was born in Brittany and studied at the Saumur Academy.[6] He and his close relatives fled the great persecution of the Huguenots around 1687 and went, not to Holland, but to England. He quickly established influential connections; in 1691 he was appointed one of the gentlemen of the privy chamber by William III.[7] He was succes-

2 Ibid 59, 107–8, 137, 201–3, 266
3 Ibid 358–9, 363
4 Ibid 362
5 Ibid 366
6 'I have his Testimonial from that Academy, dated A.1682' (Jortin, quoted in 'Advertisement' (by his son Rogers) to *Tracts, Philological, Critical, and Miscellaneous* I v–xxii, at vii).
7 'I have his Patent' (quoted ibid)

sively secretary to admirals Sir Edward Russell, Sir George Rooke, and Sir Clowdisley Shovel.[8] According to his son he was fond of passing for an Englishman and 'spoke English perfectly, and without any foreign accent.'[9] He married an Englishwoman, Martha, the daughter of Rev Daniel Rogers of Haversham, Bucks, to whom John was born on 23 October 1698 in the London parish of St Giles in the Fields.[1] John was within a day of his ninth birthday when his father perished at sea in the wreck of the *Association* (22 October 1707).

Like Knight's, Jortin's was a regular clerical career for one who, if not among the 'brightest ornaments' of his church, yet in the words of his biographer 'did his portion of good in his day' and left in his writings 'a legacy of no mean value to posterity.'[2] He was educated at Charterhouse and Cambridge (BA 1719, MA 1722). He became a Fellow of Jesus College in 1721 and took orders three years later. He early showed a 'remarkably facility' in languages and read and spoke French with 'accuracy and ease.'[3] The classical tutor at Jesus, Dr Thirlby, chose him, though still an undergraduate, to translate passages from the commentary of Eustathius which Pope was including in the notes to his translation of the *Iliad*. Pope incorporated the passages virtually unchanged. Jortin poignantly recalled his relationship with the poet: 'I was in some hopes in those days (for I was young) that Mr Pope would make inquiry about his *coadjutor*, and take some civil notice of him. But he did not; and I had no notion of obtruding myself upon him – I never saw his face.'[4] Jortin was ordained deacon by White Kennett in 1723 and priest by the bishop of Ely the following year. When he married in 1727 he had to give up his Fellowship but held a college living in Cambridgeshire for the next four years.

His return to London in 1731 – to be reader and preacher at the New Street chapel of the parish of St Giles in the Fields where he had been born – opened for Jortin 'a fair field for literary exertion.'[5] He helped found a journal, *Miscellaneous Observations upon Authors, Ancient and Modern*, a title which characterizes exactly his scholarly style, particular, conversational, confident. His chief patron in the middle years of his career was Thomas Herring, archbishop of Canterbury.

8 'Advertisement.' Cf DNB x 1089–91, at 1089.
9 Ibid
1 William Trollope 'A Brief Account of the Life and Writings of John Jortin, D.D.' xxvi
2 Ibid xxv
3 Ibid xxvi
4 *Tracts* II 521
5 Trollope 'Life and Writings' xxviii

Herring once said to Jortin that he would be to him what Warham was to Erasmus; 'and,' Jortin adds, 'what he promised he performed: only less fortunate in the choice of his humble friend, who could not be to him what Erasmus was to Warham.' In a passage which reveals the bias of his own religious and political principles, Jortin said that Herring had 'piety without superstition, and moderation without meanness, an open and a liberal way of thinking, and a constant attachment to the cause of sober and rational liberty, both civil and religious.'[6] The prospect he had at one time of obtaining the mastership or preachership of Charterhouse was not realized, but, after the appearance of his *Discourses concerning the Truth of the Christian Religion* in 1746, Herring and Thomas Sherlock, bishop of London, appointed Jortin Boyle lecturer, 'an office,' says Trollope, 'in which he was preceded and has been followed by some of the greatest of our great divines.'[7] Part of the lectures was carried over to Jortin's *Remarks on Ecclesiastical History*. Later Herring gave him the living of St Dunstan's in the East and in 1755 a Lambeth DD; 'I was willing,' Jortin remarked, 'to owe this favour to *Him*, which I would not have asked or accepted from any other Archbishop.'[8] In his last years (after the publication of the life of Erasmus) preferment was rapid: in 1762 he became chaplain to the bishop of London (then Dr Osbaldeston) and vicar of Kensington and in 1764, archdeacon of London.

Even from printed sources we obtain a congenial picture of Jortin's personality and way of life. He devoted the energies 'of a quiet and unobtrusive life to the duties of an arduous and responsible profession' and extended the 'benefits of pastoral care' by his writings.[9] One who remembered him as rector of St Dunstan's called him 'a grave, mild person,' and a good judge said of his sermons: 'Religion and sound morality appear in them, not indeed dressed out in the meretricious ornaments of a flowery style, but in all the manly force and simple graces of natural eloquence.'[1] Something of the man is revealed in his ingenuous remarks about his health: he did not follow Bacon's costly and troublesome rules for good health, 'except the general ones of Regularity and Temperance. I never had a strong constitution; and yet, thank God, I have had no bad state of health, and few acute disorders.'[2] He loved music and played the harpsichord and so, says Trollope,

6　*The Life of Erasmus* I 40 (note m)
7　'Life and Writings' xxix
8　'Advertisement' in *Tracts* xi
9　Trollope 'Life and Writings' xxv
1　Ibid xxxvi, xxxviii
2　'Advertisement' in *Tracts* viii–ix

cherished 'that placid gentleness of disposition for which he seems to have been remarkable.'[3]

Jortin's religious position is best gauged by his sentiments on subscription. If we do not allow a lax subscription, he said, then 'we must suppose that in an age, – and an age not perhaps the most learned, – an Assembly of fallible men may determine concerning all points of faith and practice for themselves, and for their heirs; and entail bondage and darkness, worse than Aegyptian, upon their posterity for ever and ever.'[4] Points like original sin and justification, over which the divines at Trent had struggled, 'should be left undecided, and every Christian at liberty to form his own judgment about them.'[5] He valued the simple, the practical, and the useful in religion and hated, above all, intemperate zeal and party spirit. 'Christianity, reduced to its principles, is more plain and simple than is commonly imagined, and is calculated for general utility.'[6] The natural bond between the human understanding and truth might be disturbed by ignorance or passion or bigotry but it could never be wholly broken. A passage (from the *Remarks on Ecclesiastical History*) following a reference to Jeremy Taylor and Tillotson admirably reveals the company which Jortin wished to keep and gives a first glimpse of his understanding of Erasmus:

> If these two excellent prelates, and Erasmus and Chillingworth, and John Hales, and Locke, and Episcopius, and Grotius ... had been contemporaries and had met together freely to determine the important question, *What makes a man a Christian, and what profession of faith should be deemed sufficient?* – they would probably have agreed, notwithstanding the diversity of opinions which they might all have had on some theological points.[7]

Jortin's priorities are clear, piety above theology, practice above profession.

Some critics accused him of facile judgments: 'He seems to make no allowance,' said one, about the *Remarks*, 'for the customary follies and weaknesses of different ages and countries, but to try all men as if they had every advantage of modern improvement.'[8] Dr Samuel Parr, on

3 'Life and Writings' xxxviii
4 *Tracts* I 419–20
5 Ibid 422
6 *Remarks on Ecclesiastical History* II 408
7 Ibid 420
8 Dr Hey, quoted in Trollope 'Life and Writings' xxxii

the other hand, who defended Jortin in one of his own more or less egregious literary feuds, found in his writings a 'rational entertainment' and 'solid instruction' offered by few others.

> Learned he was, without pedantry: he was ingenious, without the affectation of singularity: he was a lover of truth, without hovering over the gloomy abyss of scepticism; and a friend to free inquiry without roving into the dreary and pathless wilds of Latitudinarianism ... Wit without ill-nature, and sense without effort, he could at will scatter upon every subject; and in every book the *Writer* presents us with a near and distinct view of the real *Man*.[9]

Jortin was in fact a good scholar capable of sharp judgments. He had the restraint and gentleness required by his profession, but there was also a touch of the passionate resentment of the exiled Huguenots against intolerance and persecution. He shared some of the illusions of his age – its naive self-confidence and faith in improvement – but he was not uncritical, as may be seen by his tart comment on Voltaire: 'A total ignorance of the learned tongues; an acquaintance with modern books, and with translations of old ones; some knowledge of modern languages; a smattering in natural philosophy, poetical talents, a vivacity of expression, and a large stock of impiety; these constitute a *Voltaire* ...'[1]

Jortin's *Erasmus* is in two parts, a 'Life' published in London in 1758 and some 'Remarks on the Works on Erasmus' and an 'Appendix, containing Extracts from Erasmus, and from other Writers,' published two years later.[2] The *Life* may seem of little interest since it is essentially a translation of Le Clerc. Jortin frankly describes his procedure in his preface: since he could not hope to do it better and did not wish to do it differently, he took Le Clerc's biography as his foundation, translating him freely rather than superstitiously. 'I found his way of thinking and judging, for the most part, correspondent with mine; and

9 Quoted in 'Advertisement' in *Tracts* xvii. On Parr, see DNB xv 356–63. (His defence of Jortin at 359.) Cf this comment, which applies well enough to his remarks on Jortin: 'His personal remarks are pointed, though necessarily laboured' (362).

1 *Tracts* II 527. The passage concludes: '... or a modern genius of the first rank, fit to be patronized by princes, and caressed by nobles: whilst learned men have leave to go and chuse on what tree they will please to hang themselves.'

2 In what follows I use the 1758 edition of the *Life*, and for the 'Remarks' and 'Appendix' the edition of London 1808 (3 vols), which alone was available to me for those sections.

I have seldom had occasion to declare a dissent from him.'³ He recognized that Le Clerc (and Knight too) had not solved the problem of dating Erasmus' letters but argued that the year-by-year approach achieved a tolerable exactness: 'Most of the Elogies of great men are full of anachronisms; to avoid which, their lives should always be drawn up in the form of Annals.' He showed himself indeed impatient with Bayle's obsession with detail.⁴ Yet he corrected Le Clerc where necessary and elaborated what he had to say, especially about Erasmus' contemporaries and acquaintances. In the first few pages of the text there is (apart from the standard references to Beatus Rhenanus and the *Compendium*) mention of Bayle, Du Pin, and Knight, whom he called 'my deceased friend.'⁵

Despite its dependence on Le Clerc and others, Jortin's work has intrinsic interest – apart, that is, from its influence for over a century in the English-speaking world. First it contains some lively translations of and small elaborations on Le Clerc. Erasmus' writings on peace, for example, made him 'almost a Quaker.'⁶ Here is Jortin's translation of Le Clerc's report of Loyola's response to the *Enchiridion*: 'The judgement of Ignatius is altogether worthy of him; and every Fanatic in the world ... would be of the very same opinion, and would want something more pathetic and savoury, something with more *Unction*, and less morality and commonsense.'⁷ More vivid still is this comment on Scaliger's work against Erasmus: 'The whole is seasoned with arrogance, vanity, self-applause, spite and scurrility, the usual *ornaments*, not of a *meek and quiet spirit*, but of a *Ruffian* and a *Bruiser* in the Republic of Letters.'⁸

Secondly, Jortin makes significant extensions to Le Clerc. For example, at the appropriate place but in a rather disordered fashion he introduces fresh material on Luther. He owes much of this to Seckendorf; indeed he uses Seckendorf to correct Le Clerc: thus Le Clerc calls Luther on predestination a Thomist,⁹ but Seckendorf has shown how Luther abhorred Aristotle and despised the scholastics – if he favoured

3 *Life* I iii
4 Ibid 70–1
5 Ibid 169
6 Ibid 47
7 Ibid 22
8 Ibid 519. The piling up of nouns is characteristic of Jortin's style. Cf this on Dolet's dialogue against Erasmus: 'This dialogue, as to *style*, is by no means amiss; ... As to *substance*, it is full of disingenuity, chicanery, declamation, puerility, malevolence, vanity, effrontery, and scurrility' (*Tracts* II 185).
9 'Vie d'Erasme' VI 121–2

any scholastic sect it was Ockham's. Luther, Jortin adds, learned his 'fatalism' from Augustine, certainly no favourite of Jortin's.[1] (In his later remarks on the *Enchiridion*, he says that Erasmus went too far in allegorical interpretations; Dionysius and Augustine were 'two egregious triflers in that way, if ever there were any triflers in the world.')[2] Jortin could correct Seckendorf, too: in his account of the controversy between Luther and Erasmus the latter was too partial to Luther; any man in Erasmus' situation would take it hard to be called infidel, Lucian, atheist, and epicurean.[3] Jortin himself understands and acknowledges Luther's greatness, but his selections and comments betray uneasiness at features of Luther's style and thought and personality: 'Luther was rough in controversy, or rather scurrilous ... He ascribed to the Devil an amazing power and activity.'[4]

Jortin also comes to terms independently with the claims of the More biographies: 'That More exhorts Erasmus to recant, may possibly be true; for he was at last bigot enough to be capable of giving this silly advice ... But there is no relying upon such authors as these, unless they cite chapter and verse' (he is speaking of Stapleton and Cresacre More). Indeed some of More's advice to revise and amend was written early and in banter; relations between the two men were good as late as 1532.[5]

Thirdly, of the greatest interest are Jortin's departures from Le Clerc's judgments. Le Clerc often blamed Erasmus for his lukewarmness, timidity, and unfairness to the Protestants. As translator Jortin adopts these censures; in the main he shares Le Clerc's opinions, feeling himself as a Protestant more obliged to the Reformers than to Erasmus. But, he goes on, let him say once for all that much can be said on the other side in extenuation. (After all, Le Clerc himself had drawn up a 'handsome apology' for Erasmus' conduct in his preface to the Leiden edition.) Allowance should be made for the prejudices Erasmus brought from his education; he also had 'some indistinct and confused notions about the authority of the Church Catholic.'[6] He thought it not

1 *Life* I 335
2 *Life* (1808 edition) II 314
3 *Life* I 397
4 Ibid 116–17. Other authors used for the Luther section were Du Pin, Mathesius, and Sleidan.
5 Ibid 177
6 Cf Jortin's 'Remarks' on Erasmus' defence against claims that he favoured the Protestant doctrine of the sacrament: 'But he certainly was full of doubts and perplexities, and had too much erudition and too much sense to

lawful to depart from the church, corrupt as she was. He was shocked by the violent quarrels of the Reformers (Vossius wrote of their 'intolerant temper' to Grotius), especially over the Lord's Supper ('for, in those days, Zwinglius and his adherents were the only men, who talked reasonably upon that subject'). He was also shaken by 'the pestilent tumults and rebellions of the Rustics, the Fanatics, and Anabaptists.' It is not credible that Erasmus – for fear of losing his pensions – said and did things which he did not believe right. Naturally he was afraid of disobliging his best and oldest friends, not only popes and princes, but also men of the calibre of Warham, More, Fisher, and Sadolet.

There is no necessity to suppose that he acted against his conscience in adhering to the church of Rome. No: he persuaded himself that he did as much as piety and prudence required from him, in freely censuring her defects. In his conduct there might be some weakness, and some passion against the person of the Reformers; but which of us can be sure that he might not have acted nearly the same part under the same circumstances? ... This worthy man spent a long and laborious life in an uniform pursuit of two points; in opposing barbarous ignorance and blind superstition; and in promoting useful literature and true piety. These glorious projects he endeavoured to accomplish in a mild and gentle manner, never attacking the persons of men, but only the faults of the age, till hard necessity constrained him to reply to those who assaulted him with the utmost disingenuity and malice. How could a learned man of peaceable disposition be better employed? He knew his own temper and talents; and conscious that he was not fitted for the rough and bold work of Reformation, he would not attempt what was beyond his strength. But, in one sense, he was a Reformer, and the most eminent of all the Reformers.[7]

All this is a marked amelioration of Le Clerc's judgments. Jortin himself says that Le Clerc suffered much from the 'odium theologicum ... which seems not to be so violent now, as it was in his time.'[8] Le Clerc (not to mention Bayle) knew the bitterness of exile in his own person; Jortin was the son of a refugee and had made the adjustments of a

swallow without reluctance the *monster* of *transubstantiation* ... the prejudices of education seem to have stuck by him, as also a certain confused notion of church-authority' (*Life*, 1808 ed, II 417).
7 *Life* I 275–6
8 Ibid 133

second generation. Besides, the religious atmosphere had visibly relaxed; indifference and enlightenment and refinement in thought and sentiment were doing their work. Jortin did not need to be so tense and sombre as his predecessors had been about Erasmus' theological controversies and difficulties.

At the end of the *Life*, Jortin makes his own summing-up of the religion of Erasmus. He feels qualified to undertake this, he says, 'for I am unprejudiced, and have nothing to bias me.' (Is this naivety or overconfidence? Perhaps. Above all, it is that eighteenth-century sense of having overcome the party spirit of the confessional age.) If Erasmus had been free to establish a form of religion in any country he 'would have been a moderate man, and a Latitudinarian, as to the *Credenda.*' He would have proposed few articles and those with 'a primitive simplicity.'[9]

'Remarks on the Works of Erasmus' is partly a collection of excerpts about Erasmus from Giovio to the Marsollier controversies – a ready reference to the historiography of the subject – and partly an analysis of the contents of the Leiden edition (including at appropriate places some materials not found in that edition).[1] The whole performance is congenial to Jortin's mind and temperament; among the extracts from Erasmus and other writers he sows pungent comments and broad reflections, sparing on occasion neither his hero nor his hero's critics. One of the most extensive comments is on Richard Simon, who censured Erasmus 'upon things which are of no great importance' and in a carping way searched out his weaknesses, while being perfectly aware of his great strengths. 'He himself lies much more open to rebuke than Erasmus; and all that he hath set forth in behalf of tradition, and for the authenticity of the Vulgate, is mere shuffle and vile sophistry ... There is something mean and sycophantic in his accusing Erasmus of favouring Arianism.'[2] In the review of the Leiden

9 Ibid 609. Erasmus denied the charge of Arianism and 'expressed himself often upon this subject like those who were called Orthodox.' Yet he said enough 'to make himself suspected by violent and unreasonable men.' He actually defended the doctrine of subordination (ibid 610).
1 Eg, the dedication of Erasmus' translation of Plutarch's *De tuenda bona valetudine*, which Jortin took from the edition of Basel (1518), in the British Museum (*Life*, 1808 ed, II 298).
2 In another place Jortin divides Catholic writers on Erasmus into the bigots who represented him as 'a wretch void of all religion' and those who treated him with 'decency and candour.' France, especially, has produced writers of the second kind; those writing with moderation and charity are more rare in England, Ireland, Flanders, Spain, Portugal and Italy ('Some Remarks upon Mr Phillips's Life of Cardinal Pole' *Tracts* II 37–44).

edition Erasmus' writings against war and his appeals for the vernacular scripture seem particularly to take Jortin's attention. Naturally he spreads himself a little on the Reformation debates, from which Erasmus did not escape unscathed. 'When the Lutherans attack him for departing from his former and freer sentiments, he is hard beset, and makes the best retreat that he can, sometimes a poor one.'[3] In the free-will debate Erasmus had the best of the argument 'in point of reason, scripture, primitive Christianity, and the Greek fathers.' Yet Jortin, like Knight and Le Clerc, is out of sympathy with the whole controversy: 'These treatises, though written, like the other works of Erasmus, with good sense, life, and spirit, yet, I know not how, are somewhat tiresome ... The question might have been discussed, and the doctrine of divine assistance, conditional decrees, and human liberty established in a smaller compass.'[4]

The Appendix is a collection of sources for the benefit of learned readers of Jortin's work. It takes from the Leiden edition those documents which were recognized by this time to be fundamental to any biography of Erasmus: the letters to Grunnius, Servatius, and Botzheim, Erasmus' pen-portraits of Colet and Vitrier and of More, and key parts of the correspondence with More. Other extracts indicate Jortin's controversial stance or matters that especially troubled him. An example of the first is Knight's passage on Wolsey and Fiddes and of the second 'Part of a letter of Erasmus, relating to St. Hilary, and to the Arian Controversy.'[5] There are also a number of pieces not found in the Leiden edition. They include various letters already printed elsewhere (by Hardt, for example), a letter from Polydore Vergil to Edward Lee, Erasmus' great opponent, transcribed by Jortin from the original in the British Museum, letters to Erasmus from Richard Pace and from Erasmus to John Fisher similarly transcribed, and lists of the contents of bound collections of tracts which Jortin had perused (one in the British Museum had belonged to Cranmer).[6] The longest single piece in the collection is the dialogue 'Julius exclusus,' of which Jortin, without strictly accepting Erasmus' authorship, says: 'I know of no person in his days, besides himself, who can be supposed to have been both able and willing to write it.'[7] It, too, was transcribed in the British Museum – from a copy of Curione's *Pasquillorum tomi duo*.

3 On the *Epistola ad fratres Germaniae inferioris*, *Life*, 1808 ed, II 421
4 On *Hyperaspistes diatribae* ibid 415
5 Knight at ibid III 30–5; 'Part of a letter ...' at ibid 88–90
6 Vergil, ibid 46–7; Pace, ibid 50–2 (cf Allen Ep. 619, III 37–41); Erasmus to Fisher, ibid 184–5 (cf Allen Ep. 1311, V 122–4).
7 Ibid 280. Text of 'Julius exclusus,' ibid 286–308. On the vexed question of

A contemporary said that Jortin's *Erasmus* 'extended the reputation of its author beyond the limits of his native country, and established his literary character in the remotest Universities of Europe.'[8] Jortin, more than Knight, belonged to Bayle's and Le Clerc's 'Republic of Letters,' and the *Erasmus* gave him within it a modest but recognized place. He knew the European writers on Erasmus; indeed, on the very eve of the publication of his own work he was able to take the measure of the latest and greatest of them, Jean Lévesque de Burigny. He acknowledged a worthy fellow-worker in the Republic of Letters.[9]

Jean Lévesque de Burigny was born into an established family of Rheims in 1692.[1] He and his older brother, Louis-Jean Lévesque de Pouilly, who was also to become a literary man (the author of *Théorie des sentiments agréables*), were orphaned at a young age and brought up by a studious uncle. He early showed signs of the thirst for knowledge which was to give his life its peculiar character; the brothers transcribed whole libraries for their own use. In Paris from 1713 on he moved in literary and journalistic circles – his friends included both the Jesuit Tournemine and the Jansenist Jacques-Joseph Du Guet. Years later Le Courayer wrote that he felt nothing in his exile more deeply than the loss of 'the pleasure of philosophizing with you with that religious liberty which befits Christian philosophers ...'[2] He spent the years 1718–20 in Holland working with Saint-Hyacinthe on his journal, *L'Europe savante*. While there he was also close to Le Clerc.[3] He was at home in the freer, more critical atmosphere of Holland: he wrote a treatise on the authority of the pope, which he published in Paris in 1720 and prefaced with an epistle to Pope Clement XI which condemned those who from self-interest vaunted the authority of the pope and gave Protestants a pretext for rejecting the truth since it was accompanied by such great and blasphemous errors.[4] There followed in 1724 a study of the theology and philosophy of the pagans. It was a

the authorship of the dialogue, see James K. McConica 'Erasmus and the "Julius": A Humanist Reflects on the Church,' especially 467–71, and the literature cited there.

8 Vicesimus Knox, quoted in Trollope 'Life and Writings' xxxv
9 See further below, 294 n 1.
1 Michaud VI 189–90; DTC II 1 cols 1264–5; J.-M. Quérard *La France littéraire, ou dictionnaire bibliographique des savants, historiens et gens de lettres de la France* ... V 278–9; Abbé Genet 'Étude historique sur Jean Lévesque de Burigny'
2 Genet 'Etude historique' 208. The letter is of 1765.
3 J.-M. Quérard *Les Superchéries littéraires devoilées* 98
4 Reprinted in second edition, *Traité de l'autorité du pape* ... iii. Marsollier praised the work in a letter of 29 May 1721 (ibid xi).

work of Burigny's sceptical youth which incorporated his reading in the classical authors and the voyagers to new worlds and which he later perhaps regretted. It brought him notoriety, and an air of mystery and ambiguity has since hung over his religious beliefs. He completed a long manuscript of 1,595 pages in 1733, *Sur la vérité de la religion*, but it was never printed.[5] Another work – *Examen critique des apologistes de la religion chrétienne* – long circulated in manuscript and was finally printed in 1767. Burigny is one of the candidates for the authorship, though the matter is much contested.[6]

What matters is the change in Burigny between the 1730s and the 1750s. The correspondent of Bolingbroke, who wrote to him on natural religion, and the associate of Helvétius became the confidant of the Roman Cardinal Dominic Passionei (1682–1761), who was nuncio in Holland and became the Vatican librarian in 1755. The two corresponded over the proposed life of Erasmus, and the cardinal approved the biographer's understanding of his subject: 'It is very sure that he [Erasmus] was always very strongly attached to the Catholic religion and gave a great proof of that at Basel ...'[7] The work on the pagans which had been first published at the Hague in 1724 was reissued with approbation and royal privilege in Paris in 1754. The author was resolved, said the preface, 'to review the work with the greatest severity and to make in it the additions and suppressions which new reading and riper reflection have been able to suggest.'[8] Most indicative is the sequence of biographies which Burigny produced between 1750 and 1761 – on Grotius, Erasmus, and Bossuet in that order. On Bossuet he showed himself 'full of goodwill and admiration for his hero.'[9]

5 Genet 'Etude historique' 218; Ira O. Wade *The Clandestine Organization and Diffusion of Philosophical Ideas in France from 1700 to 1750* 20
6 Genet offers reasons for not attributing the work to Burigny ('Etude historique' 311); Quérard, following A.A. Barbier, takes his authorship as proved (*Superchéries* 98–102); DTC declares the proofs insufficient (II col 1265); Wade sees it as the product of a deistic group around Boulainvilliers and primarily the work of the enigmatic Nicolas Fréret, who became secretary of the Académie des Inscriptions, though Burigny made contributions (*Clandestine Organization* 202). One should recognize the impossibility of reaching agreement on these attributions, especially when the names of learned men were placed on the clandestine manuscripts. See F. Manuel *The Eighteenth Century Confronts the Gods* 229. Cf H. Dieckman *Le Philosophe: Texts and Interpretations* 321.
7 Passionei to Burigny, 30 December 1754, quoted in Genet 'Etude historique' 274–5
8 *Théologie payenne* ... liii
9 Genet's judgment ('Etude historique' 306)

In his later years Burigny became something of an institution in French scholarly life. He joined the Académie des Inscriptions et Belles-lettres in 1756 and offered there many dissertations, ranging in title from 'Memoir on the ancient history of India' to 'Memoir proving that in the preceding centuries there were many occasions of unhappiness which no longer exist today.'[1] He was an agreeable personality, 'good, simple, true, indulgent and easy.'[2]

Burigny's life of Erasmus outdid those of his predecessors in range and grasp and learning; he begins by reviewing their achievements, such as they were. Among the earliest biographies, he says, Beatus Rhenanus was much more instructive than the Compendium, which, as Bayle saw, was a work of the utmost negligence.[3] Mercier's brief life was inexact and superficial but superior to the effort of La Bizardière, who was a 'Panégyriste outré' and ill-read in Erasmus' writings. Tournemine fabricated judgments – for example, that Erasmus was flattered and honoured by the authorities in order to bind him to the church – out of pure hatred of Erasmus; he was 'refuted with great liveliness by a redoubtable adversary' (Le Courayer).[4] Knight's was not a true biography since it concerned only his English connection, which was the least part of his history.[5] Then there were the great lost biographies, Malinckrodt's and Joly's. In his earlier works, Joly spoke of Erasmus as one who knew his writings well; so the disappearance of his manuscript was regrettable.[6] But, plainly, amid these inadequate and abortive works Burigny's comprehensive undertaking was given its opportunity.

Like Le Clerc, Burigny gave close attention to the epistles, which in one place he describes as 'among the most agreeable reading-matter one can find.'[7] Erasmus' illnesses, his financial affairs, his personal relations – there is an especially moving account of his friendship with Froben[8] – are described in detail from the letters. Burigny indeed added to the common stock: Cardinal Passionei discovered several letters in the Vatican and in 1754 sent copies to his friend.[9] The work is rich in

1 Quérard La France littéraire 278–9
2 Eloge by Dacier, 1786, quoted in Genet 'Etude historique' 220
3 Vie d'Erasme I ... iv
4 Ibid v–viii
5 Ibid ix–x
6 Ibid xi–xiv
7 Ibid 387
8 Ibid 427–9
9 Included are two letters from Erasmus at Basel to Francis Asulanus (respectively 18 March 1523, Allen Ep 1349, v 252–3; 19 April 1528, Allen Ep

VIE D'ERASME,

DANS LAQUELLE ON

trouvera l'Hiftoire de plufieurs Hommes célébres avec lefquels il a été en liaifon, l'Analyfe critique de fes Ouvrages, & l'Examen impartial de fes fentimens en matiére de Religion:

Par M. DE BURIGNI, de l'Académie Royale des Infcriptions & Belles-Lettres.

TOME PREMIER.

Nomen Erafmi nunquam peribit.
Joannes Colletus, Epift. 12. L. 2.

A PARIS;

Chez DE BURE l'aîné, Quai des Auguftins, du côté du Pont S. Michel, à S. Paul.

M. DCC. LVII.

AVEC APPROBATION ET PRIVILEGE DU ROI.

Title page of Jean Lévesque de Burigny *Vie d'Erasme*
Vassar College Library

detail but, although transcending the chronicle form, it is not well organized: all is linked together in an endless chain, one topic opening into the next without break or division; there are but suggestions of a pattern in the shapeless flow.

In the biography itself, Burigny continues to use and comment critically on his predecessors. This reinforces the impression that here for the first time is a truly scholarly work. Scaliger and Lando are accused of circulating the outrageous charge that Erasmus was born of a sacrilegious union. (Even if this were so, how might it affect his own honour?) Otherwise Burigny traces Erasmus' birth, childhood, and youth from Beatus Rhenanus and the *Compendium*, though the letter to Grunnius is seen to be decisive on the existence of his older brother.[1] Bayle must be behind Burigny's solemn consideration of Erasmus' chastity: his enemies may have exaggerated his unchastity, his friends his absolute chastity – various letters admit faults.[2] Scaliger, Possevino, and most recently Tournemine have wrongly called Erasmus an 'apostate' for leaving the monastery, which he had entered 'almost in spite of himself' and under unscrupulous pressure from his guardians, but Le Courayer has rightly said that he who leaves with permission from his superiors cannot be called an apostate.[3] Is Le Clerc's remark about 'Italian posturing' likewise transposed into Burigny's approval of Erasmus' decision, despite his good relations with the Habsburgs, not to follow the court to Spain, since 'his bold and free nature' would not endear him to the Spaniards?[4] Marsollier exaggerated Erasmus' influence at the Roman court: Pope Adrian VI was not preparing to adopt his program for overcoming the German crisis.[5] From savants at Basel Burigny learned that Boissard's story about Erasmus' behaviour as rector of the university there deserved no credence. Similarly, since his meeting with Calvin 'has the warrant only of Florimond de Raemond, one is well advised to doubt it.'[6]

Despite its shapelessness, this work has recurring themes. Burigny has an interest in Erasmus' relation to places; this gives his life a sense

1989, VII 380–1) and the contract between Erasmus and Jan Laski for the sale of Erasmus' library to the latter (Burigny *Vie d'Erasme* I 124, 133, 436; II 422). Burigny, said Jortin, should have printed the whole of these unpublished documents (Jortin *Life* I 618).

1 *Vie d'Erasme* I 3, 11–12
2 Ibid 38–9
3 Ibid 33, 48–9
4 Ibid 227
5 Ibid 409
6 Ibid 454–6

of pilgrimage, a quest for unrealized satisfactions. When he spoke of settling in Holland, his compatriots themselves insisted that 'he was born to shine on a larger stage.'[7] He had a genuine attachment to England, but more than once his hopes were disappointed; still, there was consolation in his English friends, the warm regard of Warham, the tender association with Colet, the abiding friendship with More.[8] Rome wanted to retain him; after mad enmities and calumnies had forced him to leave Brabant, he spoke of returning there, but would Rome afford him the liberty and tranquillity he craved?[9] Attachment to liberty led him to Basel, where he was loved and esteemed and could oversee the publication of his works; he sought his tranquillity there.[1] The great mischance – a natural judgment for a patriot – was the failure of France to win him, despite many attempts: he was grateful for the warm sentiments of King Francis I towards him; his warm expressions in return led some to accuse him of partiality towards the French nation; though there were differences between them, Budé, the great French scholar, and Erasmus enjoyed a mutual esteem.[2] Erasmus loved France and praised her, but did not settle within her borders.

Burigny is also concerned with what later generations called the Renaissance problem. The backdrop to Erasmus' life is the barbaric condition of studies in the fifteenth century and the rapid transformation at the century's end from 'this most profound barbarism to the most varied and elegant erudition.'[3] The north followed Italy towards enlightenment and purer studies. Deventer, where Erasmus went to school, received some of the 'abundance of light' streaming from Italy.[4] Erasmus in his turn advanced enlightenment: the *Adagia* were 'the greatest literary work to appear in Europe since the revival of good letters.'[5] Erasmus may not have written with perfect elegance but he had 'an admirable ease and richness.' The Ciceronians said nothing in harmonious phrases, while Erasmus' works were full of useful and agreeable things.[6] The state of theology was analogous to that of literature. Scholasticism was barbaric theology. Now (in the

7 Ibid 70
8 Ibid 91, 154–93
9 Ibid 139–47, 285–7
1 Ibid 390
2 Ibid 100, 234–57
3 Ibid II 474
4 Ibid I 14–15
5 Ibid II 357
6 Ibid 484, 488–9

eighteenth century) it is hard, says Burigny, to conceive of the insanity of the scholastic questions. 'The scriptures were not understood, the Fathers were not read.'[7] Before Erasmus, criticism was an unknown land; he was the pathfinder. There has been nothing comparable to his critical and scientific work on the New Testament in the whole history of Christianity. Later writers, who have not always been easy to please, have praised his performance: Joseph Scaliger, Huet, Simon, and Le Clerc.[8] Like the renewal of letters earlier, a great and rapid transformation of theology came in as the theologians followed Erasmus into biblical and patristic studies.

But the great theme of Burigny's work is, of course, Erasmus' relation to Catholicism. A constant refrain runs through his two volumes: Erasmus was Catholic and a useful teacher of the church in his time, but he did not always speak with discretion. Thus Burigny begins his long consideration of Erasmus' relations with Luther: when Luther appeared Erasmus was the most highly regarded scholar in the world, but he had enemies 'whose hatred was all the more violent as religion was its cause or pretext'; the reproaches of the monks and theologians were not wholly without foundation, but men of equitable judgment were with reason persuaded that his aim was but to check abuses and so 'they made no great crime out of his indiscretions.'[9] Honest contemporaries and historians like Bossuet have recognized the justice in Luther's attacks on indulgences and other abuses.[1] Erasmus understandably saw in Luther at first 'only an indiscreet and too ardent Catholic,' but the difficulties of the middle way were soon apparent: the bull of 1520 against Luther turned him towards violence, while in Rome there ruled 'inordinate pride ... insupportable vanity.'[2] Burigny tells the familiar story of the pressures on Erasmus to write against Luther; his diatribe on free will provoked Luther to fury but did not reconcile his enemies among the monks and theologians. The story of the controversies with Beda, Carpi, and Aleander is told in a dispassionate way: of the propositions which Beda called reprehensible Burigny characteristically says: 'If some are bold or even false, the greater number can be easily justified; there are some so true that no

7 Ibid 489–90. Notice, however, Burigny's praise of Aquinas (in reference to the debate between Colet and Erasmus on the great doctor): '... une grande profondeur de raisonnement, & un esprit supérieur' (ibid I 183).
8 Ibid I 325, 349–51
9 Ibid II 1–2
1 Ibid 5–25
2 Ibid 25, 39, 54–5, 61

critic today would dare to contest them.'[3] He was too enlightened not to realize that heretics were not punished by death in the early church, but for once he prudently hid his views for fear of embroiling himself further with the theologians of the Sorbonne. Burigny sums up in Marsollier's words: Erasmus' views were essentially sound but he wrote at a time when any criticism of received opinion was suspect.[4] In a sense that excused both Erasmus and his enemies their indiscretions and extravagances. Such was the benign regard of an eighteenth-century man for the follies of his ancestors!

That Pope Paul III offered him a cardinalate was an honour to Erasmus and 'decisive for his catholicity.' The enemies of his reputation, like Tournemine, instead of reproaching Erasmus for dying in a heretical town, should have noted his last extant letter, where he expresses his longing to die in a Catholic country. He died indeed 'in giving proof of a perfect resignation to the will of God and a truly Christian patience.'[5]

Erasmus had no difficulty in convincing reasonable men of his orthodoxy on disputed questions. He was orthodox, for example, on the primacy of the pope, though he did oppose those who lifted the papal authority beyond its just limits.[6] Doubtless (Burigny goes on in a passage that outraged Jortin) he would have accepted the ruling of the Council of Trent that auricular confession was founded by Christ himself.[7] On divorce, he would like to have seen some possibility of dissolving marriages in serious and well-considered cases, but his replies to his critics showed that he was not challenging decisions of the church.[8] He was right to flay the corruption of the monastic orders, but some of his expressions went too far; yet he did not attack the state itself.[9] In the Arian controversy his orthodoxy was not in danger, but again his expressions were indiscreet, even inexcusable.[1] In judging the religion of Erasmus, Burigny concludes, there are two excesses to

3 Ibid 219. An example of the first is his notion of an adolescent repetition of baptismal vows which the Council of Trent condemned and an example of the second his rejection of Dionysius the Areopagite's authorship of the works attributed to him (ibid 227–8, 253–5).
4 Ibid 224, 259
5 Ibid 414–15
6 Ibid 508–12
7 Ibid 517. 'Are you in earnest?' Jortin exclaims. Logs of wood, he goes on, would have done as well as the Trent Fathers (*Life* I 626).
8 Ibid II 522–3
9 Ibid 524–6
1 Ibid 531–5

avoid. The first is to treat him as a heretic, as Bellarmine did and Tournemine and Father Gabriel. The second is to overpraise him as the great teacher of the church in his time, as Richard and La Bizardière did. The truth is that he was one of the ablest and most useful men of his age, but he did not always speak with wisdom and discretion, though he willingly accepted the ruling of the church.[2]

This judgment is repeated in what Burigny has to say about Erasmus' various writings. The *Moriae encomium* was 'a very ingenious satire on all conditions of life' which deserves to be read in the original for its elegant allusions to ancient literature. Not at first intending to publish it, Erasmus consulted only his own taste in his witticisms. Neither Leo x nor any of the other popes under whom he lived made him any reproach over it, but others – Dorp, whom Erasmus reconciled by a civil reply, the Sorbonne, with characteristic exaggeration – 'began ... to have a bad opinion of his religion.' Certainly under rigorous scrutiny its indiscretions cannot be fully justified.[3]

Similarly in the *Enchiridion* 'the truth is perhaps put forward with too little care.' It made him enemies. As Du Pin saw, it contains expressions not suitable for a work of piety which is to go into everyone's hands. Still, in this more enlightened age, one may speak as Erasmus did without offending anyone. Not all by any means shared Loyola's judgment that it dampened devotion, through it lacked the compunction of the *Imitation of Christ*: 'It may well be more enlightened but for the devout what is enlightenment with respect to that spirit of compunction which, after touching the soul, unites it in some fashion to God ... ?'[4]

It cannot be denied that the *Colloquia*, too, are filled with indiscretions. Erasmus should have been more prudent since he lived in stormy times with enemies always on the watch; but such was his character, as he himself recognized – he could not forgo a *bon mot*, when once it had come into his mind. Yet criticism 'served to make evident his Catholicity because he disavowed the errors attributed to him.' And in itself this was an agreeable work.[5] The last writings continued to make

2 Ibid 541–3. Only the first part of Richard's work was published but it was 'so badly done and so filled with invectives and declamations that it does not lead one to wish for the second' (ibid 547). Father Gabriel's book had order but its prejudice against Erasmus was too apparent (ibid 550). Burigny has most praise for Klefeker's thesis, the *Exercitatio critica* ... One recognizes in it the moderation of the illustrious Fabricius, Klefeker's teacher (ibid 55).
3 Ibid I 194–205
4 Ibid 288–302
5 Ibid 507–20

enemies. Of the tract on *Mending the Peace of the Church,* Burigny says: 'The Catholics did not approve all his ideas; but the Protestants were even more dissatisfied with his book ...'[6]

Of course, the works reveal the man as well as the controversialist. Burigny does not go far beyond the famous character-sketch by Beatus Rhenanus but he offers an engaging portrait none the less. Erasmus was a man of feeling and sympathy who delighted in company and loved raillery; sometimes angry, especially with pen in hand, he was easily appeased; he was neither ambitious nor avaricious but candid and sincere, sometimes to his own hurt; he loved work; he hated discord.[7]

Burigny was the best-read writer in the works of Erasmus up to his time, the first to take full advantage of the Leiden edition. He was also an astute reader, as we have many times seen, of writings about Erasmus. Indeed his own judgment often hides behind an extended critical treatment of earlier authors. By the standards of his predecessors his work was balanced and dispassionate. The outlook is essentially that of Bossuet but with an overlay of 'enlightenment,' apparent, for example, in Burigny's acceptance as self-evident of contemporary ideas on religious toleration. Erasmus is seen as orthodox in intention and in fact but prone temperamentally and in the historical circumstances to too much boldness and a certain looseness of expression.

Contemporaries recognized the importance of the work Passionei called a model for biographies.[8] 'Who,' asked Voltaire, speaking of the lives of Grotius and Erasmus, 'could better celebrate them than a man who has all their learning and shares all their sentiments?'[9] And Gibbon said:

It is a work of great reading. M. de Burigni proposed connecting with his history, a general account of the sciences and religion in his time, and has very deeply considered the subject. His style and reflections are suited to a man of science and modesty, who neither pretends to nor possesses the least share of genius. Upon

6 Ibid ɪɪ 352
7 Ibid 560–3
8 Genet 'Etude historique' 276
9 In response to the promise of Burigny's biographies, 20 March 1757
   (Voltaire *Correspondence* xxxɪ 107); his praise after reading the works, 10
   May 1757 (ibid 158–9)

the whole, the book is a perfect contrast to the fashionable French ones; since it is useful without being brilliant.[1]

1 Quoted in C. Butler *The Life of Erasmus: With Historical Remarks on the State of Literature between the Tenth and Sixteenth Centuries* 221–2. Jortin's *Life* was, as we have seen, almost printed before he could procure a copy of Burigny. He looked for instruction, he says, and was not deceived. 'How indeed should it be otherwise, since we both draw from the same spring, and employ nearly the same materials?' On religious matters a French Catholic and an English Protestant are bound to speak differently: what is bold to one is 'most agreeable and useful' to the other. 'The zealous Romanists will perhaps think that even M. Burigni is half-spoiled by keeping bad company, and that here and there he smells a little of *Erasmianism*' (*Life* I 615–16).

Conclusion

❦

The story of Erasmus' reputation may be told in three ways or, to put the point differently, it proceeds on three levels. The first is emotional. This is the level of love and hate, attraction and repulsion, taste or distaste. From his day to ours, those of a certain psychological make-up or with ideological commitments of a certain kind have found Erasmus uncongenial and have felt threatened by him. His was a singularly open spirit, a responsive, even a fluid, personality and an eclectic mind with a preference for combining rather than dividing. Those of like temperament have been drawn to him. Others – the more committed or the more exclusive, who have known very well where God and Satan, church and world, belief and unbelief, purity and impurity (be it in language or in faith) divide – have been angered. At this level there is little change over the generations. The moral value or the emotional quality of what is offered by succeeding writers in the two series, the sympathetic and the unsympathetic, has been more or less constant.

The clearest case in our period is the hostile Jesuit tradition. From Canisius to Tournemine there are expressions of distaste and disgust for Erasmus' shiftiness and evasiveness, his demoralizing wish (as it is seen) to stand in well with all parties. In a Garasse or a Raynaud these disgusts seem psychologically maiming; they pass over into hatred and hysteria. On the other hand, temperaments which find conflict hard to bear and are easily wounded by party strife feel sympathetic to Erasmus. At the beginning of the story are those who resisted emotionally the fact of religious division and fought, against the odds, for reunion – Nausea on one side and Melanchthon on the other. At the end are the irenicists of the early eighteenth century, sensing the amelioration of confessional conflict after six generations but then outraged by the threat of its revival in, say, the revocation of the Edict of Nantes. On the Protestant side, the temperamental break with orthodoxy is seen in a figure like Fabricius, who is the first among his co-religionists to recognize a moral validity in Erasmus' conscience.

Among the enemies of Erasmus, loyalty – to an institution or a doctrine – has a high place among the virtues. His Catholic critics take certain episodes in his career as indicative of apostasy: his departure from the monastery, his death (without benefit of clergy) in a Protestant town. To his unsoundness on certain doctrines they return *ad nauseam*: the Trinity (Erasmus is a neo-Arian), the authority of the church (he is a crypto-Protestant). Protestant opponents are naturally preoccupied with his relationship with Luther; he saw the force of Luther's claims but abandoned him under pressure or for more disreputable reasons. By the time of Melchior Adam a pattern is fixed: Erasmus saw the right road but was too fearful to follow it. Even Jean Le Clerc, who made so much of tolerance, had a mental block here: Erasmus must have seen the light; he must have turned his back on it in a kind of betrayal.

Among the friends of Erasmus, by contrast, party spirit is a great enemy, which he in his day struggled to overcome. The theme runs through the whole literature. It can be found at the beginning in what emerged from the Cleves circle. It is central to the Basel tradition about Erasmus. It comes to a climax in the great denunciations of partisanship by Le Courayer, Arnold, and Bayle.

In some cases, emotion arises from a sense that the drama of Erasmus' life is being replayed in a contemporary setting. Those especially who feel an affinity with Erasmus like to compare their struggles with his. Essential to the self-consciousness of the Arminians – Barlaeus and Grotius – was the feeling that their controversy with orthodox Calvinists was like, indeed in some ways was a continuation of, Erasmus' controversy with monks and scholastic theologians. This identification was characteristic of minority or defeated parties. We have found it – surprisingly, given their strong views against a doctrine of free will – among the Jansenists. It is not, on the other hand, surprising to find the pietist Gottfried Arnold defending the maligned remnant to which both he and Erasmus belonged. The same sense of continuity or of replay appears among writers unsympathetic or less sympathetic to Erasmus, usually in this form: the corrosive forces which he represented are still at work in the world. Bossuet laughed at the pretensions of an Erasmus and a Richard Simon to decide between the Fathers.

At this level, one may say, the moral or emotional flavour of the discussion about Erasmus changes little between 1550 and 1750. At the next level, however, we must recognize changing fortunes in the history of Erasmus' reputation. The balance of favourable and un-favourable judgments alters. There is, as a matter of fact, a clear pattern. This is the story over two centuries of the decline, fall, and recovery of a reputation. Arond 1550, on both sides of the widening confessional division or – to state it more accurately – within the various parties, people were still living who had known Erasmus and shared the aspirations of the Christian humanists. By the end of the century, outside a small number of limited settings, all that was forgotten or remembered only with despair, as by de Thou. Those speaking for Erasmus were few. Minds were fastened on the confes-sional differences and on the problems, which in part arose from them, of political breakdown and cultural shift. Only when Europeans drew back from the abyss and attempted a mutual accommodation of the religious differences could the recovery of Erasmus' reputation begin. With the defeat of the Arminians a first attempt was thwarted. By the end of the seventeenth century, recovery was widespread; by the middle of the eighteenth to speak well of Erasmus was the norm, to speak ill of him the rarity. This paragraph shows that this pattern cannot be described without reference to a changing climate of opinion and sensibility. To this we will return.

It might be asked: was there, superimposed on the cycle of fall and recovery, a progress in the understanding of Erasmus which can be objectively recorded? One cannot honestly say that there has been a great advance in method or approach. Even the first biographies remain unplanned, amorphous, episodic. In form, they compare unfavourably with the brief life of Beatus Rhenanus. Nevertheless, the difference in scale is significant. A work like Burigny's, or even Jortin's, requires a critical reappraisal of a host of particular questions and of their treat-ment by previous authors. Burigny's handling of Erasmus' writings offers a number of examples; here he had been anticipated by Morhof. Much earlier, Opmeer had used local knowledge to achieve a greater accuracy. Merula's publication of the *Compendium* and other docu-ments also came out of a particular local setting. This was the one major addition to the sources in the whole period, and to it all subsequent writing on Erasmus was in debt. In psychological understanding there was no advance; the Thomasius essay was the first of its kind and interesting, but the psychology was crudely determinist; otherwise, Burigny's pen-portrait of Erasmus the man was a rephrasing of that of Beatus Rhenanus of 220 years before. To ask 'What of religious

understanding?' is to return to the heart of the controversy about
Erasmus. The religious parties, within limits modern scholars too,
disagree among themselves. My judgment would be: the changes in
religious sensibility around the beginning of the eighteenth century, if
they were in danger of sentimentalizing him, nevertheless recovered
for the first time since the generation after his death the warmer
elements in Erasmus' piety, and that was immeasurable gain.

So we come to the third level. The changes in the appreciation of
Erasmus can be explained historically; they relate to particular historical settings or to large changes in what I have called the climate of
opinion and sensibility. Let me recall some of the particular settings. In
Basel Erasmus' name continued to be cherished, when elsewhere in
Protestant Europe it was at a discount. This was due partly to the
influence of Erasmus' friends and connections, partly also to Basel's
appearance as a moral rival (if a subdued one) to Geneva. In the
southern Netherlands at the end of the civil wars Erasmus' reputation
fared better than among Catholics generally. That indicates the persistence of an Erasmian tradition but also a continuing contact between
the two parts of the Netherlands despite their political separation. The
Dutch republic itself, for all the bitterness of the Arminian controversy the most tolerant society in Europe, was a congenial environment for restoring and then nurturing Erasmus' reputation.

The first of the larger changes in the moral and intellectual climate
was the slide of the first two generations after Erasmus' death into
murderous religious war. The lines – we do not need again to labour the
point – were drawn ever more sharply. Early Catholic controversialists
like Cochlaeus still used Erasmus' witness against the Reformers; by
the 1560s, Catholic polemic damned him, with them, beyond recall.
Similarly, Protestant controversialists abandoned the middle ground.
The atmosphere of the last quarter of the sixteenth century was
sombre, brutal; Erasmus, as we know, was then the possession of a
minority who saw themselves as outsiders.

The second change – in the late seventeenth and early eighteenth
centuries – makes Erasmus again a figure of the cultural majority. We
have come into the vestibule of the Enlightenment; in the Erasmus
literature we do not go beyond the vestibule. Bayle, as we have seen,
was not simply a man of the pre-Enlightenment, but the scepticism
about historical claims and the pleas for toleration in his article on
Erasmus were welcome to the next generation. Hardt fitted Erasmus
into a scheme of progress; Klefeker and Fabricius, without sacrificing
their Lutheran allegiance, could make a reasoned judgment about

Erasmus' religion, free of confessional constraints and prescriptions; Jortin, revising Le Clerc, could see in Erasmus a model of moderate religion. Catholic writers reflect the change in religious sensibility more largely, Pope in the English Catholic community, Joly, Marsollier, and Burigny amid the tumults of the Gallican church. Their purpose is to defend the Catholicism of Erasmus, but how different a Catholicism from, say, Bellarmine's. Religion, reason, sensibility must live together. In that atmosphere, Erasmus' reputation takes on a new lease of life.

If our standard is set by the question: 'Do these writers see Erasmus in his own terms or judge him still by others' claims?' then this last phase has made ground significantly. Simon, Bayle, and Jortin have applied stricter standards to the appreciation of his critical and literary work. Various writers have shown some inner understanding of his piety. Much remains superficial – a danger always in an 'enlightened' age – but the gains are real and enduring. Erasmus has begun to assume a recognizable face.

Bibliography

꙰

BIBLIOGRAPHIES

Barbier, A.-A. *Dictionnaire des ouvrages anonymes* 3rd edn, I, III, Paris 1872, 1875
Margolin, J.-C. *Douze années de bibliographie érasmienne (1950–1961)* Paris 1963
– *Quatorze années de bibliographie érasmienne (1936–1949)* Paris 1969
– *Neuf années de bibliographie érasmienne (1962–1970)* Paris and Toronto 1977
Quérard, J.-M. *La France littéraire ou dictionnaire bibliographique des savants, historiens et gens de lettres de la France ...* III, V, Paris 1829, 1833
– *Les Superchéries littéraires devoilées* II Paris 1870
Sommervogel, Carlos SJ *Bibliothèque de la Compagnie de Jésus* I, Brussels/Paris 1890
Vander Haeghen, F. *Bibliotheca Erasmiana* Ghent 1893, reprint Nieuwkoop 1961
Vander Haeghen, F., R. Vander Berghe, and T.J.I. Arnold *Bibliotheca Erasmiana* in *Bibliotheca Belgica*, 27 vols, Ghent 1891–1922; reprinted in 6 vols, Brussels 1964. 'Erasmus' vol II

MANUSCRIPTS

Harpsfield, Nicholas 'Historia anglicana ecclesiastica' Arundel MS 73, British Library
Joly, Claude 'Histoire de la renaissance des lettres dans la fin du quinzième siècle, et dans les commencemens du seizième ...' Bibliothèque de l'Arsenal, MS 4625 (transcription of part, MS 4626)

Wake correspondence MS 244, Christ Church Library, Oxford, nos 11, 21, 23, 24, Le Courayer to Wake, 12 December 1721, 25 October 1722, 12 June, 4 October 1723

PRIMARY PRINTED SOURCES

Acta eruditorum Leipzig May 1688, 267–70 (Review of Richard) Adam, Melchior Dignorum laude virorum quos Musa vetat mori, immortalitas, seu vitae theologorum, jure-consultorum & politicorum, medicorum, atque philosophorum, maximam partem Germanorum ... 3rd ed, Frankfurt-am-Main 1706

Andreas, Valerius (Valère André) Bibliotheca Belgica Louvain 1623

Arnold, Gottfried Unparteyische Kirchen- und Ketzer-Historie, vom Anfang des Neuen Testaments bis auf das Jahr 1688 Frankfurt-am-Main 1729

Aubrey, John Brief Lives and Other Selected Writings ed Anthony Powell, London 1949

Barlaeus, Caspar (Kaspar van Baerle) Casparis Barlaei Bogermannus ... in quo etiam crimina a Matthaeo Slado impacta Erasmo Roterodamo diluuntur Leiden 1615

Baudius, Dominicus Amores ed P. Scriverius Amsterdam 1638

– Dominici Baudii epistolae semicenturia auctae ... Leiden 1650

Bayle, Pierre Dictionnaire historique et critique 16 vols, Paris 1820, VI

Beatus Rhenanus 'The Life of Erasmus' in John C. Olin (ed) Desiderius Erasmus: Christian Humanism and the Reformation: Selected Writings N.Y. 1965, 31–54 (Latin text in Allen I 56–71)

Bellarmine, Robert Disputationum ... de controversiis christianae fidei, adversus huius temporis haereticos, opus ... Ingolstadt 1601

de Bèze, Théodore Correspondance de Théodore de Bèze ed Hippolyte Aubert, F. Aubert, H. Meylan and A. Dufour, Geneva 1960–

– Icones, id est verae imagines virorum doctrina simul et pietate illustrium, quorum praecipue ministerio partim bonarum literarum studia sunt restituta, partim vera religio in variis orbis christiani regionibus, nostra patrumque memoria fuit instaurata: additis eorundem vitae & operae descriptionibus ... Geneva 1580. French tr by Simon Goulart Les Vrais Pourtraits des hommes illustres en piété et doctrine, traduits du latin de Th. de Bèze ... ed G. Goguel, Saint-Suzanne 1858

– Theodori Bezae Vezelii poemata Paris 1548

Biandrata, Giorgio Antithesis pseudochristi cum vero illo ex Maria nato in D. Cantimori and E. Feist (eds) Per la storia degli eretici

Italiani del secolo XVI in Europa, Reale Academia d'Italia Studi e Documenti 7, Rome 1937, 95–103

Biandrata, Giorgio and Ferenc David *De falsa et vera unius dei patris, filii et spiritus sancti cognitione libri duo* in ibid 104–10

[Biddle, John] *A Brief History of the Unitarians, Called also Socinians: In Four Letters to a Friend* London 1687

Binauld, Guillaume (Gulielmus Binaldus) *Desid. Erasmi Roterodami colloquia familiaria, notis novis illustrata: Ad usum juventutis politioris humanitatis studiis imbuendae, apud omnes Protestantes, Britannos praesertim, & Hibernos* Dublin 1712

Blount, Thomas Pope *Censura celebriorum authorum* ... London 1690

Boissard, Jean-Jacques *Icones quinquaginta virorum illustrium doctrina & eruditione praestantium ad vivum effictae, cum eorum vitis descriptis* Frankfurt 1597

Bossuet, Jacques B. *Défense de la tradition et des Saints Peres* Paris 1763

– *Histoire des variations des églises protestantes* in *Œuvres* VII, Paris 1846

Boxhorn, Marcus-Zuerius *Monumenta illustrium virorum, et elogia* Amsterdam 1638

– *Theatrum sive Hollandiae comitatis et urbium nova descriptio* Amsterdam 1632

Brandt, Gerhard *Historie der Reformatie* 4 vols, Amsterdam 1671–1704. Eng tr *The History of the Reformation & Other Ecclesiastical Transactions in and about the Low-Countries ... In which all the Revolutions that happen'd in Church and State on Account of the Divisions between the Protestants and Papists, the Arminians and Calvinists, Are fairly and fully represented ...*, 2 vols, London 1720–1

Burnet, Gilbert *History of the Reformation of the Church of England* ed Nicholas Pocock, 7 vols, Oxford 1865, I, II

Canisius, Peter *De Maria virgine incomparabili, et Dei genitrice sacrosancta, libri quinque* ... Ingolstadt 1577

– *D. Hieronymi Stridoniensis epistolae selectae, & in libros tres distributae* ... Lyon 1592

Cary, Lucius, Viscount Falkland *A Discourse of Infallibility, with Mr Thomas White's Answer to it, and a Reply to him* ed Thomas Triplet, 2nd ed, London 1660

Castro, Alfonso de *Adversus omnes haereses libri XIIII*, Paris 1534

'Cleral' 'Replique sur la réfutation inserée aux Mémoires de Trevoux Juin 1714 de l'Apologie d'Erasme, faite par M. Marsollier' *Journal Literaire*, Hague, article XXIV, VI, pt 2, 1715: 374–81

Cochlaeus, Johannes *Commentaria Joannis Cochlaei, de actis et scriptis Martini Lutheri Saxonis, chronographice, ex ordine ab anno. domini M.D.XVII usque ad annum M.D.XLVI* ... Mainz 1549 (Gregg reprint 1968)

Curione, Celio Secundo *Pasquillus ecstaticus non ille prior, sed totus plane alter, auctus & expolitus* ... Geneva 1544

– *Pasquine in a Traunce: A Christian and learned Dialogue ... Wherein besydes Christes truthe playnely set forth, ye shall also finde a numbre of pleasaunt histories, discovering all the crafty conveyaunces of Antichrist* London [1566]

– *Pasquino in estasi nuovo* ... [1546?] [Rome?]

des Périers, Bonaventure *Cymbalum mundi* ed Peter H. Nurse, Manchester 1958

Dolet, Etienne *Dialogus, de imitatione Ciceroniana, adversus Desiderium Erasmum Roterodamum, pro Christophoro Longolio.* Facsimile in Emile V. Telle (ed) *L'Erasmianus sive Ciceronianus d'Etienne Dolet (1535)* Geneva 1974

Du Bosc de Montandré, Claude (ed) *Du Mépris du monde, et de la pureté de l'église chrétienne; Avec un discours sur l'enfant Jesus; & une lettre aux religieuses de Cantbrige de l'Ordre de saint François, qui contient un excellent éloge de la solitude: Traduction d'Erasme* Paris 1713

– *Le Manuel du soldat chrêtien ou les obligations et les devoirs d'un chrêtien, et la preparation à la mort: Ouvrages d'Erasme, traduits en François* Paris 1711

– *Le Mariage chrétien: ou traité dans lequel on apprend à ceux qui se veulent engager dans le mariage, ou qui y sont déjà engagez, les règles qui'ils doivent suivre pour s'y comporter d'une maniere chrétienne: Traduit du latin d'Erasme* Paris 1714

Du Pin, Louis Ellies *A New Ecclesiastical History of the Sixteenth Century: Containing an Impartial Account of the Reformation of Religion, and other ecclesiastical affairs* ... London 1703

Emlyn, Thomas *An Answer to Mr. Martin's Critical Dissertation on 1. John v.7. There are Three that bear Record &c.* ... London 1719

Erasmus, Desiderius *Erasme: Declamatio de pueris statim ac liberaliter instituendis: Etude critique, traduction et commentaire* ed J.-C. Margolin, Geneva 1966

– *Erasmi opuscula: A Supplement to the Opera omnia* ed Wallace K. Ferguson, The Hague 1933

– *The Colloquies of Erasmus* ed Craig R. Thompson, Chicago/London 1965

Fiddes, Richard *The Life of Cardinal Wolsey* London 1724

Foxe, John *The Second Volume of the Ecclesiasticall history con-teynyng the Actes and Monumentes of Martyrs, with a generall discourse of these latter persecutions, horrible troubles, and tumultes, styrred up by Romish Prelates in the Church* ... London 1570

Franck, Sebastian *Chronick: Geschichte und Zeitbuch aller Namhafftigsten und Gedechtnuswierdigsten Geystlichen und Weltlichen Sachen oder Handlungen von anbegin der Welt nach erschaffing des ersten Menchen bis auff das gegenwertige jar Christi* M.D. LXXXV *verlengt* ... 1585

– *Das Kriegbüchlin des Friedes* 1539

– *Das teur und künstlich Büechlin Morie Encomion das ist ein lob der torheit von Erasmo Roterodamo* ... *verteutscht durch Sebastianum Franken von Wörd* ed E. Götzinger, Leipzig 1884

Gabriel de Toulon [Vieilh] *Critique de l'Apologie d'Erasme de M. l'Abbé Marsolier* Paris 1719

Garasse, François *La Doctrine curieuse des beaux esprits de ce temps, ou pretendus tels* Paris 1623

Giovio, Paolo *Elogia doctorum virorum ab avorum memoria pub-licatis ingenii monumentis illustrium* ... Antwerp 1557

Gratianus, Verus (pseud) [Henry Geldorp] *Clariss. theologi D. Ruardi Tappaert Enchusani, haereticae pravitatis primarii & generalis in-quisitoris, cancellarii celeberrimae Academiae Lovaniensis, pridem inconsolabili suorum luctu vita functi, apotheosis* in S. Cramer and F. Pijper *Bibliotheca reformatoria Neerlandica* I Hague 1903, 567–636

Gretser, Jacob *Controversiarum Roberti Bellarmini* ... *defensio* 2 vols, Ingolstadt, 1607–09

Grotius, Hugo *Apologeticus eorum qui Hollandiae Westfrisiaeque et vicinis quibusdam nationibus ex legibus praefuerunt ante mutationem qui evenit anno 1618* Paris 1622

– *Briefwisseling van Hugo Grotius* ed P.C. Molhuysen, Hague 1928–

– *Hugo Grotii reginae, regnique Sueciae consiliarii* ... *epistolae quot-quot reperiri potuerunt* ... Amsterdam 1687

– *Parallelon rerumpublicarum liber tertius: de moribus ingenioque populorum Atheniensium, Romanorum, Batavorum* Haarlem 1801–3

von de Hardt, Hermann *Historia literaria reformationis in honorem jubilaei anno* MDCCXVII ... Frankfurt/Leipzig 1717

– *Jubilaeum humanitatis & fontium sacrorum, hebraeorum &*

graecorum, qui A. *1516 & 1517. per Erasmum & Ximenium Christianis primum exhibiti ... celebratum in Academia Julia praeliminari feria* A. MDCCXVII. *d.* XXIX *Octob.* Helmstedt 1717

Harpsfield, Nicholas *Historia anglicana ecclesiastica* Douai 1622
- *The life and death of Sir Thomas Moore, knight, sometymes Lord High Chancellor of Englande, written in the tyme of Queen Marie* ed E.V. Hitchcock, Early English Text Society, Original Series 186, London 1932

Heresbach, Konrad von *De educandis erudiendisque principum liberis, reipublicae gubernandae destinatis, deque republica christiana administranda ... libri duo ...* Frankfurt-am-Main 1570

Hermant, Godefroi *Mémoires de Godefroi Hermant sur l'histoire ecclésiastique du* XVIIe SIÈCLE *(1630–1633)* V, VI, Paris 1908, 1910

Herold, Johannes *Philopseudes, sive pro Desiderio Erasmo Roterodamo V.C. contra dialogum famosum anonymi cujusdam declamatio ...* in LB VIII 591–652

Hosius, Stanislaus *De origine haeresium nostri temporis* Louvain 1559

Hottinger, Johann Heinrich *Historiae ecclesiasticae Novi Testamenti, seculi* XVI, *pars* II ... Zürich 1665

Huet, Pierre *De interpretatione libri duo; quorum prior est, de optimo genere interpretandi: alter, de claris interpretibus* Paris 1661
- *Origeniana* in J.-P. Migne *Patriologiae cursus completus ... series Graeca* XVII, Paris 1857

Insulanus, Guilielmus *Oratio funebris in obitum Desiderii Erasmi Roterodami, auctore Guilielmo Insulano Menapio Grevibrocensi, oratore luculentissimo* in LB X 1845–59

Jöcher, Christian G. (ed) *Allgemeines Gelehrten-Lexicon* III, Leipzig 1751

Joly, Claude *Codicille d'or, ou petit recueil tiré de l'Institution du prince chrestien composée par Erasme* 1665
- *Recueil de maximes veritables et importantes pour l'institution du roy: Contre la fausse & pernicieuse politique du Cardinal Mazarin, pretendu Sur-Intendant de l'education de sa Majesté* [Paris] Holland 1653
- *Voyage fait à Munster en Westphalie et autres lieux voisins, en 1646 & 1647* Paris 1670

Jortin, John *The Life of Erasmus* 2 vols, London 1758, 1760; 3 vols, London 1808
- *Remarks on Ecclesiastical History* ed William Trollope, 2 vols, London 1846

– *Tracts, Philological, Critical, and Miscellaneous* 2 vols, London 1790

Junius, Franciscus (François du Jon) *Animadversiones ad controversiam secundam christianae fidei, de Christo capite totius ecclesiae, quam Robertus Bellarminus ... disputationum suarum libris exaravit adversus huius temporis haereticos* in *Opera theologica Francisci Junii Biturigis* ... II, Geneva 1613, cols 539–631

Junius, Hadrianus (Adrian de Jonghe) *Hadriani Junii Hornani, medici, Batavia: In qua praeter gentis & insulae antiquitatem, origenem, decora, mores, aliaque ad eam historiam pertinentia, declaratur quae fuerit vetus Batavia, quae Plinio, Tacito, & Ptolemaeo cognita* ... Antwerp 1588

Kidd, B.J. (ed) *Documents Illustrative of the Continental Reformation* Oxford 1911

Klefeker, Johannes 'Exercitatio critica de religione Erasmi, quam in auditorio gymnasii Hamb. ad d. XVIII Mart. anni MDCCXVII, jubileo secundo ecclesiae, divinis auspiciis reformari coeptae, memorabilis ...' in J.A. Fabricius *Opusculorum historico-critico literariorum sylloge quae sparsim viderant lucem nunc recensita denuo et partem aucta indice instruuntur* Hamburg 1738, 357–406

Knight, Samuel *The great Happiness of a Lawful Government: A Sermon Preached before the Honourable House of Commons ... on Saturday, May 29, 1725, Being the Anniversary of the Restoration of the Royal Family* London 1725

– *The Life of Dr John Colet, Dean of St Paul's in the Reigns of K. Henry VII. and Henry VIII. and Founder of S. Paul's School* London 1724

– *The Life of Erasmus, More particularly that part of it, which He spent in England; wherein an Account is given of his Learned Friends, & the State of Religion & Learning at that Time in both our Universities* Cambridge 1726

Kortholt, Christian *Historia ecclesiastica Novi Testamenti, a Christo nato usque ad seculum decimum septimum* ... Hamburg 1708

De La Bizardière, Michel David *Histoire d'Erasme, sa vie, ses mœurs, sa mort et sa religion* Paris 1721

Lando, Ortensio *In Des. Erasmi Roterodami funus, dialogus lepidissimus* Basel 1540

Le Clerc, Jean *An Account of the Life and Writings of Mr John Le Clerc (Philosophy and Hebrew Professor in the College of the Arminians at Amsterdam) to this present year 1711* London 1712

– *Parrhasiana ou pensées diverses sur des matières de critique, d'histoire, de morale et de politique* Amsterdam 1701
– 'Vie d'Erasme tirée de ses lettres …' *Bibliothèque choisie* (1705) v: 145–282, vi: 7–238
Le Courayer, Pierre-François *A Dissertation on the Validity of the Ordinations of the English, and of the Succession of Bishops of the Anglican Church* Oxford 1844
– 'Réponse à la Réfutation de l'Apologie d'Erasme', *Mémoires litteraires de la Haye* 1716, 355–94. Republished as *Matanasiana, ou Mémoires litteraires, historiques, et critiques, du docteur Matanasius* i, Hague 1740
De l'Estoile, Pierre *Mémoires-Journaux* ed G. Brunet, A. Champollion, E. Halphen, 12 vols, Paris 1875–96
L'Estrange, Roger (ed) *Twenty Select Colloquies, Out of Erasmus Roterodamus* … London 1680
Lévesque de Burigny, Jean *Théologie payenne, ou sentimens des philosophes et des peuples payens les plus célebres, sur Dieu, sur l'âme et sur les devoirs de l'homme* 2 vols, Paris 1754
– *Traité de l'autorité du pape, dans lequel ses droits sont établis & réduits à leurs justes bornes, et les principes des libertés de l'église gallicane justifiés,* Vienne 1782
– *Vie d'Erasme, dans laquelle on trouvera l'histoire de plusieurs hommes célèbres avec lesquels il a été en liaison, l'analyse critique de ses ouvrages, & l'examen impartial de ses sentimens en matière de religion* 2 vols, Paris 1757
Lindanus, Wilhelmus (Willem van der Lindt) *Dubitantius de vera certaque per Christi Jesu Evangelium, salutis aeternae via libris III instructus: quibus populariter docetur, veram certamque salutis aeternae viam, nisi apud Catholicos, non inveniendam* … Cologne 1565
Locke, John, Review of Richard in *Bibliothèque universelle et historique* vii (1688): 122–41
Loos, Cornelius *Illustrium Germaniae scriptorum catalogus: Quo doctrina simul et pietate illustrium vitae, & operae celebrantur* … Mainz 1582
Luther, Martin *D. Martin Luthers Werke: Kritische Gesamtausgabe (Weimarer Ausgabe) (WA). Briefwechsel* vii; *Tischreden* iv
– *Works* (American edition) liv *Table Talk* ed and tr Theodore G. Tappert, Philadelphia 1967
– *Works* (American edition) xlix *Letters* ed and tr Gottfried G. Krodel, Philadelphia 1972

Lydius, Martin *Apologia pro D. Erasmo Roterodamo* in LB X 1759–80

Maimbourg, Louis *Histoire du Lutheranisme* I, Paris 1681

Von Malinckrodt, Bernard *De ortu ac progressu artis typographicae dissertatio historica* ... Cologne 1639/40

– *Die Autobiographie des Münsterchen Domdechanten Bernhardt v. Mallinckrodt, 1635* ed H. Keussen, Bonn 1911

Marsollier, Jacques *Apologie, ou justification d'Erasme* Paris 1713

Mathesius, Johannes *Ausgewählte Werke* III *Luthers Leben in Predigten* ed G. Loesche, 2nd ed, Prague 1906

Melanchthon, Philippus 'Oratio de Erasmo Roterodamo; recitata a M. Bartholomaeo Calkreuter Crossensi, 1557' in *Corpus reformatorum: Phillippi Melanchthonis opera quae supersunt omnia* XII, Halle 1844, cols 264–71

– *Phillippus Melanchthon, declamationes* ed Karl Hartfelder, I, Berlin 1891

Menckenius, F.O. *Historia vitae et in literas meritorum Angeli Politiani* Leipzig 1736

Mercier, Nicholas (ed) *Desiderii Erasmi Roterodami colloquia familiaria: in usum studiosiae iuventutis* 3rd ed, Paris 1661

Merula, Paullus (ed) *Vita Des. Erasmi Roterodami ex ipsius manu fideliter repraesentata; comitantibus, quae ad eandem, aliis. Additi sunt epistolarum quae nondum lucem aspexerunt, libri duo: quas conquisivit, edidit, dedicavit S.P.Q. Roterodamo Paullus G.F.P.N. Merula*, Leiden 1607

Milton, John *Tetrachordon: Expositions upon the foure chief places in Scripture, which treat of Mariage or nullities in Mariage* London 1645, in *Complete Prose Works* II 1643–8, New Haven/London 1959, 577–718

– 'Post-Script' *The Judgment of Martin Bucer, concerning Divorce* ... London 1644, in ibid 478–9

Miraeus, Aubertus (Aubert le Mire) *Bibliotheca ecclesiastica sive de scriptoribus ecclesiasticis* ... Antwerp 1649 (republished in J.A. Fabricius *Bibliotheca ecclesiastica* ... Hamburg 1718)

– *Elogia illustrium Belgii scriptorum, qui vel ecclesiam Dei propugnarunt, vel disciplinas illustrarunt, centuria, decadibus distincta* Antwerp 1602

More, Cresacre *The Life of Sir Thomas More, Kt. Lord High Chancellour of England under K. Henry the Eighth, and His Majesty's Embassadour to the Courts of France and Germany* London 1726

Moreri, Louis *Le Grand Dictionnaire historique, ou le mélange curieux de l'histoire sacrée et profane* ... II 4th ed, Lyon 1687

Morhof, Daniel Georg *Polyhistor, literarius, philosophicus et practicus* ... 4th ed, Lübeck 1747

Nas, Johannes *Centuriae* Ingolstadt 1565–70

Nausea, Friedrich *Friderici Nauseae ... in magnum Erasmum Roterodamum, nuper vita functum, Monodia* in LB I

New Memoirs of Literature ... IV (July 1726): 85–90. Review of Knight *Erasmus*

Nicéron, Jean Pierre *Mémoires pour servir à l'histoire des hommes illustres dans la république des lettres* II, Paris 1720

Nichols, John *Illustrations of the Literary History of the Eighteenth Century* II, London 1817

– *Literary Anecdotes of the Eighteenth Century* V, London 1812

Nöthiger historischer Unterredungen im Reiche derer Lebendigen auf Erden: Vierdtes Gespräche zwischen Erasmo Roterodamo, und Diogene Cynico, welcher insgemein derer Gelehrten ihr Eulen-Spiegel genennt wird ... Frankfurt 1720

Opmeer, Petrus *Opus chronographicum orbis universi* Antwerp 1611

Pantaleon, Heinrich *Prosopographiae heroum atque illustrium virorum totius Germaniae* ... Basel 1565–6. German tr *Teutscher Nation Heldenbuch* Basel 1567–70

Pope, Alexander 'Essay on Criticism' in E. Audra and Aubrey Williams (eds) *Pastoral Poetry and An Essay on Criticism* London 1961

– *The Correspondence of Alexander Pope* ed George Sherburn I 1704–18, Oxford 1956

Possevino, Antonio *Apparatus sacer ad scriptores Veteris & Novi Testamenti, eorum interpretes, synodos & patres Latinos ac Graecos, horum versiones, theologos scholasticos quique contra hereticos egerunt, chronographos & historiographos ecclesiasticos* ... 2nd ed, Cologne 1608

– *Bibliotheca selecta qua agitur de ratione studiorum in historia, in disciplinis, in salute omnium procuranda* Rome 1593

– *Judicium de confessione (ut vocant) Augustana ... de Des. Erasmo ad quem novi Ariani provocant* Posnan 1586

– *Judicium, de Nuae militis Galli, Joannis Bodini, Philippi Mornaei, & Nicolai Machiavelli quibusdam scriptis ... item ... de confessione Augustana, ac num admittendi sint haeretici ad colloquium publicum de fide, de Desiderio Erasmo, & secta Picardica iudicium* Lyon 1593

Prateolus, Gabriel (Du Préau) *De vitis, sectis, et dogmatibus omnium haereticorum, qui ab orbe condito, ad nostra usque tempora, &*

veterum & recentium authorum monimentis proditi sunt, elenchus alphabeticus ... Cologne 1569

De Raemond, Florimond *L'Histoire de la naissance, progrez et decadence de l'heresie de ce siècle* Rouen 1623

Raynaud, Théophile *Erotemata de malis ac bonis libris deque iusta aut iniusta eorundem confixione* Lyon 1653

Richard, Jean *Sentimens d'Erasme de Roterdam, conformes à ceux de l'Eglise Catholique, sur tous les points de controversez* Cologne 1688

Roper, William *The Lyfe of Sir Thomas Moore, knighte* ed E.V. Hitchcock, Early English Text Society, Original Series 197, London 1935

Rüdiger, Johann Christoph (Adolphus Clarmundus) *Vitae clarissimorum in re literaria virorum: Das ist Lebensbeschreibung etlicher hauptgelehrten Männer, so von der Literaturprofess gemacht* ... 3rd ed, Wittenberg 1708

Ruvio, Antonius *Assertionum catholicarum adversus Erasmi Roterodami pestilentissimos errores libri novem* ... Salamanca 1568

Scaliger, Joseph *Autobiography of Joseph Scaliger* ed George W. Robinson, Cambridge, Mass. 1927

– *Scaligerana ou bons mots, rencontres agreables, et remarques judicieuses et scavantes de J. Scaliger* Cologne 1695

Scaliger, J.C. *Jul. Caes. Scaligeri epistolae aliquot nunc primum vulgatae* Toulouse 1620

– *J. Caes. Scaligeri pro M. Tullio Cicerone, contra Desid. Erasmum Roterodamum* Oratio I, Toulouse 1620

Von Seckendorf, Veit Ludwig *Commentarius historicus et apologeticus de Lutheranismo, sive de reformatione religionis ductu D. Martini Lutheri magna Germaniae parte aliisque regionibus, & speciatim in Saxonia recepta & stabilita: in quo ex Ludovici Maimburgii Jesuitae historia Lutheranismi ... libri tres ... Latine versi exhibentur, corriguntur, & ex manuscriptis aliisque rarioribus libris plurimis supplentur; simul & aliorum quorundam scriptorum errores aut calumniae examinantur* ... Leipzig/Frankfurt 1692

Simon, Richard *Critique de la bibliotèque des auteurs ecclesiastiques et des prolegomenes de la Bible, publiez par M. Ellies Du-Pin* ... I, Paris 1730

– *Histoire critique des principaux commentateurs du Nouveau Testament depuis le commencement du Christianisme jusques à notre tems* Rotterdam 1693

– *Histoire critique des versions du Nouveau Testament* ... Rotterdam
1690. Eng tr *The Critical History of the Versions of the New
Testament* London 1692
– *Lettres choisies de M. Simon* III, Amsterdam 1730
– *Nouvelles Observations sur le texte et les versions du Nouveau
Testament* Paris 1695
Slade, Matthew *Cum Conrado Vorstio ... de blasphemiis, haeresibus
et atheismis a ... Jacobo ... primo ... in ... Vorstii de Deo tractatu ...
notatis scholastica disceptatio* Amsterdam 1612
– *Matthaei Sladi Anglo-Britanni disceptationis cum Conrado Vorstio
theol. doctore pars altera. 'De immutabilitate & simplicitate Dei.'
Qua docetur serenissimum ac sapientissimum Magnae Britanniae
... Regem Jacobum huius nominis primum ... justè ac merito
notâsse blasphemum Vorstii dogma, 'Deum esse mutabilem & ac-
cidentibus subjectum' adferentis* ... Amsterdam 1614
Sleidan, Johannes *Joan. Sleidani de statu religionis et reipublicae,
Carolo Quinto Caesare, commentarii* Strasbourg 1555. Annotated
ed, ed C.C. am Ende, Frankfurt 1785–6
Stapleton, Thomas *Tres Thomae, seu de S. Thomae Apostoli rebus
gestis. De S. Thoma Archiepiscopo Cantuarensi & Martyre. D.T.
Mori Angliae quondam Cancellarii vita* ... Douai 1588. Eng tr P.E.
Hallett *The Life and Illustrious Martyrdom of Sir Thomas More*
London 1928
Stillingfleet, Edward 'Several Conferences between a Romish Priest, a
Fanatick-Chaplain, and a Divine of the Church of England, con-
cerning the Idolatry of the Church of Rome' in *Works* VI, London
1710
Surius, Laurentius (Lorenz Sauer) *Commentarius brevis rerum in
orbe gestarum, ab anno salutis 1500 usque in annum 1568 ex
optimis quibusque scriptoribus congestus* ... Cologne 1568
– *Vitae sanctorum* I, Cologne 1617
Sweertius (Sweerts), Franciscus *Athenae Belgicae* Antwerp 1628
Tappaert, Ruard *Explicationis articulorum venerandae facultatis sac-
rae theologiae generalis studii Lovaniensis, circa dogmata
ecclesiastica ab annis triginta quatuor controversa, una cum re-
sponsione ad argumenta adversariorum, tomus primus* Louvain
1565
Tentzel, W.E., Commentary on Seckendorf in *Monatliche Unterredungen einiger Guten Freunde von allerhand Büchern und andern
annemlichen Geschichten* III (1691): 762–82

Thomasius, Christian (ed) 'Icon Desiderii Erasmi Roterodamensis'
Observatio xxi *Observationum selectarum ad rem litterariam
spectantium* iv, Halle 1701, 440–62
De Thou, Jacques-Auguste *Histoire universelle* 11 vols, Hague 1740, i
– *Mémoires de la vie de Jacques-Auguste de Thou, Conseiller d'Etat,
et Président à Mortier au Parlement de Paris* Rotterdam 1711
De Tournemine, René-Joseph 'Refutation de l'Apologie d'Erasme'
Mémoires pour l'histoire des sciences et des beaux-arts [*Journal de
Trévoux*] Articles lxvii–viii (June 1714): 935–72
Trollope, William 'A Brief Account of the Life and Writings of John
Jortin, d.d.' in Jortin's *Remarks on Ecclesiastical History* (ed Trol-
lope) 2 vols, London 1846, i xxv–xxxviii
Verheiden, Jacob *Praestantium aliquot theologorum, qui Rom.
Antichristum praecipue oppugnarunt, effigies* ... Hague 1602
Von Watt, Joachim (Vadianus) *Chronik der Aebte des Klosters St
Gallen*, in Ernst Götzinger (ed) Joachim von Watt *Deutsche Hi-
storische Schriften* i, ii, St Gallen 1875, 1877
Weise, Chr. *Dissertationem de spuriis in Ecclesia et re litteraria claris:
Von gelehrten Huren Kindern* ... Wittenberg 1735
Whitaker, William *A Disputation on Holy Scripture against the
Papists, especially Bellarmine and Stapleton* tr and ed William
Fitzgerald, Cambridge 1849
Voltaire, F.M.A. de *Correspondence* ed T. Bestermann xxxi, Geneva
1958

SECONDARY WORKS

Allgeier, Arthur 'Erasmus und Kardinal Ximenes in den Ver-
handlungen des Konzils von Trient' *Spanische Forschungen des
Goerresgesellschaft* 1, 4 (1933): 193–205
Anderegg, Michael A. 'The Tradition of Early More Biography' in
R.S. Sylvester and G.P. Marc'hadour (eds) *Essential Articles for the
Study of Sir Thomas More* Hamden, Conn. 1977, 3–25
Armstrong, Brian G. *Calvinism and the Amyraut Heresy: Protestant
Scholasticism and Humanism in Seventeenth-Century France*
Madison 1969
Aubert, F., J. Boussard, H. Meylan 'Un premier recueil de poésies
latines de Théodore de Bèze' bhr 15 (1953): 164–91, 257–94
Backvis, C. 'La fortune d'Erasme en Pologne' *Colloquium Eras-
mianum* Mons 1968, 173–202

Bainton, Roland H. *Erasmus of Christendom* New York and London
1969
- 'The Continuity of Thought of Erasmus' *American Council of
Learned Societies' Newsletter* 19, 5 (1968)
Barnes, Annie *Jean Le Clerc (1657–1736) et la République des Lettres*
Paris 1938
Bataillon, Marcel *Erasme et l'Espagne* Paris 1937
Baron, Hans 'Erasmus-Probleme im Spiegel des Colloquium "In-
quisitio de Fide"' ARG 43 (1952): 254–63
Baur, F. Ch. *Die Epochen der kirchlichen Geschichtsschreibung*
Tübingen 1852
Van Berchem, Denis 'Grotius à l'Université de Leyde' *Hommage à
Grotius* Études et documents pour servir à l'histoire de l'Université
de Lausanne 4, Lausanne 1946, 9–18
Bennett, G.V. *White Kennett, 1660–1728, Bishop of Peterborough: A
Study of the Political and Ecclesiastical History of the Early
Eighteenth Century* London 1957
Bernays, Jacob *Joseph Justus Scaliger* Berlin 1855
Bierlaire, Franz *La familia d'Erasme: Contribution à l'histoire de
l'humanisme* Paris 1968
Bietenholz, Peter G. *Basle and France in the Sixteenth Century: The
Basle Humanists and Printers in their Contacts with Francophone
Culture* Geneva/Toronto 1971
Blok, F.F. *Caspar Barlaeus, From the Correspondence of a Melan-
cholic* Assen/Amsterdam 1976
Bolgar, R.R. *The Classical Heritage and its Beneficiaries: From the
Carolingian Age to the End of the Renaissance* New York 1964
Bornkamm, Heinrich *Luther im Spiegel der deutschen Geistesges-
chichte* Göttingen 1955
Bracken, Harry M. 'Bayle Not a Sceptic?' *Journal of the History of
Ideas* 25 (1964): 169–80
Brandi, K. *Emperor Charles v* London 1939
Brissaud, Jean *Un Libéral au xviie siècle, Claude Joly (1607–1700)*
Paris 1898
Brodrick, James sj *Saint Peter Canisius* London 1963
Büchsel, I. *Gottfried Arnold: Sein Verständnis von Kirche und
Wiedergeburt* Witten 1970
Buscher, Hans *Heinrich Pantaleon und sein Heldenbuch* Basler Bei-
träge zur Geschichtswissenschaft 26, Basel 1946
Bush, Craig R. *Montaigne and Bayle: Variations on the Theme of
Skepticism* Hague 1966

Büsser, F. *Das katholische Zwinglibild: Von der Reformation bis zur Gegenwart* Zürich/Stuttgart 1968

Butler, C. *The Life of Erasmus: With Historical Remarks on the State of Literature between the Tenth and Sixteenth Centuries* London 1825

The Cambridge History of Poland Cambridge 1950

Cantimori, D. *Italienische Haeretiker der Spätrenaissance* Basel 1949

Carroll, Robert Todd *The Common-Sense Philosophy of Religion of Bishop Edward Stillingfleet 1635–1699* Hague 1975

Chrisman, M.U. *Strasbourg and the Reform: A Study in the Process of Change* New Haven/London 1967

Christie, R.C. 'The Scaligers' *Selected Essays and Papers* London 1902

Clark, George *The Later Stuarts, 1660–1714* 2nd ed, Oxford 1955

Colie, Rosalie L. *Light and Enlightenment: A Study of the Cambridge Platonists and the Dutch Arminians* Cambridge 1957

Crahay, R. 'Les censeurs louvanistes d'Erasme' *Scrinium Erasmianum* I 221–49

– 'Recherches sur le "Compendium vitae" attribué à Erasme' HR 6 (1939): 7–19, 135–53

Cranston, Maurice *John Locke: A Biography* London 1957

Crisan, Constantia 'Erasme en Roumanie' *Colloquia Erasmiana Turonensia* 2 vols, Paris 1972, I 175–85

Cytowska, Maria 'Erasme en Pologne avant l'époque du Concile de Trente' *Erasmus in English* 5 (1972): 10–16

Degroote, G. 'Erasmiaanse Echo's in de Gouden Eeuw in Nederland' *Scrinium Erasmianum* I 391–421

Delcourt, Marie 'Recherches sur Thomas More: La tradition continentale et la tradition anglaise' HR 3 (1936): 22–42

Desautels, Alfred R. *Les Mémoires de Trévoux et le mouvement des idées au XVIIIᵉ siècle 1701–1734* Bibliotheca Instituti Historici, s.J. 8, Rome 1956

Dieckmann, H. (ed) *Le Philosophe: Texts and Interpretations* St Louis 1948

Dolan, John Patrick *The Influence of Erasmus, Witzel and Cassander in the Church Ordinances and Reform Proposals of the United Duchies of Cleve during the Middle Decades of the Sixteenth Century* Reformationsgeschichtliche Studien und Texte 83, Münster 1957

Doolin, Paul *The Fronde* Cambridge, Mass. 1935

Dörries, H. *Geist und Geschichte bei Gottfried Arnold* Göttingen 1963

Droz, E. 'Les étudiants français de Bâle' BHR 20 (1958): 108–42

Dumas, Gustave *Histoire du Journal de Trévoux depuis 1701 jusqu'en 1762* Paris 1936

Elliott, J.H. *Imperial Spain 1469–1716* London 1963

Erasme, l'Alsace, et son temps Publications de la Société Savante d'Alsace et des Régions de l'Est, collection 'Recherches et Documents' 7, Strasbourg 1971

Erskine-Hill, Howard *The Social Milieu of Alexander Pope: Lives, Example and the Poetic Response* New Haven/London 1975

Evans, R.J.W. *Rudolf II and His World: A Study in Intellectual History 1576–1612* Oxford 1973

van Eysinga, W.J.M. *Huigh de Groot: Een Schets* Haarlem 1945

Fairfield, Leslie P. 'John Bale and the Development of Protestant Historiography in England' *Journal of Ecclesiastical History* 24 (1973): 145–60

Faux, Jean 'La fondation et les premiers redacteurs des Mémoires de Trévoux (1701–1739) d'après quelques documents inédits' *Archivum Historicum Societatis Jesu* 23 (1954): 131–51

Febvre, Lucien 'Une histoire obscure: La publication du "Cymbalum Mundi"' *Revue du seizième siècle* 17 (1930): 1–41

– 'Origène et Des Périers ou l'enigme du *Cymbalum Mundi*' BHR 2 (1942): 7–131

– *Le Problème de l'incroyance au XVIe siècle: La religion de Rabelais* Paris 1962

Feller, R. and E. Bonjour *Geschichtsschreibung der Schweiz vom Spätmittelalter zur Neuzeit* I, Basel/Stuttgart 1962

Fenlon, D. *Heresy and Obedience in Tridentine Italy: Cardinal Pole and the Counter Reformation* Cambridge 1972

Ferguson, Wallace K. *The Renaissance in Historical Thought: Five Centuries of Interpretation* Cambridge, Mass. 1948

Flanagan, Cathleen 'Aubertus Miraeus, An Early Belgian Librarian' *Journal of Library History* 10 (1975): 341–53

Flitner, A. *Erasmus im Urteil seiner Nachwelt: Das literarische Erasmus-bild von Beatus Rhenanus bis zu Jean Le Clerc* Tübingen 1952

Fraenkel, Peter and Martin Greschat *Zwanzig Jahre Melanchthonstudium: Sechs Literaturberichte (1945–1965)* Geneva 1967

Frappell, L.O. 'Interpretations of the Continental Reformation in Great Britain during the Nineteenth Century' unpublished PH D thesis, Macquarie University 1972

Friedensburg, W. *Johannes Sleidanus: Der Geschichtsschreiber und die Schicksalmächte der Reformationszeit* Leipzig 1935

Freydank, Hanns 'Christian Thomasius der Journalist' in Max Fleischmann (ed) *Christian Thomasius: Leben und Lebenswerk* Halle 1931, 345–81

Fritzsche, O.F. 'Johan Heinrich Hottinger' *Zeitschrift für wissenschaftliche Theologie* 11 (1868): 237–72

Fueter, Eduard *Geschichte der neueren Historiographie* Munich 1936

Garstein, Oskar *Rome and the Counter-Reformation in Scandinavia* 1, Bergen 1963

Geisendorf, Paul F. *Théodore de Bèze* Geneva 1949

Genet, Abbé 'Etude historique sur Jean Lévesque de Burigny' *Travaux de l'Académie Nationale de Reims* 66 (1878–9): 201–334

Gerlo, Alois 'Erasme, homo batavus' *Commémoration nationale d'Erasme, Actes* Brussels 1970, 61–80

Geyl, Pieter *Napoleon: For and Against* London 1949

Gilmore, Myron P. 'Anti-Erasmianism in Italy: The Dialogue of Ortensio Lando on Erasmus' Funeral' *The Journal of Medieval and Renaissance Studies* 4, 1 (1974): 1–14

– 'Erasmus and Alberto Pio, Prince of Carpi' in T.K. Rabb and J.E. Seigel (eds) *Action and Conviction in Early Modern Europe* Princeton 1969, 299–318

– 'Italian Reactions to Erasmian Humanism' in H.A. Oberman (ed) *Itinerarium Italicum: The Profile of the Italian Renaissance in the Mirror of its European Transformations* Leiden 1975, 61–115

Golden, Samuel A. *Jean Le Clerc* New York 1972

Gossart, Ernest 'Un livre d'Erasme réprouvé par l'Université de Louvain' *Académie royale des sciences, des lettres et des beaux-arts de Belgique: Classe de lettres: Bulletin* 4, 4 (1902): 427–45

Goubert, P. *Louis XIV and Twenty Million Frenchmen* New York 1972

Grendler, Paul F. *Critics of the Italian World (1530–60): Anton Francesco Doni, Nicolo Franco and Ortensio Lando* Madison 1969

Grootens, P.L.M., SJ *Dominicus Baudius: Een Levensschets uit Leidse Humanistenmilieu* Nijmegen/Utrecht 1942

Haag, Eugène and Emile *La France protestante* VI, Paris 1856

Haak, S.P. *Paullus Merula 1558–1607* Zutphen 1901

Hall, Vernon Jr *Life of Julius Caesar Scaliger (1484–1558)* Transactions of the American Philosophical Society, New Series 40, pt 2, Philadelphia 1950, 85–170

Haller, William *Foxe's Book of Martyrs and the Elect Nation* London 1963

Harrison, A.W. *The Beginnings of Arminianism to the Synod of Dort* London 1926

Harrisse, Henry *Le Président de Thou et ses descendants, leur célèbre bibliothèque, leurs armoires et les traductions françaises de J.A. Thuani historiarum sui temporis* Paris 1905

Hartmann, A. 'Beatus Rhenanus: Leben und Werke des Erasmus' *Gedenkschrift* 11–24

Hazard, Paul *La Crise de la conscience européenne 1680–1715* Paris 1935. Eng tr *The European Mind (1680–1715)* London 1953

Herte, A. *Das katholische Lutherbild im Bann der Lutherkommentare des Cochläus* 3 vols, Münster 1943

Heyd, Michael 'A Disguised Atheist or a Sincere Christian? The Enigma of Pierre Bayle' BHR 39 (1977): 157–65

Hirsch, E. *Geschichte der neuern evangelischen Theologie im Zusammenhang mit den allgemeinen Bewegungen des europäischen Denkens* II, Gütersloh 1951

Hoendedaarl, G.J. 'The Debate about Arminius outside the Netherlands' in Th. H. Lunsingh Scheurleer and G.H.M. Posthumus Meyjes *Leiden University in the Seventeenth Century: An Exchange of Learning* Leiden 1975, 137–59

Holborn, H. *A History of Modern Germany: The Reformation* New York 1959

Hudson, H.H. 'Current English Translations of "The Praise of Folly"' *Philological Quarterly* 20 (1941): 250–65

Hyma, A. *The Life of Desiderius Erasmus*, Assen 1972
– *The Youth of Erasmus* 2nd ed, New York 1968

James, E.D. 'Scepticism and Fideism in Bayle's *Dictionnaire*' *French Studies* 16 (1962): 308–23

Jedin, H. *History of the Council of Trent* 2 vols, Edinburgh/London 1957, 1961
– *Geschichte des Konzils von Trient* III, Freiburg 1970

Johnston, Edith Mary *Ireland in the Eighteenth Century* Dublin 1974

Jordan, W.K. *The Development of Religious Toleration in England from the Accession of James I to the Convention of the Long Parliament (1603–1640)* Gloucester, Mass. 1965

Jourdain, Charles *Histoire de l'Université de Paris, au XVIIe et au XVIIIe siècle* Paris 1888

Juhász, Ladislaus 'De carminibus Nicolai Olahi in mortem Erasmi scriptis' *Gedenskschrift* 316–25

Kaegi, W. 'Erasmus im achtzehnten Jarhundert' *Gedenkschrift* 205–27

- 'Machiavelli in Basel' *Historische Meditationen* Zürich 1942. 121–81

Kalkoff, Paul 'Die Anfangsperiode der Reformation in Sleidans Kommentarien' *Zeitschrift für die Geschichte des Oberrheins* new series 32 (1917): 297–324, 414–67

Kardos, Tibor 'L'esprit d'Erasme en Hongrie' in *Colloquia Erasmiana Turonensia* 2 vols, Paris 1972, I 187–214

King, James 'Pope and Erasmus' "Great, Injur'd Name"' *English Studies* 55 (1974): 424–7

Kinser, Samuel C. 'The Historiography of Jacques-Auguste de Thou' PH D thesis, Cornell University 1960 (University Microfilms)

Kommoss, Rudolf *Sebastian Franck und Erasmus von Rotterdam* Germanische Studien 153, Berlin 1934

Kossmann, Ernst H. *La Fronde* Leiden 1954

Koyré, A. *Sébastien Franck* Paris 1932

Kristeller, P.O. 'Le mythe de l'athéisme de la Renaissance et la tradition française de la libre pensée' BHR 37 (1975): 337–48

Kutter, M. *Celio Secundo Curione: Sein Leben und sein Werk (1503–1569)* Basler Beiträge zur Geschichtswissenschaft 54, Basel/Stuttgart 1955

Labrousse, Elisabeth R. 'Les coulisses du journal de Bayle' in Paul Dibon (ed) *Pierre Bayle: Le Philosophe de Rotterdam, Etudes et documents* Paris 1959, 97–141

- *Pierre Bayle* I: *Du Pays de Foix a la Cité d'Erasme*, II: *Heterodoxie et rigorisme* Hague 1963–4

Lebeau, Jean 'Erasme, Sebastian Franck et la tolérance' in *Erasme, l'Alsace, et son temps* Publications de la Société Savante d'Alsace et des Régions de l'Est, collection 'Recherches et Documents' 7, Strasbourg 1971, 117–38

Lecler, Joseph 'Un adversaire des libertins au début du xviie siècle: Le P. François Garasse (1585–1631)' *Etudes* 209 (1931): 553–72

- *Histoire de la tolérance au siècle de la Réforme* 2 vols, Paris 1955

Léonard, Emile G. *A History of Protestantism* II: *The Establishment* London 1967

Lindeboom, Johan 'Erasmus' Bedeutung für die Entwicklung des geistigen Lebens in den Niederlanden' ARG 43 (1952): 1–12

Manschrek, C.L. *Melanchthon: The Quiet Reformer* New York/Nashville 1958

Mansfield, Bruce E. 'Erasmus and the Mediating School' *Journal of Religious History* 4 (1967): 302–16

- 'Erasmus in the Nineteenth Century: The Liberal Tradition'
  Studies in the Renaissance 15 (1968): 193–219
- 'Erasmus of Rotterdam: Evangelical' *Erasmus in English* 6 (1973):
  1–5
Manuel, F. *The Eighteenth Century Confronts the Gods* Cambridge,
  Mass. 1959
Margival, Henri *Essai sur Richard Simon et la critique biblique au XVII*
  siècle Paris 1900
Margolin, Jean-Claude 'Guy Patin, lecteur d'Erasme' *Colloquia Eras-*
  miana Turonensia 2 vols, Paris 1972, I 323–58
- 'L'inspiration érasmienne de Jacob Cats' *Commémoration nationale*
  d'Erasme, Actes Brussels 1970, 113–51
- 'La politique culturelle de Guillaume, duc de Clèves' in Franco
  Simone *Culture et politique en France à l'époque de l'humanisme et*
  de la Renaissance Turin 1974, 293–324
Marriott, J.A.R. *The Life and Times of Lucius Cary Viscount Falkland*
  London 1907
Mason, H.T. 'Pierre Bayle's Religious Views' *French Studies* 17
  (1963): 205–17
McConica, James K. *English Humanists and Reformation Politics*
  under Henry VIII and Edward VI Oxford 1965
- 'Erasmus and the "Julius": A Humanist Reflects on the Church' in
  Charles Trinkaus and Heiko A. Oberman *The Pursuit of Holiness in*
  Late Medieval and Renaissance Religion Leiden 1974
- 'The Riddle of "Terminus"' *Erasmus in English* 2 (1971): 2–7
McManners, John 'Paul Hazard and the "Crisis of the European Con-
  science"' *Arts: The Proceedings of the Sydney University Arts*
  Association, 2, 2 (1962): 73–86
Meinecke, F. *Die Entstehung des Historismus* Munich 1965
Meinhold, Peter *Geschichte der kirchlichen Historiographie* 2 vols,
  Munich 1967
Menchi, Silvana Seidel 'Spiritualismo radicale nelle opere di Ortensio
  Lando attorno ad 1550' ARG 65 (1974): 210–77
- 'Sulla fortuna di Erasmo in Italia: Ortensio Lando e altri eterodossi
  della prima metà del Cinquecento' *Schweizerische Zeitschrift für*
  Geschichte 24 (1974): 537–634
Mesnard, P. 'La dernière traduction française de l'Enchiridion'
  Scrinium Erasmianum I 325–32
- 'La tradition érasmienne' BHR 15 (1953): 359–66
- 'The Pedagogy of Johann Sturm (1507–1589) and its Evangelical
  Inspiration' *Studies in the Renaissance* 13 (1966): 200–19

Metzner, J. *Friedrich Nausea aus Waischenfeld, Bischof von Wien* Regensburg 1884

Meylan, Henri 'Grotius théologien' in *Hommage à Grotius* Etudes et documents pour servir à l'histoire de l'Université de Lausanne 4, Lausanne 1946, 19–41

Michel, A. *Histoire des Conciles* x: *Les Décrets du Concile de Trente* Paris 1938

Miller, L. *Geschichte der klassischen Philologie in den Niederlanden* Leipzig 1869

Morrison, Ian R. 'The *Cymbalum Mundi* Revisited' BHR 39 (1977): 263–80

Mozley, J.F. *John Foxe and His Book* London 1940

Müntz, Eugène 'Le Musée de portraits de Paul Jove: Contributions pour servir à l'iconographie du moyen âge et de la Renaissance' *Mémoires de l'Institut national de France: Académie des inscriptions et belles-lettres* 36 pt 2 (1901): 249–343

Murdock, K.B. *The Sun at Noon: Three Biographical Sketches* New York 1939

Näf, Werner *Vadian und seine Stadt St Gallen* 2 vols, St Gallen 1944, 1957

Nauwelarts, M.A. 'Erasme à Louvain: Ephémérides d'un séjour de 1517 à 1521' *Scrinium Erasmianum* I 3–24

Nelson, Axel 'Hugo Grotius: Quelques observations sur ses débuts comme philologue, sur ses études de droit romain et sur ses relations avec J.-A. de Thou, historien et président au Parlement de Paris' *Kungl. Humanistika Vetenskaps-samfundet* Uppsala 1952, 33–63

Nigg, W. *Die Kirchengeschichtsschreibung: Grundzüge ihrer historischen Entwicklung* Munich 1934

Nobbs, D. *Theocracy and Toleration: A Study of the Disputes in Dutch Calvinism from 1600 to 1650* Cambridge 1938

Noordenbos, Oene *In het voetspoor van Erasmus* Hague 1941

Norskov Olsen, V. *John Foxe and the Elizabethan Church* Berkeley 1973

– *The New Testament Logia on Divorce: A Study of their Interpretation from Erasmus to Milton* Tübingen 1971

O'Connell, Marvin R. *Thomas Stapleton and the Counter Reformation* New Haven/London 1964

Oelrich, K.H. *Der späte Erasmus und die Reformation* Reformationsgeschichtliche Studien und Texte 86, Münster 1961, 134–48

Olin, John C. *Desiderius Erasmus: Christian Humanism and the Reformation, Selected Writings* New York 1965

- 'Erasmus and St Ignatius Loyola' in Olin (ed) *Luther, Erasmus and the Reformation* New York 1969, 114–33
Oncken, H. 'Sebastian Franck als Historiker' *Historischpolitische Aufsätze und Reden* I, Munich/Berlin 1914, 275–319
Orr, R. 'Chillingworth versus Hooker: A Criticism of Natural Law Theory' *Journal of Religious History* 2 (December 1962): 120–31
Palmer, Robert R. 'The French Jesuits in the Age of Enlightenment' *American Historical Review* 45 (1939): 44–58
Pastor, Ludwig *History of the Popes from the Close of the Middle Ages* XX, London 1952
Pattison, Mark 'Joseph Scaliger' *Essays* I, Oxford 1889
Payne, J.B. *Erasmus: His Theology of the Sacraments* 1970
Peuckert, W.-E. *Sebastian Franck: Ein deutscher Sucher* Munich 1943
Phillips, Margaret Mann 'Erasmus and Propaganda: A Study of the Translations of Erasmus in England and France' *Modern Languages Review* 37 (1942): 1–17
Pintard, René *Le Libertinage érudit dans la première moitié du XVIIe siècle* 2 vols, Paris 1943
Plath, Uwe *Calvin und Basel in den Jahren 1552–1556* Basler Beiträge zur Geschichtswissenschaft 133, Basel/Stuttgart 1974
Popkin, Richard H. 'Pierre Bayle' *Encyclopaedia of Philosophy* 8 vols, New York 1967, I 257–62
- 'Pierre Bayle's Place in 17th Century Scepticism' in Paul Dibon (ed) *Pierre Bayle: Le Philosophe de Rotterdam, Etudes et documents* Paris 1959, 1–19
Préclin, E. *L'Union des églises gallicane et anglicane: Une Tentative au temps de Louis XV: Pierre-François Le Courayer (de 1681 à 1732) et Guillaume Wake* Paris 1928
Préclin, E. and E. Jarry *Les Luttes politiques et doctrinales aux XVIIe et XVIIIe siècles* in *Histoire de l'église depuis les origines jusqu'à nos jours* XIX 2, Paris 1956
Räber, K. *Studien zur Geschichtsbibel Sebastian Francks* Basler Beiträge zur Geschichtswissenschaft 41, Basel 1952
Von Ranke, Leopold *History of the Popes* I, London 1847
Rébelliau, A. *Bossuet, historien du Protestantisme* Paris 1891
Reedijk, C. 'Das Lebenende des Erasmus' *Basler Zeitschrift für Geschichte und Altertumskunde* 57 (1958): 23–66
Reesink, Hendrika J. *L'Angleterre et la littérature anglaise dans les trois plus anciens périodiques français de Hollande de 1684 à 1709* Zutphen 1931

Rétat, Pierre *Le Dictionnaire de Bayle et la lutte philosophique au XVIIIe siècle* Paris 1971

Reusch, F.H. *Der Index der verbotenen Bücher: Ein Beitrag zur Kirchen- und Literaturgeschichte* I, Bonn 1883

Rex, Walter 'Bayle's Article on David' *Essays on Pierre Bayle and Religious Controversy* Hague 1965, 197–255

Reynolds, E.E. *Thomas More and Erasmus* London 1965

Ritter, G. *Erasmus und der deutsche Humanistenkreis am Oberrhein* Freiburg-im-Breisgau, 1937

Rupp, Gordon *Patterns of Reformation* London 1969

Ryan, E.A. *The Historical Scholarship of Saint Bellarmine* New York 1936

Sandberg, Karl C. *At the Crossroads of Faith and Reason: An Essay on Pierre Bayle* Tucson 1966

Saulnier, V.-L. 'Les dix années françaises de Dominique Baudier (1591–1601): Etude sur la condition humaniste au temps des Guerres civiles' BHR 7 (1945): 139–204

– 'Le sens du "Cymbalum mundi"' ' BHR 13 (1951): 43–69, 137–71

Schlüter, Joachim *Die Theologie des Hugo Grotius* Göttingen 1919

Schmidt, C. 'Celio Secundo Curioni' *Zeitschrift für die historische Theologie* 30 (1860): 571–634

Schöpf, Johann B. *Johannes Nasus, Franziskaner und Weihbischof von Brixen (1534–90)* Bozen 1860

Seeberg, E. *Gottfried Arnold: Die Wissenschaft und die Mystik seiner Zeit: Studien zur Historiographie und die Mystik* Meerane 1923

Seebohm, Frederic *The Oxford Reformers of 1498: A History of the Fellow-work of John Colet, Erasmus and Thomas More* London 1867

Sherburn, George *The Early Career of Alexander Pope* Oxford 1934

Shriver, Frederick 'Orthodoxy and Diplomacy: James I and the Vorstius Affair' *English Historical Review* 85 (1970): 449–74

Smith, Preserved *Erasmus: A Study of His Life, Ideals and Place in History* New York 1963

Sowards, J.K. 'Thomas More and the Friendship of Erasmus, 1499–1517: A Study in Northern Humanism' University of Michigan dissertation 1951

Spitz, L.W. 'Seckendorf as a Church Historian' University of Chicago microfilm 1946

Spörl, Johannes 'Hugo Grotius und der Humanismus des 17. Jahrhunderts' *Historisches Jahrbuch* 55 (1935): 350–7

Stadelmann, R. *Vom Geist des ausgehenden Mittelalters* Halle 1929

Stauffer, R. *Luther vu par les catholiques* Neuchâtel 1961

Stegmann, André 'La réhabilitation de l'orthodoxie chez Erasme par Jean Richard (1688)' *Colloquia Erasmiana Turonensia* 2 vols, Paris 1972, II 867–76

Steinmann, Jean *Richard Simon et les origines de l'exégèse biblique* Paris 1960

Sykes, Norman *William Wake Archbishop of Canterbury* 2 vols, Cambridge 1957

Teichmann, W. 'Die kirchliche Haltung des Beatus Rhenanus: Eine kirchengeschichtliche Studie' *Zeitschrift für Kirchengeschichte* 26 (1905): 363–81

den Tex, Jan *Oldenbarnevelt* 2 vols, Cambridge 1973

Thompson Craig R. 'Erasmus and Tudor England' *Actes du Congrès Erasme Rotterdam 27–29 octobre 1969* Amsterdam 1971, 29–68

Tolmer, Léon *Pierre-Daniel Huet (1630–1721), Humaniste-physicien* Bayeux 1949

Trencsényi-Waldapfel, Imre 'L'humanisme belge et l'humanisme hongrois liés par l'esprit d'Erasme' *Commémoration nationale d'Erasme, Actes* Brussels 1970 211–24

Trevor-Roper, H.R. 'Desiderius Erasmus' *Encounter* 4, 5 (May 1955): 57–68

Van der Blom, N. 'The Erasmus Statues in Rotterdam' *Erasmus in English* 6 (1973): 5–9

Volz, H. *Die Lutherpredigten des Johannes Mathesius: Kritische Untersuchungen zur Geschichtsschreibung im Zeitalter der Reformation* Leipzig 1930

De Voogd, G.J. *Erasmus en Grotius: Twee grote Nederlanders en hun boodschap aan onze tijd* Leiden 1946

Wade, Ira O. *The Clandestine Organization and Diffusion of Philosophic Ideas in France from 1700 to 1750* New York 1967

Weber, Kurt *Lucius Cary Second Viscount Falkland* Columbia University Studies in English and Comparative Literature 147, New York 1940

White, Helen C. *Tudor Books of Saints and Martyrs* Madison 1963

Wilbur, E.M. *A History of Unitarianism: In Transylvania, England and America* Boston 1952

Williams, G.H. *The Radical Reformation* London 1962

Wolf, D. *Die Irenik des Hugo Grotius nach ihrem Prinzipien und biographischgeistesgeschichtlichen Perspektiven* Marburg 1969

Yates, Frances A. *Astraea: The Imperial Theme in the Sixteenth Century* London 1975

Zeeden, E.W. *Martin Luther und die Reformation im Urteil des deutschen Luthertums* 2 vols, Freiburg 1950

Index

๛

Erasmus Studies

A Series of Studies Concerned with Erasmus and Related Subjects